DATE DUE

FEB 19 2008	
MAR 04 2008	
FEB 10 2015	

BRODART, CO.   Cat. No. 23-221-003

Managing the President's Message

MANAGING
the President's
MESSAGE

The White House Communications Operation

Martha Joynt Kumar

THE JOHNS HOPKINS UNIVERSITY PRESS | BALTIMORE

10886568

© 2007 The Johns Hopkins University Press
All rights reserved. Published 2007
Printed in the United States of America on acid-free paper
9 8 7 6 5 4 3 2 1

The Johns Hopkins University Press
2715 North Charles Street
Baltimore, Maryland 21218-4363
www.press.jhu.edu

Library of Congress Cataloging-in-Publication Data

Kumar, Martha Joynt.
    Managing the president's message : the White House communications
operation / Martha Joynt Kumar.
        p.   cm.
    Includes bibliographical references and index.
    ISBN-13: 978-0-8018-8652-2 (hardcover : alk. paper)
    ISBN-10: 0-8018-8652-X (hardcover : alk. paper)
    1. Government and the press—United States. 2. Press and politics—
United States. 3. Presidents—Press coverage—United States.
4. Communication—Political aspects—United States. I. Title.
    PN4738.K86 2007
    352.3'840973—dc22   2006037724

A catalog record for this book is available from the British Library.

To Ann Marie Devroy,
1948–1997, *Washington Post*

A reporter who set the standard for fine coverage of the
contemporary presidency
and the modern White House.

Contents

Acknowledgments

Many White House staff members and reporters were instrumental in enabling me to undertake research at the White House for an extended period of time. Press Secretaries Mike McCurry, Joe Lockhart, Jake Siewert, Ari Fleischer, Scott McClellan, and Tony Snow graciously agreed to interviews and tolerated my presence around the Press Room. White House communications directors during the same time period interrupted their own busy schedules to discuss their work. Among those who provided interviews are Dan Bartlett, Karen Hughes, Nicolle Devenish Wallace, and Kevin Sullivan from the administration of President George W. Bush; Loretta Ucelli, Ann Lewis, Don Baer, and George Stephanopoulos from the Clinton administration; and Tom Griscom from the Reagan White House. David Gergen, from the Ford, Reagan, and Clinton administrations, spoke with me as well. Chiefs of Staff John Podesta, Andrew Card, and Joshua Bolten also agreed to interviews about presidential communications and White House operations.

Reporters have also been gracious in welcoming me to the basement of the Press Room, where I parked first at the desks of a variety of news organizations before settling at the *National Journal* desk. *National Journal* White House correspondents Alexis Simendinger and Carl Cannon have supported my work from the early days of the Clinton administration, when my regular visits to the White House for this project began. They graciously created a more permanent place for all three of us to observe and write about daily events. Alexis has been particularly helpful in talking with me about White House staff and communications patterns.

The denizens of the basement of the press room were willing to discuss their work and institutional operations, which helped me understand reporting patterns and the pressures. Among the most informative were radio reporters Mark Smith, Associated Press; Tina Stage, Bloomberg Radio; April Ryan, American Urban Radio Network; Greg Clugston, American Standard Radio; Don Fulsom, United Press International; Mark Knoller, CBS; Don Gonyea and David Green, National Public Radio; Bob Deans and Ken Herman, Cox Newspapers; and Keith Kofler, *Congress Daily*. Television reporters and their producers kindly helped me develop an understanding of the rhythms of their working life. First among them was Bill Plante, White House correspondent for CBS. He read and commented on every chapter of this book as well as the early drafts of conference papers and articles that form the underpinnings of those chapters. Other television correspondents who were particularly helpful include Jim Angle and Wendell Goler of Fox News. Also located in the basement in the area where I worked were several fine photographers who cover the White House for our nation's newsweeklies. Of these, I would like to thank *Time* photographers Brooks Kraft and Christopher Morris, *Newsweek* photographers Charles Ommanney and David Hume Kennerly, *US News and World Report* photographer Chick Herrity, and *New York Times* photographer Stephen Crowley.

Newspaper and magazine reporters also took time to stop and talk about their work. Ann Devroy, White House reporter for the *Washington Post*, stood out for the thoroughness of her reporting and for the degree to which she was able to part the White House publicity curtain to discover the facts associated with many policies, actions, and events. For the high standard she set, this book is dedicated to her.

Presidency scholars were helpful in reviewing and encouraging my work. The foremost of these was Michael Grossman, my coauthor on *Portraying the President: The White House and the News Media*. The present volume benefits from that earlier work. Many of the patterns we discovered are still valid twenty-five years later. As a good friend and managing editor of *Presidential Studies Quarterly*, Professor George C. Edwards at Texas A&M University read and encouraged my work and published articles of mine, including material found in chapters 3, 4, 5, and 7. Professor Timothy Cook of Louisiana State University read most of the manuscript and encouraged me at every turn, as did Professor John Kessel of Ohio State University and Professor Terry Sullivan of the University of North Carolina. Kenneth Simendinger was also invaluable to the project. He gathered information on presidential press conferences from Woodrow Wilson to George W. Bush. He also served as a good sounding board on issues related to communications operations.

Support for the book came from several sources. I particularly wish to thank the University System of Maryland for the two Wilson H. Elkins grants that supported my course on White House communications and my research work in 2003 and 2005. The work on presidential press conferences was funded from the Elkins grants. The Pew Charitable Trusts supported my work on White House publicity offices through the funding they provided to the White House Interview Program. The Joan Shorenstein Center for Press Politics at the Kennedy School at Harvard University gave me a place to hang my hat as I wrote about White House information sessions. Towson University has been generous in funding my work through the release time granted to me and through development grants from the Towson University Foundation. Towson University presidents Robert Caret, Dan Jones, and Hoke Smith all supported my research work, as did Provosts Jim Brennan, Dan Jones, and Robert Hager. My thanks go to my department chairmen, James Roberts and Eric Belgrad, who championed my case at many levels within the university over a period of many years, as did the rest of my colleagues in the department of political science.

In preparing the manuscript I had the strong support of my editor, Toby Marotta. Henry Y. K. Tom, executive editor at the Johns Hopkins University Press, supported and believed in the project for a longer time than he might have wished. So too did my husband, Vijay Kumar, and our sons Zal and Cameron, who all encouraged me at every point in the writing of this book.

Introduction

No matter their programs, their party, or their political circumstances, modern presidents regularly communicate with their fellow citizens to inform them of their plans, decisions, and views on world and domestic events and to encourage them to action or patience, as needs require. The general public expects to hear from the chief executive on domestic, foreign policy, and national security issues, and so too do the special constituencies a president has among government officials and interested individuals and nongovernment groups important to his initiatives.

The president's need to communicate derives from the nature of our representative political system and from the reality that he must continually seek support for everything he does. Informing the public about presidential decisions and initiatives is an important aspect of a democratic political system. Whether in the context of a crisis or a policy discussion, citizens expect a president to clarify his choices and decisions. On September 14, 1926, President Calvin Coolidge emphasized to journalists the need to keep citizens informed as the reason for his twice-weekly news conferences with them: "I regard it as rather necessary to the carrying on of our republican institution that the people should have a fairly accurate report of what the president is trying to do, and it is for that purpose of course that those intimate conferences are held."[1]

An emphasis on presidential communications can also be traced to the reality that chief executives are guaranteed no victories by dint of their election. Election provides them with the opportunity to persuade those whose support they need, but they must be able to exploit the resources and opportunities available to them. In order to identify and to take advantage of circumstances, presidents have done two things. First, in an effort to enhance their chances of success, they have considered communications as an important factor in their policy and political initiatives. Second, they have developed staffs responsible for identifying communications resources and opportunities, creating and coordinating presidential themes, developing publicity plans and strategies to further those themes, making arrangements for events and speeches, and coordinating with others in government.

While most presidents have pursued a strong relationship with the public that involves the president educating, persuading, and energizing citizens, how they have done so has evolved over the course of the first forty-three presidencies. During the years of a limited White House staff structure, presidents directed their own relations with the public. In the modern period, however, as presidents increased not only their public appearances but also the number and scope of their policy initiatives, they developed staff units to manage their public communications.

Understanding the modern presidency requires recognizing the importance of communications to everything that a president does and becoming familiar with what it is he and his staff members do to further his public presidency. A president today is presented with something of a puzzle when he takes office. How can he regularly reach and motivate support for initiatives and goals using the vehicle of what most chief executives consider to be a critical press? If news organizations are independent of administrations, how can a president use them to carry his messages to the general and specialized publics?

This book is about how the president and his staff solve that puzzle and use news organizations to communicate his messages to the public in a manner that suits his policy, political, and personal needs. In addition, the chief executive and his White House staff need to determine how much to communicate to the public through news organizations. How do they explain their policies in terms they find favorable in a media structure designed as much to critique as to praise? The public is where a president's political strength lies, but the president's chief vehicle to reach them is the major news organizations. Getting media attention means designing strategies that fit in with the routines and respond to the demands of news organizations.

Delivering coherent messages to the public is not as easy in today's media environment as one might assume, notwithstanding the resources and opportunities the president has available to him. Today the public has access to a huge amount of information from cable television, network evening news programs, morning newspapers and updates on their websites, magazines, talk radio programs, and Internet blogs. It is difficult for the public to sift through this vast amount of information and opinion to understand what is happening in government and in the presidency. How does the president reach the public with a message of his design through what he may consider to be a "filter," as President George W. Bush refers to the press?[2] And where does the public's need for information fit with what a president perceives as his interests?

To develop coherent messages, a president and his staff members need to integrate communications choices into their plans for governing. Communications is central to governing, and if a president does not fold communications into the policy process and does not have a multifaceted communications operation, he risks failure of his political, electoral, and policy goals. Whether it is promoting a presidential initiative or campaigning for reelection, a president must make communications a part of everything he and his staff do because persuasion is so central to presidential accomplishments. A president needs supporters, and it is through effective communications that he builds winning coalitions on issues. If he is to achieve his goals, he must persuade interested groups and public officials to support them.

Presidential communications shape policy outcomes. Underestimating the importance of communications can sink presidential initiatives. In February 2006, the administration signed off on the sale of a British company (Peninsula and Oriental Steam Navigation) responsible for container operations in six major ports in the United States. Because it was a foreign company doing business in a sensitive security area, the P&O sale to Dubai Ports World, a Dubai state-owned company, required presidential approval following a report from the Treasury Department's Committee on Foreign Investments in the United States. The approval process called on the Congress to review the decision.[3] Presidential allies and critics in Congress made clear they were going to oppose the deal, which ultimately led the company to announce that it would sell its terminal operations by October. On February 13, 2006, Senator Charles Schumer (D-NY) held a news conference criticizing the decision before President Bush made any public statement about the need for Congress to approve the sale.[4] The same day, talk show radio host Michael Savage began what became a continuing discussion of the ports issue with his audience of roughly nine million people on 370 radio stations.[5] Very quickly and without fully realizing it, the White House staff was soon confronted by what the president described to his aides as a "prairie fire."[6] President Bush twice addressed the subject with reporters on February 21, but by that time even the Republican leadership in the House and Senate had distanced themselves from the sale.[7] President Bush publicly spoke to the issue so late in the process of congressional consideration of the decision that there was little chance that he could achieve his policy goal of supporting the U.S.-friendly Arab government. Critics framed the administration's decision as a potential national security threat because Dubai is an Arab state. In explaining the differences between the two events, President Bush's senior communications advisor, Dan Bartlett said, "The biggest difference was Hill notification—having people not surprised." While the Dubai Ports World issue occurred during a congressional recess, the second act took place while Congress was in session. "It's always a challenge on the message when they are scattered to the wind," Bartlett said. "It is hard enough coordinating with them when they are in town. . . . Secondly, the issue of ports was just ripe at that time, the debate about port security and port funding. But most importantly, people were caught unawares. There was not a good notification process for the Hill." When it came to the second Dubai issue, "in the wake of [the first Dubai issue], we were much more sensitive to it, we did a lot better scrubbing, a lot more preemptive briefings with key members, so they couldn't say, 'Ah, I didn't anything know about this,'" he said. "Once you get somebody invested in that process, you can control it a little bit better," Bartlett said.[8]

Less than two months after the Dubai Port World deal fell through, however, with no fuss from members of Congress, President Bush approved the sale of a British company to Dubai International Capital, which is owned by the government of Dubai.[9] The sale involved nine manufacturing plants, some of which supply parts to the U.S. military, including ones for tanks and aircraft. In the second case, President Bush and his staff were well aware of the potential communications damage associated with the issue and worked early with members of Congress to make certain that the administration, and not their opponents, defined the stakes in the sale. The first public statements came from the administration, not their critics. The administration had learned the high cost of not having communications integrated into policy decisions.

Whether the chief executive is a liberal or a conservative, a Republican or a Democrat, he must make communications a part of his governing strategies and must create a multifaceted communications operation that includes senior and middle-level staff as well as a vast support operation to put on events and carry out strategies. The organizational structure includes not only all senior level staff who have communications as an important aspect of their jobs but also specific White House units devoted to presidential publicity, particularly the Office of Communications, the Press Office, and their satellite units and operations. This book looks both at what publicity work senior staff members perform and at how the communications organizations operate. Both are important to understanding White House communications operations.

Studying White House Communications

This book fills a gap in the available literature about White House operations by including the perspective of those who work there. Rather than view the subject from the outside, it aims to build from inside the White House an understanding of the importance of communications to all that a president and his staff do. By tracing the daily discussions of senior White House staff, the meetings of communications officials, and the operations of communications units, we can see how the president and his White House staff operate in an area essential to our understanding of the modern presidency. A president and his staff spend a great deal of time on communications issues because they view publicity as integral to presidential leadership. The book focuses on those who work in the White House, not those who study it from the outside.

In order to explain how presidents and their staff develop their communications strategies, I interviewed senior administration officials from the last four administrations as well as conversed with officials who served in earlier years. In order to get a fresh perspective, I interviewed people as close as possible to the time of their service in the White House. Over a twenty-five-year period, I interviewed more than a hundred people, including repeat interviews with some key officials and reporters. I moved to Washington in 1997 because I realized that the only way to get a good grasp on how White House communications operations worked was to be present at the White House to observe the interactions between officials and reporters, to witness events organized by communications staff, and to interview officials and reporters about their work.

In addition to interviews with administration officials, I observed White House briefings and publicity events. In December 1975, my colleague Michael Grossman and I came to the White House to begin our on-site research for *Portraying the President: The White House and the News Media*.[10] For five years, we regularly observed White House publicity operations and spoke with officials and reporters about their work. Through the first year of the Reagan administration, we watched the press secretary's daily briefing and occasional events.

Since then, I have spent a great deal of time watching White House publicity operations unfold and talking to officials and reporters about the evolution of their work. During the Reagan and George H. W. Bush administrations, I watched the operations from a distance, although I did talk to communications officials during each administration and at the end of both. In 1995, I came into the Press Room for an extended stay, taking up a spot in the basement among radio, cable television, magazine, and some newspaper reporters. From there, over a period of eleven years, I saw up close how reporters did their work and monitored changes in the news business and in the White House publicity organization.

Observing at close hand was useful for two reasons. First, it gave me an understanding of the rhythms of White House publicity. If one relies on isolated instances to generalize about the relationship between the two partners—the White House and the media—and about the motivations that drive each side, one can easily miss the rhythms of the relationship that emerge over weeks, months, even years. By regularly attending briefings and events, for example, I could appreciate the cooperation that generally characterizes the public exchanges between officials and reporters, especially in those sessions in which cameras are not present. Even in the occasional period of intense acrimony, cooperation governs the relationship.

Second, viewing a variety of events and publicity circumstances provided me with an information base for interviewing officials and reporters about their work. Participants on both sides of the presidential-press relationship were generous in discussing their work. A familiarity with their routine contributed to productive interviews.

My perspective, however, was that of an observer, not a participant. I looked at how events were staged and what similarities and differences existed among administrations in how they chose to communicate with reporters and other members of the Washington community. In this book, I do not take a position about how an administration should have organized its communications but rather relate how several presidents and their staffs did choose to organize their publicity, the reasoning behind those choices, and the consequences those decisions had on their operation. Though I was just an observer, I hope that by providing information on how officials in several administrations conducted their publicity, my work can contribute to an understanding for future White House officials of what has preceded them.

While I focus on the words and actions of White House officials, the political science literature on White House organization is also important to this book. The work of presidency scholar Richard Neustadt, who linked the importance of persuasion to the conduct of the presidency, is particularly essential. Inspired by his observations while serving on the political staff of President Harry Truman, Neustadt in *Presidential Power* focused the attention of those interested in the presidency on the difficulties presidents have convincing others to follow their lead.[11] Few others have both worked in a White House and served in the academic world. Neustadt, who taught at Columbia University and Harvard University, studied and taught the presidency after leaving the Truman White House and the Bureau of the Budget.

In 1996, thirty-six years after *Presidential Power* was published, Neustadt, at a Columbia University conference highlighting his work and the state of the study of the presidency, encouraged attendees to study White House operations. Neustadt worried that the records of White House operations that now exist "disguise or distort the living purposes, the interchanges, struggles, and reactions of the people involved, and their outlooks on the world at the moment." He thought we, as scholars, should try to make up for that deficit by talking to participants in White House decision-making and to do so as close as possible to the time when the officials made their choices. "The only way to partially make up those lacks is by interviewing, where the interviewer knows the record and can conjure up the atmosphere, while the interviewee still fully commands memory, inevitably imperfect, and both are eager for a genuine reconstruction.[12] I have tried to do just that. By being at the White House as regularly and as often as I have been, I could talk to officials and reporters as events unfolded and their memories were still fresh.[13]

Managing the President's Message builds on *Portraying the President*, which Grossman and I published at the beginning of the Reagan administration. In it, we focused on the nature of the relationship between the White House and the press and on the ways that each side used the other to further its own goals. We found the relationship to be a continuing and cooperative one. From one administration to the next, both sides need each other, so they tend to cooperate with one another. Since the earlier book was published in 1981, there have been new developments in the relationship even if the basic contours remain the same.[14]

The tensions in the relationship are greater now than they were then. Indeed, the frustrations of reporters covering the White House are more noticeable today than during most of the earlier periods since World War II. Over the years, expectations of how much information the president and his surrogates will release to the public have increased. There have been enormous changes in the news business, among them the proliferation of types of media, the development of the Internet and blogs, financial problems in the newspaper industry and at the traditional three television networks, and the development of cable television. All of these changes have accelerated the pace at which news is reported; this in turn has required White House staff to be ready to dispense information virtually around the clock. The traditional venues for disseminating news that we explored in *Portraying the President,* such as the press secretary's daily briefings and presidential press conferences, have evolved to take advantage of and to respond to technological advances. Even so, the traditional White House information venues remain.

In the intervening years, presidents have increased their public appearances, which has given rise to an even larger White House persuasion operation. Since the publication of *Portraying the President,* the long-range planning operation has increased its scope and number of personnel. In addition, Democrats as well as Republicans have developed communications planning units. Presidents Kennedy, Johnson, and Carter saw no need for such an operation, but President Clinton did and future Democratic presidents probably will as well.[15]

What This Book Covers

In its individual chapters, this book explores effective communications first by identifying the basic functions that communications operations address. In recent administrations, publicity operations have advocated for presidents, defended chief executives from their critics, explained administration actions and policies, and coordinated government-wide publicity. Advocating for the president involves promoting the policies and goals of the chief executive in a variety of venues. Explanation entails responding to queries as well as providing supporting information and fleshing out presidential initiatives. Defending the president calls for a different set of strategies and people who can respond to criticism of him and his policies as well as clean up after presidential mistakes. Coordination includes bringing together White House units with governmental organizations and outside groups to publicize the presidential actions. Those basic demands recur no matter who is president. Yet there are differences as well as similarities among presidents in how their White House staffs deal with these basic communications needs.

Using these four categories of presidential communications tasks, we will look at how the Clinton and George W. Bush administrations organized their communications operations, created publicity strategies, and then carried out those strategies. Where did the various aspects of communications fit into the overall governing plans of these two administrations, and how did they shape their strategies? To what extent do the personal differences of presidents determine how they organize their administrations and how they communicate? By viewing who was involved in communications decisions and in what ways publicity came up in decision-making settings, I could see how important communications has been, in both Democratic and Republican administrations. I will consider the manner in which communications fit into their overall White House operations. The communications operations of Presidents Clinton and Bush demonstrate the range that a president has in how he arranges his publicity units and what they do.

In order to understand the place of communications in an administration, it is important to study the performance of the two established White House communications units tasked with presidential publicity, the Office of Communications and the Office of the Press Secretary. The book has chapters explaining the workings of both units over the course of several administrations. As the two most significant offices consistently involved with publicity, by studying them we can get a good sense of how communications strategies are developed and carried out.

All recent administrations have had communications advisers in charge of the Office of Communications, which is at the center of the administration's persuasion efforts. It is an office tasked with creating communications strategies that are aimed at news organizations and designed to win support for the president and for his initiatives. It is also the unit that coordinates governmental agencies and resources for the president's events. The second unit crucial to presidential publicity is the Office of the Press Secretary. Since Herbert Hoover was president, every administration has chosen to have a senior assistant assigned to press relations, and their operations are detailed in a chapter here. Traditionally, the press secretary is critical in shaping strategies for handling the daily release of presidential information and for establishing the official presidential record. His twice-daily briefings place the president's thinking and actions in the public record.

In addition to exploring the part the two publicity office operations play in creating and staging communications strategies, this book details the basic information sessions where White House communications strategies are played out. It looks at how recent administrations have used traditional information venues as well as settings of their own choice to provide information. Both briefings and press conferences involve choices designed to meet the president's needs but also to respond to the demands and interests of reporters. The press secretary's two daily briefings and the president's press conferences are major venues where communications strategies dictate the organization of the sessions and the scripts prepared for the president and his surrogates. During the press secretary's morning briefing, known as the "gaggle," and his or her televised afternoon briefing each day, an administration's publicity strategies are on display. Less frequent but more significant are sessions where the chief executive responds to reporters' queries—in recent years, two such sessions are his press conferences and his short question-and-answer sessions with journalists. It is important to consider the dynamics of the basic sessions where the president and his surrogates speak as a matter of routine. Two of the chapters do so. The book concludes with a summary chapter on presidential communications operations in which I explore the recurring elements of presidential communications operations, the benefits they provide to presidents, their limitations, and the lessons they impart about the modern presidency.

The Development of White House Communications Operations

The White House communications apparatus developed through a combination of need, opportunity, and presidential inclination. As presidents and their senior staff members began regularly interacting with the growing number of reporters covering the White House, they gradually found that they needed organizational support to meet these new communications demands and goals. Reporters came to the White House when they sensed an increase in presidential policymaking activity on the domestic and then international fronts, a willingness of the chief executives and their staffs to talk about their policies and philosophies, and a curiosity on the part of the public as to the White House.

The century and a quarter or so from the 1880s to today is a period in which presidents and their staffs dealt with an expanding number of reporters and types of news organizations. Furthermore, presidents increased their public appearances in a country growing in both population and territory.[16] The White House organizational structure gradually grew from its incarnation at the end of the nineteenth century, focused on providing official information to reporters, into its current form, where the focus is advocating for the president as well as giving out official information. In terms of offices, in the late nineteenth century the responsibility for dealing with reporters most often fell to the president's secretary, who had only a small staff. The senior staff expanded in 1929 to include an official, informally known as the press secretary, whose job was to answer reporters' queries. Forty years later, the Office of Communications was created to focus on advocating for the president. These two offices, the Press Office and the Office of Communications, and their satellite units form the core of the White House communications efforts. The process of creating them took more than a century, a period that can be broken down into four stages for the purposes of tracking the development of White House communications organization.

The Early Organizational Years: 1880–1932

During the period from 1880 to 1932, the presidency became the national political news center as problems moved to the chief executive's desk in times of peace as well as war. It was during these years that the chief executive became a world leader and took a more public domestic role than he previously had. As he did so, interest in him grew, so his expanding staff needed to focus on his relations with news organizations.

In the post–Civil War period, as presidents increased the distance and frequency of their travels and newspapers and wire services expanded their reach, chief executives and their staffs spent more and more of their time dealing with reporters and providing them with information. During these years they established communications precedents that succeeding presidents adopted—and built on.

Presidents traveled increasing distances with a press contingent along for the ride. Rutherford B. Hayes was the first president to take an official trip to the west coast. He wanted to bring the presidency to the people in new territories and states. This was extending the presidential tradition of what was known as the "swing around the circle," a tour away from Washington, D.C, dating back to George Washington's presidency. In 1880, Hayes had the first transcontinental trip, which originated in

Washington on August 26 and returned him to the capital on November 6. During the seventy-one-day trip, the president and the first lady visited several cities in California and Oregon, among many other cities on the way. They traveled by train except in those areas where they had to ride by stagecoach. In one segment, General William Tecumseh Sherman rode shotgun through New Mexico Indian Territory. His trip was followed by similar journeys, including one in 1891 by President Benjamin Harrison, who went by the newly completed cross-country rail line and had two wire service reporters in his presidential party.[17]

Presidents recognized that they needed reporters to make their trip a reality to people around the country. Presidents William McKinley and Theodore Roosevelt followed with their own cross-country journeys. When in 1906 he took a journey to Panama and Costa Rica, President Theodore Roosevelt became the first president to travel outside of the United States in an official capacity, which fit into his agenda of demonstrating the United States as a world power and the president as a world leader. The number of reporters traveling along on such trips grew steadily.

As their travels increased, presidents brought with them staff members who were familiar with press routines and who understood new technologies. In other ways, White House officials realized that they needed to provide presidential information to the public, and reporters were often the vehicle for doing so. The president's annual message to Congress was a printed one provided to Congress rather than one delivered in person. In addition to giving it to members of Congress, the message was delivered to newspapers around the country on an embargo basis: the news organizations had to agree not to publish it before a given date in order to get an early copy. White House officials developed and directed the distribution process.

Tragedy also increased the presence of reporters around the president and the White House. When President James Garfield was shot in 1881, he lingered for two months at the White House before dying. During that time, at least one reporter, an Associated Press wire service correspondent, was there during the night to report on the status of the president's health.[18] The presence of reporters was a recognition of the public's right to know about their president. When President McKinley was shot in 1901 in Buffalo, New York, his secretary, George B. Cortelyou, spoke with reporters several times to pass on updates about his condition.[19]

With their growing travel and public activity, presidents recognized a need for experienced staff. As far back as the first administration of President Grover Cleveland, the president's chief aide, his private secretary Daniel Lamont, had a press background. Cleveland's successor, Benjamin Harrison, also had an aide with a press background, Elijah Halford, as did William McKinley, who followed Cleveland's second term. McKinley had John Addison Porter, who owned the *Hartford Post,* as his senior aide. Having as their top aide a person with a press background helped the president get answers to reporters without their having public interaction with journalists themselves.

When Theodore Roosevelt entered office, he brought with him from his governorship a tradition of responding to reporters' queries. He did the same as president, though the sessions were off the record and thus could not be used by reporters in their stories. In addition, he chose his audience; the sessions were not available to all reporters. His aides, first George Cortelyou, who first came to the White House in the Cleveland administration, and then William Loeb, paid great attention to reporters' information needs and exploited the newfound possibilities of using news organizations to meet presidential needs. The work they did responding to reporters' queries and planning presidential publicity foreshadowed the work press secretaries would do in the near future and communications directors would do decades down the road.

While President William Howard Taft allowed reporters to retain their White House space, journalists did not get the kind of frank discussions reporters had with President Roosevelt. He met with reporters from time to time, not on a regular basis. The fact of their continuing presence, though, firmly established the importance of the White House as a place where reporters should be stationed.

President Woodrow Wilson increased the public presence of the chief executive by returning to the practice of Presidents George Washington and John Quincy Adams of presenting the State of the Union message in person to members of Congress. He also established presidential press conferences open to all reporters on an equal basis, although, as with Roosevelt, his sessions were off the record. Though there were many of them in his early years in office, he abandoned the sessions when the war came. His secretary, Joseph Tumulty, handled press relations as a central part of his work until World War I came and Wilson created the Committee on Public Information.

Headed by newsman George Creel, the Committee on Public Information was the precursor of the White House Office of Communications. The earlier committee designed and implemented strategies to promote the importance of U.S. participation in World War I. In addition to its wartime censorship role, the committee identified places where information flowed to the public, such as movie theaters, and developed dissemination strategies accordingly. When the war was over, the committee was abandoned.[20]

In the 1920s, the public demands on the president increased, as reporters and their news organizations now viewed the chief executive and his White House as a news center. Reporters regularly spoke with Presidents Harding, Coolidge, and to a lesser extent Hoover, in what became regular press conferences held in the president's office. In fact, President Coolidge held more presidential press conferences than any of his successors.[21] While there often was little news, reporters regarded whatever the president was thinking or doing as important. Presidents and their staffs learned to make use of such technological advances as radio so that the president could deliver messages to the public personally, using the technology of news organizations without having reporters determine which part of their statements would be carried. Entire presidential addresses were carried by radio; President Coolidge was the first chief executive to have his State of the Union radio broadcast in 1923, and President Hoover made frequent radio addresses to the public as well.

Once White House staff increased, a senior position was reserved for the tasks associated with press relations. While the title for the post, created in the Hoover administration, was assistant to the president, the person occupying that role was responsible for press relations and became popularly known as the press secretary. George Akerson, who first served in the post, had handled communications issues for Hoover when he was secretary of commerce in the Coolidge administration. Hoover, however, did not follow the practices he established when he was commerce secretary—in his earlier post he had regularly spoken with reporters in a frank manner. In his sessions with reporters as president, he offered up scant information.

Speechwriters came on the staff in the 1920s. In the Harding administration, the first presidential speechwriter, Judson Welliver, was hired to serve on the White House staff. In addition to his speechwriting duties, Welliver regularly chased down information to provide to reporters who posed queries in Coolidge's press conferences.

The President at the Center of News: 1933–1952

Under Franklin Roosevelt presidential communications became a central aspect of the presidency because of the two crises the country endured during his time in office—the Depression and World War II. President Roosevelt spoke directly with the public at important times through his occasional "fireside chats" and with reporters at his twice-weekly press conferences. With so much government activity on both the domestic and foreign fronts, the White House had become the center of national news. Reporters enjoyed reporting on the administration's many actions and liked covering a president who so clearly enjoyed their company.

Though the position of press secretary was created during the Hoover administration, it was during Roosevelt's years in office that the post became an important one. Stephen Early, Roosevelt's appointee, was the first press secretary to have the confidence of reporters as well as of the president. He spoke for the president in his daily briefings and was the first press secretary to be regarded as a credible and well-informed source. The president relied on him as much as reporters did. He served in the post from the beginning of the administration until its last month.

The basic White House communications structure of a press secretary with some speechwriters on the staff continued in the Roosevelt administration. In addition, Roosevelt used an ad hoc system where several aides would be involved in publicity issues. He sometimes brought government officials to his press conferences to give reporters information on individual subjects, such as the budget. With budget officials arrayed nearby, President Roosevelt annually briefed reporters on his budget. He wanted to be the person who explained the administration's priorities.

Others in the administration were involved in publicity too. Cabinet secretaries, such as Harold Ickes, who headed the Department of Interior, were involved in publicity on important policy issues. Ickes authorized using the Lincoln Memorial as a place for opera singer Marian Anderson to perform after the Daughters of the American Revolution refused to allow her to sing before an integrated audience at Constitution Hall, which the organization owned. Some of his White House aides, such as Harry Hopkins and Marvin McIntyre, dealt with reporters as well. People who did political work were involved in writing speeches.

The president was not the only Roosevelt of the time who had an active relationship with reporters. For the first time, not only did the president have press conferences on a regular basis, but his wife, Eleanor Roosevelt, did as well. The first lady discussed substantive domestic policy issues as well as ones related to women. Her impact on the press corps was a lasting one, as she required news organizations to send women to cover her press sessions. In addition to her interchanges with reporters, she also wrote a column, "My Day," that was published in newspapers throughout the country.

When President Roosevelt died, Harry Truman followed Roosevelt's practice of meeting with reporters, even if only once a week. The sessions, however, were not the same informal ones of Roosevelt's tenure, with reporters clustered around his desk. As the press corps had grown, Truman moved them to a larger, more formal space. His series of press secretaries spoke for the president on a daily basis. Like Roosevelt, Truman used his political staff for a variety of communications tasks, including writing his speeches, as did aides Ken Hechler and Richard Neustadt.

Organizing the Presidency for Television: 1953–1974

In the 1950s, technology, changes in presidential press conferences, and the development of a hierarchical White House staff structure all led to the basic structure of White House communications operations we know today. It was during Dwight Eisenhower's presidency that television became a factor in presidential publicity and that presidential press conferences moved from being off-the-record events to ones open for broadcast and reporting by all media. In addition, President Eisenhower replaced the relatively free-flowing staff system of his Democratic predecessors with an organized operation that attached responsibilities to particular positions. While it disappeared during the years Presidents John F. Kennedy and Lyndon Johnson were in office, it returned under Richard Nixon.

It was during this period that the idea of long-range communications planning took hold, even though there was no special organizational structure to support it. That arrived in the Nixon administration. During the Eisenhower administration, Press Secretary James Hagerty extended the information-sharing role of the press secretary and his office by planning communications strategies and coordinating publicity for the entire executive branch. In addition, pro bono public relations and television advisers joined the communications team as a part of the president's publicity circle. Eisenhower relied on some part-time people, such as Hollywood producer Robert Montgomery and pro bono people including

New York advertising executive Sigurd Larman of Young and Rubicam, who advised him how to use television and how to blend public relations strategies with the governing process.[22]

Today, the work that Hagerty did all by himself in 1959 merits two prominent offices, the Press Office and the Office of Communications, staffed by leading presidential advisers, a handful of subsidiary units with specialized portfolios, and several layers of White House staff.

Hagerty's work was particularly important because as the 1950s wound to a close, the administration's friendly relationship with reporters was fraying. With the disclosure in 1960 that the administration had lied about a government plane shot down over the Soviet Union, reporters adopted a more critical attitude toward information coming from the White House. The incident brought an end to the willingness of reporters to accept an administration's version of events, which they had done during the war years, for example. In this instance, a U.S. military plane was shot down by the Soviets in their airspace. The State Department announced that it was a weather plane. Unknown to them, the pilot had survived the downing of the plane, was captured, and had acknowledged that the aircraft he was flying was a U-2 spy plane. Now that the administration had been caught in a lie, Press Secretary Hagerty was the one who would feel the heat. From that point forward, the president and his White House staff would have to work even harder to persuade reporters to accept their information. They needed additional strategies to get their messages to the public.

Presidents Kennedy and Johnson did not have a sustained communications planning operation, although both men had regular press conferences with reporters. In Kennedy's case, the press conferences attracted a great deal of attention, as they were broadcast live and not for later broadcast, as Eisenhower's had been. Kennedy was witty, and the sessions were viewed as events benefiting both the president and news organizations. Television was an important presence in the Kennedy administration and remained so under Johnson. During both of these administrations, reporters publicly questioned the accuracy of the information they were receiving, particularly as it related to the government's actions during the Vietnam War. The relationship became acrimonious on a regular basis during the Johnson years and became even more hostile during the Nixon administration. Not only did Nixon have to contend with information issues related to the Vietnam War, the Watergate scandal went on for the last two years he was in office. While not all newspapers were immediately interested in the issue, all media began focusing on it in early 1973 and stayed on it until Nixon left office August 9, 1974.

President Nixon, whose vantage point as Eisenhower's vice president permitted him to see the value of Hagerty's expansion, created the Office of Communications to permit planning over and above the daily routines required of the press secretary. Through the creation of that office, a new group of paid officials was added to the staff to promote the president and his programs. The office was also involved in establishing relationships with out-of-town news organizations, which they regarded as more friendly to the administration than what they perceived as a hostile White House press corps. While the office has been shaped and used in different ways, the Office of Communications has mostly been used to establish and maintain contact with local news organizations. Nixon did accept established precedents, such as having a press secretary who daily briefed the press and holding presidential press conferences, but he dramatically reduced the number of such sessions.

While the current organizational structure of the White House communications operation was in place and fully functioning by the end of the Nixon administration, Presidents Reagan and Clinton fine-tuned it to deal with the explosion of new media, particularly cable television and the Internet.

Established White House Communications Operations: 1981–2007

In the Reagan administration, the president's communications planning team took advantage of a telegenic president and a setting in which each day most citizens received their news through one or more of the three television networks in the early evening. They used their planning and daily press operations to dictate how the president would be covered by television and staged an event a day to establish the pictures they wanted on the evening news. By 2007, the White House was confronted with an environment in which there were five networks, all of which provide news all day long, starting with their morning news programs through to their traditional evening newscasts and on to local TV news in the late evening. In addition, they faced a dwindling number of newspapers, with almost no evening papers still publishing, and the rise of the Internet, an increasingly important source of news, especially for younger voters. The focused system for delivering news of the Reagan years had transformed into one in which the presidential press staff worked throughout the day to provide information for a fractured media system with different time and information demands. The national moment for delivering administration news in a unified way in the Reagan years was replaced by the somewhat chaotic system of 2007, with the media industry still in transition.

In the Reagan years, the new medium of cable television came to the White House, with CNN receiving space there. Gradually, cable TV would allow the White House to produce dramatic settings for the president to deliver carefully scripted appearances for delivery throughout the day, not just for the evening news broadcasts. The Reagan team fine-tuned the organizational structure created during the Nixon period by developing its own television studio as well as a staff to book appearances for those representing its administration on cable and network programs. Reagan built on the presidential stages discovered by Nixon, such as televised prime time press conferences from the East Room of the White House.

By the time Bill Clinton and George W. Bush reached the White House, there were publicity units available for them to use or not use and to shape as they wished. Both used the structure of the offices, albeit in somewhat different ways. Both had to adjust organizationally to the opportunities and minute-by-minute information demands presented by the growth of cable television networks and the development of the Internet.

By the last years of the Clinton administration, with three networks plus two cable networks following the president's speeches and remarks, there was every incentive for the president to speak frequently. His public speeches could easily be televised, as the technology to broadcast live from remote locations was in place once news organizations moved from shooting on film, which needed to be processed, to using videotape, which didn't. That change occurred during the Reagan years.

In the relatively short period of 1953 to 2001, presidential public appearances grew at such a rapid rate that presidents needed well-established communications operations to help them select, design, and stage their appearances. That period is bounded by the beginning of Dwight Eisenhower's two terms and the end of Bill Clinton's eight years in office. With 193 press conferences, many of which were available for television and radio to broadcast, the Eisenhower White House needed a press team to prepare the president for those sessions.

Twenty-five years later, the numbers alone demonstrate the move from an ad hoc White House communications operation to a well-established and professional one. During his eight years in office, President Clinton too had 193 press conferences. In addition, though, he also met with reporters for interviews and short question-and-answer session 1,500 times. Eisenhower's interchanges with reporters were almost all in the press conference format. By the same token, presidential speech numbers rose almost sevenfold in the same period. Clinton had 4,500 speeches and remarks in his eight years as compared to Eisenhower's approximately 700. Between those two presidencies, it was inevitable that chief executives would develop organizations to handle their growing public presentations. This book is about the White House communications organizations that were developed to handle that growth in presidential publicity needs.

Managing the President's Message

1

Creating an Effective Communications Operation

Presidents have communications opportunities and resources unmatched by any elected official in the American political system. Each modern president has a press secretary, a senior communications adviser, and many speechwriters and researchers, with support staff of up to 350 backing up each of them so they can create and stage events, deliver messages of the president's choosing, and respond to critics. They have media ready for live coverage of the president's words and those of his staff members as well. On the driveway outside of the West Wing there is a facility with hookups for sixteen individual television crews to produce live broadcasts from the White House. Inside, approximately a hundred newspaper, magazine, television, radio, and wire reporters plus camera people come through the Press Room each day. Elsewhere in Washington, there are hundreds of people in news organizations backing up those who work at the White House on a daily basis. Yet with all of these resources and opportunities, presidents find effective communications difficult to accomplish.

Getting what a president and his staff want in terms of coverage of the administration requires more than identifying presidential resources and opportunities. They must be able to navigate their way through a system where power is distributed among the branches of the national government and among the levels of government. A president needs to make his way through the "noise" of the Washington community where elected officials and many holding positions in executive departments and agencies have goals that conflict with those of the president.

Presidential Communications Challenges

In today's information environment, the president and his staff are confronted with a challenge in communicating with the American people.

For their part, citizens are presented with so much information that it is difficult to make sense of it all. There is a constant stream of news on their cable television networks and computers. Even the newspapers they read have websites updating their own stories from earlier in the day as well as reporting on new ones. Because the news pace moves so quickly, there is less emphasis on providing context for the news the organizations are reporting. The emphasis is on getting information out as soon as news organizations get it. Our situation is defined by an abundance of information but a lack of understanding of what it means. It is difficult for consumers, who want to make sense of it all, to sift through facts coming in from so many different and often conflicting sources—continuous television network and cable news programs, radio news and talk programs, Internet blogs representing media companies as well as interest groups and individuals, each with its own take on the news, newspapers, news magazines, and policy journals. That situation presents problems to a modern president and his staff, who must try to bring coherence to the available information about their administration.

The challenges for the White House communications team were much simpler in the Reagan years, when the staff focused on developing one public presidential event a day and a message to go along with it. When Ronald Reagan assumed the presidency in 1981, television was the dominant medium, as it is today. All three networks, CBS, NBC, and ABC, used the same news format with their resources concentrated on a thirty-minute evening news program broadcast throughout the country at 6:30 or 7:00 p.m., depending on when local affiliates aired it. Together, the three evening newscasts had a large audience, which got most of their news from those programs. On a daily basis, the president and his staff used these broadcasts as their primary vehicle to relay information to the American people because they knew that that was the way people got their news.

Having a common source for people to get their news meant that the White House could use that time to bring people together and tell them what they thought was important. They knew that they could regularly get people all at once, so they built their news cycle around that one time slot. "Keeping people well informed, getting folks involved in whatever the public discourse was, was easier because you had several dominant players that really set the tone for most of the media," observed Bill Clinton's press secretary Mike McCurry.[1] The same is not true today: "We don't gather around the network campfire every night and listen to Walter Cronkite tell us that's the way it is. We have lost that coherence."[2]

Today the White House is dealing with a vastly different situation because instead of three networks, anchors, and correspondents who constitute the main purveyors of your events, you have a rapidly changing news environment with little center to it. In addition to the developments in the news arena described above, the public is not watching those newscasts in the numbers they once did, and there is a shrinking audience for newspapers as well. With cable news networks looking for a constant stream of news and with newspapers updating news stories throughout the day on their websites, the White House today has a very different configuration of news outlets to deal with than was the case in the Reagan years. "We have multiple story lines developing on an hourly basis, in which . . . images have to constantly be fresh and innovative. We've got to continually be ahead of the news cycle," commented senior communications adviser Dan Bartlett. When they are dealing with issues and media from Afghanistan and Iraq, for example, they are dealing with "a news cycle that is six to nine hours ahead of you and with a different standard of reporting than we're even used to dealing with here."[3]

What presidents and their staffs have confronted in the last two administrations is a fast-paced flow of information from a variety of sources, some accurate and some not. All media have chosen to emphasize speed in their competition with one another. It has been to the detriment of accurate reporting, suggests Mike McCurry: "But the faster you report, the less reliable the information will be. Because it hasn't been tested, and verified, and determined to be authentic. That's why we have miners miraculously surviving disasters, who actually in fact are dead."[4] The result has been less trust of the media. That is something too a White House needs to take into account.

The White House has reacted to the presence of a fast-paced news cycle and the media credibility issue through discipline and planning. The George W. Bush administration is the first one to deal with five networks and a maturing Internet for all of its years in office. Right from the start, the Bush administration aimed at developing a message and staying on it. Bartlett described why discipline is so important to their communications process: "What we feel is, particularly since there is so much competition and so much news content out there, that it requires even more discipline to stay on message and stay on what you want to talk about, or you're not going to have success in getting anything across to the American people."[5]

In addition to choosing what they want to talk about, the Bush White House has also identified the targets of the president's conversation and then sought out the appropriate way of reaching them. That has meant developing a communications operation directed toward local media as well as the national press corps. They have needed a structured communications operation in order to do so.

The Contemporary White House Communications Operation

When President Bush arrived at the White House in January 2001, there was in place a tradition of strong communications operations in Republican administrations and in the recent Clinton one as well. The Bush operation built on these earlier efforts. In the fall of 2000, as soon as his election was certified, George W. Bush asked campaign spokesperson Karen Hughes to take charge of his incoming communications operations. When Hughes decided to return to Texas in the summer of 2002, she was replaced in her role as communications director by her deputy, Dan Bartlett. In 2005 he was appointed counselor to the president, which was the title and position Hughes had held.

Contemporary communications operations involve several units and many people. The domain of Bush's first two communications directors extended from the Offices of Communications, Media Affairs, Speechwriting, and Global Communications to the Press Office and the Photography Office. In 2005, after the Office of Global Communications was eliminated, the remaining offices had sixty-three full-time employees. Add another twenty-one working on communications and the press in the Office of the Vice President, the Office of the First Lady, and the National Security Council. Include also the twenty-four staff members working in communications for ancillary operations in the Executive Office of the President (who are not White House staff members), at the Office of Management and Budget, the Council on Environmental Quality, the Office of National Drug Policy, and the United States Trade Representative. These officials regularly coordinate their activities with the press secretary and the communications director. This communications staff of 108 was far larger than the sixty-seven people working in the White House economic and domestic policy operations, specifically in the Domestic Policy Council, the Council of Economic Advisers, and the National Economic Council.[6]

Other officials have responsibilities that include some aspect of communications, especially those in political offices. Another forty-two staff members have worked in the four offices supervised by Karl Rove, senior adviser to the president, whose responsibilities have included promoting administration messages via his contacts with government and Republican officials at the state and local levels as well as with representatives of supportive interest groups.[7] Getting to particular groups of supporters with information the president and his staff want to convey outside of the mainstream news organizations has been an important aspect of Rove's work.

In addition to these 150 front-line employees, there were nearly 200 people working in communications-related support operations, from the chief of staff to those transcribing presidential speeches. Some of them staffed the offices responsible for scheduling public appearances, making travel arrangements, and analyzing all of the public correspondence (paper and electronic) that arrives at the White House. Each office provides information important to the development of communications strategies.[8]

If one were to count into the communications orbit all of those White House staff working on the presentation of the president and the development of his communications, the number would indeed be large. A conservative estimate at the beginning of his second term has approximately 350 people in the Bush White House working in communications and supporting operations, from senior communications officials down to the military personnel who operate the recording equipment for presidential speeches, press conferences, and briefings and who transcribe the sessions.

While the numbers may vary, communications has been an important component of most White House staff operations. When asked about the numbers in the Clinton White House devoted to communications, Mike McCurry responded with this observation: "I'd say 25 to 30 percent of the paid White House staff devotes at least two-thirds of its time to communications and shaping the storyline. But the truth is, just about everybody who has any serious, consequential role at the White House, from the chief of staff on down, has to be mindful of, cognizant of playing a role in how are we going to communicate, how are we going to present our message, how are we going to put our best argument forward?" The reason administrations pay so much attention to communications is that the stakes are so high: "The modern presidency revolves around this question of how you use or how you penetrate the filter of the press to go directly to the American people, which is your ultimate source of political strength."[9]

Functions of White House Communications Operations

An effective White House communications operation is one that is multifaceted, that can perform four functions: it advocates for the president and his policies, explains the president's actions and thinking, defends him against his critics, and coordinates presidential publicity within the administration and outside Washington.

These four basic communications functions can work at cross purposes, which is why such operations are difficult to pull off successfully. They call for a variety of people with different skills working together on timetables that are often hard to reconcile. Advocating a policy, position, law, or program is not the same thing as releasing all of the relevant information about it. Because different people interpret information in different ways, simply airing it can impede advocacy and stymie cooperation.

Defending the president often calls for a different tone and action timetable than advocating for the chief executive. And efforts to maximize support for the president by coordinating positions and publicity can undermine the building of broadly based consensus by making doubters and dissenters feel manipulated, ignored, overlooked, and left out.

Advocating for the President

Every president needs communications operations that advocate for policies, laws, and programs using events and arguments that will advance his goals. Increasingly, the president and his staff use their sophisticated communications apparatus to make the case for presidential programs. The publicity organization also promotes his brand of leadership and his political priorities. These are disciplined operations in which White House staff determine what communications actions they want to take in support of the president, such as scheduling and writing speeches, and then coordinate them with the introduction of legislative initiatives.

Getting the attention of the public is not as easy as it once was, because people are not following the news through traditional outlets. Comparative data from the Newspaper Association of America vividly demonstrate the relatively rapid fall of newspaper readership. In 1967, at least 70 percent of every age group from 18 years old to those 55 and up read a newspaper every day. Today, less than 40 percent of those under 35 years of age read a daily newspaper, and only 53 percent of those from

35 to 54 read one. In the 55 and up category, only 67 percent now read a daily newspaper, as compared with 76 percent in 1967.[10] Television has become important more as a vehicle for communication except for young people, who increasingly get their news from the Internet.

The next challenge for the president and his staff is getting to the public before their critics do, in order to forge favorable opinions of the president and his policies. Advocating for a president is particularly challenging because once the public's views solidify on a given issue, it is very difficult to change them. To begin with, it is often difficult to get their attention.[11] In explaining the president's programs and goals to the public, White House communications operations have to get in early, before the public has developed opinions on issues or events. In his classic work *On Deaf Ears,* presidency scholar George C. Edwards found that once they develop, the predispositions of the public are difficult to change: "Although sometimes they are able to maintain public support for themselves and their policies, presidents typically do not succeed in their efforts to change public opinion."[12] Fully aware of the difficulty of changing public opinion, what presidents seek to do is form opinion in the first instance, not come in after it has already hardened. For that, a president needs a proactive communications operation ready to focus on presidential priorities in the phase where they can still define issues and priorities.

In addition to the normal difficulty of developing favorable public attitudes, presidents now work in an environment where they vie with their critics and other policy advocates in defining what the public needs. Each president has his own ideas about how best to use these occasions to advance his policymaking agenda. To some extent, his priorities and performances will depend on whether he is campaigning or governing (or both). Either way, his messages must be fashioned for and sold to a variety of constituencies. They must also vie for attention and support with other demands for public attention.

When it comes to raising and discussing issues, Washington has become an increasingly sophisticated city. Its residents include many with long careers of White House service and even more professionals who know how the West Wing operates. Every lobbying group has a public relations staff. Even as the president deploys his communications operation to cultivate his image and to promote his agenda, others are trying to steal the spotlight. In 2005, there were somewhere between 12,000 and 30,000 people working as lobbyists registered with Congress; if you include all of the support people who are not registered as lobbyists, that number jumps to approximately 100,000, political scientist James Thurber has estimated.[13] These people coordinate their priorities and activities to compete with the president and his staff for the time and attention of the media.

Presidential Speeches

The most important advocate of presidential initiatives and priorities is the president himself. Surrounded by critics who use television and other media to make their case to a skeptical public, presidents have stepped up their speaking schedules. The president and his staff have increasingly taken advantage of the additional opportunities to get on television when and where they want. With cable and network television, radio, wire services, and newspapers with constantly updated websites, the president has no shortage of opportunities to present his ideas.

Table 1 demonstrates President Bush's appearance patterns during his tenure. During his six years in office, he has averaged 1.6 speeches a day if you include his Saturday radio address. In three of his five years in office, Bush gave approximately 500 addresses and remarks a year.

President Bush's appearances are very much in line with the number of public presentations President Clinton had, as we see in table 2. Clinton averaged 1.8 addresses and remarks a day if one assumes a six-day week. Once cable television began carrying presidential speeches on a regular basis, presidents could count on reaching voters directly, because cable carried their speeches in their entirety rather than the brief snippets the three established networks play on their evening newscasts. It was during the latter half of the Clinton administration that cable news broadened beyond CNN to include MSNBC and Fox News. While CNN came to the White House in 1980, the other two channels established a presence in 1996 and almost immediately became an important part of White House communications plans.

For both administrations, the high volume of presidential speeches called for a planning operation to control the flow and determine that where the president was speaking was related to his goals.

Establishing the Policy Agenda

More than any other official in the nation's political system, the president has a large impact on the agenda of policy issues. But he has competition from a broad group of contenders, including members of his own and of the opposition party in Congress, interest groups, and the news media.

In order to get ahead in letting the public know the administration's priorities, the president's staff uses a calendar before the year begins to think through how they want to space out his pronouncements. As a guide, the communications staff first isolates the events that warrant speeches. The highlights are the State of the Union and budget addresses after the winter holidays, commencement appearances in the late spring, the G-8 session with world leaders in the summer, the Asian-Pacific Economic Cooperation meeting and the opening of the United Nations General Assembly in early autumn, and the budget negotiations as the year draws to a close. All are anticipated events that the White House can use to set the year's calendar for the president's priority initiatives.

From the perspective of the White House staff, the key to successful advocacy is controlling the public agenda. In the spring of 2002, Karl Rove explained how the Bush White House managed to dominate it so thoroughly. "Our view is that there's a period of time at the beginning of the year—this year and last year—where we control the agenda," he said. "Then the calendar begins to take hold and we lose some control to events, which is the way you expect it to be." The White House staff needs to compile the events they have to attend as well as those they want to create: "Here's the big tube, fill it up with stuff, and eventually at some point the nature of what's in the tube is going to begin to determine what you're saying and doing." In order to bring about a discussion of priority issues, Rove indicated that you need to coordinate among White House units, in this case the Office of Legislative Affairs and the Office of Strategic Initiatives.

When Congress is out of session, the White House takes advantage of its absence. As Rove put it in 2002: "That was our strategy when they broke last year, and it will be our strategy again this year. Absolutely. When they are out of town and when they first come back, it gives us a real good chance to set a message and sort of put people in a pattern."[14] In the latter part of the Clinton administration and in the Bush administration, the president made use of congressional recesses, particularly the one leading up to the State of the Union message.

State of the Union Message

Central to White House communications efforts is the annual State of the Union address. The State of the Union message is important for an administration in two key ways. The annual message is a point when the entire nation turns its attention to what the president has to say, even if

Table 1. President George W. Bush's Addresses and Appearances Available for Use by News Organizations

	2001	2002	2003	2004	2005	2006	First Term	Second Term to January 20, 2007	Totals
Addresses to the Nation	7	4	7	1	7	3	19	11	30
Oval Office	1	0	1	0	1	2	2	3	5
Other White House Venues	1	1	4	0	2	0	6	3	9
Joint Session of Congress, including State of the Union and Inaugural	3	1	1	1	2	1	6	3	9
Other	2	2	1	0	2	0	5	2	7
Weekly Saturday Radio Addresses	48	51	52	52	52	52	206	108	314
Addresses and Remarks	453	485	331	482	361	464	1,772	836	2,608
Total Appearances Available for Media Use	508	540	390	535	420	519	1,997	955	2,952

Source: This category represents those instances where the president gave an Address or Remarks. If the president had "Remarks" followed by an "Exchange with Reporters," the two were counted separately because they required work by separate staff operations, the Office of Communications and the Press Office. Only the "remarks" segment is counted in this chart, while the "exchange" segment is counted in Table 3. These are categories of remarks found in the Weekly Compilation of Presidential Documents and Public Papers of the Presidents of the United States.

The Public Papers of the Presidents of the United States has three document categories that can be used in combination to bring together the public appearances in which the president makes remarks. Those document categories are: "addresses to the nation," "weekly radio addresses," and "addresses and remarks." The first category includes State of the Union messages, inaugural addresses, and speeches designated "Address to the Nation." The radio address category includes the president's weekly radio address played on radio and television, usually on Saturday morning. The final category includes the bulk of the president's speeches and more informal remarks.

Table 2. President Clinton's Addresses and Appearances Available for Use by News Organizations

	1993	1994	1995	1996	1997	1998	1999	2000–2001	1993–1996	1997–2001	1993–2001
Addresses to the Nation	7	5	3	2	2	5	3	3	17	13	30
Oval Office	4	4	2	0	0	1	2	1	10	5	15
Other White House Venues	0	0	0	1	0	2	0	1	1	3	4
Congress	3	1	1	1	2	2	1	1	6	5	11
Weekly Saturday Radio Addresses	47	50	51	52	49	51	51	56	200	207	407
Addresses and Remarks	410	475	426	531	438	545	567	645	1,842	2,195	4,037
Total Appearances	602	530	480	585	489	601	621	704	2,059	2,415	4,474

Sources: This section includes State of the Union messages as well as Inaugural addresses and other addresses found in the Document Category, "Addresses to the Nation" found in *Public Papers of the Presidents of the United States, William J. Clinton*. The categories are the same as those in Table 1.

only for a brief time. The speech is important as well for the internal role it has in letting those in the administration and in the Washington community know what the president's priorities for the year are.

The public audience for the State of the Union message is the largest a president and his staff can count on for his annual set speeches. Even if viewers and listeners do not hear all of it, they will hear segments of it on television newscasts and read about it in newspapers. When Ronald Reagan was president, he could count on a sizeable segment of the public listening to the speech, in whole or in part, or reading about it later. Reagan pollster Richard Wirthlin found that a consistent number of people heard or read nothing about the speech. For the seven State of the Union addresses Reagan gave between January 1982 and January 1987, the number of people knowing nothing about it varied only between 30 and 36 percent, with 43 percent for his message in 1988.[15] While some people do read about it later, an annual average of 48 percent of those polled by Wirthlin's organization saw all or part of seven of Reagan's State of the Union addresses.

In the Clinton administration, the State of the Union was watched in whole or in part by 50 and 72 percent, respectively, of the respondents in several polls. In between those two administrations, however, the numbers watching the State of the Union address of President George H. W. Bush in 1990 and 1992 were a much lower 40 and 48 percent.[16].

Because of the prominence of the speech with the public, official Washington stops and listens to the president as well. The president and his staff view it as a prime publicity opportunity for the president's leadership and his policies. "The centerpiece is the State of the Union," said Mike McCurry, President Clinton's second press secretary. "That has become sort of the public relations work plan for the year. And it is always loaded up with the themes and the messages that you're going to reinforce as you go forward. So you work yourself up to late January and give the speech and then amplify out of it with various cabinet people and the president himself on the road."[17]

In the last thirty years, it has become customary for presidents to follow their State of the Union addresses by traveling around the country, tailoring versions of it for various regions and localities. Anyone the president fails to reach on the night of the speech can be reached at the local level. Then the president returns his attention to Congress. In the Clinton and Bush administrations, the president traveled for several days after the State of the Union address, as did many cabinet secretaries, with messages related to the agenda items and themes of the president's latest address.

According to McCurry, the State of the Union "usually identifies what then immediately becomes the give and take with Congress on the legislative agenda. So you go into the cycle of the budgetary process, in which a lot of your initiatives are front and center that you spelled out in the State of the Union. The work plan, as you go through working up to a summer congressional recess, generally tracks the issues you've tried to identify and address in the State of the Union."

Karen Hughes describes President Bush's 2002 State of the Union address in similar terms: "I think if you'll look at what we did this year, we started off talking about jobs, talking about economic security, what economic security really meant was jobs for Americans." Before the speech, the president went on the road several times in the month of January to address the issue of jobs because they knew they were receiving criticism on it. "We went to a lot of the blue-collar plants, and went to California, and talked about jobs for a couple weeks, where we positioned the buildup to the State of the Union in a way that I think helped focus on the economy and on jobs for Americans," said Hughes. "Then coming out of the State of the Union, we did it a little differently. . . . We did a series of follow-up speeches to expand and further describe a lot of the domestic agenda that we didn't go into as much detail" in the speech itself.[18] In different appearances around the country, the president could speak about specific initiatives of particular interest to his individual audiences.

Promotion Campaigns for Specific Agenda Items

The Bush White House followed the 2002 State of the Union address with a monthly routine consisting of three "pillar events" designed to highlight three basic policy areas about which they wanted the public to follow and understand what the president was doing. As Communications Director Dan Bartlett explained it, "What we have done with this from a messaging standpoint, we basically take the State of the Union, which outlines the president's national goals for the year—winning the war on terrorism, protecting the homeland, defeating the recession—and knowing over the course of the next year we're going to want to keep coming back to those three core themes."

By focusing on those three policy areas, the president and his staff reminded people about his actions on what the White House believed were the most significant issues to the public. "So what you can at least do is think about some pillar events, pillar messages for each month going forward," continued Bartlett. "You're always going to want to talk about the war in a given month. You're always going to have the president talking about protecting the homeland in a given month, and you're going to want him talking about the concerns of those who have lost their jobs and such as we recover from a recession. Those kinds of things you can plan pretty far out."[19]

Bush's communications team was intent on promoting a few introduced themes as effectively as it could. Clinton's communications staff was more concerned about the audiences the president should visit and what these groups wanted to hear. "Scheduling decisions get based on two things," explained Joe Lockhart in 1998, after he succeeded McCurry as press secretary. "One is, there are groups that we want to go speak to. We're going some time in July to speak to the National Education Association in New Orleans. It's just an important group to go talk to. I don't know what we'll say. Then there are other times when we decide what we want to say and we go looking for a group that's receptive to that message or interested in the subject."[20]

Agenda items go onto the presidential agenda for scheduling reasons as well as presidential preference. Because the president is committed to appearing at certain national and international events and to meeting with particular people, he and his staff have to think through his goals for each event. Lockhart indicated that certain speaking engagements were required by events scheduled by influential others. "The president is committed to going to EU meetings once a year. He's committed to seeing Boris Yeltsin once a year. He's got to go up to the UN general assembly a couple times a year. There are just fixed things in the schedule that you've just got to do. . . . Our trick is to make sure that we stay ahead and we keep setting the agenda rather than reacting to what Congress is doing." When he appears at those meetings, he needs to speak to the interests of the individuals and groups before whom he is appearing. Their agendas can intrude on his. How to minimize that intrusion is a challenge for the White House staff.

The communications team has to work with other governmental institutions as well as with the routines of news organizations. Asked for an example that illustrated her point about salesmanship, Mary Matalin spoke of persuading the Congress to adopt the president's energy program in 2001: "That one was really hard because . . . there was a pretty big instant dislike for our position on energy. It got all tied up with the environment." Once Matalin and the communications staff began their work, it was a boilerplate operation. She wrote the original communications framework after the energy plan was drawn up. Their plan was "very structured, because if you don't stay structured, it just—it gets away from you."[21]

Whether it was energy or other significant issues, the Bush White House considered regional media central to its communications rollouts. Hughes was another senior staffer who emphasized this point: "I think one strategic decision that we made—perhaps this was because many of us came from state government, part of it is maybe my background in local television—we had a strong feeling about the importance of local and regional media in conveying the White House message. . . . I think we work that very hard and very effectively."

Since 2001, administration officials and White House staffers have traveled around the country and garnered coverage by local media that way. They also spoke to regional media outlets based in Washington and hosted conference calls and televised sessions from the White House. "When we did a budget, we did [it] state by state and really worked the regional media hard," said Hughes, who regularly handled out-of-town press people, as she did when the administration announced the creation of the homeland security department. She also talked to the editorial boards of regional and local publications. Editorial boards are established by news organizations, usually print publications, as a vehicle for bringing their top officials and reporters into contact with, if possible, the president and, short of that, with his senior White House staff knowledgeable about the subject of discussion: "Our chief of staff did a lot of that," said Hughes. "We had a very complex . . . local media plan to brief local media around the country. So it's not just the White House Press Secretary's Office that deals with the White House press."[22] Much of their energy was spent on using the Media Affairs office to deal with local press.

Explaining Presidential Decisions and Actions

Advocating for the president is not the same as explaining his decisions and actions. Advocating involves talking about what you want to discuss and on your terms. Explaining presidential decisions and actions and answering questions of those inside and outside of government includes providing supporting materials.

Explaining Presidential Choices

Explanation involves letting people know about the context of a presidential action. While the communications office and its subunits handle advocating for the president, the press secretary is involved in explaining presidential initiatives and actions on a daily basis. Explanation involves discussing the hows and whys of policy as well as the details. That is what the press secretary does twice a day when the president is in Washington. To varying degrees, the Clinton and Bush administrations also included briefings by other officials as an important way to explain presidential actions and decisions. Briefings are discussed in detail in chapter 6.

Both the Clinton and Bush administrations have had to face explaining presidential actions in an environment where the news cycle is outpacing the facts at hand. An example from the Bush administration demonstrates the difficulties of providing context for presidential decisions. The administration's decision to embed reporters with military units when American troops entered Iraq in March 2003 led to a situation where reporters on the ground had information before the generals did. While administration officials were pleased with the program, it caused them some difficulties as they sought to explain what was happening in all parts of the military incursion into Iraq, not just where the individual embeds were assigned.

While the embed program worked to the administration's benefit and disadvantage, it also demonstrated the difficulty of anticipating problems. The program was a "net plus," according to Dan Bartlett. "The plus was, the public was getting emotionally invested in what was going on because they felt like they were there . . . invested in what our soldiers were doing." The 1991 Gulf War had a "distant feel." Reporters were not there as the soldiers moved into Kuwait and Iraq. "It looked like an arcade game. It really didn't look like a war, feel like a war, because you didn't see it or feel it there with them." The program of embedding reporters with military units would change the "feel" of the invasion into Iraq.

The White House anticipated that the program would give the public a feel of the troop movements for the first few hours of the invasion. Bartlett said that they had no idea that technological advances would allow reporters to broadcast for such an extended period of time: "We never thought it was going to be as successful as it was from a technical standpoint," Bartlett said. We were convinced that forty-eight, seventy-two hours into the . . . military campaign that they would have lost . . .

the technological capabilities to link up." They underestimated how long those television images would be coming back home—and the questions that would arise from them.

Television reporters such as NBC's David Bloom equipped with his "Bloom Mobile" could provide video images all the way into Baghdad. If one tuned into NBC's *Today Show* in the morning, one could "watch David Bloom and the Bloom Mobile go firing across the desert every morning." One morning, "here goes David Bloom, he's going like a bat out of hell and he's . . . saying . . . 'we've covered 300 miles in forty-eight hours.' Then all of a sudden they stopped for seventy-two hours. During that time, his camera is showing the troops hanging out and doing little. They don't move. And the television audience is asking, 'Why are we all of a sudden bogged down? Boy, they must be bogged down.' What people didn't know was that there was a great deal of activity elsewhere. It was like viewing the war through a straw. . . . because if you were associated with one of the embeds, or a couple of these embeds, you were only getting a thin slice."

Because reporters were in the field with the soldiers, they did not have to rely on generals briefing them. "And the whole Schwarzkopf model from '91, in which the general came out and told you what was happening," was basically irrelevant for the reporters in the field, who were seeing it for themselves and therefore didn't have to wait for the command structure back in Doha, Qatar, to tell them information. Reporters in the field provided information to their network reporters stationed in Doha, where the generals held their briefings. "So they would reel it back to Qatar to their reporter there and say, 'We've just learned that there was a bomb that took out three tanks' or whatever, and they [the generals] couldn't confirm it."

The situation confronting both the White House and news organizations was how to provide context for what was happening out in the field, how to tie it all together. "So you had this big disconnect between those who were trying to give context to it to those who were in the field reporting it. So I think that was the challenge of it," Bartlett said. Their situation was made more difficult because the commander of the operation, General Tommy Franks, did not like to do briefings: "And then the challenge was, Tommy Franks was the ultimate un-Schwarzkopf. He didn't want to be the briefer. . . . So our one guy who could really break through and come out and put things into context did not want to go out in front of the cameras."[23]

While the embed program gained the public's attention and let view-ers become emotionally invested in the military campaign in Iraq, the ad-ministration lost control over defining events—news organizations were doing that for themselves. While their embedded reporters were not al-lowed to go from unit to unit to see what was happening elsewhere, the major television networks assigned reporters to Baghdad, where the mili-tary had little control over their movements. In an administration that prizes control, officials lost the power to direct how news organizations covered the war. In the end, though, the administration found that the program worked to their benefit and did not try to stop it. Reporters and their organizations worked at freeing themselves to cover the war from a variety of locations, not just from military units.[24]

Theoretically, explaining presidential policy, actions, and decisions is an area where the interests of reporters and officials are similar. A presi-dent needs to explain his decisions in order for the public to be informed, and reporters want background on decisions and actions. Mike McCurry explained how he viewed the intersection of the interests of reporters and officials when he was press secretary: "There's ultimately only one real constituency, and that's the American people. And if the president believes in his program and thinks his program is what the American people want, it's in his interest to try and get as much accurate, reliable in-formation out to the American people about what he's doing, in theory."[25] Reporters are interested in accurate information about what the president is doing and thinking: "Where they come in conflict, of course, is when the perspective is different about what matters most." For McCurry, the divergence in what information reporters wanted to talk about and what the president wanted to talk about was most apparent during the period when the president's relationship with intern Monica Lewinsky was in the news. McCurry wanted to move the issue out of the Briefing Room, while reporters were demanding answers about the president's behavior. In theory, officials can see where the interests of reporters and officials overlap, but it is more difficult than it might seem to do so in such a way that the White House maintains control over subject matter.

Presidents Meet the Press

As with advocating for the president's policies and programs, the most effective official to explain this thinking is the president himself. As with speeches great and small, presidents have increased the number of times they answer queries from reporters. There are three basic kinds of interchange presidents have with reporters. First, there are presidential press conferences. In recent years, press conferences can be divided into two types: solo press conferences and joint sessions, most often with foreign leaders. The first is what one often thinks of as the traditional press conference, where the president alone answers questions, usually for about forty-five minutes. In such sessions the president calls on anywhere from ten to fifteen reporters. Joint press conferences are generally held with foreign leaders on their official visits to the United States. Following a statement by the president and the visitor, each answers a limited number of questions from the visiting press corps as well as the White House press corps.

The second type of presidential interchange with reporters is the short question-and-answer format. In those, the president meets with a pool of reporters, a rotating group of reporters who attend events in the White House and on the road where it is not practical to allow the whole press corps. The print pool representative writes up a description of the event for distribution to other reporters. The radio and television pool representatives provide sound and video to their colleagues. That way, reporters and news crews can get a full reading of what happened in the event even if they were not present. Formed of reporters and photographers from the wire services, television networks, and print outlets, the pool might get to ask a question or two of the president in the Oval Office when he is meeting with a visitor, in the Rose Garden following an announcement of an appointment or initiative, or perhaps the South Lawn as he leaves for a trip. There is usually little official warning that the president will take questions, which differs from press conferences, where there is advance notice.

The third type of exchange with reporters that presidents use to discuss their thinking and their policies are interviews with individual reporters or groups of them. Sometimes those sessions are held to explain a particular action or situation. When the CBS program 60 Minutes carried photographs of the abuse of Iraqi prisoners by American soldiers in the Baghdad prison of Abu Ghraib, President Bush did an interview with Arab television networks Al Arabiya and Al-Ahram International.[26] Before he went to St. Petersburg, Russia, for the G-8 meeting in July 2006, he met with reporters from Germany and Russia to talk about his priorities for his visits to the reporters' respective countries.[27] On the domestic front, when President Bush was facing criticism for his administration's slow response to the unfolding Middle East crisis that summer, he agreed to an interview with Fox News talk show host Neil Cavuto on August 1, 2006. Such sessions can be used to explain an action or to shift the focus to a positive aspect of the president's record. In the case of the interview with Cavuto, Bush talked about his administration's role in improving the economy. His interview took place in Miami, where there is a substantial Jewish population interested in hearing his response to the Israeli missile strikes on Lebanon. In addition to talking with Cavuto, the president spoke with reporters from the local ABC and Fox affiliates.

The patterns of press interchanges found in table 3 demonstrate the relatively high number of press contacts in the first year of the administration and then the different balances that are struck in different years among forums where President Bush entertains reporters' queries. In 2001, he had a weekly average of 4.1 press contacts in a five-day week, while in 2006 it was down to 2.4. But in 2004, the president gave a very high number of speeches. The president gave multiple speeches a day during his reelection campaign, but his team wanted to reduce his vulnerability to unpredictable problems by reducing the occasions in which he responded to press queries.

In the early days of an administration, when the president was introducing his programs and his new appointees, there was little to fear in having the president answer a few questions on a regular basis. As critics emerge and the questions become tougher, the frequency of the sessions falls off. The election campaign is a time when short question-and-answer sessions and solo press conferences are cut back because they are relatively risky.

Joint press conference numbers are more consistent from year to year than solo sessions, as the latter have their own rhythms. Joint sessions have come to have more diplomatic than domestic political importance. These are occasions where the president and the visiting foreign dignitary describe their meetings. It suits the purposes of any administration as it reduces the possibility of the visitor stepping outside of the White House and giving his or her own explanation of events without the president present to give his.

The interchanges that President George W. Bush has had with reporters are less frequent than those of President Clinton, but Clinton had more interchanges with reporters than any recent president. Table 4 demonstrates the very high number of contacts he had with reporters, particularly in his first two years in office. In looking at their figures in terms of how their administrations progressed, President Bush increased the number of solo press conferences in his second term, while President Clinton had far fewer of them in his second. That is significant, as the solo press conference is the forum where presidents are most vulnerable to questions about issues and events they don't want to talk about.

No matter what the exact numbers, both Clinton and Bush answered reporters' questions relatively frequently. In order to prepare them for those sessions, they required a strong staff operation to gather information on possible questions and, of course, responses. As we will see in chapter 7, the two presidents prepared for such sessions in different ways, but in both cases their staffs did preparatory work.

Defending the President against Critics

Defending a president calls for different strategies, timetables, and skills than advocating for a chief executive or providing explanations reporters will accept. Defensive communications operations are responsive ones with a short timetable. Defense is necessary when a president, his staff, or members of his administration make mistakes or are faced with criticism or unanticipated events. It is also necessary when the president takes a newsworthy action that his critics view as an opportune moment to steal some of the spotlight by making statements reporters will also consider newsworthy. Defense also calls for press secretaries to challenge reporters when the president and his staff find a news story unfair.

Critics act quickly when the president is involved. When President George W. Bush in early 2006 replaced Chief of Staff Andrew Card with Joshua Bolten, head of the Office of Management and Budget, his critics almost immediately provided reporters with information critical of the administration's budget policies and Bolten's role in them. President Bush made his announcement in the Oval Office at 8:31 a.m. At 9:52 the Democratic National Committee sent out a statement attacking Bolten: "From stonewalling Congress about Katrina relief and the cost of the Medicare drug benefit to creating a 'shadow budget' with costs that will explode in 2009 to concealing the true reasons for the ballooning deficits this Administration has created, Josh Bolten is responsible for this Administration's long series of policy failures."[28] Shortly after the DNC message, Senate Minority Leader Harry Reid criticized the appointment of Bolten, as did House Minority Leader Nancy Pelosi.

At 11:11 a.m., approximately an hour after statements from the Democratic National Committee and the congressional Democratic leaders, the Center for American Progress, a think tank operated by former Clinton

Table 3. President George W. Bush's Public Interchanges with Reporters

	2001	2002	2003	2004	2005	2006	First Term	Second Term to January 20, 2007	Totals
Public Question and Answer Sessions other than Press Conferences, by Location	143	96	66	47	40	38	355	75	430
White House, including Camp David, Air Force One, Blair House	92	48	36	26	22	22	204	42	246
In Washington, D.C.	9	8	3	1	6	2	22	7	29
Outside of D.C., inside the U.S.	32	31	18	18	7	8	99	15	114
Outside of the U.S.	10	9	9	2	5	6	30	11	41

Press Conferences	19	20	26	24	32	29	89	62	151
Solo	4	3	4	6	8	10	17	18	35
Joint	15	17	22	18	24	19	72	44	116
Interviews with News Organizations	49	34	45	69	45	55	209	96	305
Total Interchanges with Reporters	211	150	137	140	117	122	653	233	886

Source: The interview numbers here are provided to me by the White House. It does not include off-the-record interviews. The numbers found in the Weekly Compilation of Presidential Documents and Public Papers of the Presidents of the United States reflect only a portion of the interviews conducted. Those conducting the interview traditionally own the recording and control its release. The White House, however, does release interviews with foreign reporters where a translation is involved, as it has an interest in making certain there is an accurate record in English of what was said by the president. The figures for round tables with reporters refers to sessions with journalists from foreign countries prior to a trip to those countries and with specialty reporters, such as those focusing on economic issues and those from a state or region where the White House groups together several reporters for an interview with the president.

The Public Papers of the Presidents of the United States has two document categories, "exchanges with reporters" and "remarks and exchanges," which cover sessions in which the whole event is one where the president takes questions from reporters and brief remarks with questions afterward. These sessions differ from presidential press conferences in their shorter length, their restricted access, and, on occasion, their restriction to a particular subject or subjects. Press conferences include those sessions categorized in the Public Papers as "news conferences."

Table 4. President Clinton's Public Interchanges with Reporters

	1993	1994	1995	1996	1997	1998	1999	2000–2001	First Term	Second Term	Totals
Public Question and Answer Sessions other than Press Conferences, by Location	242	142	107	125	122	88	99	117	621	421	1,042
White House, including Camp David, Air Force One, Blair House	202	92	84	88	90	58	62	82	471	287	758
In Washington, D.C.	5	2	1	6	1	1	3	4	14	9	23
Outside of D.C., inside the U.S.	26	28	12	19	17	7	9	18	85	51	136
Outside of the U.S.	9	20	10	12	14	22	25	13	51	74	125
Press Conferences	38	45	28	22	21	13	18	8	133	60	193
Solo	12	17	9	6	7	2	6	3	44	18	62
Joint	26	28	19	16	14	11	12	5	89	42	131

Interviews with News Organizations	53	80	35	24	16	36	36	94	192	182	374
Total Interchanges with Reporters	333	267	170	171	159	137	153	219	946	663	1,609

Sources: The Weekly Compilation of Presidential Documents and *Public Papers of the Presidents of the United States* has two document categories, "Exchanges with Reporters" and "Remarks and Exchanges," which refer to sessions where either the whole event is one where the president takes questions from reporters or the event consists of remarks where he takes questions, usually following his speech. These sessions differ from presidential press conferences in their shorter length, their restricted access, and (sometimes) their restriction to a particular subject or subjects. Press conferences include those sessions in the "news conferences" category in the *Weekly Compilation* and the *Public Papers*. The annual figures are calculated by calendar year rather than by elapsed time in office. The number of interviews found in the *Weekly Compilation of Presidential Documents* and the *Public Papers of the Presidents* does not reflect the total number of interviews conducted. In the Clinton administration, there are transcripts that have not been made public, especially ones with print media. Additionally, there are interviews, especially radio ones in the Clinton administration, where no permanent record was made of the President's remarks. On November 6 and 7, 2000, for example, President Clinton conducted 21 and 27 "get out the vote" radio interviews from his home in Chappaqua, New York. No transcripts were made. These figures come from an internal record kept by staff in the Clinton White House. "William Jefferson Clinton, Presidential Radio Interviews, As of January 15, 2001." A staff member who was present for the interviews said that they were "individual interviews one after another after another. We started at about 2:00 p.m. on Monday the 6th and went until about 7:30 p.m. that night," she said. "And then on the 7th went from about 6:30 a.m. to 8:00 a.m. and 9:30 a.m. until 2:00 p.m." Background information. I have included television interviews not in the public record that are found on a list kept internally by White House staff: "President William Jefferson Clinton: Presidential Television Interviews 1993–2001."

chief of staff John Podesta, released its own attack on the newly named Bolten: "Replacing Andy Card with Josh Bolten is like rearranging chairs on the deck of the Titanic." Like the Democratic National Committee, the Center for American Progress released background briefing information on Bolten.[29] The information they provided went into the early news stories on the appointment and led to the questions asked at the press secretary's televised briefing with reporters that afternoon.

With the myriad of attacks on the president requiring a quick response, the press secretary becomes a crucial part of the White House response team. The press secretary can help defend the president by mediating with news organizations. Mike McCurry was known as a press secretary who was especially effective in defense strategies. Following President Clinton's reelection, the administration sought to pave the way for a fresh start by providing reporters with documents relating to questions they had raised in the closing weeks of the campaign. Reporters wanted to know whether President Clinton had used the White House as a venue to discuss policy with an Indonesian billionaire named James T. Riady.

Responding to reporters' demands for details, McCurry and the communications staff gave out the relevant information. For example, after the election, McCurry brought in Stephen Labaton of the *New York Times* to give him details about the dozen or so White House visits of James Riady, who discussed trade policy with the president in some of the sessions.[30] "We started off right after the election in 1996 going into 1997 with a lot of effort to dump information and clear the decks." McCurry dealt with an unfolding campaign fundraising scandal by releasing information in bulk. "We certainly got a lot of the information out there before Congress could use it to beat Clinton up with, but I don't think we got any particular credit with the press for being more forthcoming."[31]

The release of fundraising documents did not satisfy the president's harshest journalistic critics. In recounting the efforts the White House staff made to give reporters information during the impeachment days, McCurry smarted at the criticism that the Clinton White House was not forthcoming with documents and other information. "I remember how— that's why I got so angry at Howell Raines and his editorials in the *New York Times*, and at those in the *Washington Post*, for talking about how this White House always puts information out in dribs and drabs. I spent two Saturdays in a row bringing these reporters in, sitting them down with [Deputy White House Counsel] Cheryl Mills, who walked them through all the records that we had."

Defending a president sometimes requires a press secretary to take issue with the facts or slants of particular news stories. Ari Fleischer remembers placating President Bush by complaining about televised reports on a speech that he delivered on Wall Street on June 10, 2002. Fleischer called Jim Lehrer, anchor of the PBS program *NewsHour*, and John Roberts, White House correspondent for CBS, about the coverage by their evening news programs of the president's speech: "CBS News began its broadcast by talking about how, despite the president's attempt on Wall Street to restore confidence, 'the stock market has dropped 480 points in two days since the president's speech.' And I took great umbrage to that, because it implies to people there was a causal connection. It actually went up 26 points an hour and a half after his speech, and it plunged an hour and a half later. These were the facts. . . . I told Jim [Lehrer], linking this to the stock market behavior—nobody knows why these stocks go up or down. So how can you link it to the president's speech, particularly when the market went up strongly and then went down."

Fleischer went on to observe that Bush could be as sensitive to press criticism as Clinton was—and as assertive in dealing with it: "Well, if he thinks somebody was unfair, if he thinks there's just something not right, he'll call up again and he'd say, 'You need to get on it.'" When a president is upset with reporters, he turns to his press secretary, who must do his best to keep the president and the news organizations talking. Citing another example, Fleischer recalled, "When Terry Moran asked the president the question about—that started this whole controversy about the Harken [Energy Corporation] stock—the president was pretty mad at Terry. But I told the president that I don't think this was Terry, this was Terry's editors telling him to ask that question." Press secretaries often defend reporters by suggesting that an offending question or remark came at the insistence of an editor. "But he still was pretty upset. But that's exactly where I'll try to let the president know why they do it the way they do it. And I still know we have to talk to Terry."[32] Moran vaguely remembered Fleischer calling him, but he distinctly recalled he developed his question without an editor involved.[33]

Gauging Success of Communications Operations

Another aspect of defending the president is assessing how well the communication efforts are working. On a regular basis, communications and political staff troll for information to evaluate the effectiveness of their publicity efforts by talking with their allies in governmental, party, and interest group organizations. In recent years, communications staff has assembled information demonstrating how their publicity efforts were covered in the local press in areas visited by the president or his senior officials. They also work off of the traditional method of assessing their work: listening to television news and reading the day's newspapers.

One of the basic tools administrations use to judge their coverage directly is the White House News Summary, which circulates each day among senior staff members. In it, officials can view how the administration is covered on key issues by international and national media, including the news and editorial pages of the major national newspapers and the network and cable news shows. The News Summary leads with an issue the president is involved in and presents the different ways it was covered by the major media and, in some instances, by the local press as well. On December 3, 2003, for example, the White House News Summary led with the president's dilemma on the issue of steel tariffs. The summary included coverage of the issue and his appearance the day before in Pittsburgh by, in order, ABC, CBS, the *Pittsburgh Post-Gazette*, the *Pittsburgh Tribune-Review*, *USA Today*, the *Wall Street Journal*, the *Washington Post*, the *New York Times*, the *Los Angeles Times*, KDKA-TV, WPXI-TV, WTAE-TV, and MSNBC's *Hardball*.[34]

There are other instruments to measure how they are doing. White House communications operations have become increasingly professional at gauging the success of their efforts. They do so by making use of the White House political apparatus and the polling operation, most often located in the incumbent party's national committee headquarters. Political scientists Lawrence Jacobs and Robert Shapiro have demonstrated the importance of polling to recent presidents.[35] The notion of the public presidency includes presidents receiving information on the public as much as it refers to the president presenting himself and his priorities to the citizenry. A president and his staff want to know where he stands with the public, both in terms of what voters know and think about ideas and initiatives important to him and what their perceptions of the chief executive are. As Jacobs and Melanie Burns put it, "What presidents say, how they say it, and where they make their comments is a function of what the White House learns from the public."[36] Polling is a key tool for presidential staffs seeking to learn how their president and his ideas are viewed.

President Bush's chief political operative, Karl Rove, plays a particularly important role in the polling assessment process. Matalin emphasized the importance of his polling, noting that in Rove's office where a large number of polls are gathered, "they take a measure on the key issues over time."[37] They want to know the direction and consistency of the public's perceptions of issues and personalities.

The response of the president himself is important in judging the success of their operations and what is in and on the media. His willingness to follow the media treatment of his administration and his response to what he reads and sees constitute gauges of success for the communications team. Fleischer emphasized that sizing up the effectiveness of communications efforts means keeping track of mass media. In fact, after suggesting that listening to what others were saying on behalf of the president could amount, very literally, to listening, he launched into a discussion of Bush's reading and listening habits. "He's a pretty keen student, although he doesn't let it on," he began. "He'll read the papers pretty carefully, squawk at me about them. Pretty much all the papers, major national dailies, any types of papers. He'll read those. He's fond of saying that he's in a news blackout when he's deep in the thick of the news. He's kind of funny about it. He won't watch a lot of TV news. He'll get that from me or from Mrs. Bush. Typically, he'll call up. On a big day where there's something hot, he'll call me up after the networks and say, 'How did it go?' But he's a big reader."

In the end, however, communications staffers in both the Clinton and Bush administrations agreed that their efforts to gauge the success of their salesmanship tended to be partial and impressionistic rather than comprehensive and scientific. Ari Fleischer attributed it to the lack of time to look back and take stock: "This is where probably government is not as efficient as the private sector. We move too fast to look back and have some type of empirical analysis or empirical accounting system like that. I think other than the use of your gut, you don't really do it."

As a result, he was most inclined to rely on informal impressions, scattershot hearsay, and the very media they were aiming to influence. At the end of the day, there is a nightly wrap-up meeting. "At 6:15 at night, we'll gather and we'll go over everything, and then we each report on what we're picking up from the press."[38] Staff members go over how they have been portrayed on television and report on their various media efforts during the day. Press secretaries Scott McClellan and Tony Snow had the same daily staff meeting concluding the day.

Coordinating Presidential Publicity

Communications staff coordinates White House publicity efforts with those of other governmental institutions and with recruited supporters in the private sector. They coordinate administrative departments and agencies and allies in Congress and at the state and local level from the White House. Interest groups come in to back up administration efforts and work with the White House on promoting their policies to specific constituencies through news organizations.

We can view how coordination works by considering how the White House works together with executive branch units. In the chapters on the Clinton and George W. Bush administrations, we will also look at other types of coordination, such as with the president's reelection campaign.

In a political system with multiple power centers competing for dominance on individual issues, an executive branch atomized into departments and agencies, and a news world with widely dispersed media outlets, the president's chances of building broadly based consensus are enhanced when he can count on supportive public relations efforts in other government agencies. For that reason, the president and his staff pay a great deal of attention to coordinating their messages through the efforts of those in the White House communications units. In addition to the communications offices, such coordination involves additional offices such as the Office of Chief of Staff, the Office of Political Affairs, the Office of Legislative Affairs as well as the Domestic Policy Council. Staff members coordinate with departments and agencies within the executive branch and with administration supporters in Congress.

Coordinating Publicity within the Executive Branch

The coordination of communications requires using the resources of the White House and the departments and agencies under it, including the cabinet secretaries and agency heads. In their coordination with others, White House officials try to exploit their wide range of resources to promote presidential priorities. Officials appear as surrogates for the president, as did, for example, Treasury Secretary John Snow in the 2005 discussion of Social Security reform. When the administration came up with a program to promote its personal accounts for Social Security, White House and Treasury officials promoted it as "60 stops in 60 days."[39] In the 60-day campaign, the following officials spoke at the specified number of stops: President Bush spoke at 18, Vice President Cheney 5, Secretary Snow 13, Social Security administrators 29, Secretary of Commerce Carlos Gutierrez 5, Treasury officials 7, Secretary of Health and Human Services Michael Leavitt 5, Secretary of Labor Elaine Chao 10, Secretary of Housing and Urban Development Alphonso Jackson 5, Administrator Hector Barreto of the Small Business Administration 13, and several White House officials. Deputies to cabinet secretaries appeared as well. All over the administration officials felt the call to take part in selling the president's program. What all of this work was not able to accomplish, though, was win the support of the public or of members of Congress, even those in the president's party.

President Bush was interested in systematic communications coordination from his first days in the White House. Among other things, he made it clear that he wanted his White House communications team to coordinate its own public relations efforts with those of executive branch units as a matter of routine. Andrew Card, his first chief of staff, knew that it was part of his job to coordinate publicity with the departments: "I make sure our communications team is not just a team in the White House. It is a communications team for the executive branch of government."[40]

One aspect of departmental coordination is regular meetings with public affairs officials. Leaders of the Bush communications team, in turn, hold regular sessions with public affairs staffers working in departments and agencies. Dan Bartlett, the deputy who replaced Hughes as communications director, explained what these meetings were for when Hughes was at the White House: they tried "to meet with the head of public affairs for each agency once a month [to focus] on the bigger picture." These sessions, which take place every four to six weeks, often in the Roosevelt Room, have continued throughout the administration.

Within the White House, there is daily coordination with departments on press matters. In order to prepare for the press secretary's two daily briefings, the Press Office has daily contact with departments and agencies on issues related to the news of the day. "Our Press Office is in a daily conference call that is what we call the three-meter target dealing with the news of the day or maybe tomorrow at most," said Bartlett. The White House communications team also deals with the public affairs team in the departments on longer-term issues by having White House meetings to discuss possible publicity moves: "But what we try to do is bring them in and say, 'This is what the president is going to focus on in the next couple of weeks. . . . How can you contribute? Here are some concerns or things we'd like you to help us address or we ought to coordinate on.'"

In some cases, Bartlett also dealt with these public affairs officers on an individual basis, especially those assigned to the State and Defense Departments: "It's usually issue-specific, and it depends on the agency. I talk to Torrie [Clark] at the Pentagon at least three or four times a week. I talk to [Richard] Boucher at State." In addition to daily contact with the public affairs people at State and Defense, Bartlett will deal with similar officials in the other departments on an issue-by-issue basis. For example, he talked to the public affairs director for the Department of Housing and Urban Development "about 'home ownership month' for June. She wanted to lay out everything they were doing. So that is one of the more regular contacts I have." In addition, Bartlett speaks with people outside of the Washington community: "We don't have a formal process but a very informal process when it comes to people in state houses or people out there who are just kind of my informal network or eyes and ears."[41]

In the chapters to come, we will see how the Clinton and George W. Bush administrations used their communications teams to design programs advocating for the president and his initiatives. We will also look at the vehicles they used to explain presidential actions and decisions and to respond to queries about the president's programs. Both administrations had defensive operations in the White House that responded to presidential critics. And coordination was also an important part of what their communications teams did.

2

The Communications Operation of President Bill Clinton

A study of the Bill Clinton and George W. Bush administrations demonstrates the consistent ingredients in a White House communications operation and identifies some of the differences. Both administrations worked with basic communications office units, in particular the Office of Communications and the Press Office, but did so in ways that reflected their presidents and the ways in which they came into office. Each had an effective communications operation, but at different points in their terms and at times when particular strengths were called for. The Clinton operation was especially effective at flexibility and adaptation, while the Bush one is noted for the success of its discipline and planning operation, particularly in the president's first term.

While the operation that George W. Bush put in place was ready when he came into the White House, the same was not true for President Clinton. It took some time for the Clinton communications operation to evolve into its eventual shape. When President Clinton took office in January of 1993, his cabinet was in place, but his White House staff was afloat. Most of them received their assignments less than a week before the inauguration. All but a few spent months getting a feel for their jobs and learning how to work with one another. Confusion existed in the first year of the administration about Hillary Clinton's role in the governing process. Vice President Al Gore was a key player too, as he was the only one on the team who had congressional experience. Since staff members were expected to work on many different issues, they were neither restricted to certain realms of responsibility nor generally assigned to specific meetings. As the administration progressed, this free-floating system acquired a strong chief of staff who tightened up the organization and emphasized planning.

The Clinton communications operation reflected these general patterns of organizational development. In the early days, when there was little staff focus on planning, the communications operation also tended to be ad hoc. The vagueness and overlap in staff assignments were also reflected in the communications area, with George Stephanopoulos both functioning as the director of communications and handling press secretary responsibilities, such as conducting daily afternoon press briefings. In addition, he worked on policy decisions.

Although the communications system tightened up, there was never one person or a single organizational unit in charge of presidential publicity. It remained a team effort, with Clinton himself involved in all of the central decisions about policy and publicity. Most of these decisions were made in group meetings, such as the residence meetings and the early morning sessions organized by successive chiefs of staff. Both policy-making and communications decisions were carried out by clusters of staffers assigned to handle particular issues.

While they became better at planning out their events, the clusters were best known for their ability to respond to events quickly. Their ability to deal with unfolding developments in the presidential campaign in 1992 became the characteristic strength of this administration's communications operation. Whether promoting particular policies or dealing with an arising scandal, its communications clusters made effective use of both President Clinton and his staff.

Coming into Office

President Clinton had a rocky start in all presidential areas, not just communications.[1] His operation reflected his disinclination to impose discipline on what he talked about, to whom, and when he did so. "I don't want to be the mechanic-in-chief," President Clinton told David Gergen, his new counselor, in 1993. "I don't want to be the guy that has his hands under the hood all the time. I want to be the guy that's in the driver's seat figuring out where the road is," Gergen commented. "He came to the right conclusions, but he had a very hard time resisting that temptation."[2] In his first year and a half in office, President Clinton focused on whatever was happening at any given time and devoted scant organizational resources on trying to get ahead of events.[3]

President Clinton's omnipresence was reflected in the images the public saw of him on television and in the newspaper. There were few issues he would not comment on and few questions he would not answer. "When he first became president, he was so charged up about having won the election and unseated an incumbent president that he never shied away from answering our questions," commented Mark Knoller, veteran White House correspondent for CBS Radio, who covered him throughout his eight years.[4] "If we shouted a question, he'd stop and talk. Every time he would run by us on a jog, we'd shout a question and, in between huffs and puffs, he'd give us a one- or two- or three-word answer."

In his early months, the president was not interested in creating a system of discipline, although he did move in that direction after he had difficulty getting traction on issues important to him. Three months into President Clinton's term, the headline on the front page of the *Washington Post* read: "Panetta: President in Trouble on the Hill."[5] The subheading elaborated: "Agenda at Risk, Trade Pact Dead." Budget director Leon Panetta, speaking on the record to a group of reporters, had expressed doubts about the administration not only on the economy but on health care, aid to Russia, and the North American Free Trade Agreement as well. It was a disappointing start for a week in which the White House had hoped to highlight the accomplishments of its first hundred days to sustain momentum for the agenda ahead.

Meanwhile, over at the Office of Media Affairs, director Jeff Eller and his crew were preparing to distribute thousands of copies of a handout lauding the president's feats. "What will come from what we accomplished here—more economic growth, comprehensive health and welfare reform, a new system of national service, and the like—is new opportunities for achievement, empowerment and progress for middle-class Americans, and a new direction for us all. It is indeed America's season of renewal," declared the White House assessment of this administration's first hundred days.[6] Coming from a high-ranking official, the Panetta interview generated two days of front-page stories that served as lead-ins for the traditional "first hundred days" pieces. The Media Affairs handout went unnoticed by the press—except as a futile effort to put fresh shingles on a leaky roof. Initially, President Clinton was said to be "unhappy and exasperated" by this turn of events. When he went on the record, he supported his budget director. "I need for him to get his spirits up," he explained. "He had a bad day yesterday because he got his spirits down. I want to buck him up. I don't want to take him to the woodshed."[7]

If Clinton showed an inability to exercise discipline over his communications, his staff shared the inclination, which worked to his disadvantage. In addition, President Clinton's staff sometimes scheduled events for him over which he had little control. Early in the Clinton administration, before David Gergen was brought aboard to manage the communications operation, the lack of planning hurt the president when his staff arranged for a town hall meeting to be held in the White House Rose Garden. Harry Smith and Paula Zahn, the hosts of CBS's *This Morning,* appeared with an audience of approximately 200 tourists just outside the White House gate.

After asking the president about his low performance in recent public opinion polls, Smith delivered a personal critique that many would find humiliating. "I know you don't pay attention to this sort of stuff—polls. You never pay attention probably, right? The negatives are now higher than the positives in the polls," Smith said. "I think people in America want to see you succeed, but I just want to see a raise of hands this morning—and don't be intimidated just because you're in the Rose Garden—(laughter)—do you feel like he could be doing a better job?" He told the president, "A lot of folks feel that way." He then asked the president, "What went wrong?" The president had provided a network television host with a forum who used it to encourage ordinary voters to show how little they thought of him. Accepting the anchor's premise, President Clinton responded, "We've done a lousy job of cutting through the fog that surrounds this town."[8]

In complaining about the Washington fog, Clinton was smarting from what he considered to be a press uninterested in the achievements of his administration. At the beginning of 1993, Bill Clinton came into office still sensitive over criticisms he had received from his adversaries during his campaign. In the spring of 1993, at a question-and-answer session held during the American Newspaper Association's annual convention, he described just how little control he felt over how his administration was covered by journalists. "When you're not in a campaign, when you have to stay there and go to work, you are at the mercy of press coverage." To his way of thinking, the defeat of his $16 billion economic stimulus package had received "fifty times the press coverage" accorded his successfully negotiated budget resolution, which involved vastly more money. This relative lack of coverage he attributed to the budget resolution being a victory rather than a defeat: "Because we won. And we won in record time and in short order." He concluded, "That's just the way this deal works."[9]

Being always willing to respond to issues others had brought up had consequences for the president in a policy context. He quickly lost control of his agenda and was buffeted about by those who wanted his attention.

The energy he wanted to use to talk about the economy was directed toward side issues that cost him political support, such as gays in the military. It took him the better part of two years to develop a disciplined organization and process that reined in his tendency to speak on issues early in the process as well as often. He learned he had a communications apparatus that could do some of the work for him.

The first step was appointing David Gergen as a counselor to the president. Gergen had worked in three previous administrations, all of them Republican, but he had become known as a master of presidential public relations while serving in the Reagan White House. "I'm in trouble. I need your help," Clinton told Gergen in a thirty-minute post-midnight telephone conversation in which the president asked Gergen to come work in the White House. Gergen recounts that President Clinton appealed to him with the following points: "How my experience and judgment could help him out. How I could serve as a bridge to the press, to Republicans, and to people I respected in Washington. How much it mattered to the country: Would I please consider it?"[10]

During his succession of White House years, Gergen had established productive relationships with many reporters. Both his experience and these relationships worked to Clinton's benefit during the time Gergen served as his counselor. Staff members complained about his presence to reporters covering the administration, but his advice benefited the president, particularly with the passage of the North American Free Trade Agreement.[11]

Clinton's new hopes for communications reflected a comparable evolution in his thinking about White House organization. Bruce Lindsey, deputy counsel to the president for special projects and perhaps the senior staffer closest to him, noted that the decision-making process Clinton brought into the White House is "not a real structured sort of deal."[12] With Thomas "Mack" McLarty, an Arkansas friend whom he had known since grade school, installed as his chief of staff, his administration lacked the centralized professionalism that might have permitted it to be proactive on publicity.

By late 1994, Clinton had been burned enough by his public relations missteps to believe that his administration required a top-rate communications team. He realized he needed to get traction for his presidency, and using the news media effectively was front and center on his list of necessary changes. For her part, First Lady Hillary Clinton made the same adjustment. By the second year, she had learned the importance of communications in the policymaking process through her unsuccessful promotion of the administration's health care proposal. She retained her West Wing office, a first for a presidential spouse, but by 1994 was no longer viewed as a major player in the administration's decision-making process, except perhaps on appointments.[13] For example, she did not attend the important weekly executive residence meetings in which the president met with his top aides and political advisers to discuss administration initiatives.

After he left office, President Clinton stated his belief that his early days were marked by two shortcomings: "I spent so much time on the cabinet that I hardly spent any time on the White House staff, and I gave almost no thought to how to keep the public's focus on my most important priorities, rather than on competing stories that, at the least, would divert public attention from the big issues and, at worst, could make it appear that I was neglecting those priorities." As his presidency unfolded, though, he spent more time selecting his senior White House staff, and he learned to stay focused on his major political and policy objectives.[14]

Advocating for the President

The president's view of communications matured from his complaints in the early days about the lack of coverage of his economic package to a broader belief in the need of the president to focus public attention on issues of importance to him—and to use the media to do so. Gradually, he and his staff developed an operation where they thought through their planning so that issues important to the president got the media attention they wanted. Presidential speeches were an important part of advocating for his initiatives.

President Clinton paid a great deal of attention to his speeches, according to John Podesta, who closely followed the president's speech patterns while he was deputy chief of staff and then chief of staff. Podesta said that Clinton took great pains to use language that had meaning for people. Clinton was "the major blue pencil on the eloquence. Take it all out. This is bullshit. His favorite expression was 'words, words, words.' He'd just scratch it all out because it . . . sounded good but it didn't mean anything."

The other point about his speech preparation was his emphasis on people understanding what he was saying: "Every time you'd put a text in front of him, he'd make you stand over his chair. He'd struggle over a phrase or a word—I'm talking in radio addresses that nobody paid attention to—because he viewed his words to the public as being an opportunity really to help them understand what he was trying to do or where he was trying to go in the country." He spent a great deal of time on his State of the Union address: "It was more than just programs. It was really him trying to tell a story about, where I want to go. And I think that he thought the public didn't have much opportunity to hear in an unadulterated way what he was thinking about, what he thought was important, what he thought they should think is important and where the country ought to go."[15] He wanted to make the most of those opportunities where he knew he had a substantial audience listening to a whole speech rather than thirty-second clips played on television newscasts.

An example of a speech where President Clinton sought to create public awareness was one he gave dealing with global warming. Early in October of 1997, before the Climate Change Conference held later that fall in Kyoto, Japan, Clinton spoke in the East Room of the White House. His audience was a group of television weather forecasters from around the country. Clinton and his communications team wanted to reach an audience beyond those who followed politics. In this case, the president spoke after the Senate had voted two months earlier, by a 95-0 vote, to reject a Kyoto agreement that did not include restrictions on undeveloped as well as developed countries. With a cool reception to U.S. participation in a Kyoto agreement, President Clinton sought to raise awareness of what global warming meant to society.

In his welcoming remarks, Clinton discussed the challenge of making people aware of a problem when it is not clearly in evidence, calling it a challenge that applied to many issues, not just the gradual but inevitable warming of the earth: "If we have a problem that is a clear and present danger, that we can see and feel, we get right on it," he began. "How did we get to the Moon? Because the Russians beat us into space, so we knew how to keep score, we would beat them to the Moon."

He told the assembled group that as experts on the weather, they could educate people on the issue of global warming. He said that he wanted the general public to be educated because "right now, while the scientists see the train coming through the tunnel, most Americans haven't heard the whistle blowing. They don't sense that it's out there as a big issue. And I really believe, as President, one of my most important jobs is to tell the American people what the big issues are. If we start with a certain set of principles, we nearly always come to the right place."[16]

In concluding his remarks, the president segued to a discussion of how he had built a consensus about the need for a balanced budget by showing various interested parties how it addressed their specific concerns. Critical to the passage of his deficit-reduction plan was creating public awareness not only of the problem but of the ingredients required for a solution as well: "That's how we have to deal with this climate change issue. We have to say, 'There's a challenge out there, we have to respond to it, here's the principles we want in our response.' And then we have to get after it. But we can't do it until we build the awareness of the American people."[17]

The Clinton White House asked the weather forecasters to the White House and encouraged them to use the North Lawn to do their weather reports back home with their local audiences because they were interested in reaching people who were not necessarily interested in politics. The president and his staff realized that people watch local television in greater numbers than the national network evening news programs. By having the weather forecasters at the White House, they would get good publicity in local areas throughout the country.

Press Secretary Mike McCurry explained their thinking in bringing in the forecasters: "There are times when you really need to try to shake things up and really reach a whole different universe of people," McCurry said. "In order to build interest in the policies of global warming, we brought weather forecasters to the White House." They were appealing to an audience interested in more than politics. "Everybody watches the [local] news, irrespective of whether they're a political junkie or not. Everyone watches the weather." The Clinton communications team understood the value of focusing on particular segments of the population: "You try to find different and interesting ways to engage different audiences at different times. But the truth is, most presidential communications are not aimed at the entire country; they're aimed at different segments of the total population."[18]

In five years, Clinton's view was that news organizations had become biased antagonists who had acquired the conviction that they were the key to crucial consensus building. And he himself had gone from being an unpolished off-the-cuff speaker to a savvy communications professional. His communications team now had a good sense of how to find new audiences, including ones chosen from beyond the political realm.

As his knowledge of presidential publicity resources and opportunities grew, Clinton folded communications into his goals, including when he traveled. The views he expressed to the weather forecasters were echoed in his pleasure at the exposure that his 1998 trip to Africa received back in the United States. At the conclusion of his visit to six sub-Saharan African nations, President Clinton and Press Secretary Mike McCurry indicated a link between the goals of the trip and the coverage it received. When asked by reporters if the president was frustrated over press coverage of his trip, McCurry indicated a far different presidential response. "It has been spectacular. It has been great. [President Clinton] has several times told me that he's been somewhat surprised at how much you all have been able to report on this and get good placement and good air time for the story. And he feels that's important because one of his goals in this trip was to introduce Americans to the potential and possibility that is Africa today and will be Africa in the twenty-first century. And the coverage has been great."[19] With a goal of having the American public view African nations as modern states, only news organizations could deliver the sights and sounds President Clinton wished the public could see and hear. Succeeding meant getting good publicity, which he did. There were few policy initiatives associated with the visit.

Executive Residence Meetings: Policy, Politics, and Publicity

As President Clinton's view of his role as president matured, so too did his White House staff operation. During the first year or so, except for discussions on economic issues, the president and his staff found that most of their time was spent responding to what others wanted to talk about. Theirs was an operation responding to the queries of others rather than one focusing on planning. This did not change until 1994, when Leon Panetta came in as chief of staff and assembled a staff with his designees heading the major White House units. After that, the communications operation reflected a more centrally organized White House.

In establishing an operation that could go on the offensive and create and communicate the president's agenda, the Clinton White House placed a high value on bringing together the politics, policy, and publicity people involved in his agenda. One important element of the Clinton White House operation from 1995 on was the regular meeting the president held with his staff and others to talk about the agenda. By that time, preparing for his reelection campaign, Clinton had become directly involved in communications issues himself.[20] He hosted weekly meetings in the Executive Residence devoted to issues related to politics and governance. In these residence meetings, which began in 1995 and continued through the rest of his administration, Clinton brought together his policy staffers with professionals inside and outside of the White House who were knowledgeable about the use of official events to promote policy agendas.

Described as a "floating craps game," by Mike McCurry, the pivotal sessions varied both in what was discussed and in who took part.[21] Rahm Emanuel, then serving as an assistant for communications planning, described the basic interests that were usually represented: "You had people around the room that agreed ideologically, thought about things from a picture standpoint, from a word standpoint, from a political standpoint, from a policy standpoint, and then from a scheduling standpoint."[22] Among the media-savvy political professionals brought into these meetings were pollsters, political consultants, present and past White House staff members, and two cabinet members. This group of approximately two dozen people included Vice President Gore; pollster Mark Penn; consultants Dick Morris, Bob Squier, Ann Lewis, and Paul Begala; and White House aides involved in politics, communications, and policy.[23]

In these weekly sessions, the assembled group combined people with political and governing experience to achieve their combined goals of enacting the president's program, responding to his critics, and winning reelection. One of the continuing subjects of discussion was the television ads they developed to promote the president's deficit reduction proposals and to identify Republicans as the ones responsible for cutting social programs as well as for shutting down the government. The ads ran in twenty key states from the summer of 1995 until the Democratic convention a year later and grew to include other issues as well. "We decided not to advertise in New York City or Washington, D.C., and to run ads only occasionally in Los Angeles," commented Dick Morris.[24] "These are the cities where journalists live and work. If the ads had run there, the press would have grasped the magnitude of what we were doing." Their aim was to reach the public directly through their local television stations, an information source people generally trusted. The president himself was very involved in the creation of the ads. "He worked over every script, watched each ad, ordered changes in every visual presentation, and decided which ads would run when and where," said Morris. "The ads became not the slick creations of admen but the work of the president himself."[25]

In addition to hosting the residence meetings, President Clinton began meeting with a smaller circle of advisers for the specific purpose of learning how to use communications to advance his policies as well as his reelection campaign. They began by clarifying, aggregating, and simplifying the welter of positions that he had taken throughout his first term. "We meet with the president separate from all of those [other] people to sort of hone and develop and provide a sense of shape and form to all of these things that he is doing," recalled Don Baer, director for strategy and planning, who was included in this circle. The themes they worked on harked back to the agenda he developed when he first prepared to run for president: "The truth of the matter is, they were developed by Bill Clinton in 1991 and 1992, and we have really tried to amplify a lot of the themes, the visions, the purposes of the presidency that we believe he brought to it." As the link between political consultant Dick Morris and the White House team during 1995 and 1996, Baer had special insight into the strategic decisions that were made. He added, "This administration has spent a lot of time putting a lot of points up on the canvas, and it's only now . . . that a lot of that is taking shape and coming into sharper relief for people to see, what the purpose and the larger images are all about."[26]

As Clinton immersed himself in the challenge of planning his administration's communications strategy, he also became more involved in developing his schedule. "All scheduling decisions go back to him," noted Communications Director Ann Lewis. "Once we do a plan, the schedule, we bring it back to him. Sometimes we have that meeting directly with him; sometimes they just bring it back to him."[27] Mike McCurry described Clinton's direct involvement in the following way: "For almost four years that I was there he would make some pretty fundamental decisions about allocation of his time." Clinton decided what topics he wanted to discuss and where. "He would make those kinds of decisions that dictated a lot about message and about communications." Further decisions on scheduling came up at the residence meetings, recalled McCurry. "That's where the political people would often present an argument—you have to go out and make an argument on this—and he would either, say 'I'm willing to develop that or let's wait and see how that plays out,' or 'Let's have the policy people look in to it some more.' "[28]

By 1996, with his reelection campaign looming, Clinton had acquired both a savvy, well-oiled communications operation and a new attitude about the press. He remained convinced that the media was narrow-minded, unwieldy, and biased against him, but he saw that it had valuable potential as a resource both for making the public aware of problems and for advancing his administration's approaches to solutions. The challenge was to learn how to work it. As the fall of 1998 approached, White House staff members believed they had worked out a system of using

their president effectively. "One of the better things about the management of the White House six years in is that the people around him are
better at using him wisely than using him everywhere," commented Joe
Lockhart, who replaced McCurry as press secretary in 1998.[29]

The Organizational Setup

In the Clinton White House there was no single staff pivot of White
House communications. Instead, they were governed by a shifting group
of official staffers, sometimes acting individually, sometimes collectively,
who did their best to shape the way the president and his policies were
portrayed by the mass media. Instead of a single, overarching office, there
were four entities that shared responsibility for public relations initiatives, the pillars of its communications operation: the Press Office, the
Office of Communications, the Office of the Chief of Staff, and various
"communications clusters," including a "scandal squad." In most of these
clusters, White House staffers worked on special projects with outside experts. Which leaders dominated any particular effort depended not only
on the issue but also on timing, personalities, expertise, and ultimately,
the wishes of the president himself.

In the Clinton White House, the press secretary served as the communications point man responsible for daily routines involving information. Every afternoon when the president was in residence, the press
secretary—first Dee Dee Myers, then Mike McCurry, Joe Lockhart, and
Jake Siewert—would walk into the White House Briefing Room, which
had a fire alarm fastened over the doorway. Metaphorically speaking, Myers and her successors would spend the bulk of their time preventing,
controlling, and extinguishing fires.

Unlike Clinton's communications directors, each of whom served for
about two years, the four press secretaries had stints that varied greatly
in length. Mike McCurry, who held the job for almost four years, had
the longest tenure, Joe Lockhart and Dee Dee Myers each served for two
years, and Jake Siewert stepped in for the final three months. While each
of the four brought a different style to his or her job, they faced comparable challenges in carrying out well-established routines. In their twice-
daily briefings, they were obliged to reconcile the multifaceted needs of
their three main clients—the president, the rest of the White House staff,
and news organizations—while establishing the official public record of
the president they were serving. Off the podium, they spent their time
meeting with reporters in private and dealing on the phone with their su-

periors—bureau chiefs, editors, and producers. At all times, their job was both to authenticate information that they had released on behalf of the White House and to supplement it to the satisfaction of those expected to convey this information to the public.

Inevitably, their journalistic constituents would express some complaint about a White House action, project, or response. In addition to everything else, as the administration's official spokesman, the press secretary was expected to endure, deflect, and defuse criticism that would otherwise be directed at the president and his staff. While accommodating the needs of fellow officials and of journalists, the press secretary's first priority was to protect his president. Nevertheless, while the press secretary was responsible for presenting official information about all aspects of the administration from the White House podium, the communications director was in charge of overall long-term strategic planning.

The communications post proved to be one with a tempo to its turnover. George Stephanopoulos, the first director, lasted in the job barely four months. Mark Gearan, Don Baer, Ann Lewis, and Loretta Ucelli, his four successors, each held on for approximately two years. Interestingly, their titles varied from director of communications—George Stephanopoulos, Mark Gearan, Ann Lewis, Loretta Ucelli—to the title held by Don Baer, coordinator of strategic planning and communications. Sidney Blumenthal, assistant to the president, who also worked on communications issues, had a portfolio as broad as his title.

To some extent, this difference in title reflected differences in responsibilities. The initial shakedown period was one in which Stephanopoulos operated as communications director but also delivered the afternoon press briefing traditionally given by the press secretary. Blurring these lines proved confusing to reporters and others who had to deal with Stephanopoulos. Nonetheless, from spring of 1993 until January 2001, the responsibilities associated with the communications post were shaped by the basic rhythms of the Clinton presidency. In election seasons, especially during the campaign for reelection, the communications portfolio extended to political strategy and coordination with the various party units. At other times, the post was primarily a vehicle developing and organizing events to promote the president's policy initiatives.

Scheduling the Discussion of the President's Program

The planning by Clinton's staff began with the understanding that there were well-established traditions and predictable rhythms to a presidential year. "We try to think in terms of bookend periods," said Emanuel. "We thought of December all the way to the budget rollout as one window. The next window will be from the budget to the Easter recess."[30] Each of these "windows" featured occasions that warranted important presidential speeches. First and foremost was the annual State of the Union address in January.[31] Then came the introduction of the budget; the two-week congressional recess that preceded Easter; Independence Day, Labor Day, and Christmas; the annual autumn opening of the United Nations General Assembly; and the annual international economic conferences, APEC (Asia-Pacific Economic Conference) and G-8, the group of eight Western countries who meet in summer.

It was traditional for the president to start his year off by outlining his policy priorities in a carefully crafted speech about the "state of the union" delivered with much fanfare to a joint session of Congress crammed with invited guests and dignitaries. According to Lewis, "You will have a State of the Union address, which will include much of our agenda for the year, and a lot of what we do during the year is then live up to, carry out, implement, follow through on that State of the Union."[32] In the Clinton years, it became their policy framework.

Once the scheduling cluster came up with an event warranting a presidential appearance, they would work up a scenario for using it to highlight particular themes while illuminating larger pictures and broader story lines. "Our long-term goal is [to reinforce the image of] an activist president with bold ideas and reflective thinking moving his agenda forward," said Emanuel, when talking about Clinton's launch of his anti-smoking campaign. "The tobacco thing is an opportunity for you to fill in a dot in your larger mosaic."[33] Ensuing appearances became opportunities for the president to reemphasize his concern about the health and welfare of Americans in strategically staged and publicized speeches and appearances while developing his themes in interviews with major news organizations, local as well national.

Once they had scheduled presidential appearances, envisioned effective scenarios for them, and discussed related follow-ups, senior advisers would assemble multifaceted teams to flesh things out. As Ann Lewis put it, "There's the policy shop talking about what policy is involved. Here's the legislative and intergovernmental shops to be sure that the right elected officials are going to be part of this. Here's communications and speechwriting, to be sure that they know what point we're trying to make."[34]

The test of their advocacy system was the ability to maintain the president's strong ratings in public opinion polls in spite of his being impeached by the House of Representatives and then the subsequent trial in the Senate. President Clinton continued his daily routine of giving policy speeches and statements in spite of the ongoing legal proceedings. His communications staff had a good sense in 1998 and 1999 of how to run an alternate storyline challenging the portrait of the president then being presented by the Republican Congress.[35]

Explaining Presidential Actions and Decisions

The Clinton administration was the first to face the fast-paced news cycle that came with having three cable television news networks reporting from the White House and the growth of the Internet. In terms of explaining the president's programs, the pace made it difficult to gather all of the facts before providing presidential responses. Early in the administration, CNN reporters were camped regularly on the North Lawn of the White House with up-to-the-minute reports for their news audiences, just as network correspondents had been doing for decades, albeit only for the evening broadcasts. MSNBC and Fox joined them in 1996.

Access to the President and His Thinking

The president himself is the most important person to explain events. He has several options in doing so. He can integrate a response to an unfolding event with a statement at the beginning of a speech or event—a "topper," as it is known. If it is something requiring an immediate response, as international events often do, then a pool of reporters might come into the Oval Office or the Roosevelt or Cabinet Rooms, for a few questions. If he wants to explain a major policy or multiple policies, then a presidential press conference is appropriate.

President Clinton enjoyed talking about policy and did so on a very frequent basis, particularly early in his first term. If he was out around town jogging, reporters would often ask him questions while he was finishing up, still in his running gear. He was happy to respond to their queries. As the White House brought more discipline to their communications process, he didn't do his jogging in public to the same extent. And he did not answer questions, as he did in his first two years. During that time, Clinton's communications process was often dominated by his comments made in response to reporters' queries, not by the topics he wanted to talk about. While he regularly held sessions in which he answered reporters' questions, his interchanges with reporters fell from an annual average of 299 such sessions for his first two years to 170 a year for the next two years. In his second term, he maintained similar figures, with an annual average of 148 sessions for 1997 through 1999. In his final year, he increased the amount to 220.

Explaining Events in a Fast-Paced News Environment

The presence of news organizations wanting to report immediately with information they have or need from the White House has made explaining presidential decisions and actions very difficult for the president and for his staff as well. Mike McCurry discussed the situation they faced with CNN reporting on unfolding events. "CNN was dominant and carried much more of our day-by-day flow of information, and to the detriment of the effort to try to be coherent in discussing policy," he said. When the president and the staff were thinking through how they were going to respond to a situation, they would find that CNN had gotten ahead of them. They would look up at their television sets and "here would be Wolf Blitzer . . . based on God knows who he had talked to, beginning to shape the story that you were still trying to think through. It had the effect of accelerating and then compressing the time available to actually get on top of news."

What McCurry tried to do was slow down a White House response until a sufficient number of facts were in place. Rather than lie to reporters, which he said a press secretary must never do, he said he would "tell the truth slowly." When you are not prepared to give a full answer, "you have to bob and weave and steer and say, 'We're not quite ready to address that.' And I generally tried to make sure the press at least was aimed in the right direction, even when I couldn't necessarily confirm something or say something on the record."

He put off reporters when they demanded a presidential response and none was ready. For example, in July of 1998, when a TWA plane went down off of the coast of Long Island in New York, McCurry responded by beginning his first press briefing with the announcement that President Clinton would be making a statement later the same morning and so would not be taking questions now. He was blunt in explaining why. "He's dying to take questions, but there aren't many answers, quite frankly," he told assembled reporters. "Our concern, as always at any moment like this, is that stories do not race faster than facts."[36] Without all of the facts, the press secretary's job was to go through the process administration officials were using to gather accurate information, rather than try to establish what happened.

On a regular basis beginning in 1995, Clinton's communications team sought to discipline the information process more effectively so that the president's central message of the day could get out while staff members responded to press questions on a variety of topics. McCurry explained the need to be responsive to reporters' demands for information on subjects other than the message the administration wanted to get out that particular day: "If the White House adopts the attitude, we're not talking about that today because that would be 'off message,' . . . they look like they're stonewalling, not being forthcoming."

The difficult task is to make your message interesting enough that reporters will use it: "So the test is, can you satisfy those questions and try to minimize them and create greater interest in the larger story of what the presidency is doing? In other words, can you create a storyline that trumps whatever the press is having on its agenda on a particular day? And that's the heart of the job of managing this relationship day in and day out. It's the days in which the president's message and program rises above whatever the clatter is that's normally in the background because of the headlines of the day. Those are the days in which the White House feels that it's come out ahead at the end of the day."

Providing answers to reporters' questions in the Clinton White House included regularly bringing in officials from around the government to brief reporters. Rather than have anonymous sources talk to reporters or have briefers talk on background, meaning that they would not be identified, they came to the Briefing Room for on-the-record sessions. "It just seemed to me that it was more reliable and authentic to have the deputy assistant undersecretary who had worked on the policy to be out there and help explain what the president had just announced," McCurry said. Rather than have staff work in the shadows because of the fear of taking the spotlight off of the president, McCurry maintained that really was not a factor in presidential publicity. "I never saw a situation in which the president failed to get the lion's share of the credit, the lion's share of the attention." The advantage of having the administration specialists brief was that they could deal with the substance of policy: "I worked hard at trying to get the answers and to understand well enough that I could answer as best as I could, but it was always to the reporters' advantage, and I thought the public's advantage, to have the real experts there."[37]

Getting Scandal Out of the Briefing Room

Scandal was an area McCurry thought should not be handled collectively, so he had a group of lawyers and their assistants discuss the issues with reporters individually. Limiting the damage to the president and preserving the credibility of the press secretary sometimes called for the press operation to move the issue to another White House venue. Harold Ickes, assistant to the president and deputy chief of staff for policy and political affairs in Clinton's first term, cited McCurry's experience to explain why Whitewater and related fundraising scandals finally led the administration to adopt a new strategy for limiting the damage and distraction posed by scandal. Essentially, it amounted to walling off such problems by transferring responsibility for them to designated higher-ups. As Ickes explained, "Mike knew one thing about the damage control stuff: that he would never know all the facts. . . . He knew, one, he didn't have time, and, two, it would tarnish his credibility, and, three, he would never know all of the facts. So whatever he said on X day, there would be new facts developed that would belie that, and pretty soon he wouldn't have any credibility, and he'd be cooked."

As a result, he agreed that it was wisest to shift the responsibility for dealing with scandal-related news from the Press Office to the Counsel's Office. As Ickes put it, "So, better to have somebody like [Special Associate Counsel Mark] Fabiani, who we had confidence in that he could handle the press, let him sit over there and let his credibility [be at stake]—that's his problem—and preserve the main guy, which makes sense."[38] It did make sense: if McCurry's statements were not regarded as legitimate, then no one would believe what he was saying on the basic policy issues the administration was addressing.

Developing a Credible Briefing Operation

Early in the Clinton White House, confusion reigned in the Briefing Room. There were two staff members briefing the press, not one, as is usually the case. White House Communications Director George Stephanopoulos gave the regular afternoon briefing, a portion of which was televised. In the morning, Press Secretary Dee Dee Myers gave the briefing. Having two people brief as the official spokespersons for the president led to confusion, as Myers sometimes did not have the same information Stephanopoulos did. Since reporters require information all day long, it was unclear who to go to and what information was accurate. The situation led to grumblings from reporters, who wanted to resolve it. Stephanopoulos left the communications post in May 1993.

In January of 1995, Dee Dee Myers, Clinton's first press secretary, was replaced by Mike McCurry. By that time, the president had recognized that there were questions about the credibility of White House information and that the situation needed to be rectified. Later, McCurry recalled, the "marching orders, I felt, were pretty clear. I was to put the operation in shape, re-center the podium as a place where there was good, credible, authoritative information coming out of the White House, and look for opportunities to get the president's program considered in a new light." "Re-centering the podium" meant making it a place where official information was provided and allowing it to be viewed by reporters and others as credible. Still, according to McCurry, the president's assumption was that more effective communications would provide a "better opportunity for our side of the story to be heard, not necessarily better press coverage."

In order to perform these functions, McCurry had to hire and manage his own staff while staying in touch with those of his associates. McCurry, who did the most to help the Clinton administration professionalize its communications operations midway through its first term and into its second, employed approximately forty people in the complex of offices that stretched along the first floor and basement of the West Wing and across West Executive Drive in the Old Executive Office Building. These staffers supplemented their face-to-face outreach with handouts placed in bins in the Press Room hallway; with announcements delivered over the PA system wired to reach the assigned alcoves set up in the basement below the Press Room and on the Briefing Room level; and with ongoing messages via pager and telephone.

The press secretary was the White House official responsible for responding to any query a reporter covering the presidency might have. By the time McCurry took over, this job was an all-consuming daily routine. Asked in 1998 to describe it, he emphasized the unceasing pressure: "I just do not think of anything beyond today as my responsibility. Two-thirds of your day is doing the briefing and then the rest of the one-third is just staying on top of whatever the story is."[39] The press secretary's portfolio was too full to include planning the communications strategy that it had taken the lead in implementing, which is why the administration also needed a director of communications.

Each of Clinton's press secretaries grappled with the issues and rhythms thrust on them by the political environment of the years in which they served. All dealt with issues posed by scandals of various kinds, but they handled them in different ways. Dee Dee Myers and Joe Lockhart, who came from the partisan world of campaign politics, brought sensitive political antennae to the podium. Myers was a senior member of the loosely organized White House of the early Clinton years, so she was less exposed to what was going on in the administration than her successors were. In fact, to compensate for the degree to which she appeared uninformed and out of touch, experience in the administration or at least close contact with senior administration officials was made a prerequisite for future press secretaries.

Defending the President

The longest-lived and most significant of Clinton's communications clusters was the scandal squad. During their first campaign for the presidency, Clinton and his team had learned how important it was to respond quickly to news reports, especially if they were critical. During the weeks before the New Hampshire primary, when a former Arkansas state employee and nightclub singer, Gennifer Flowers, alleged an affair with Governor Clinton, his response team acted quickly to contain the story. His staff created rapid response teams charged with making sure that their side of a story, their view of an event or an issue, was publicized as soon as possible after a story containing charges or criticism appeared. In the Flowers case, she made her charges in an interview bought by the tabloid *Star*.[40] Two days after Flowers made her charges in a press conference sponsored by the tabloid, Governor and Mrs. Clinton appeared on the CBS program *60 Minutes* to rebut the charges. In their interview with Steve Kroft, Governor Clinton "acknowledged wrongdoing" and said "I have acknowledged causing pain in my marriage."[41] The Clinton campaign team learned to respond swiftly and strongly.

Once in the presidency, they also created a rapid response team to deal with any breaking news that might be harmful, especially if it included a whiff of scandal. The resources they marshaled included specialists in conducting political intelligence and research, professionals able to shape and deliver targeted messages, including attacks, and a sense of when to say little and how to stonewall. All of these campaign assets proved to be crucial, as scandal after scandal dogged the Clinton White House.

Whenever a reporter raised a scandal-related issue during McCurry's twice-daily press briefings, he or one of his deputies referred the journalists to the White House Counsel's Office, which included staffers who specialized in such matters. Building on character-related issues that had been raised during Clinton's first campaign for the presidency, the scandals that drew the most attention in his White House were, in chronological order, the Whitewater land deal, the firings of Travel Office officials, the unauthorized acquisition of several hundred FBI files by persons working in the White House, reelection-related fundraising practices of the president and vice president, the Paula Jones sexual harassment case, the Kathleen Willey harassment charges, and, finally and most sensationally, the president's intimate relationship with one of his interns, Monica Lewinsky.

Early on, this administration was reluctant to cooperate with scandal-minded reporters by allowing its lawyers to give interviews or to release documents. Even though David Gergen had counseled both the president and Hillary Clinton to release documents related to Whitewater, none were released in the early years. By the middle of the first term, however, the communications team reversed course, opting for a strategy of openness and defense.

With the arrival of controversy over the fundraising undertaken for the 1996 campaign, especially the questions of whether inappropriate use was made of the Lincoln Bedroom and whether "soft money" raised for party-building purposes had been misused, the top echelon communications team responded by appointing a group of staffers to deal exclusively with scandal-related issues. This allowed the rest of the White House to stay focused on their major policy initiatives. If the staff was to keep scandal out of the Briefing Room, they needed another place in which it would be discussed with reporters. In a break with tradition, the Clinton White House assigned a member of the Counsel's Office to handle all of its scandal-related publicity. The first two staffers assigned to this duty, Mark Fabiani and Lanny Davis, were lawyers who had other responsibilities as well. Davis set the pattern for handling scandal-related information that prevailed from 1997 on, especially where campaign fundraising was concerned. It consisted of two basic approaches: first, provide a great deal of information to reporters, and second, supply thorough explanations of the administration's case to selected reporters.

When documents were subpoenaed, the scandal squad released all of the documents members of Congress had requested, and sometimes more. For example, when the House Government Reform and Senate Governmental Affairs Committees subpoenaed documents belonging to Deputy Chief of Staff Harold Ickes, the scandal squad released three large batches of documents in 1997, well before the hearings were held. By having the full set of documents in the public domain prior to the congressional hearings that would deal with them, they made sure that there was little new damage that committee members could do to the president and his White House.

Some days the scandal squad released so many documents that reporters had to scour 500 pages at a time in order to report on what they contained. Since this team wanted to wall off the rest of the White House from the scandal-related issues, they always released their documents in a locale other than the White House. Lanny Davis made himself regularly available to reporters. But neither he nor any of his associates spoke from the podium in the White House Briefing Room. They appeared before reporters on the North Lawn of the White House or, for on-camera interviews, in its West Wing driveway or in the Indian Treaty Room across the way in the Old Executive Office Building.

Davis also presided over the release of videotapes subpoenaed by congressional committees. On October 16, 1997, he arranged for tapes of White House coffees produced by the White House Communications Agency to be played continuously from early in the morning to early evening on a day when the president was returning from a trip to Venezuela and Brazil. Reporters were free to come and go as they pleased. They could ask officials to replay a video or selected parts.

Perhaps the most sensational of the tapes showed President Clinton on December 7, 1995, telling Democratic Party patrons at a luncheon at the Hay Adams Hotel how he had successfully used their "soft" money designed for party-building activities to produce and run television ads aimed to convince the public that the government shutdown in the fall of 1995 was the work of congressional Republicans.[42] Clinton told his audience that the advantage of using soft money to pay for ads is that "we could raise money in $20,000 and $50,000 and $100,000" amounts rather than be subject to usual maximum campaign donations from individuals of $1,000.[43] Critics in Congress and interest groups immediately seized on the Clinton remarks, which indicated a possible violation of campaign laws relating to soft money. In the end, however, no legal action was taken against the president or the Democratic National Committee. By making the tapes available through the White House rather than waiting for Republicans to release them on the Hill, the staff got the sting of the bad publicity out of the way prior to the congressional hearings for which the videotapes had been subpoenaed.

This communication cluster worked other scandal issues with the same degree of thoroughness. In 1999, when Kathleen Willey, a former staffer in the White House Social Office, capitalized on the fallout from the Monica Lewinsky scandal by making charges about a presidential grab-and-grope in an on-camera interview with Ed Bradley on CBS's *60 Minutes*, the scandal response team was at its seasoned best. The very next day the White House released a spate of letters that Willey had written to the president over the course of several preceding years, including after their alleged encounter in the hallway to the Oval Office.[44] This quick and thorough response was effective enough to prevent the Willey charges from catching hold.

To supplement their document release strategy, Davis and other lawyers responsible for dealing with reporters placed the potentially most harmful documents with journalists they believed were able and willing to look at all aspects of a scandal. Davis himself characterized this strategy as developing "predicate" stories.[45] Predicate stories were ones for reporters or news organizations selected specifically to provide fair treatment to damaging information. "By its very nature, a predicate story takes time to investigate and time to write, and thus does not lend itself to the competitive pressures and imminent deadlines that are inevitable when there is a general release to all news organizations," according to Davis.[46] Because it takes so long to work through a damaging story with many sides, it is important to supply the raw material to a reporter or news organization believed willing to do a thorough job.

Those who worked scandal-related issues carefully chose the news organizations they provided information to. They based these choices on how they best could control the spread of the story. Davis said that when they had damaging stories with many angles requiring investigation, they would often give it to the Associated Press. "Not only was the AP's team of investigative reporters first-rate and notoriously fact-oriented and fair, but we found that when an AP story went out on the overnight wires, the major daily national newspapers, such as the *Washington Post* or the *New York Times,* would not be inclined to give it front-page play. If they printed it at all, it was often buried on an inside page. More important, if an AP story was comprehensive and accurate—meaning, if it was an effective predicate story—it was less likely that the major dailies would have much left to report the following day."[47]

During 1998, as personal scandals involving the president gathered steam, further refinements were made to this White House strategy. When the Monica Lewinsky scandal broke, Jim Kennedy was hired to specialize in related press inquiries and media strategies. Appointed communications director for the White House Counsel's Office, he was the first staffer without legal training to occupy it, as well as the first expected to focus exclusively on the communications aspects of scandal.

Having communications specialists in the Counsel's Office responsible for scandal allowed the press secretary to avoid answering scandal-related questions in his briefings. Kennedy was the first to point out that Mike McCurry still had to answer questions from television people "just because they're looking for something on camera and they're going to get it one way or the other." Yet the communications team preferred to have Kennedy deal individually with reporters inquiring about the scandal du jour rather than have their press secretary respond to queries in his daily televised briefings. "It's much easier to manage it if it's dealt with on one-to-one phone calls," Kennedy noted. "The questions are not as provocatively worded. The questions they get at the podium are worded much differently than the questions I get because they're looking for an on-camera response. . . . [in the televised briefing] it's more of a duel. With me it's just more of a general search for information, and I can deal with them a lot more fluidly because I can jump back and forth between on the record, for background, deep background, off the record."

The scandal squad had the flexibility that comes from having a small group put in extended hours to deal with issues as they arose. Kennedy remembers that they often consulted via conference calls, especially on weekends. "There may be a work conference phone call on Sunday to just monitor what's happening on the Sunday shows. That's not an every Sunday thing, but a number of times we'll have a Sunday conference call and then decide whether we have to react to anything on the shows." In addition to their weekend conference calls, they met in the Counsel's Office to discuss scandal-related communications issues.

Almost every day Kennedy spoke with reporters from most of the major news organizations: "In terms of the breakdown of who I talk to, there's a regular group of people I talk to virtually every day, which includes CNN—Bob Franken, Frank Sesno, and Wolf Blitzer. I talk to several CNN people several times a day. And then I usually talk to people at ABC, NBC, CBS, Fox, CONUS [a group representing stations in smaller markets] on a fairly regular basis. I can't say every single day somebody from every one of those places calls me, but on a quite frequent basis. And then I virtually always have a talk with somebody at the *Washington*

Post and the *New York Times*. And also the *Washington Times* is frequent." The other contacts he listed were the *New York Post*, the *New York Daily News*, the *Arkansas Democrat-Gazette*, the *Dallas Morning News*, the *Houston Chronicle*, the *Baltimore Sun*, the *Boston Globe*, the *Los Angeles Times*, the Associated Press, Reuters, *Newsday*, Scripps-Howard, Knight Ridder, and National Public Radio. He also spoke with commentators who had specialty shows, such as CNN's *Crossfire*, MSNBC's *Geraldo*, and Court TV. There were no media forms he did not work with.

While working in the White House, Kennedy attended both the daily meeting devoted to general communications and the 8:30 a.m. follow-up restricted to scandal. But he saw the two sessions as being very different, characterizing the first one as offensive and the second as defensive. The first meeting "is more active and it's more logistical; it's more kind of nitty-gritty planning—here's what's going to happen; here's how it unfolds; here's what we need to do to get ready for it—and then looking ahead maybe a day. Here's a speech that needs tinkering with. It's more affirmative; it's more detailed." The scandal meeting was where they were "operating with less information and more a matter of defense-oriented handling incoming [salvos] and how it can be deflected, deal with it or turn it around."[48]

To prepare for their rapid responses to scandal-related charges, clusters of insiders and outsiders would assess the issues, assemble information, shape effective messages, and choose the right messengers to deliver them. White House political adviser Paul Begala often appeared on television to respond to questions about scandal, as did communications director Ann Lewis and special assistant Rahm Emanuel. James Carville was always ready to appear on television with sharp responses to Clinton critics. Senior adviser Sidney Blumenthal was deemed more effective off camera. Behind the scenes, everyone relied on the polling expertise of outsider Mark Penn and his associates.

Gauging Success of Presidential Communications Programs

In defending a president, it is crucial to judge the effectiveness of the communications operation and discern public responses to the president and his initiatives. Gauging the success of communications efforts is something that takes place each day in any modern White House. As with most modern administrations, the daily measurement for the Clinton White House was how their storyline fared on the evening news and in the newspapers the following day. It is clear what methods worked "when you turn on your network news at night or begin to look at the Internet and see what the next day's newspapers will look like," said Mike Mc-Curry. "So by mid-evening most days, every White House knows whether their story defined what story the White House was about that day, or whether they were taken off their message plan by some other issue that began to interrupt their ability to get their best argument in front of the American people. So you get a pretty good and usually pretty accurate measure."

The other measure administrations use to judge how they are suc-ceeding in reaching their communications goals is polling. News orga-nization polls and presidential ones as well have two measures that were important to the Clinton White House, McCurry said. "The favorable/unfavorable rating that every president now gets on a pretty regular ba-sis, and then the larger, broader, and probably more significant political measurement—'Is the country on the right track or the wrong track?'—which is a pretty good test of how that president is faring in the public mind and whether, as of now, a one-term president will have a chance to be reelected."[49]

Joe Lockhart, who served as President Clinton's press secretary from October 1998 to September 2000, revealed his take on the role of poll-ing in gauging public relations effectiveness: "Polling gives you kind of a scorecard. It's kind of the ultimate broad measurement. You'd have to be an expert these days to read them, but it tells you whether people think favorably or unfavorably, whether they approve of your job or don't. And each of those has their own little intricacies to them. And then it tells you where people are on a particular issue which gives you a sense of the marginal movement of how effective you are in making your case." Ac-cording to Lockhart, polling is done less to determine the level of public approval for a president's options or actions than to figure out how best to sell what the president wants: "What polling does get used for is once you've decided what your position is, deciding how you communicate it . . . the words you use, the way you argue it, can have an important impact on how people view it."[50]

The president and his staff use polls gathered and made public by news organizations, but they use their own as well. The major difference between the presidential polls and those of news organizations is the fo-cus on how best to state the president's case. "Presidential pollsters tend to ask more questions that are what we would call message testing," ex-plained McCurry.[51] "They are questions that kind of read somewhat like this: 'Some people say this, other people say that. Which is more close to your own point of view?' So you try to get some measurement of how people hear arguments and how they respond to different arguments."

Generally their pollsters sought two sets of numbers pertaining to the president's actions. "One is, did you hear anything about Clinton doing x? [The second is] Does that make you more or less supportive of him?" explained Mike McCurry. "So obviously what we want is high recall and big numbers saying it's more likely to be supported. A great example was the Tuskegee apology. About 85 percent had heard something about it, and 80 percent [said it] made them feel more supportive of Clinton because of it."[52]

An issue where polling was helpful was the administration's support of the Mexican peso to ease that country's financial problems late in 1994. McCurry said, "Bill Clinton looked at every poll there was on whether or not we ought to expend resources from the United States of America to bail out the Mexican economy in 1995. And there was good reason at the beginning of a reelection cycle that you would do that." The polls showed that such an action was unpopular, but Clinton wanted to do it anyway. He brought a group of congressional leaders to the White House to talk about it. Speaker of the House Newt Gingrich, who supported the bailout, gave them advice based on his party's polling: "He said, 'In our polling we know that economic conservatives will react to this particular argument particularly well and you ought to try stressing that . . . in your communications that are aimed for a more broader audience.' It was right on point, and it was, how do you talk to conservative audiences in a way that they will buy into this more so than your traditional liberal friends on the Democratic side?"[53] While the president did not get the congressional support he needed, he was able to take action through a combination of federal loan funds and support from a combination of international organizations and the Federal Reserve.

Lockhart agreed that observing the effects of PR efforts was the best way to supplement polling in gauging their success. He added another measure to test how you are doing: "Another way you can judge effectiveness is by watching the behavior of others. An example I'll give you is we have been pushing now for six, seven, eight months this health care bill of rights. The numbers haven't changed that much as far as support for it. It's always been supported—where you can measure your success is here looking at the activity and action of the opposition."

In this case, Lockhart knew that his administration was making progress when the Republicans in Congress began to grapple with it. They began looking for "something that's acceptable to their political beliefs but is an attempt to take the wind out of ours." Watching the opposition is "often the best way to judge whether what you're doing is working or not, because they are all sitting around calculating the same things."[54]

Communications Coordination

The approach that the Clinton White House developed to handle campaign-related public relations shaped its approach to publicity in general. Building on procedures evolved during the 1992 presidential campaign and institutionalized in the 1996 quest for reelection, this approach amounted to having a core group assemble ad hoc teams, or clusters, of in-house policy staffers and outside political and media advisers to plan and to execute communications rollouts. Eventually, there were three basic types of communications clusters in the Clinton White House. One type handled issues pertaining to the scheduling of events involving the president. The second type arranged for policy promotion events of various kinds. And the third type coped with scandals.

The most valuable resource a White House has is the president. Helping him decide how he should go about promoting himself and his goals is the job of the first type of communications cluster. David Gergen described the big picture and those responsible for its various specific initiatives: "There is any number of events . . . over the course of the year, and you've got to think through the coverage, and how a particular episode is going to unfold," he explained. "It's not one story on a particular day. It's how a large story unfolds over time, and what that story has to say about the person who's in the office, and what it has to say about his term. In other words, how is this story going to unfold over three, four, five weeks as opposed to, are we going to get a good deal on this one day?"[55]

In addition to the Executive Residence sessions, three kinds of meetings were held to orchestrate presidential publicity initiatives. First, there were sessions devoted to identifying events that could warrant or occasion major public relations efforts. Then came weekly planning meetings held to decide what the focus of a particular rollout should be. Finally, there were meetings to work with relevant officials and policy shops on fleshing out scripts for presidential appearances.

For most of Clinton's second term, four people, with others added as needed, were responsible for determining when, where, and how various publicity rollouts would unfold. What became known as the "Gang of Four" consisted of senior staffers John Podesta, Mike McCurry, Rahm Emanuel, and consulting political adviser Paul Begala. Communications director Ann Lewis dubbed them the "Gang of Four," but as happens with most White House meetings, the addition of new participants made its nickname obsolete. The way Lewis described it, "We have what we call the 'Gang of Four,' which is about ten people at last count, who sit down once or twice a month and go through a list of requests for interviews and make recommendations."[56]

The Gang of Four meetings were infrequent during the period when impeachment was an issue. Joe Lockhart commented, "You don't have to sit around and think about how you say no. But there are occasional things that come in that the president wants to do or that make sense to do. You've got to litigate those." While the Gang of Four meeting was held less frequently, a new meeting was added during Joe Lockhart's tenure as press secretary. As a former television producer, Lockhart was interested in making certain they were doing all they could to coordinate television appearances by administration officials and to prepare information on issues they wanted to have television cover: "We do a meeting that I've instituted once a week, now generally on Wednesday or Thursday, that's called the TV Meeting, where we basically try to work with Mark [Neschis], who handles TV requests, and figure out what we're doing on the Sunday shows, and also figure out, looking out a week, if there are any issues we can pitch to television, which generally need a little more lead time than print."[57]

Whether it was scheduling for the Sunday programs or other programs, the staff thought hard about their audience and about what they could accomplish by having an administration figure appear. John Podesta commented, "We never worried much about what was going on on the cable shows that no one watched." Even cable programs that had a sizeable audience did not prove useful in terms of getting across a policy agenda: "Larry King or this or that, every once in a while you could use it as an opportunity," he said. "It was like, that was totally Chinese food. It never had any staying power. It never moved public opinion, never moved message, never did anything, which is interesting because there's so much media attention to it. Yet I think it's just like complete froth. It just goes away."[58] Other administrations have made similar calculations with their officials' appearances on personality-based television interview programs.

This idea of using clusters of advisers full-time alongside consultants to work on various policy issues had been developed during Clinton's 1992 campaign, enhanced during his first term, and used even more effectively during his 1996 campaign. When George Stephanopoulos, serving as senior adviser to the president for policy and strategy, appointed mixed teams to deal with affirmative action and welfare, communications considerations were central to their strategies for policymaking. During the reelection campaign, these so-called policy clusters devoted even more time to devising themes, messages, and even slogans that would summarize their policy positions in the simple terms needed to make them widely accessible. The "crime cluster," for example, included political consultant Dick Morris, who had identified crime as an issue; Clinton pollster Mark Penn, who conducted polling designed to detail what the public thought about it; and Special Assistant Rahm Emanuel, who set up events to publicize Clinton's views about the value of increasing numbers of patrolmen and found uniformed officers willing to help with ads. Communications Director Don Baer wrote the speeches, while Bruce Reed, a deputy in the domestic policy shop, found a way to work police proposals into overarching themes about social health and welfare.

Several of these policy-oriented communication clusters tapped cabinet secretaries and their aides for ideas, policies, rhetoric, and props. During the 1996 presidential campaign, the White House sponsored a host of events designed to dramatize Clinton's positions on domestic issues, such as education, crime, and housing. Frequently, a cabinet secretary, often Secretary of Housing and Urban Development Henry Cisneros, Health and Human Services Secretary Donna Shalala, or Secretary of Education Richard Riley, would come to the White House to join the president in an event and then proceed to the Briefing Room to discuss policy details with reporters. On June 6, 1996, for example, the president and Secretary Cisneros visited the South Lawn of the White House to join a young family buying their first home. Behind them, as a visual, was a cardboard house. The purpose of the event was to promote the president's proposed middle-income home-buying initiative. Similar events were routinely staged in the Rose Garden, the Roosevelt Room, Room 450 of the Old Executive Office Building, and, though less frequently, in the Oval Office itself.

Once long-term schedules and their scenarios had been planned, as the policy cluster groups proceeded with their work, the challenge was to keep everyone and everything on track. "You do try to take a window of time, and remember what your strategic plan is," said Emanuel. "It's a conflict between day-to-day management . . . and, on the other hand, what is your long-term goal?" The biggest threat came from unanticipated events. And in Clinton's case, they were likely to involve scandals. "Every day the deck of cards is thrown at you," Emanuel recalled. "I don't know of any other profession, except probably one, where the deck of cards is every day shuffled on you."[59]

The Chief of Staff

The chief of staff or a deputy chief of staff operated as the overseer of communications. President Clinton came into the White House intending to maximize his control by operating with few controls exercised by his chief of staff. Mack McLarty made no attempt to promote policies with publicity initiatives designed to produce a consensus favorable to their passage and successful implementation. As expected, he left the job of initiating to the president himself. In addition to the president, the first lady was very involved in policy in the first months of the administration, chairing a health care task force and then trying to develop congressional and public support for it. Both efforts failed, and she then adopted a less public role with the president at the center of the policy stage.

Soon, however, Clinton came face to face with the consequences of his arrangements, wherein the substance of policy was not linked to the selling of it. "Give me a strategy!" he was said to exclaim early on, as he and his aides struggled to get their economic stimulus package adopted by the Democratic controlled Congress. "That's all I get is analysis. I never get a strategy. I never get a plan."[60]

To address this problem, Clinton replaced McLarty with Leon Panetta, the savvy former congressman whom he had earlier appointed to be the director of the Office of Management and Budget; he had also served in the House of Representatives, rising to the position of chairman of the House Budget Committee. Panetta immediately established an aura of control. John Podesta, who later served as Clinton's fourth chief of staff, recalled that there was a "notion that there was a completely sloppy pizza-at-midnight dorm atmosphere in the White House. The truth is, from Leon on, it was a pretty tight place." The impetus for this newly disciplined system came from the president himself, according to Podesta: "I think he [Clinton] at least had a sense that 'I've got to have people who are hard-edged, hard-assed and disciplined around here if I'm going to succeed.'"[61] As part of their effort to discipline their process of governing, Panetta and his successors held daily meetings devoted to the development and promotion of legislation. In these early morning meetings, senior White House staff discussed not only policy initiatives but also their communications angles.

By 1995, the Clinton White House had an effective communications operation to supplement its policymaking shop. The chief of staff was a crucial player, although Panetta and his successor, Erskine Bowles, had different approaches to communications. "Leon had a keen interest in how we were responding; he enjoyed dealing with the press and talking to the press and was very hands-on," noted Mike McCurry. "And Erskine was almost exactly the opposite." Bowles, for example, did not believe that there was any value in his appearing on the Sunday morning interview programs. "He hated it and said, 'You said I need to do this in order to be taken seriously as chief of staff. I think I can figure out on my own how to be taken seriously without having to waste my entire weekend getting ready for an interview show.'"[62]

As much as he might have disliked appearing on the Sunday programs, Bowles made certain that communications issues were addressed by handing that portfolio to his deputy, John Podesta. Moreover, it soon became clear that his avoiding the sessions had a payoff when he was negotiating budget issues with Republicans in Congress. "I think any objective observer would have to argue that it was a real asset when we were doing the balanced budget negotiations to have Erskine go up there with an enormous reservoir of goodwill with Republicans to get this thing done," said Joe Lockhart. "I'd further argue that if he were out on the Sunday talk shows day in and day out, it would be a little bit harder."[63] Bowles's television interviewers would have pressed him to be critical of Clinton's opponents, which would have generated antagonistic headlines and news stories, which in turn would have compromised his ability to negotiate with the opposition.

Podesta himself emphasized how much Clinton's approach to communications evolved during his two terms. "Gone are the days where you bring in a few reporters to sit around the desk in the Oval Office and chitchat them up and that's your communications strategy," he observed. Instead, they developed strategies that gave them the flexibility to change direction decisively and swiftly: "The thing that amazes me is how much we can turn on a dime. It's actually something I always attribute to learning from [David] Gergen . . . that you can stop, assess that you're going in a bad direction, turn on a dime, and go someplace else rather than just keep going down."

As it was, the ability to change direction quickly became one of the hallmarks of the Clinton communication operation, especially when it came to handling the continuing stream of unfolding scandals. Now everyone in the White House seemed aware of the power of the press and the need to focus on the coverage of their administration. Podesta explained why, in the most intimate of terms: "The fact that these people live in your house and are constantly trying to give you a proctologic examination means that you have to respond to that and organize your life around it."

Erskine Bowles came to devote a substantial portion of his early-morning staff meetings to publicity issues. But he instructed John Podesta to follow up on his more substantive sessions with meetings devoted primarily to communications issues. The consensus was that communications angles had to be handled by the chief of staff's office—if not by the chief of staff himself, then by his deputy.

Early in the second term, mornings in the Clinton White House began with four meetings overseen by the chief of staff. According to Podesta, all of these meetings included concrete references to "what kinds of things are reported and what things we want to report." Publicity concerns were a top item in each of the meetings of the senior and middle-level aides. Having all of the aides involved meant that everyone would know the specific issues that the senior staff wanted to emphasize and how they wanted them treated. The first meeting, which began at 7:30 a.m. in Bowles's office, was restricted to the chief of staff and his top advisers. At 7:45 they were joined for half an hour by the entire senior staff and selected appointees. At 8:15 came the meeting devoted primarily to the communications angles of policy initiatives, held in the office of John Podesta. The final 8:45 meeting, also run by Podesta, dwelt on ongoing and prospective scandals, each considered from a public relations perspective.

7:30 a.m.: The first morning meeting convened by Erskine Bowles was devoted to anticipating the day. Those attending were Deputy Chiefs Sylvia Matthews and John Podesta, Counselor to the President Doug Sosnik, Senior Adviser to the President for Policy and Strategy and Executive Assistant to the Chief of Staff for Policy Rahm Emanuel, Assistant to the President Paul Begala, and, sometimes, Assistant to the President Sidney Blumenthal. Podesta explained its purpose this way: "We try to identify what's going on. . . . That's a kind of what's in the paper, what are we having to deal with today, what's a problem?"

7:45 a.m.: Approximately twenty-five assistants to the president, representing all of the White House shops, join the 7:30 core group for a comprehensive senior staff meeting. In contrast to the sessions before and after, this is "a kind of report meeting, letting more people figure out what is going on that day," Podesta recalled. "That is, have you turned in your combined federal campaign forms, and what's the president doing today? It's kind of like each assistant to the president has a chance to report on what's going on, do you know what's going on the Hill. You get a little report from the NSC [National Security Council]; you get a report from OMB [Office of Management and Budget]."

Knowing that White House meetings were open and important as well, former staff members holding positions elsewhere in the administration gravitated to senior staff meetings in order to keep current with internal politics. Although not White House staffers, Secretary of the Treasury Robert Rubin and OMB Director Franklin Raines attended this second morning meeting. Both were aware of the importance to their duties of knowing what White House priorities were. "Rubin has kept participating in White House activities, which he started [doing] as head of the NEC [National Economic Council], and he never gave up when he went to Treasury," said Podesta. Larry Haas from OMB, later on the vice president's staff, was there as well. Through the information provided in this meeting, "we usually get a fairly good sense of what's going on."

8:15 a.m.: After this senior-staff roundup came the communications meeting overseen by Podesta. "That's kind of a huddle on what's our communications plan for the day," he explained. As they discussed what stories were playing in the papers and on television that day, they considered what they should add to previously developed plans. "We really try to scope out: Is the president going to be available to the press? What is the storyline? What questions are going to be asked? What questions do we have to ask?"

In addition to its host, the staffers who attended this meeting on a regular basis included middle-level as well as senior aides and those representing political and policy domains. Rahm Emanuel, Mike McCurry, one or more of the deputy press secretaries (Barry Toiv, Joe Lockhart, and Amy Weiss-Tobe), presidential speechwriter Michael Waldman, Communications Director Ann Lewis attended, as did the vice president's chief of staff, Ron Klain; his press secretary, Larry Haas; political advisers Paul Begala and Sidney Blumenthal; and domestic and economic policy advisers Bruce Reed and Gene Sperling.

There was also "a sort of collection of whoever else wants to show up if they have a particular issue that's working," added Podesta. "We usually don't have the NSC there, unless there's something they're doing that day, in which case we'll ask somebody to come." The meeting itself he characterized as "kind of a as-many-people-as-can-fit-in-a-room sort of meeting. . . . We figure out what we need to do," Podesta explained. "We add material to the speeches; we change communications direction." If they decide on a speech change, "we'll say, 'Michael [Waldman], we need a topper on this or change direction on that.' He'll usually execute that."

One of their goals was how to get the most publicity for a policy they wished to showcase. "If we're going to leak something—if we're putting out a new policy on health care or whatever—if we know we're doing an event the next day, do we want to preview it on a network?" said Podesta. Generally, showcasing a policy initiative called for a spot on the evening news the day before a related event was to occur. Some stories, though, did better when placed in a newspaper. "If we're doing a report on cyberterrorism, my view is you probably have got to use USA Today," he noted. "All things computer get on the front page of USA Today."[64]

While considering how to shape a story in a manner favorable to the president, and how to get the attention of news organizations, the participants in this first communication meeting would decide who should take the lead, who should make what announcements, and who should operate behind the scenes. "The president could say something. The vice president could say something. Rahm could say something," remembered Mike McCurry. "There are only a few people who actually speak both on the record and on background," he added. In addition to himself, "we basically have got Doug Sosnik, Rahm Emanuel, and Paul Begala, and, to a lesser extent, Ann Lewis and Sidney Blumenthal, who I think spend a large portion of their time dealing with the press. . . . I think we've been reasonably tight on how we do it," he said, referring to the team's ability to maintain confidentiality when necessary.[65]

After deciding who would get put out front and who would brief behind the scenes, the communications team would then decide on the most effective media outlet to use. "There are vehicles to get stuff out," said John Podesta. The Associated Press was considered good for launching a topic into the news stream. "You can put it in to AP and get everybody going. If there's a wire thing on it, that will just get everybody rocking and rolling."[66] Newspapers were the choice for important announcements about policy. Television was the place to go with something accompanied by visuals.

After the Monica Lewinsky scandal broke, a communications staffer was assigned to the Counsel's Office. Initially, Jim Kennedy, given the title special adviser to the counsel, handled all of the relevant public relations. Yet he also attended the morning communications meeting. "It's good for me just to get a sense of what's going on in the real world of the White House outside of my operation," he remembered. "It also helps give me a sense of when the president is going to be exposed to questions in case we need to work on possible Q&A's for that."[67]

8:30 a.m.: In the final morning meeting held every day under the auspices of the chief of staff, John Podesta considered how the media was covering various scandals. Basically, he said, "it's press, strategy, opposition, what are we doing?" The point was to discuss public relations affecting scandals in a separate session so that, in the other sessions, staffers could focus on substantive issues: "We have learned to try as much as we can to isolate and keep away from the people who do the normal work and the important work in the White House, that cluster of crap that we deal with day in and day out. So that just stays isolated with a few of us and the Counsel's Office."[68]

All told, the questions answered between 7:30 and 8:45 were: How is policy to be served with publicity? Who will lead the day's publicity charge? Will he or she speak on the record, off the record, or both? What kind of media and which news organizations should we use? How do we grab attention and sustain it? What surrogates, especially cabinet secretaries, should be used to follow up on an initiative? Who will do the background briefings necessary to provide reporters with supporting information?

The chief of staff's office was also central to coordinating publicity during the 1996 reelection campaign. In addition to developing the message, the deputy chief of staff in charge of politics, Harold Ickes, was made responsible for ensuring that campaign spokesmen, the Democratic National Committee, and the White House staff were all saying the same thing. "I think there was very little daylight, so to speak, between what the White House was saying, what the DNC was saying, and what the reelection campaign was saying," said Ickes. "It was a pretty tightly run operation. And we ran it from the White House. We made no bones about it. The DNC is a creature of the White House. The campaign is a creature of the White House. We control the message. If you don't like it, get another job."[69]

The chief of staff's office also controlled communications meetings with Democratic congressional leaders. In the last few years of the Clinton administration, top White House officials met with their party congressional leaders every Friday to discuss how they could help each other advance legislation. In the closing days of the Clinton administration, senior adviser Joel Johnson, who reported to Podesta, described how White House officials attempted to help its allies in the Senate: "We look at the week ahead. We try to figure out what the leadership strategy is, what issues they're planning to move on, and how the president can help amplify something that they're trying to accomplish up there. They may tell us on Friday that [Senate Minority Leader Tom] Daschle on Tuesday afternoon is going to try to amend the pending bill with minimum wage." Once the White House staff knows the plans of its allies on the Hill, it can adjust the president's schedule to lend a hand: "So we might alter our plans to have the president out in the morning talking about the minimum wage and try to build a little momentum for a story and for some action that can elevate what they're doing up there in terms of coverage."

Johnson concluded by offering some broader perspective on the Clinton communications strategy: "You try to keep your agenda mix fresh and moving and rotating in a way that keeps public interest in the issue high, keeps the Congress from simply running and hiding from an issue." The president and his staff must also be careful not to "talk about it so much that you don't get covered anymore."[70] News organizations like to cover new issues, not ones where people are familiar with the president's position and his statements and actions.

When the administration came into office, there was little time or inclination for the president and his staff to view communications as a priority just as important as their political and policy priorities. Governor Clinton came into office with little organization to his White House staff and with much to learn about news organizations and how they fit into governing. With little shape or discipline in his communications operation, the Clinton White House eventually developed both. As his administration progressed, he assembled a savvy team of White House staff members with a sense of how to integrate communications into governing.

Clinton went from having two principal spokespeople and little distinction between the communications and press office operations to an organization that effectively handled daily operations and planned out communications events on the annual calendar. The Clinton communications operation matured from an organization in 1993 that could not figure out how to get good publicity for the president's economic plan into one that provided an alternate scenario of a governing president after the Monica Lewinsky scandal broke in 1998. Each day the president could be seen speaking to groups, discussing his policy initiatives, and generally engaged in government business. It took a development in the president's own thinking for the change to come about.

President Clinton's operation was very much a reflection of what he brought with him to the White House. During his campaign he had a strong defensive operation, which he adapted to his benefit once he came into the White House. While he and his staff learned how to plan his publicity ventures, often their operation had an ad hoc air about it because there were so many events and initiatives of others they had to deal with, including his impeachment.

3

The Communications Operation of President George W. Bush

Prior to his inauguration, George W. Bush and his advisers spent a substantial amount of time considering how they would organize their staff. Karen Hughes, the designated senior communications adviser, worked through possible ways of organizing the communications operation well before January 2001, settled on how she wanted to set it up, and then staffed it. Other parts of the White House were composed similarly, so they were ready to go as well. In fact, they were so intent on coming in prepared that the senior White House staff staged mock senior staff meetings in the month prior to the inauguration.

Not only did Clinton and Bush differ in how they planned out their White House organizations, they also set up systems emphasizing different functions. In the communications area, the Clinton operation was characterized by its flexibility and adaptability in handling unanticipated events and issues, especially where defending the president was involved. Damage control was their strong suit. Their operation was quick to discover and assess problems and to respond when they were confronted with trouble or with opportunity. Other than the State of the Union address, they were less successful in planning events and policies in advance. Their timeline was closer to a week than two or three months ahead. Advocating for the president was often done on the fly because so many plans were interrupted by unanticipated issues, particularly the Monica Lewinsky and impeachment episodes, which took up the better part of twelve months.

The communications operation of George W. Bush was strong where the Clinton one was weak and weak where Clinton excelled. The Bush operation did a good job planning ahead on policy and establishing a disciplined White House staff that held presidential information very closely.

Bush's staff thought through how to develop publicity for the issues he wanted to discuss and focus on what they thought was important. The communications staff emphasized the issues they thought crucial and avoided discussing what was on the minds of others. Considerable effort went into prioritizing issues, creating events to emphasize a limited number of priorities, and rounding up people to talk about them.

Where the Bush team proved less responsive was in listening to others, including members of Congress, and developing a communications operation that could adjust to changing circumstances. While they changed personnel over the years, as the administration began its sixth year, the shape of the White House organization remained similar to what they had set up in the first days. The challenges they faced in 2006 were quite different than the ones they faced in early 2001, but the organization was not.

The Bush operation did not prove adept at taking advantage of unanticipated opportunities and dealing with unexpected problems. When information crises arose, it often took weeks for the White House staff to get the matter off of the front pages of the newspapers and off the evening news programs. Protracted problems arose, for example, from President Bush having said in his 2003 State of the Union address that Saddam Hussein had attempted to buy yellowcake uranium from the state of Niger, which the administration later admitted was not the case. Their efforts to handle and then correct his earlier statements brought in all of the senior staff and the president himself, taking approximately six months in 2003 to get it under control. Even then, the issue resurfaced in 2005, 2006, and 2007, in part because the staff sought to avoid correcting their errors in the first instance.

In the second term, the communications team experienced a great deal of political difficulty because of the ebbing public support for the president's Iraq policy and the lack of support of the president's signature issues, such as the addition of personal retirement accounts to the Social Security program and the guest worker program as part of the proposed immigration bill. With criticism coming from members of the president's own party in Congress as well as from the Democrats, the communications team was under fire, as was much of the White House staff.

In April 2006, as his job approval standings in public opinion polls reached the 30s in all of the major national polls, the president replaced his chief of staff and his press secretary. The president and his staff also made an effort to turn things around by trying a strategy not associated with this administration: putting Bush and his surrogates in vulnerable

situations where they would respond to critics of their policies and reporters asking questions about the president's weaknesses. Rather than
provide less information, which they would have done in the first term,
currently the president and his staff are providing more information.
"We are doing a lot more briefings where we put forward administration spokesmen, administration policymakers either on background or
on the record before we do policy," said Karl Rove in early 2007. On Air
Force One on the way to policy events, for example, they have briefings
by "Nerdnicks from the National Economic Council or the guy from Science and Technology, or the person from Domestic Policy, or people from
Education."[1] In addition, they developed a unit responsible for quick response to news articles that they consider to have misinformation. The
rapid response unit in the Office of Communications regularly puts out
information countering press stories that White House officials find inaccurate or that simply require an official response.

The current phase of openness dates to the period after the president's
reelection when Bush increased the frequency and regularity of his solo
press conferences as well as the number of speeches where he appeared
before an audience untested for its support of the president and his programs. In addition to speaking to groups that included a number of critics, he took questions from them on the state of the war in Iraq and the
lack of weapons of mass destruction there, the president's low approval
ratings, issues related to the leaking of national security information, and
the NSA wiretapping program.

Coming into Office

The organization that President Bush brought to the White House emphasized planning and maintaining control over the subjects they wanted
to talk about.[1] The operation was set up to be an advocacy operation with
the emphasis on his choices of subjects. They wanted to make news on
the president's terms and spend little time responding to the agenda of
others, including that of reporters.

George W. Bush came into office with both an interest in presidential
communications and a familiarity with the established rules for dealing
with news organizations. He was aware of the importance of his own
words and the need for him to take responsibility for what he said. Like
many lessons, he learned the hard way. In this case, he learned the resonance of his words. In 1993, when he was preparing for his first run for
governor, in an interview with *Houston Post* reporter Ken Herman, Bush

said, "Heaven is open only to those who accept Jesus Christ." This subject had come up in the context of a discussion about family. "The way it came up was, we were talking about his family," Herman recalled. "And the reason for putting it in the story was that he and his mother had a disagreement [about] whether you have to accept Jesus to go to heaven. So they called Billy Graham to get involved. Which shows that they are a little different from the average family, that they can call a man some people consider God's right hand down here."[2] There was substantial fallout from the interview. "And eventually he had to do some explaining to some groups about it. In fact, I think he learned something from that. You have to be careful about what you say."

Five years later, in 1998, the subject of religion came up in another discussion between Bush and Herman. Bush was at a convention of the Republican Governors Association. He and his brother, newly elected Governor of Florida Jeb Bush, held a joint news conference. Afterwards, the Texas governor invited state reporters to his hotel room for a little press conference. He revealed that he was about to go to Israel. According to Herman, it was "an indication he is thinking nationally, thinking about running for president. A good news story."

After the session, Herman was waiting at the elevator. "And then Governor Bush walks up to me with this glint in his eye that he gets when he is about to crack wise," Herman remembered. "So he walks up to me and says he was going to Israel. [I respond by saying] 'That is interesting governor, that should be an interesting trip.' And without making the connection, but clearly making the connection to our previous conversation, he looked at me and he said, 'Do you know what the first thing I am going to say over there is?' And I said, 'No, governor.' He said he would tell them that they 'are going to hell.' It clearly was a self-deprecating joke. He was clearly joking."[3]

It may have been a joke, but Herman's editors wanted it used in a story. "So we put it in a story, and clearly [presented it as] a self-deprecating joke, made fun of himself for previously having said something that upset some people. There was no doubt that it clearly was a joke."[4] This story caused another dust-up. "The next day I hear through sources that the governor may not be happy with me. I don't know why. So I called to Karen Hughes and said, 'Do I need to see the governor?' Hughes advised him to do so. Governor Bush, who had just returned from jogging, met with Herman near a pool outside the Governor's Mansion. "And I said to him, 'What's the deal; where am I here?' He told me he was disappointed the comment was published. He thought it was a joke between two acquaintances."[5]

Bush had been caught off guard by a situation that officials and reporters often find themselves in, especially at the state and local level. As Herman explained, "You get to know these people, you spend a lot of time with them, you get to know their families, and they get to know your family. It can be problematic, and you just wonder if there is some time when you have to say, from this time forward, we may not have put it in the paper in the past, but now we need to put it in the paper."

Bush understood that he and Herman had reached that point. He told Herman that he could have prevented it from being in the paper by just not saying it. By 1998, Bush had learned two lessons: Good relations with reporters are crucial to communications, but self-discipline was essential when dealing with cohorts who consider it their professional obligation to inform the readers about holders of public office. He remembered these lessons as he set up his White House communications organization.

Bush avoided some errors early in his term by having an experienced communications and politics team. He launched his political career in Texas with the help of Karl Rove and Karen Hughes, who felt rewarded enough by his two terms as governor to become mainstays of his presidential campaign and chief strategists of his first administration. Hughes had worked as a reporter in Dallas television stations and as executive director of the state Republican party before becoming his gubernatorial communications adviser. Rove, whom Bush had known when his father was vice president, had served as Bush's political adviser until he ran for governor and then advised Bush in office while running his own consulting firm. Professionally, Hughes and Rove represented the marriage of communications and politics that had made Bush's style of governing an extension of his style of campaigning, and vice versa.

Even before Bush's election was certified, Rove went to work on a 180-day plan for pursuing the goals they had touted and discussed during the campaign. Chief among them were building up military defense, improving the quality of education, tax cuts, and faith-based initiatives. As soon as he was inaugurated, Bush began to introduce this governing agenda by devoting a week to each of these goals in turn. To expand on the ideas he had discussed in his campaign, he explained exactly how he hoped to accomplish each one. For that entire first year, the president and his staff transformed their campaign agenda into an agenda for governing.

Advocating for the President

The primary rule discussed in the last chapter holds true here as well: the most important advocate for an administration is the president himself. President Bush has a demonstrable interest in his communications and, in the case of the global war on terrorism, the challenges involved in getting people to understand the issues and the urgency of response. Mary Matalin said that shortly after September 11, 2001, "he pulled us together and said, 'Communications is critical on this because fighting this war is not going to be like anything that Americans or the world have seen. There's no storming of beaches. There's no CNN cameras, you know, watching grainy pictures at night. It's going to be a lot in the shadows, a lot that does not lend itself to visuals, breaking up financial networks,' and other actions taking place outside of a theater of war."[6]

He told his senior staff that administration communications strategies were going to be important and that he wanted to be at the center of them. He pushed the staff in terms of making certain that activities related to our response to the events of September 11 rose to his level. Dan Bartlett discussed the president's interest in being at the center of administration actions: "I remember our first big opportunity to prove we knew what we were talking about we failed because the following weekend they sent some documents up to Camp David for him to sign." The documents dealt with freezing the financial assets of groups on the administration's list of terrorist organizations. "He called Karen, pulled her out of church on Sunday," Bartlett said. "She got me on the phone. He was furious. He said, 'Why am I just signing this document and Secretary [Paul] O'Neill is announcing this tomorrow? This is the first strike in this new war against terror. It's not with a missile. It's with a stroke of a pen.' "[7] The communications operation put together a Rose Garden signing event for the following morning, with President Bush signing the documents. He made it clear that he wanted to be the one taking the action, not his cabinet members. He wanted to assert, at the beginning of the terrorism campaign, that he was the one in charge.

Advocating for the President as a Person and as a Leader

With a public generally more moderate than many of the president's policies, the president's communications team focused on developing his image as a person and as a leader, particularly in his handling of the September 11 attacks and their aftermath. The leadership role that he established in his first term paid off well in his reelection campaign. President Bush has often joked about the limitations of his own speaking style, but he knows that people understand what he means and, most important, who he is. During the last month of his reelection campaign, the line that received the hardiest applause in his stock campaign speech was about what the public knew of the president. In city after city, he told his audiences he had learned a great deal during his first term: "In the last four years, Americans have learned a few things about me, as well. Sometimes, I'm a little too blunt. [Applause.] I get that from my mother. Sometimes, I mangle the English language. I get that from my dad. [Laughter.] But all the time, whether you agree with me or not, you know where I stand and where I'm going to lead this nation."[8]

No matter how tangled his nouns and verbs or his pronunciation of words, voters were confident they knew the president's thinking and understood and approved of his brand of leadership. The public understood him when he said, "I know how a president needs to lead. As presidents from Lincoln to Roosevelt to Reagan so clearly demonstrated, a president must not shift in the wind; a president has to make tough decisions and stand by them." His appeal to Americans for support was based on the brand of leadership he established beginning with his response to the attacks of September 11.

Focusing on presidential personality and leadership was a strategy that paid off well. He scored much higher with the public on his leadership qualities than on his issue positions, where many Americans differed with him. In an October 2004 CNN / USA Today / Gallup poll, when people were asked if George W. Bush "has the personality and leadership qualities a president should have," 57 percent of the respondents agreed and 41 percent disagreed. When asked in the same poll whether people "agreed or disagreed with George W. Bush on the issues that matter most to you," there was an even split, with 49 percent agreeing with the statement and 49 percent disagreeing.[9]

The high standing with the public has been a goal of the Bush White House communications team. Dan Bartlett discussed his strategy to get reporters to cover the president as a person: "My strategic goal as communications director for the president, and what I think is in the president's best interest, is the more reporters are covering the person and not the institution, the White House, I think is better for us from a communications standpoint." They wanted to show him as a person because, Bartlett said, "one of his strengths is his personality."

There are several ways of making the presidential connection with the public, some of which represent new media opportunities. One of the methods used by Bartlett and others on the communications teams is to use unconventional media to reach people. In the 2004 campaign, they reached what Bartlett called the "hook and bullet crowd" by bringing to the White House correspondents for "all the hunting magazines, fishing magazines, conservation magazines, which reach millions and millions of Americans. We brought them in and did a roundtable with the president." Some media organizations, such as *Runner's World* and *Field and Stream,* did one-on-one interviews at the White House. Reporters for *Sports Illustrated* and *Bicycling* came to Bush's Crawford, Texas, ranch to go biking with the president and conduct a short question-and-answer session with him. Three other reporters for news organizations, regular bicyclists all, went along as well.

"By design, by knowing who we're reaching, we're going to help craft our message to make it as attractive as possible. You can't change your position, but you can talk about it in a certain way in which we'll brief the president and make sure he knows what's on their minds so he can kind of play to their interests and speak to the issues that they're concerned with," said Bartlett. The benefit is that the sessions are more informal than many he does: "In these nonconventional forums, of news forums, that they tend to be conversations that are more personal and . . . not so focused on politics and process. It's more about, what do you think about this and why." During the campaign, they used the same approach of running ads on unconventional channels, such as the Golf Channel.

In the second term, the staff continued to look for unconventional media to carry presidential messages that are difficult to get through by traditional media. The president's work on AIDS in Africa and his Millennium Challenge Accounts both received little attention in American media. Bartlett explained a basic problem they face is the lack of space for foreign news on television news programs. "On the evening scripts or on the story boards for the morning shows or for the major papers, there is only so much room for foreign policy. When you have to cover Iraq, you have to cover some element either of Iran or North Korea, those things. There is only so much of the attention span of the public that you can get." With these practical limitations, they focused on nontraditional media. "Our best media PR has been coming through Bono—because it is unconventional media. It hasn't gone through the national news, it has gone more through Oprah or this or that or whatever." Those are places where their African AIDS initiative has been highlighted.[10]

From the White House, the communications staff try to attract people to presidential information found on the website (www.whitehouse.gov) by getting them to the site with attractive items, such as the BarneyCam that followed the president's dog around the White House during the Christmas season in 2002: "We were trying to take an unconventional way of getting people's attention. It drives them to the website and then they might say, 'Oh, I wonder what he's saying about education,' and they might click on something next to where the Barney video is."[11]

Another way of driving home the personality of the president is by getting others to talk about him, especially people in a community. One such strategy was adopted early in the administration. When the president travels around the country, he is typically welcomed by officials from the city or region where he is landing. In addition, there is a USA Freedom Corps member who meets him and receives the President's Volunteer Service Award. These greeters are chosen by the White House office of USA Freedom Corps as part of the Presidential Greeters Program. They are volunteers who work in the community and are the subject of local media interest both before and after the president comes to town. Invariably, they speak of their visit with the president in very positive ways. Della Amos, for example, a volunteer with Foster Grandparents in Springfield, Illinois, was the subject of an article in the *State Journal-Register*. The article followed her day from the award given her by President and Mrs. Bush, who brought her along with them in the motorcade, to the dedication ceremony of the Abraham Lincoln Presidential Museum. "It was great," she said of her trip.[12]

When President Bush traveled to South Bend, Indiana, he presented the volunteer's award to Lucy B. Kumincez for her work sewing for the group Busy Hands. An article in the local paper, "She Cherishes Kiss from President Bush," focused on her work and her meeting with the president.[13] Large city newspapers as well as small ones write about their local volunteer award winners. The *Milwaukee Journal Sentinel* wrote about Beverly Christy-Wright, who won the award for her efforts with the Northside YMCA's Black Achievers Award. Christy-Wright also spoke of her meeting with President Bush. "He said, 'Keep up the good work,' and he really likes what I am doing in the community," she said.[14] In Seattle, Sheryl Sheaffer, who has three sons serving in Iraq and Afghanistan, said that her meeting with President Bush "will fulfill a longtime wish by joining the greeting party for Bush when Air Force One lands at Boeing Field." She told a reporter, "I've always dreamed of meeting him."[15] Publicity for the volunteers is not limited to the day when they receive the award. Some profiles run days after the presidential visit. When Lou Dantzler of Los Angeles died, his obituary mentioned that he had received the president's USA Freedom Corps Call to Service Award in 2004 as well as receiving a Thousand Points of Light award in 1992 from President George H. W. Bush.[16] Since the Presidential Greeters Program began in 2002, over 550 volunteers have met the president to receive their award.[17] The program is run by the Office of Communications.

Communicating on the President's Terms: Establishing Discipline

Jim Wilkinson, director for planning in the Office of Communications during the first term and later chief of staff to Treasury Secretary Henry Paulson, said that the president's goal as a communicator is "to make news on his own terms."[18] A lot of the strategies that the administration adopts derive from the effort of the administration to have the president covered when and how he and his staff want. Their information release strategies are based on the president as the focus of their efforts, including having him do the announcements without a lot of buildup in the press. As the staff sets up events, they do so in a way that works for them, including responding to press queries on their terms.

First, the president, not his staff or cabinet members, is the focus of presidential communications. Ari Fleischer defined the president's desire in specific terms: "The president really believes, one, he's the newsmaker, not the staff."[19] That translates into White House news policy in two ways. First, the president does not want to see the staff in the news. An important result of the focus on presidential policy pronouncements is the rarity of having policy specialists use the Briefing Room to provide background information on policy in a televised session. That represents a substantial change from earlier administrations, as most recent presidents have had a support operation for most of their initiatives in which on-the-record sessions are held with policy specialists, including cabinet secretaries, explaining a presidential program.

In the Clinton administration, for example, cabinet secretaries Donna Shalala (Health and Human Services), Richard Riley (Education), and Henry Cisneros (Housing and Urban Development) regularly gave on-the-record briefings in the White House Briefing Room, as did economic adviser Gene Sperling, domestic policy adviser Bruce Reed, and budget chief Jack Lew. The benefit for the president was that reporters there included material they had received in the Briefing Room in their daily stories coming from the White House.

In the Bush administration, cabinet secretaries do not use the Briefing Room to explain presidential initiatives. During the first term, only National Security Adviser Condoleezza Rice regularly came out to brief reporters, and in the second term her successor, Stephen Hadley, did as well. But recent actions by the administration have involved several layers of White House officials going further than they previously have to explain the president's thinking and policy goals. Cabinet secretaries are viewed as part of the "echo" of what the president has already said rather than a voice in the initial stages of explaining the president's policies. They are used to keep a presidential theme going rather than to go deep into policy explanations.

As part of the focus of having the president announce policy in the first instance, there was relatively little buildup to presidential announcements in the first four years. Ari Fleischer explained how they worked releases when he was there in the first term: "You see a lot less of the pre-leaks before announcements. When he has something to say, he says it and everyone hears it typically from him for the first time. It's our policy that . . . the American people should hear it from him first."[20]

In his second term, Bush has been more willing than he was in his first term to have his staff advance policy initiatives with releases of information beforehand. Press Secretary Scott McClellan said that the staff sometimes advances a presidential announcement by giving the information to the wire services the night before, with a time restriction: "We may go to the wires and say, 'Look, we don't want this to appear in papers tomorrow, but you can put it in your overnight, meaning they put it on the wires at 2:00 or 3:00 in the morning when all of the morning papers are already put to bed, but then they have the story out there before the president announces it," said McClellan. Unlike newspapers, the wire services work with little space for a story. They have sufficient room to explain the initiative, but not enough to get reaction from a variety of sources. Releasing it to the wires "helps kind of frame things before it starts leaking out on someone else's terms and maybe is not being framed or not getting across the message you want to get across."[21]

Second, having the president covered on his terms means that the ad-

ministration decides what its communications goals are, what information the president and his staff give to reporters, to whom they give it, and
when they do so. That discipline is at the heart of the Bush communications strategies. According to Dan Bartlett, the Bush White House is reluctant to respond to media opportunities because they often do not fit in
with the plans they have laid out. Bartlett explained how the Bush White
House works the news cycle: "We'll pass up opportunities if something
presents itself in the headlines that day or if television broadcast hits with
some news." He continued, "We're not as eager to jump on something
and ride that wave, so to speak, if it's not fulfilling or consistent with our
strategic communications goal for that week, or that month, or that quarter or whatever it may be."[22]

They stick to the plan even though controlling the discussion upsets
certain reporters who want responses from the White House on their issues, not just the ones the president and his administration want to speak
about: "So I think in that regard we kind of approach the news cycle a
little bit differently which can be frustrating for the press corps because
they're in that news, that's them." From Bartlett's viewpoint, reporters
want to get you to respond to their news priorities, which he calls getting
dragged into the "deep end." "They're in the news cycle and they're wanting to play in that and they're trying to invite you into the deep end," he
said. "We tend to look at our long term goals or our midterm goals and
say, 'Does it fit our communication's priorities to do so?'"

In the second term, when they found themselves down in the polls,
the president and his staff were more willing than they had been earlier to
take communications risks. In 2006, with low presidential job approval
poll numbers, they had little to lose by taking risks. The administration
was facing criticism from a variety of political sources, including from
their own party, and the president's job approval numbers in the major
public opinion polls were in 30s. The issues they chose to focus on for
the second term, personal retirement accounts as the centerpiece of Social Security reform and comprehensive immigration reform, met with
strong opposition in the general public and within the Republican party
ranks as well, including among his party members in Congress.

Instead of steering clear of risk, they courted it by allowing both staff
and the president to answer questions from audiences likely to pose unwanted questions. In the spring of 2006, the president appeared before
audiences that were not handpicked by administration or local party officials, a situation he had avoided in the latter part of his first term. He

faced questions dealing with issues the president and his staff would prefer not to focus on. White House staff found that news organizations were more likely to cover the president's remarks if he included questions from an audience with people the White House had not cleared. Instead of appearing solely before local Republican audiences or friendly business ones, the president mixed in venues such as the School for Advanced International Studies at Johns Hopkins University, where on April 10, 2006, after his speech, he faced a student audience with tough questions on U.S. policy toward Iran, the leak of information involving Ambassador Joseph Wilson's wife, Valerie Plame, and the president's democracy initiative.[23]

Events with an unscripted element are more attractive to news organizations, and the public also pays more attention than to partisan events with a handpicked crowd. Such sessions "definitely raise the interest level with the public and the press," said Scott Sforza, deputy communications director for television production, who arranges the stage settings for presidential events. "Reporters ask, 'What is going to happen?' And the president doesn't even know."[24] Those are situations likely to be covered by television, which is good for the administration, and such events also have the benefit of demonstrating that the president hears opinions that may conflict with his own.

When the president went to Yuma, Arizona, on May 18, 2006, to discuss his immigration initiative in connection with border control issues, the communications staff informed all five television networks that their correspondents would have an opportunity to conduct individual short interviews there with the president. As the staff fully expected, the reporters went beyond the immigration subject to ask the president about his low poll numbers as well as other issues the administration would have preferred not to address. In interviews with President Bush on immigration, NBC White House correspondent David Gregory brought up the subjects of Iraq and the president's low numbers in public opinion polls, as did CNN's Suzanne Malveaux.

A third element in the approach of the Bush White House of making news on the president's terms is planning. President Bush followed a set of management principles in his days as a businessperson and as governor of Texas. His core set of principles call for setting goals, developing plans for getting to the desired goal, assigning operational responsibilities, and then allowing staff to implement the plans.[25] Karl Rove described the system Bush followed: "Set the goal; bring everybody together; focus them on the goal; let people find how to get from point A to point B; be clear about methods; be clear about philosophy; be clear about the goal. Define limits within which people can operate, but make them wide and expansive." The principles derive from Peter Drucker, Karl Rove indicated, and Bush practiced them: "These are all things, whether it's because of his training or his nature, he does."[26] The emphasis here is for the president to establish how the system is to work rather than managing the system himself. President Bush prefers to let others carry out the assignments he, the chief of staff, and others give them. He gets involved when he wants to.

Karen Hughes explained where the president's management system fits into the communications system: "He'll want to know the plan. 'What's the plan? How are we rolling out?' "[27] Mary Matalin described it this way: "He throws out big projects, big goals, and then you come back with pieces of it," she said. "It's more meeting and talking, but tasks are given out, assignments are made."[28] Rove said, "Our starting point was really the president's [Bush's] office in Texas, and then the campaign, where there had been this close integration between policy and politics and publicity."[29] In both the first and second terms, those three elements come together in Karl Rove's domain, a crucial one for planning out the publicity for the president's program.

A good example of how politics, policy, and publicity come together is the planning group that Rove created and managed. Rove chaired a monthly or bimonthly meeting of what he dubbed his "strategery" group. This name was borrowed from a skit on the television comedy program *Saturday Night Live,* which made fun of Bush's speech and syntax difficulties by having him say *strategery* for the word *strategy.* Early in May of 2002, Rove illustrated what his "strategery" group did by describing what he expected for the year ahead: "Right now, for example, we had a strategy meeting last night, and we were talking about August. We have a model for between here and the end of the year, in terms of what we are attempting to achieve, what are our goals." For the shorter term, they had filled out their schedules three to four months out. "But in terms of, for example, planning the president's travels, and focusing on message, and focusing on thematic, and sort of helping make sense of our time here, we have a good handle on June. We've got the model for July; we've got the framework for August. Shortly we will have July filled out."

Although they plan way ahead, they are aware that plans can easily go awry: "But last year, when we started, we were eight weeks ahead, and at other times we've been four weeks ahead, and at other times we've been twelve weeks ahead. We had September, October, November mapped out, and guess what?" Even if they are blown off course by unpredictable events, as they were on September 11, 2001, their long-term strategizing gives them the stability of an overriding direction. In Rove's words, "It is better to walk into a day and say, 'This is our model and we're going to discard it,' than it is to say, 'What is our model for today? What are we going to try to do?'" They work from a general planning document that identifies major scheduled events. "Then the thematic for the day, then a specific POTUS [President of the United States] activity, and then the days that we're traveling are so indicated in green," Rove said while pondering a sample document. "This is just sort of the general, long-range planning calendar. There is a more detailed description of every one of those days."[30]

Karen Hughes was involved in setting out the communications part of that general schedule; Dan Bartlett succeeded her in that role. At the start of the administration, Hughes held weekly communications planning meetings on Wednesdays and Fridays so that the senior staff could map out high points of the president's schedule for the next three to four months. Based on the general goals that the president and his top associates had laid out, they would plan publicity events in which he could explain, promote, and illustrate his more specific aims. As soon as this schedule was set, perhaps two dozen staffers from various White House offices would work on implementing particular events with their counterparts in relevant cabinet departments and with supportive officials in both governmental and nongovernmental units at the state, regional, and local levels. Once an event was scheduled, a senior person was assigned responsibility to work with the operations team, overseeing the deputies to sketch it out in detail. This could be a communications, process, or policy person. This strategist would make certain that the purpose of the event was clear and that its proposed staging would achieve that aim effectively. The same process continues under Chief of Staff Joshua Bolten. "Every issue has a home, in the White House . . . a patron, a sponsor, and only one home," said Bolten. "Lots of people get to play, everybody who has any legit interest gets to play in the process," he continued. "The person and whichever apparatus is responsible for bringing the policy forward has a responsibility to make sure that everybody with an interest gets to play, but there is only one avenue in to the president." He learned from his service in the first Bush administration that it was often difficult to discover how an issue had come to the Oval Office because there were so many ways in.[31]

The discipline of the Bush White House team has become legendary. Staff members hew to their course of deciding when and where they want to speak and who is going to talk. There are fewer unwanted leaks than has been true in most recent administrations. Earlier administrations, including the Reagan and George H. W. Bush ones, Bartlett said, had "real divided camps within the White House, and they litigated their differences through the press." There were leaks by the forces led by Chief of Staff James Baker and leaks provided to reporters by those loyal to Edwin Meese. Bartlett said the administration was not immune from it, as "the most obvious kind of public kind of 'toing and froing' you get is between the State Department and the Department of Defense, Rumsfeld versus Powell. You hear about that all of the time."[32] But in the White House there is little of it, because they have drawn on people who have worked for the president for a long time and then brought in some people with Washington experience to complement them.

In part, White House discipline is related to President Bush's emphasis on control and to the experience White House senior staff had working together on the 2000 campaign. Chief of Staff Josh Bolten, who headed the policy operation during the 2000 campaign, commented on Bush's discipline and organization: "One of the reasons that this president's White House has been such a potent White House from the very first weeks, which isn't always the case . . . is that he has always had that style, and he brought into the White House much of the same team he had on the campaign and he ran the campaign that way too." The group of people coming into the White House as close aides—Bolten, Karl Rove, Dan Bartlett, and, earlier, Karen Hughes—had all worked on the 2000 campaign. Bolten said that Governor Bush gave him his "first substantive direction" early in the campaign. Bush told Bolten, "I want to campaign the way I am going to govern." He told Bolten that "he wanted the policy process [in the campaign] to work in the same way that it would actually in government." As a result, in setting up their White House organization, "he wanted to be able to simply take everything that he said in the campaign, the structures he built, and transplant them if and when he got to the White House."[33] Together, the discipline, the direction, and the mix of people have combined to make a "potent White House."

The Organizational Setup for Communications

George W. Bush raised public relations to unprecedented prominence in his presidency by choosing as his senior strategists a communications expert and political expert who worked closely and effectively with one another. Karen Hughes and Karl Rove showed other senior staffers how to plan effective publicity for the president's agenda, work with the operations-level staff to bring together the elements of strong event plans, and then oversee their implementation. For carrying out their plans they relied heavily on the four offices that had traditionally been responsible for such matters, namely, the Press Office, the Office of Communications, the Office of Media Affairs, and the Speechwriting Office. Together they make up the operations component of the Bush communications operation.

As table 5 shows, the number of employees these offices required remained about the same after Bush took over. In 1998, six years into the Clinton administration, they were staffed by thirty-nine employees. By 2001, in the early days of the Bush White House, the staff had been increased to forty-three.[34] But the emphasis had changed. The Bush White House invested heavily in long-range planning operations, while the Clinton White House focused on daily press operation.

In the Bush White House, White House publicity was the responsibility of Counselor to the President Karen Hughes. All of the offices reported to her during her tenure and, later, to Dan Bartlett who used the title assistant to the president for communications. In 2005 he became counselor to the president. In the Clinton White House, however, there was no one responsible for all of its communications offices. Instead, the Press Office and the director of the Office of Communications reported separately to the chief of staff and to the president.

The Strategists: Karen Hughes and Karl Rove

To insiders, it was clear that the president benefited from the marriage of political expertise and communications expertise represented by Rove and Hughes. Karen Hughes retained the title counselor to the president, which put her in charge of all of White House publicity and additional responsibilities President Bush assigned her. Karl Rove's title, senior adviser, allowed him to focus on political affairs as well as other assignments the president was interested in assigning him. Their titles indicated what

Table 5. Staffing of White House Publicity Offices

White House Publicity Offices	G. W. Bush May 2005	G. W. Bush July 2002	G. W. Bush July 2001	Bill Clinton July 1998
Counselor's Office	4	5	4	—
Office of Communications	12	8	8	8
Speechwriting	16	13	11	8
Office of Media Affairs	10	10	10	Part of Press Office
Office of Global Communications (created July 2002; removed March 2005)	—	2	—	—
Press Office	12	12	10	23
Press Office Staff Handling Traditional Media Affairs Responsibilities*	—	—	—	13
Total Communications Staff	54	50	43	39

Source: Tabulated by the author from White House phone books, Bureau of National Affairs, "Daily Report for Executives," White House Phone Book, Number 116, June 17, 2005. I also used earlier ones, Number 155, August 13, 2001 and Number 140, July 22, 2002.

*Not counted as communications staff.

everyone on the staff knew: both Hughes and Rove operated in a broad spectrum of White House and administration activities.

As one senior aide put it in the spring of 2002, referring to the president's plans to further Republican fortunes in that fall's midterm elections, "Karl is about the business of elections and taking back the Senate, if possible, and holding the House. There's a whole lot of things that he does that help accomplish that, but that's what his goal is right now." This same aide spoke of Rove's exceptional knowledge and skilled use of presidential resources: "He uses all the tools that one might, in a campaign. There's the principal's time, and where do you place him, and what relationships are being developed, what outside organizations that will be helpful for fundraising, that will be helpful for votes, that will be helpful for getting enough votes for the candidates we'd like to see win, in the Republican Party and the administration. So that's what Karl does. He looks at all policy, then, with an eye toward his objective, which is the preservation of the political support for the president and then the congressional midterm elections."

According to this same aide, Karen Hughes brought a broader perspective to the administration's strategic planning. "Karen is much broader: What is the message of the American public? What do we need to educate the public on, or now, more broadly, the global public? Are the president's policies being understood? Is there support for the president's policies? How can we build more support for the president's policies? She has all the things that [one] might use in an issue campaign on the outside underneath her: the speechwriting, media affairs, television, press secretary, and communications."[35] In addition to her sense of perspective, Ari Fleischer spoke of the control she had over how something moved in the administration: "Karen's really the big picture. Karen kind of changes the fundamental direction of something that's moving, or puts speed into it when something is moving."[36]

The personalities of these two senior aides were also complementary. The aide discussed how their personalities fit the type of work they did: "Karl is just sort of harder-edged, and Karen has that sort of easy, sit-down-and-tell-me-your-ideas kind of style. It's a little different. So the president is probably served well by these two highly intelligent people that come at things from a different style and different way."[37]

Beyond the fact that Rove and Hughes are the president's most trusted long-term political and communications advisers, having their complementary perspectives at his disposal provides him with a more fleshed-out picture of what he might want to see or do. Over the course of a year he must operate in cultural as well as political environments, the former warranting nonpartisanship, the latter hard politics. As Mary Matalin puts it, "He also understands in different environments, you've got to be in the environment you are. This is a political environment. Then discuss it in ways that people can understand."[38] So when he was discussing homeland security in the weeks prior to the 2002 and 2006 congressional elections or the 2004 presidential election, he portrayed his agenda in stark political terms. But when it was time for the State of the Union address, where bipartisanship is more expected, he addressed his remarks to citizenry, country, even the world at large.

During the first term of the Bush White House, most days began with a strategy meeting presided over by the president. "We have a meeting every morning where we sort of talk about strategic direction and issues and approaches," said Karen Hughes in 2002, prior to leaving the White House and returning to Texas. "This morning we covered a wide range of things. So that's me and Andy and Karl and the president and vice president, and Condi sometimes on foreign policy stuff. If we have a foreign policy discussion, Condi sits in on it."[39]

That first meeting of the day was followed by a meeting devoted to implementing and putting into operation the agreed-upon goals. In her capacity as director of the Office of Communications, Hughes herself chaired this follow-up meeting, as her deputy Dan Bartlett did later.

Karl Rove illustrated the operations side of this process by discussing an event held in Wisconsin in May of 2002 to promote the president's educational policy. "We have a series of working groups about each event in which there is participation by what are called project officers. The only people who can be project officers are assistants to the president," he began. Those assistants to the president are the operations people on the events: "So, for example, today in Wisconsin, [domestic policy chief] Margaret Spellings and I were the co-project officers on the education event. So that means that we have deputies who sit in a meeting with communications people and with all the other requisite inquirers and work out the event and the message and come to closure about what it is we're precisely trying to achieve there, which includes advance."

The chief strategists want to make certain that the themes of scheduled events are communicated in effective terms. As Rove explained, "But generally the object of each one of these thematics in the planning process, in the groups, is to see—like today, our object was, in Wisconsin, to say there are 116 low-performing schools in Wisconsin, [but] that under the new education reform act, there are 70,000 kids in those schools that as of this fall will be eligible to attend another public school in their area, better-performing school in their area. And there are an unknown number of those kids—we'll shortly know that number—which are eligible for supplemental services, because their schools have been failing for three years in a row." He concluded, "The object is to get those things worked up far enough in advance so that here at the last minute we can triangulate. Today we need to make a statement on Pakistan, on the Pakistan bomber."[40]

Hughes's biweekly communications planning meetings scheduled events for as much as three months in advance in order to set in motion the process of bringing together the resources needed to implement them. Her daily communications meetings, on the other hand, were devoted to finalizing arrangements and making last-minute changes called for by immediate contingencies. At this daily operations level, the decisions were about how a strategy was going to be carried out and how stories with differing degrees of complexity would be marketed.

Susan Neely, communications director for the Department of Homeland Security, detailed the process they came up with for handling the release of information pertaining to homeland security: "Some of our workaday stuff is just dry and complicated and tends to lend itself better to print. So we've done much more of giving something, a fact sheet or a backgrounder, to the right reporter the night before, for an exclusive the next morning, in the interest of getting it right—assuming it would be more of a print story. Then the broadcast will kind of follow."

Some information lends itself to print publicity. Other material is suitable for publicizing on television. "The more complex and unvisual the story, the more it lends itself to print, obviously," said Neely. "Then it's sort of, what's going to be the connect to the public with this story? That helps determine how far you can get with TV and radio, because, if it's going to connect with the public, then you usually have the ability to turn it into a simpler message, something that will be really relevant with the public. So you can work the morning shows, which is a great way to reach a lot of people, leading up to the press briefing that gets everybody else. And then you've got CNN and Fox going all day long with the echo of your message that you started with in the morning."[41]

For her daily session, held at 8:30 a.m., Hughes assembled about twenty staffers with communications responsibilities for a predictable routine. "Someone from the Press Office, Ari [Fleischer], or one of his deputies, Scott [McClellan] or Claire [Buchan], covers the news of the day, and what's hot, look at the week that's coming up, what speeches the president has," said one regular participant. "It's day-to-day and weekly oriented. And then, periodically, depending on the flow, how pressed everyone is, Karen will inject sort of a larger communications concern." This staffer said that Hughes had a sense of how all of their messages fit together and where they were not achieving their communications goals. At the time—2002—the staff member said that Hughes told her communications team the following: "Recently, it seems, we're having too many small events, so that nothing's penetrating. We have so many messages, there isn't a message. What would I tell the American people the message is right now?" she asked. "Because I'm not sure what the message is. You look at this schedule, and it's fitness, early childhood development, aviation security, and this whole mixture. She'll generate—again, sort of that easy style—discussion and draw on people for their ideas."[42]

Touting one main message a day is one of the ideas they came up with to reduce the risk of overloading the circuits with competing messages. "The idea is to give the press one thing to cover," said a White House staff member chosen to work on these message issues. "You are going to get the president's words once a day, so if they are running a story, they have to use his words, and if they only get those words—and it seems simple, but that's why Karen's so good at it, breaking it down to the most simplistic terms."[43]

In the second term, the news cycle is much faster than it was in the first term, with the result that messages are more difficult to sustain. With the rapid growth of Internet news sources, in 2006 there are more places where information is distributed than was true in 2001. In addition, many White House correspondents have increased information needs for the multiple reporting tasks they are performing. Dana Perino, deputy press secretary, spoke about the continuing stream of information the White House needs to provide to individual reporters who, in addition to their print writing, might contribute to a blog or appear on television. Many reporters now have the information needs of wire reporters, who work on breaking news stories and need a continuous stream of White House information. She referred to Mike Allen of *Time* magazine as "an example of someone who has changed the way a magazine reporter works. He files on the Web a lot, and he has a blog, and he does TV. He does radio. . . . As a journalist, it is almost like everybody is doing everything."[44]

Explaining Presidential Decisions and Actions

While the communications adviser heads the persuasion operation in the White House, the press secretary is responsible for the information explaining presidential decisions and actions. President Bush told reporters the day he appointed Tony Snow as his press secretary that Snow would be the person to explain his decisions: "My job is to make decisions, and his job is to help explain those decisions to the press corps and the American people. He understands like I understand that the press is vital to our democracy. As a professional journalist, Tony Snow understands the importance of the relationship between government and those whose job it is to cover the government. He's going to work hard to provide you with timely information about my philosophy, my priorities, and the actions we're taking to implement our agenda."[45] Explaining the president's philosophy, priorities, and actions requires the press secretary to work with the president on the official wording. "One of the things I regularly do is go into the office and I'll review with him the way I think I ought to lay something out. I want to get the voice and the policy and the context right. He is always willing to do that. If I've got any questions about how to frame it, I don't sit around and try to fake it, I just go in and ask. . . . There have been a couple of occasions where he says, 'I think we ought to say it this way,' but usually he leaves it up to me." In addition to getting a sense of the president's voice, Press Secretary Snow indicated that he and his staff needed to do a considerable amount of legwork to get information for reporters. "There is something unique with the White House press corps, which is, everybody is cooped up. The White House press corps doesn't have the ability that the Capitol Hill press corps has, to wander in and out of offices. They don't have easy and continuous access to senior members of the administration and the president. So, in many ways, the press corps really does have to depend upon what the Press Office supplies, and that is not only in terms of fact sheets but access to people within the administration."[46] Thus, explanation is a multilayered task for those working in the Press Office.

Explaining Events while Focusing on the Presidential Message

Explaining differs from advocating. Reporters, the president's critics, and the public all have information points and needs that White House staff must deal with. "One of my responsibilities is to make sure that people are getting an accurate picture of decisions we're making and policies we're pursuing," commented Scott McClellan. Both the White House and the press have a "shared commitment," he said, to getting that accurate picture across. But there is going to be "contention" over "what an accurate picture is." From the press secretary's point of view, the staff wants to "make sure certain points are in those articles or in news coverage. And it might not necessarily be picked up unless I continue to make those points over and over."[47]

Because the press secretary's briefing is now televised, the president's communications team sees the daily event as an opportunity to discuss what they want to talk about, as opposed to the session's traditional use, responding to reporters' queries. Dan Bartlett spoke about the dual nature of the televised session and the position of those administration figures who take the Briefing Room podium: "Not only are they responding to reporters' questions, but they've got an audience out there that are watching, and you're communicating a message to them. And sometimes there's a tension between those two goals. You have a communications goal and a responsiveness-to-the-press goal."[48]

With television present, the Bush White House wants to use the briefing venue to focus on what they want to say, rather than what reporters want to hear about. The communications team does not want to see reporters' questions drive the direction of the briefing. "Our goal is to, as much as possible, stay on the messages we want to in a press briefing, and then try and get those questions answered off the podium and away from the camera," said Bartlett. Whether it is explaining presidential actions to a group of reporters in the Briefing Room or elsewhere in the White House, the communications team is concerned about how information is used. Rather than have a group of policy experts come to the Briefing Room to respond to questions raised by reporters, Bartlett was reluctant to have those involved in the creation of policy explain their work and the president's thinking.

For Bartlett, dealing with reporters reduces rather than enhances the president's flexibility. He explained his thinking this way: If the administration were to bring in a reporter to discuss Medicare with a policy expert "about the complexities of Medicare" and "where we are in the Medicare debate and talk about how this is such an important issue but has complexities," it would be very risky, since the policy people are not trained to deal with the press. The policy person might make news in an unintended way because, as Bartlett argued, reporters are more experienced in such discussions than officials are: "That reporter is very smart [as to] how to ask questions to a policy person who doesn't deal with the press—and they say well, you know, Tommy [Thompson, secretary of health and human services], he really has this idea, but somebody over here has this [conflicting] idea."

What ends up in news articles can be harmful to the administration because it reduces the president's options. Bartlett observed, "The screaming headline the next morning, 'White House Divided Over Medicare' or, you know, 'White House Clashes.'" Neither the president nor the staff wants to see those kinds of stories on policy options in the public domain, so they opt not to have the policy people speak, especially in preparation of an event or presidential speech. As Bartlett explained, "And that's the challenge we have, that we want to do that, we want to enrich the reporting, we want to give context to reporting. At the same time it's difficult, particularly in policymaking, because the best thing that we can do for the president when he's trying to make a policy decision is to give him the most flexibility as possible."

In the second term, White House staff also exhibited more of an interest than they had earlier in providing informed people to answer questions on the president's speeches before the fact. When President Bush laid the groundwork for his address to the nation on immigration on May 15, 2006, for example, the preceding Friday a senior administration official with a publicity rather than a policy specialty briefed two groups of reporters from electronic and print publications, respectively. The idea was to inform reporters about the basic provisions of the president's immigration initiative without focusing on the staff person providing the information. In the afternoon prior to the speech, two administration officials elaborated on the points of the speech. By so doing, White House reporters, who most often are generalists, could go through the particulars and implications of the programmatic angles of the speech with officials. The White House is interested in informing the stories reporters write, but it wants to do so in a way that does not draw attention to staff.

The day of the speech, senior White House staff members involved in the preparation of the address talked to reporters shortly before the president was to deliver it. Four aides, communications chief Dan Bartlett, Press Secretary Tony Snow, homeland security adviser Frances Townsend, and Deputy Chief of Staff for Policy Joel Kaplan answered questions from reporters for an hour. Rather than discuss the policies in any depth, the four aides talked about the speech itself and what the president wanted it to accomplish.

Contrary to Bartlett's stated reluctance to let reporters query cabinet secretaries in an open setting, policy specialists discussed the issue of border security the day after the president's immigration speech. The officials included the secretary of the Department of Homeland Security, the immigration chief, the head of the border patrol, an assistant secretary of defense, and the chief of the National Guard. Rather than avoid letting reporters get an opportunity to talk to the policy specialists for fear that reporters might get them to say something off the program, the communications staff created the event with the four policy specialists. In both sessions, reporters questioned officials for at least half an hour following the initial remarks made by staff members. Immigration has proven to be a very difficult issue to sell, and the White House has tried a variety of ways of getting out the information. The explanations provided by the four policy specialists received broad coverage; their comments were included in immigration stories in the *New York Times* and the *Washington Post* as well as in regional newspapers in Texas and California.

Flexibility involves maintaining control over information so that you are not forced by others to do what they want you to do. Bartlett said that the staff wants the president to be in the position to "entertain as many options as possible, but as soon as those options are in the public domain and given a certain characterization it then starts boxing him in, or her, but in his case it would say you're now putting a perception on a policy position or a certain way it's being communicated or reported makes it more difficult for him to have a free hand in deciding what he wants to do."[49]

Daily Press Operations

In the modern White House—during the Bush era too—the focus of the Press Office is limited to daily operations whose central task is to provide explanatory information on current presidential actions and initiatives. Next week, next month, and next year belong to the Office of Communications and others working on general strategic planning. The main responsibility of the Press Office remains providing reporters with information during the morning and afternoon briefings conducted by the press secretary and in one-on-one or small group conversations. While the Press Office is involved in the advance work done for trips, most of what the office does concerns daily information coming from the White House.

The press secretary plays little role in developing overall communications strategies because of the volume of work the office must deal with each day. Ari Fleischer, who served as President Bush's first press secretary, put it this way: "The Press Office is much more operational, much more implementation." The Press Office is where daily press relations are handled, where plans for daily coverage developed elsewhere are carried out.

As Fleischer carried out his work, he consulted with Hughes but was not micromanaged by her. He explained, "Once it's moving, Karen's not the type who said, 'Here are the words you have to use.' If I have questions or doubts to what's sensitive, I always reached out to Karen, and still will, because she really is good. So she can help me think it through and sort out generally as to how far do you want to go, on what don't I go. I can count probably on one hand how many times Karen and I actually sleuthed the words, 'Here's the way to say [it]. Say these words, don't say those words.'"[50]

In the Bush White House, the Press Office was slightly pared down. In the Clinton years, under Press Secretary Mike McCurry, it employed twenty-four people. But it had ten staffers in 2001 and thirteen in 2005. One major difference is that in the Clinton White House, the operation now known as the Office of Media Affairs belonged to the Press Office. Today it is responsible to the assistant to the president for communications because it has a central role in the advocacy operation.

Dealing with Local Press

While the Press Office is responsible for the White House and Washington press corps, the out-of-town press is handled through the Office of Media Affairs. This office extends the Bush administration's initiatives as far and as wide as possible. It interacts with the regional and local press, special interest media, and ethnic news organizations. It promotes designated themes and messages via newspapers, radio, and television and on the White House website. In this administration, the office emphasizes follow-up coverage for presidential events. When President Bush goes on the road to make a major speech, for example, the Office of Media Affairs handles both pre- and post-event coverage in the local press.

The Media Affairs operation is broken down into regional portfolios. Those handling particular regions are responsible not only for conveying information to news organizations within their assigned areas but also for finding out how administration initiatives are playing in those locations. One of the responsibilities of its director, especially when there is an important speech or event taking place, is to set up calls between White House officials and representatives of regional news organizations.

Working with the cabinet is another important aspect of endowing presidential publicity initiatives with a loud and far-reaching "echo." For a summer housing initiative in 2002, the Office of Media Affairs called on Secretary of Housing and Urban Development Mel Martinez to talk with a wide range of reporters. "With the housing rollout, we had—we kind of guided and directed HUD's activities," said Nicolle Devenish Wallace, who headed the office in the first term. "We asked Secretary Martinez to do something with the Hispanic press. There was an undersecretary that did something with the African-American press. I think we set up some conference calls with reporters from all around the country. And it's a little bit—I won't say low tech, but a lot of it is just getting our reporters to get on a conference call."[51]

The White House communications team focuses on local coverage

Table 6. Popularity of Media Outlets, 2004 (%)

Media Source	Every Day	Several Times a Week
Local Television	51	19
Local Newspaper in Your Area	44	14
Cable News: CNN, Fox News, MSNBC	39	16
Nightly Network News	36	16
Morning News and Interview Programs	27	12
Radio Talk Shows	21	12
National Newspapers, such as the *New York Times, Wall Street Journal,* and *USA Today*	7	4

Source: Gallup poll, December 5–8, 2004, selected categories. Available at pollingreport.win.

because the president generally receives positive coverage when he travels to localities around the country and people have a high degree of trust for their local newspapers and television news programs. When a president travels to a local area, he often receives full coverage of his trip, beginning with the landing of Air Force One at the local airfield. His public remarks receive television coverage, and people meeting with the president get airtime as well. Rather than have short edited footage of the presidential visit and remarks that cable news might or might not run, local television will air the full speech and interview others connected with the event, such as the Freedom Corps volunteer award winners discussed earlier in the chapter.[52] Such coverage gives local viewers a fuller portrait of the president than national coverage will. That is what the president and his staff seek.

Getting local media coverage is important because it is a more trusted source of news than national newspapers and television. Dan Bartlett said that when the Bush staff spoke with communications staff from earlier administrations, "the most common piece of advice we received from every administration, both Democrat and Republican, was don't ignore, and, in fact, give more priority to local media than to national media." The reason is people get their news locally. "They don't rush out and grab the *New York Times*; they rush out and grab their local paper. They don't always click on to the CBS Evening News; they click on their local news-

Table 7. Public Perception of Media Outlets, 2004 (%)

News Source	Favorable	Unfavorable	Can't Rate
Local Television News	73	20	7
Daily Newspaper You Are Most Familiar With	72	18	10
Network Television News such as ABC, NBC, CBS	68	23	9
Cable News: CNN, Fox News, MSNBC	67	18	15
National newspapers such as the *New York Times* and *Washington Post*	38	25	37

Source: Pew Research Center for the People and the Press/Project for Excellence in Journalism Survey, Princeton Survey Research Associates International, June 8–12, 2005. Available at pollingreport.com/media.htm.

casters that they rely upon. And if you reach them through the medium in which they typically trust more often, their local newscaster, their local paper, their local reporters, the better opportunity you're going to have to get your message across. And we have done that. We've spent a lot of time focusing on the regional media operation and local media operation because it is true."[53]

Polling data back up Bartlett and his predecessors. People do heed and trust their local media to a greater extent than they do the national ones, as tables 6 and 7 show. A Gallup poll conducted in December 2004 demonstrated the news habits of the public. The question asked was, "Please indicate how often you get your news from each of the following sources: every day, several times a week, occasionally, or never."

Polling data demonstrate that the White House communications unit is correct—the public trusts local media. A Pew Research Center for the People and the Press survey focused on people's trust levels. Poll respondents were also asked to rate various media outlets as "very favorable, mostly favorable, mostly unfavorable, or very unfavorable." Collapsing the responses into "favorable" and "unfavorable," the data were as shown in Table 7.

Talk radio is one of the areas the Office of Media Affairs has targeted to give information for reporters not based in the White House. The strong support they receive from conservative talk radio programs is what led the administration to host three days of interviews for fifty radio hosts, who set up shop from 6:00 a.m. to 7:30 p.m. in tents on the North Lawn of the White House and spoke with the available administration officials, including all of the White House senior staff and almost every cabinet secretary.[54]

Communicating through Pictures

The Bush White House staff focuses on controlling those aspects of presidential communications that are possible for them to manage successfully. How the president is portrayed in pictures is one of the areas in which the White House has both an ability to control what is released and an interest in doing so. Communications staff members think through how to explain what the president is doing, right down to the pictures they want to see on television. As in earlier administrations, especially those of Presidents Reagan and Clinton, communications staffers in the Bush White House invest heavily in producing memorable pictures. Because presidential appearances are now covered live from beginning to end on cable television, every detail of such events can affect their effectiveness at conveying messages.

Karl Rove traces the high point of media sophistication in this regard to the Reagan administration: "I think in the post-1980 era, we all owe it to [Michael] Deaver, who said, 'Turn off the sound of the television, and that's how people are going to decide whether you won the day or lost the day: the quality of the picture.'" He explains, "That's what they're going to get the message by, with the sound entirely off. And I think that's simplistic, but I think it's an important insight. There is a reason why that old saw, a picture is worth a thousand words—how we look, how we sound, and how we project—is important. So winning the picture is important, and [so is] having a president with the right kind of people to drive and hone the emphasis of the message, [so he will] be seen in a positive, warm, and strong way."[55]

After White House strategists determine what themes they want to communicate, their implementation people decide how to structure an instructive event, and their operations people set everything up and frame the pictures so that they will communicate what the planners and implementers want to convey. Communications assistant Scott Sforza capitalizes on his background in television and his experience with White House policymakers to make sure that both sides are handled well. As he said, "I sort of use the rule of thumb, if the sound were turned down on the television when you are just passing by, you should be able to look at the TV and tell what the president's message is. If you are passing by a storefront and see a TV in the window, or if you are at a newspaper stand and you are walking by, you should be able to get the president's messages in a snapshot, in most cases."

Among other things, Sforza is the official who designs the backdrops that appear behind the president when he speaks in indoor locales around the country. For a speech about homeland security delivered in Kansas City, this "wallpaper" was lined with the phrase "Protecting the Homeland," interspersed with profiles of a firefighter. At the White House, where these message banners are only occasionally used, the preference is for scenic locales in and around the White House itself. In his effort to produce precisely the pictures he wants, Sforza leaves no detail to chance. The background before which the president appears is chosen with the aim of maximizing the impact of the "tight" shots that television cameras are most likely to use. And the president speaks from a special podium tagged "Falcon" because its top seems to hunch over a thin stem, which has been crafted to allow televised close-ups to show as much of a selected background as possible.

According to Sforza, "Falcon" is "designed so that you can see the lower portions [of a picture]. You can see around it. So it really opened up the shot for us, and you could see the process behind it." He continues, "It made for a much, much better event. When you look at the photos, you can tell it's really—it's a striking difference. So it has had just really terrific results. We have had great results with it, even in events where we have message banners. You can see the banners much better, because this sits lower, and it really plays well with that backdrop, so it doesn't dominate the show."[56]

Until the end of the twentieth century, presidents had very few choices when they wanted to go live on television with a speech. Most of them used the Oval Office as their setting. In addition to the eleven addresses he delivered to Congress during his eight years in office, President Clinton made nineteen formal "Addresses to the Nation." Fifteen of them came from the Oval Office.[57] By December 15, 2006, in Bush's sixth year, setting aside his two inaugurals and his seven addresses to Congress, only five of his twenty "Addresses to the Nation" took place in the Oval Office. Seven of them were delivered in locales other than Washington, namely Crawford, Texas; New York; Cincinnati; Atlanta; New Orleans; Fort Bragg, North Carolina; and an aircraft carrier.[58] The remaining eight were staged in other White House locations—three from the Cabinet Room; four in Cross Hall (located on the first floor of the White House midway between the East Room and the State Dining Room), and one from the White House Treaty Room.

Thanks to the fiber-optics technology that was in place by the time he was elected, thanks to the Clinton communications operation, President Bush can appear live on television in a matter of minutes from several locations in the White House itself, in the West Wing, and on the White House grounds, such as the South Lawn and the East Garden. While the Clinton communications team was responsible for acquiring this technology, only the Briefing Room and the East Room were wired when Clinton left office.

On October 7, 2001, when President Bush addressed the nation to announce a campaign of military strikes against Al Qaeda and Taliban targets in Afghanistan, he spoke from the Treaty Room in the White House, so named because it was where President McKinley signed the treaty that ended the Spanish-American War. He began his speech at one o'clock in the afternoon. Through the window behind him one could glimpse the midday traffic on Constitution Avenue.

No president had delivered a speech from this room before. President Bush and his staff selected it because they felt the visuals themselves would convey important messages. "The president wanted to really address the nation in a different way than he had before," remembered Sforza. "He enjoyed the history of the room, and what it was all associated with." He also wanted the traffic in the background: "We wanted . . . [to] send a message to the world that we're still in business here."

In earlier times, a satellite truck arriving the day prior to the event would have been needed for a television broadcast, and it would have taken a lot of time to set up all of the necessary equipment. The existence of fiber-optic lines "really enabled us to go on the air much quicker than we ever would have been able to the old way, the way it was ten years ago," said Sforza. "So this way it's a very short cable line. You just plug it in and you're ready to go. And with that speech in particular we had as little time as possible to notify the networks." Instead of the previously required hour-and-a-half warning, "we were able to notify them in fifteen minutes, twenty minutes before we would go on the air."[59]

"Winning the picture" is important for any administration. But Bush's communication staffers are more sensitive than their predecessors to the need to reach particular segments of the public through television. Even though the Internet is attracting a large number of readers, television is an important source of news for most who follow it. The goal of "winning the picture" influences how departments and agencies showcase presidential policies as well as what the White House and the president do. The creation by outside contractors paid by government departments and agencies of video news releases to be shown at the regional and local levels in addition to the national one is a practice that builds on traditional efforts to shape newspaper coverage.

The "picture" is an area where the White House can make use of changes in technology as well. When asked the differences in broadcasting the presidential image between 2002 and 2006, Sforza pointed to some of the developments. "It's a lot easier to get a satellite signal out. It's easier to do the video taping, a lot of the networks, the locals have the ability to turn stories around much more quickly now that there is an advancement in the editing capability and the software that's available." These changes require staff to assess how networks and local television stations broadcast in order to make the most of their opportunities getting television time.

When President Bush announced what the administration considered to be the end of military operations in Iraq, he and his staff did so in a dramatic location. Through developments in video technology, they were able to broadcast live from the Pacific Ocean while the USS *Abraham Lincoln* was moving. That was something that previously was not possible, Sforza said, as the transmitters would "always hit black holes when . . . traveling through the ocean." For the USS *Abraham Lincoln* event where President Bush landed in a Navy S-3B Viking fighter jet, improved technology allowed a clear, stable signal for transmitting the president's arrival and his speech given at dusk: "That was the first time that we used this new technology, which was a Sea-Tel Antenna . . . that could lock in to a KU-band satellite signal while moving." That meant continued transmission for all news organizations without any loss of signal while they journeyed toward San Diego.

The USS *Abraham Lincoln* event demonstrated the problems that can arise when a communications operation focuses so heavily on the technology of an event that one misses the larger communications problems. The White House made a sign that served as a backdrop when President Bush spoke. The sign read "Mission Accomplished." Sforza said that the derivation of the sign was a request by the commander of the ship, who wanted it because the crew had been at sea for eleven months. The president's critics portrayed the sign as a presidential announcement that the war in Iraq was over, which proved to be far from the case. Sforza said that the sign "took on a life of its own, and to this day they still try to apply it like an anniversary of the 'Mission Accomplished' speech." Though the president was reluctant to declare an end to hostilities, the sign seemed to indicate that he had. The communications staff learned that "the image overrides even sometimes the truth."[60]

Difficulties in Explaining Unanticipated Situations and Selected Policies

The Bush White House was at its best in situations calling for long-range plans and creating events to match. The communications operation was far less successful at dealing with unanticipated situations. That was true for those that represented opportunities as well as ones where criticism unexpectedly surfaced requiring a response. In addition, there were certain policy areas where even a series of events did not bring credit the administration deserved. In particular, the president received little credit from the public for a strong economy and there was little awareness, even in the African-American community, of his Africa initiatives.

When Libya renounced its weapons of mass destruction program, the Bush communications system failed to take advantage of a real victory. On December 19, 2003, President Bush came out to the Briefing Room at 5:30 p.m. with ten minutes allotted to make the announcement that Libya's leader Col. Moammar Gaddafi agreed to renounce its nuclear, biological, and chemical weapons and to allow international inspections. The agreement, which was the result of British and American efforts, "will make our country more safe and the world more peaceful," Bush declared.[61]

In fact, even Democrats acknowledged that it was a breakthrough agreement. Ashton B. Carter, who served in the Clinton administration as an assistant secretary of defense, told the *New York Times*: "One certainly hopes that what we did in Iraq put countries like Libya on notice that we're really serious about countering proliferation."[62] The agreement was indeed significant, but the administration sought—and received— little credit for reaching it. There was hardly any publicity of the victory because there was no advance notice given to reporters and no follow-up briefings from the White House to encourage reporting of the story. As with bad news, the White House had difficulty with news for which they had no operational plan.

The communications team also had difficulty recognizing the growth of problems. In the 2004 campaign, President Bush consistently cited corporate responsibility as one of the major issues arising during his term in office. Yet when Enron collapsed in 2001 and WorldCom along with it, the administration was slow to appreciate how important the issue of corporate responsibility was. Even with a long lead time, there were some issues where the president received little credit for a policy on which he had a solid record.

Starting with the collapse of Enron in the autumn of 2001, for months stories in newspapers and on television news programs detailed the depth of the issues, including, for example, the connections some of the corporate players had with the White House. Articles such as one appearing in January in the *Washington Post* ("Enron's Influence Reached Deep into Administration: Ties Touched Personnel and Policies") left questions that were not answered until much later.[63] By the time the president did speak about it in July, the bar representing success was fairly high. While the first-day stories following the president's Wall Street speech focused on the President's rhetoric ("Bush Crackdown on Business Fraud Signals New Era"), the day-two and day-three stories focused on the speech's lack of effective enforcement mechanisms ("How a Clear Strategy Got Muddy Results").[64] He followed up on the subject in August with a one-day conference in Waco, Texas, on corporate issues.

Defending the President

Operating in a fast-moving news cycle has not been the strength of the Bush White House. Dan Bartlett described how much better Democrats responded to the needs of the news pace: "The best way that I can describe it is that in the daily news cycle they're kind of more day traders and we're more like long-term investors. They play the cycle much better than we do. They're very flexible, very agile."[65] The Bush White House communications operation worked with its strength: planning and coordination. They laid out their agenda and stuck with it. Proportionately, they spent far less time in a mode where they defended the president outside of the issues they were intent on discussing.

Three years later, in the fall of 2006, Bartlett said that his views had evolved. As far as being a day trader or a long-term investor, "it can't be either/or. It has to be hybrid. You have to be more disciplined in this news environment with your message, or your message will scatter and never penetrate. I still feel very strongly about that. I think the more news channels, the more media outlets, whether it be Internet or elsewhere, how even more important it is to stay focused, and disciplined, and on message." There is an upside to the fast news cycle because bad stories are subject to fast burnout, just as good ones are. "The burnout rate on stories is so much quicker," he said. With a climate of an even faster news cycle, "I think we have to show a little more flexibility to play off what's in the news of the day." He pointed to their response to a spate of highly publicized school shootings in mid-October 2006. He noted the difference from what they would have done in the early years of the administration. "The first term Bush shop probably wouldn't have turned on a dime and pulled something together and organized a conference on gun safety in four days. The fact that we did that this time is an evolution in thinking in how we should deal with the news climate." What they have had to do with news that is out there is "play into it a little bit more," he said, "be more willing to take a more assertive role in shaping it, the press conference the president held on Wednesday, the [increased] number of press conferences we are doing."[66]

As is true with most administrations, the Bush team learned their lessons the hard way. At one time, they were slow in responding to problems, and it cost them heavily. One of the issues where the Bush communications team had trouble getting traction as they defended the president was the issue of the accuracy of the president's statement in his 2003 State of the Union address that Saddam Hussein had tried to buy yellowcake uranium in Africa: "The British government has learned that Saddam Hussein recently sought significant quantities of uranium from Africa."[67] The president and his staff were reluctant to admit that they had given out incorrect information. The issue was important because it became part of the larger question of what types of weapons Saddam Hussein had and what types he had attempted to buy.

In the summer of 2003, memoranda began to surface casting doubt on the claim's accuracy. Initially, CIA Director George Tenet accepted blame for the error. He said that the "CIA should have ensured that it was removed." Yet, the CIA also put out the message that the White House shared in the fault. In the same article, the *Washington Post* reported that "the CIA director also made clear that it was members of the president's National Security Council staff who proposed including the questionable information in drafts of the Bush speech, although the CIA and the State Department had already begun questioning an alleged attempt by Iraq to buy uranium from Niger."[68]

Day after day in the Briefing Room, reporters hammered Press Secretary Ari Fleischer with questions about who was at fault. Even his last briefing later that summer was dominated by questions related to the issue of what became known as the "sixteen words" in the State of the

Union address.[69] Weeks after the issue first came up, White House officials decided to take the issue out of the daily briefing by having a senior administration official take questions in a half-hour briefing devoted to the topic.[70] They provided selected pages from a National Intelligence Estimate that discussed the issue. Even that did not stop the flow.

Finally, four days later, Steve Hadley, deputy national security adviser, took the blame in a briefing he gave with communications director Dan Bartlett. In the briefing, they "revealed the existence of two previously unknown memos showing that Director of Central Intelligence George J. Tenet had repeatedly urged the administration last October to remove a similar claim that Iraq had tried to buy uranium in Africa."[71] After that, the issue moved to the background—but it had dominated White House information sessions for weeks.

Yet there was an aftertaste from the State of the Union incident that affected the relationship between the White House and reporters. Reporters were weary of the product the White House was selling. Two years later, in October 2005, the issues came up in a daily briefing in which Press Secretary Scott McClellan received a large number of questions related to President Bush's Iraq speech earlier in the day. David Sanger, *New York Times* White House correspondent, asked McClellan for support on the president's description of ten attempted terrorist attacks halted by security forces. Sanger said, "After the '16 words incident' sometime ago, we are more interested than usual in having—seeing the footnotes that go with the speech. So just as a matter of maintaining credibility, it would be good if we could get at least outlines of the brief [on terrorism incidents]."[72]

Closely related to the issue of the uranium claims were the questions surrounding what White House aides Karl Rove and Lewis Libby, Vice President Cheney's chief of staff, had said to reporters Matthew Cooper, Judith Miller, and Robert Novak about CIA operative Valerie Plame. Day after day the press secretary was put on the spot to vouch for the credibility of what others in the White House had said and done on this issue and was bombarded day after day with reporters' demands to make public the president's National Guard records and answer questions about the quail hunting accident in which Vice President Cheney shot his friend and the like. Ultimately, the lack of accurate information coming out of these briefings was a major factor in compromising Scott McClellan's credibility.

Coalition Information Centers

The one expressly defensive operation created by the Bush White House dealt with external issues. The White House experimented with a rapid response team in the days after September 11 when it created an operation to defend against anti–United States statements coming from the Taliban from its base in Islamabad, Pakistan. The first effort was an operation called the Coalition Information Centers. When that operation became viewed as no longer needed, the president and the communications staff developed a permanent White House operation designed to defend against erroneous claims of U.S. conduct and to get ahead of issues of special interest to the Arab world.

After September 11, with the aim of responding to publicity critical of the United States in Afghanistan and in other Muslim countries, the Bush administration created the Coalition Information Centers to make its communications operation a global one. The aim was to respond within the same news cycle to information coming out of Afghanistan and surrounding countries. Tucker Eskew, who headed the Office of Media Affairs at the time of the September 11 attacks, moved to London to coordinate this new publicity initiative with Alastair Campbell, spokesperson for Prime Minister Tony Blair. The plan was to have an offensive and defensive operation where the American government and its allies could generate news and responses in the same news cycle as its opponents, most especially the Taliban.

Eskew explained the impetus for extending the existing communications operation: "We were being inflicted with disinformation, misinformation, outright lies, largely by a Taliban public information officer based in Islamabad in the days following the beginning of the bombing in Afghanistan," he said. He related that officials in Tony Blair's government had told the White House that they were lagging behind in the news cycle: "I think we acknowledged that we needed to respond more aggressively, more rapidly, to defend ourselves in that global news cycle, and to do it more quickly so that we weren't letting the ten hours lapse from Islamabad's morning to D.C.'s morning." Once these discussions began, then "Alastair [Campbell] and Karen [Hughes] cooked up this idea of Coalition Information Centers designed to more effectively, rapidly, respond and coordinate information resources across agencies within the United States government and between governments in the coalition. . . .

So there's a briefing process at the White House. There is certainly one at Number 10 [Downing Street] as well."

Because the challenge was to counter publicity resulting from Taliban briefings conducted in Islamabad, Campbell and Hughes decided that they needed a briefer there on the spot: "We had to do it because the press was getting briefed by this Taliban information officer. . . . The campaign became so successful that we didn't just rout the Taliban from most of Afghanistan; we routed that guy out of Islamabad. There was somewhat less need to respond to all of that but still a concentration of international media and regional media that was often very conspiracy-minded and in some ways anti-American. So throughout November and December particularly, we briefed, briefed frequently and regularly, daily in fact, and we knocked down some stories."[73]

Four months after it was created, it was disbanded in favor of a longer-term operation designed to sell the administration viewpoint in a more coordinated way than the response operation represented by the Coalition Information Centers. Its successor was the Office of Global Communications.

Despite early hopes and grand expectations, by 2005 it ended up doing little beyond sending daily e-mails containing information favorable to the administration to a sizeable mailing list. Generally, each e-mail contained two snippets of information: The first was the "Fact of the Day," some fact or anecdote about progress in Afghanistan or Iraq, and the second, "Global Messenger," reproduced quotations from presidential speeches together with upbeat war reports. On March 11, 2005, for example, the Global Messenger section gave information on the status of Iraq from the viewpoints of the Defense and State Departments. One bulleted item reported: "President Bush and his counterparts not only turned the page on Iraq, they wrote a new chapter. All 26 NATO allies are now contributing to the NATO Training Mission in Iraq."[74] On March 18, 2005, the messages unceremoniously stopped. The director and deputy directors of the office left for other assignments, and the unit was quietly moved to the National Security Council. Executive Order 13283 creating the Office of Global Communications was signed on January 21, 2003, and was officially revoked on September 30, 2005.

The phasing out of the Office of Global Communications coincided with the return to the Bush administration of Karen Hughes. When Condoleezza Rice became secretary of state at the beginning of George W.

Bush's second term, Karen Hughes returned to Washington after a three-year absence to take the position of undersecretary of state for public diplomacy. Her job was to improve the image of the United States in the Muslim world. Nicolle Devenish Wallace, director of the Office of Communications, indicated that since the White House Office of Global Communications was in charge of the image of the United States abroad, there was a good chance that efforts would be unnecessarily duplicated. The administration wanted to move the image function. "And I think that Secretary Rice believes that this is a priority for the State Department," said Wallace.[75] When she announced the Hughes appointment, Secretary Rice outlined her mission: "I can think of no individual more suited for this task of telling America's story to the world, of nurturing America's dialogue with the world and advancing universal values for the world than Karen Hughes."[76] Building understanding and good will in the Muslim world proved as difficult for Hughes, as it had for her predecessors. Before she came to the State Department, public relations executive Charlotte Biers and Margaret Tutwiler, former White House communications director at the end of the George H. W. Bush administration, tried to get control over the public diplomacy portfolio. It was difficult for them and has proven similarly difficult for Karen Hughes to come up with victories.

Gauging the Success of White House Communications Efforts

In some ways, measuring communications success remains somewhat the same from one administration to the next. Whether the Clinton or the Bush administration, staff members watch and record the network evening news for the tone of the coverage, assess stories in newspapers and magazines, and get summaries of the White House comment line phone calls and e-mails to the president. Did they get covered the way they wanted? What stories are newspapers carrying? What does their polling say about the president and his policies? What do independent polls say? "We try to look at all the different venues and outputs and determine if it punched through or not to a certain level, editorial support or lack thereof," said Dan Bartlett. Both the Clinton and Bush administrations viewed the process of reaching the public a matter of "punching through" a welter of conflicting messages sent by others inside and outside of the political system, including the president's critics in Congress and individuals representing interest groups.

Assessing the success of their efforts is different depending on whether the president and his team are communicating in a campaign cycle or a governing cycle. Dan Bartlett explains the difference in terms of the horizon they work with and the nature of their goals. In a campaign the horizon is Election Day: "Your communications goals are much more what I call the three-meter target. They're right in front of you. And you really get to a point where you're trying to just win as many news cycles as possible. You're fighting or competing against your opponent, and you try to accumulate as many victories as possible in a given news cycle." Measuring success in governing mode is more difficult because that process does not lend itself to daily wins and losses. "Communications in governance has much more long-term scope," Bartlett said. "You're trying to accomplish a goal, whether it be implementing a piece of legislation or affecting public opinion over a period of time, whether it be [over] the tenure of your presidency."[77]

During election periods, the test is more specific: did they win the day? Nicolle Devenish Wallace, who was in charge of communications for President Bush's reelection campaign, explained the daily cycle of winning and losing: "Karl [Rove] used to call at the end of every day around eight o'clock, not the end of every day but after the network news, and say, 'Did we win today?'" She said, "Every day someone inches ahead of someone else, either in the rhetorical debate or in the polls or in their standing in the state."[78] The network news is at the end of the daily cycle, the beginning of which is the morning newspapers. The papers she followed included five national ones, the *Washington Post,* the *New York Times,* the *Wall Street Journal, USA Today,* and the *Washington Times,* and thirty regional papers and TV markets.

Gauging success in local television coverage is an area where technology has made assessing success easier than it once was. Rather than having to rely solely on people at the local level to gather and send information to White House political and communications officials, it is now possible to follow local news programs all over the country following their broadcast. Today the White House relies on ShadowTV, a private sector company that has the "ability to search and record television by key words, or by time/date of broadcast. You can monitor, access and email video materials instantly over the Internet. . . . ShadowTV searches live and archived broadcasts for important stories and advertisements based on key words provided by you."[79] Then ShadowTV e-mails the video segments and the transcripts of the clips. "Now that you have ShadowTV and things like that you can pick up on a local feed and see what the news was like there in a local market," said Scott Sforza, who runs television production for the White House.[80]

An additional way to measure success is tabulating how many people the communications staff reached on a particular day with the president's message. Take one medium, radio, as an example. "You add up the number of radio shows that there were . . . and we know their numbers. . . . [from] Sean Hannity, who gets in the millions, to NPR, who gets tens of thousands at any given moment . . . and you added them all up," said Bartlett.[81] "You say, 'on this day we at least reached 20 million people or 30 million people.' That alone to us is a way to gauge success." Radio has what Bartlett calls a "long-term benefit" because when a talk show host interviews an administration official, the host will often refer to the interview for several days.

Coordinating the White House Communications Operation

The communications staff coordinates White House publicity efforts with those of other governmental institutions and with recruited supporters in the private sector. From the White House, they create and then coordinate with administrative departments and agencies and allies in Congress and at the state and local levels. Interest groups come in to back up administration efforts and work with the White House on promoting their policies to specific constituencies and news organizations and other channels.

Chief of Staff

Chief of Staff Andy Card set up a system with two deputies and fairly independent positions for Senior Advisor Karl Rove and Counselor Karen Hughes. Except for Karl Rove, staff members had specific assignments and responsibilities. Rove was a floater who could move among all three areas of policy, politics, and publicity. In Card's system, staff members other than Rove worked in one of the areas, not all three.

Card described that system as a "compartmentalized" one. "In my job, I am the chief of staff, and so I am responsible for the staff. I am just a staffer responsible for the staff." Card described his system of communications with the staff, which was based on sharing only information he determined to be relevant for what individual staff members were doing: "I try to first of all have good communications with the people on the staff. But it is based on the 'need to know' rather than the 'want to know.'

And right after the war I had that discussion with the entire senior staff where I said we are going to now be very disciplined about 'need to know' and 'want to know.' All of you will want to know everything. I am asking you to discipline yourself to recognize that you will be told what you need to know. And if you come to me and you say you need to know something else, if it is a real need to know, you will know it. But focus on that which you have been assigned rather than try to get into that which you want to go."[82] The emphasis of the system on "need to know" restricted people to their assigned tasks, which in the communications area meant creating and carrying forward presidential messages.

Although this system was efficient in terms of avoiding overlap in staff duties, it turned out to be one in which the staff, including the president, was caught by surprise on some major issues, including the status of legislation, resignations, nomination difficulties, and program problems. The system was effective at getting out messages related to presidential priorities, but it ran into trouble picking up on problems outside and inside the White House. Two major embarrassing issues for the White House where clear warnings did not filter up the system were the prison conditions at Abu Ghraib prison in Baghdad and administration approval for Dubai Ports World to manage container operations at several U.S. ports (see p. xv). Detailed International Red Cross reports about conditions at Abu Ghraib came to the National Security Council at the White House but did not rise to the presidential level. Both situations were important issues that should have been handled as early as possible.

The public learned of the extent of abuses by American guards at Abu Ghraib prison in Baghdad through photographs contained in an April 28, 2004, piece by Scott Pelley on the CBS program *60 Minutes II*. As did the White House. "As far as I know, everyone here learned about it after it aired on *60 Minutes II*," said Press Secretary Scott McClellan.[83] The White House was put in a position of catching up to a very bad story already shaped by photographs the public had seen of American prison guards humiliating Iraqi prisoners. The communications staff was left to explain why the president had not known about the situation even though the National Security Council staff was aware of allegations contained in a twenty-four-page report prepared by the International Committee of the Red Cross, which included graphic descriptions of types of alleged torture techniques.

Presidential aides told *Washington Post* reporter Mike Allen that the "graphic images" of abuse "took the president by surprise."[84] Although the story would have been bad whether or not the president had known about the extent of the prison abuses, coming on the problem so late left the president and his White House team with nothing left to do but respond to a story that had already been defined by others. The system failed the president in a basic way. "The White House staff is there to insure there are no surprises," noted Reagan's senior communications adviser Tom Griscom.[85]

The White House was also taken by surprise on issues involving other parts of the government. When Harvey Pitt, the embattled chairman of the Securities and Exchange Commission, turned in his resignation, the *Washington Post* reported that "White House sources said they were surprised by the timing but were very relieved."[86] When legislation with a competitive outsourcing amendment sponsored by a Democrat, Christopher Van Hollen of Maryland, passed the House of Representatives, Deputy Director of the Office of Management and Budget Clay Johnson spoke with the *Washington Post* about the legislation: "Johnson acknowledged that the Van Hollen amendment took the administration by surprise, and he said the debate over job competitions has been marked by 'a lot of misunderstanding and a lot of misinformation.'"[87] When Senator James Jeffords of Vermont switched parties from Republican to Independent, the White House was said to be surprised. And when Republican Senator George Voinovich of Ohio opposed the nomination of John Bolton for the post of ambassador to the United Nations, the White House was similarly surprised by his opposition.

Coordinating Executive Branch Agencies

We can view how coordination works in the Bush administration by considering how the White House works together with executive branch units. Coordination within the executive branch involves several points. As we saw earlier with the use of administration people in the 2005 Social Security debate, the president and his staff make use of the resources of the departments and agencies as he communicates his programs to the public. All of these appearances by the president and his cabinet had little effect.

In the Social Security debate and on other issues, the White House made use of their communications team in the executive branch. Having a communications team for all of the executive branch has entailed controlling appointments to the public affairs offices in the various departments, coordinating executive branch communications officials with

White House senior officials, and making certain that statements coming out of the departments and agencies conform to administration programs and presidential goals.

One of the early decisions of the Bush White House was to have senior staff control several appointments at the department and agency level. Public affairs was one of the five offices at the administration level over which the White House wanted total control. The five positions are secretary, deputy secretary, legislative liaison, counsel, and public affairs. Asked if controlling who serves as public affairs officers means that White House officials can be comfortable knowing the briefings are tied into the White House, Card said, "I believe that to be the case." In order to make certain that the public affairs people are aware of White House themes and interests, "there is a call every morning with the communications teams from all of the cabinet agencies. And I know [Deputy Chief of Staff for Policy] Josh [Bolten] keeps in touch with their policy wonk types and [White House Counsel] Al Gonzales with the lawyers, and so White House liaison people are very important too."[88] So communications was one of several efforts to tie the White House together with the departments in a way that created message consistency throughout the administration. In addition to their daily calls, the White House communications team has regular meetings in the Roosevelt Room at the White House to discuss administration programs and plans with departmental and agency public affairs officials.

The goal of this control over departmental publicity efforts is to make the most of administration resources and to ensure coordinated messages and initiatives. All recent administrations have tried to do the same. But the George W. Bush administration has been willing to put in more resources than its predecessors, especially in the public affairs area. In the period between September 2000 and September 2004, public affairs officers have increased slightly, according to *Newsday* reporter Tom Brune: "The number of public affairs officials rose 9 percent, from 4,327 to 4,703, in executive-branch agencies, according to U.S. Office of Personnel Management statistics. Meanwhile, the federal work force grew 6 percent." Moreover, despite talk of cost consciousness and budget control, the funding for public affairs increased: "The cost of public affairs staffing has grown by more than $50 million, records show, from $279 million in 2000 to $332 million in 2003, the last year for which figures are available."[89]

In the second term, the administration faced criticism for actions taken by public affairs officers viewed as trying to enforce consistency in presidential messages too vigorously. Scientists working for the National Oceanic and Atmospheric Administration (NOAA), the U.S. Geological Survey, and the National Aeronautic and Space Administration (NASA) publicly chafed at what the scientists regarded as administration efforts to interfere with their public descriptions of their own findings. One area of contention is the issue of global warming. The *Washington Post* reported that the scientists "say they are required to clear all media requests with administration officials, something they did not have to do until the summer of 2004."[90] An official for NOAA, Kent Laborde, said that they were enforcing preexisting policies on clearing interviews. "We've always had the policy, it just hasn't been enforced," Laborde told Juliet Eilperin of the *Washington Post*. "It's important that the leadership knows something is coming out in the media, because it has a huge impact. The leadership needs to know the tenor or the tone of what we expect to be printed or broadcast."

Other scientists publicly complained about the monitoring of their press contacts. In the case of NASA, scientist James Hansen complained that when he posted information on the agency's website indicating that 2005 might be the warmest year on record, he was told to take it down "because he had not had it screened by the administration in advance."[91] It wasn't long before congressional Democrats got into the discussion and critical stories appeared.

In addition to public affairs officers conveying messages consistent with those of the president, departments developed publicity contracts designed to promote particular programs. Several of the contracts caused trouble for the administration. Long a source of friction with congressional committees responsible for overseeing the priorities and operations of various departments, departmental practices in this regard created so much resentment that the president himself felt compelled to put an end to certain routines.

President Bush spoke out against government contracts to media personalities who promoted administration policies without disclosing that they had been paid to do so.[92] The contract generating the most criticism was one granted to conservative talk show personality Armstrong Williams. Williams was paid $240,000 by the Department of Education to promote the administration's "No Child Left Behind" program. He often appeared on television and radio to discuss it. When he advanced the administration's programs, he never indicated that he was being paid by the government.[93] After reporter Greg Toppo revealed the existence of Williams's contract in *USA Today*, contracts to media commentators

Maggie Gallagher and Michael McManus were also reversed.[94] It was not long before the president called for an end to the practice of paying media personalities.

In a report requested by Senators Edward Kennedy (D-MA) and Frank Lautenberg (D-NJ), the Government Accountability Office found the payments to Armstrong Williams to be illegal, while the contract with Maggie Gallagher was permissible. The Department of Education responded through spokesperson Susan Asprey that "we've said for the past six months that this was stupid, wrong, and ill-advised."[95]

In addition to the contracts to media personalities, several departments sponsored the creation and distribution of videotapes for television created specifically to appear as if they were news stories. Although the videos sent to local television stations identified the source, the stations often edited the videotape, removing the identification of government origin. The result was that the audience had no idea that the film had been created by the government. The Comptroller General criticized such programs, found in the Office of National Drug Control Policy and the Department of Health and Human Services. In its report, the Government Accountability Office noted propaganda prohibitions found in law: "Television-viewing audiences did not know that stories they watched on television news programs *about the government* were, in fact, prepared *by the government*."[96] Video news releases, however, remained in place as the president and his staff felt that they had identified the source of the information. If there was fault, administration officials reasoned, it belonged to the local television stations, not to the administration.

In addition to deploying departmental resources for presidential agendas, controlling departmental public affairs offices allows the president and his staff to avoid having such units serve the goals of cabinet secretaries over the president's goals. The foundation of such control often lies in appointing to the departments people who have already demonstrated their loyalty to the president and his goals by working in his campaigns. Torrie Clark, the first public affairs officer at the Pentagon, worked in the presidential campaigns of George H. W. Bush and George W. Bush. Mindy Tucker, who had worked the Florida shift in the wake of the contested 2000 election, was placed in the public affairs operation at the Justice Department. In the second term, several staff members went from the White House out to departments and agencies, including White House Deputy Press Secretary Clare Buchan to Commerce and Jennifer Millerwise Dyck from Vice President Cheney's office to the public affairs job at the CIA. By sending out people loyal to the president and vice president, the administration was ensuring that the messages coming out of the departments and agencies would be in sync with those of the White House.

In a setting where compartmentalization is a defining element of the organizational structure, communications is a crucial cross-cutting force. "It's important because it keeps people on priority and on message," said former chief of staff James Baker. "It keeps people on the reservation, so that you don't have some cabinet officer running off and doing something that will destroy or compete with . . . your story."[97]

The strength of the Bush communications operation was the ability in the president's first term to set priorities, plan ahead, and coordinate among government units. The president and his staff focused on what they wanted to talk about and make news on the president's terms. Where they were less successful in the first term was handling unanticipated situations and criticisms of the president. Both require a staff capable of quick surveys of a situation and a fast response. And an ability to deal with the problem by assigning a communications team that responds to information inquiries. Those were qualities the communications team did not exhibit in the National Guard records issue or the White House response to the charges the president misstated the facts when he said in his 2003 State of the Union message that Saddam Hussein had sought yellowcake uranium from Niger. The unwillingness to deal with those charges quickly led to an expanding problem that engulfed all of the senior staff, including those of the vice president.

In the second term, the communications team experienced a great deal of difficulty because of the ebbing public support for the president's Iraq policy and the lack of support of the president's signature issues, such as the personal retirement accounts as part of the Social Security program and a guest worker program in an immigration bill. With criticism coming from members of the president's own party in Congress as well as the Democrats, the communications team was under fire as was much of the White House staff. As his standing in public opinion polls reached the 30s in all of the major national polls, in early April the president replaced his chief of staff. In the fall, their problems increased manyfold when Democrats replaced the Republicans controlling the House of Representatives and the Senate. It did not take long for the Democratic Committee chairman to schedule hearings probing administraion policy and management problems, including Iraq War support contracts.

4

White House Communications Advisers

No president today would come into office without appointing a communications adviser to handle his publicity and to oversee a variety of existing White House organizational units. In the modern White House, the communications adviser manages the words, pictures, publicity schedules, and events connected to the president. All of these are important in letting the public know what information the president wants them to have about him and his administration.

No matter who is in office and how he assigns tasks and creates structures, the president and his staff must put together a publicity operation that will perform two basic tasks. First, the communications operation must advocate for the president and his goals and initiatives. Units within the office are responsible for crafting the words and choosing and staging the events that showcase presidential priorities. Second, the adviser and his or her operation coordinate the selling of the president and his program, both within government and to organizations and publics at the national, state, and local levels. These objectives have remained White House public relations priorities even as the job of communications director and the offices it commands have varied in their specific tasks and structure.

A president's chief communications adviser usually heads the Office of Communications, but in some administrations the same person directs all of a chief executive's publicity initiatives. President George W. Bush's chief communications adviser, Karen Hughes, for example, served as counselor to the president while controlling all of the publicity units, including the Press Office, the Office of Communications, and the Office of Media Affairs. Other presidential communications advisers, such as David Gergen in the Ford administration, headed the Office of Communications and had no control over the Press Office. What the chief communications advisers have in common, though, is that they control the long-range publicity planning operation, including speechwriting, events management, and coordination of department and agency resources. The variation in the organizational title and responsibilities of the communications adviser is a sign of the variety that exists in the office from one administration to another and even within the years of a single administration, particularly in a two-term presidency.

The role of a modern communications planner and coordinator goes back to the Eisenhower administration, when presidential publicity took root in an organizational way.[1] James Hagerty, President Eisenhower's press secretary, was the first White House publicity officer to understand that his office could do more than merely respond to current press demands. He performed the functions of press secretary and communications director, though the latter job did not formally exist when he was in office. In addition to the basic tasks of a press secretary, he coordinated cabinet publicity officials, made recommendations on presidential speaking engagements, set up trips to highlight particular issues and presidential qualities, and made sure that reporters had a raft of handouts emphasizing the president's activities and leadership.[2]

In reorganizing the White House staff structure, President Nixon, who served as vice president during the Eisenhower years and was very aware of Hagerty's work, created an office to do what Hagerty had routinely done by himself. The mission of the Office of Communications was to portray his administration and its effects favorably to news organizations around the country.[3] The office was set up to arrange speeches on behalf of the president and to have a separate staff to handle out-of-town print and broadcast media.[4]

It was traditional for the press secretary and the press office to interact with the Washington press corps. Nixon wanted an office that would reach media far and wide. The Kennedy administration occasionally brought out-of-town news organizations into the White House for a day of briefings and an event with the president. The Nixon administration institutionalized state and local outreach efforts as part of the presidential communications process. Nixon's communications office sent information to out-of-town and foreign news organizations. Its director dealt with their editors and publishers, both individually and in their professional association settings.

President Nixon needed the office to help organize the news coming out of the White House so that reporters would have one event a day to cover. Brit Hume, a veteran White House observer who worked as a reporter in Washington during those years, commented that Nixon did more than set up the communications structure: "He also created the contemporary model for the event. He did the one-event-a-day [model], and they did it to an incredible degree."[5] Photographers noticed the same trend. David Hume Kennerly, who was President Ford's official photographer, spoke of event setups in the Nixon years: "The Nixon administration really perfected the photo op here [in the White House]. . . . [It started] during the campaign, [and] it carried through his presidency where they had this incredibly well-staged event, and a lot of attention went into the angles and this and that."[6]

Environment in Which the Communications Director Works

The demand for communications services is great, as is the pressure on the person who heads the operation—so much so that the turnover rate of top communications advisers is the highest among senior White House staff. The shape of the communications operation changes frequently as well, depending on what the president and the chief of staff want from their communications operation. All of these factors come together to make the communications adviser a crucial yet particularly vulnerable official in most White Houses.

Growing Speech and Event Demands

While President Nixon was the one who created the Office of Communications, the need for an organization that would perform the speechwriting, planning, and coordination tasks gradually grew from Hagerty's days in the Eisenhower administration. When President Eisenhower was in office, his speech and event obligations and press contacts were modest by today's standards. So was his communications organization—Eisenhower gave an average of less than a hundred speeches a year.

Forty years later, a president's public speaking appearances have increased sixfold. During his eight years in office, President Clinton gave an annual average of 559 addresses and remarks (see p. 11). This includes, at the top, addresses to the nation and, on an everyday basis, set speeches inside and outside of Washington as well as remarks made under less prepared circumstances, such as in the Oval Office, the Cabinet Room, or the Roosevelt Room before or after a meeting. This increase in presidential appearances requires an organizational structure to supply appropriate speech texts, locations, and scenarios that reinforce delivered words and maximize the resulting publicity.

While presidential speeches vary in importance, all of them are taken seriously because his words and his delivery communicate important information about his thinking. In the view of Terry Edmonds, chief speechwriter for President Clinton at the end of his administration, "All of what the president says is important. There's no sort of hierarchy of importance, because whenever the president speaks, it's the president speaking, and his words have sometimes global impact." As a result, "I treat every speech, whether it's pardoning the Thanksgiving turkey or the State of the Union, as a very important speech. . . .Of course, we put a little bit more effort into the State of the Union than we do into pardoning the turkey, but all of them are important."[7]

What is true of formal speeches and prepared remarks also applies to the president's answers to questions from reporters. In this case, too, the amount of work required by the president's communications staff has steadily increased.

Presidential responses to questions posed by reporters were treated as off the record until the arrival of the Eisenhower administration. Eisenhower held a total of 193 press conferences during his eight years in office. But he did not participate in the short, transcribed question-and-answer sessions with reporters that more recent presidents have regularly engaged in at the White House. In addition to his 193 press conferences—both Eisenhower and Clinton had the same official number—President Clinton had 1,410 other exchanges with reporters. By the time his term was over, this kind of presidential give-and-take had come to include regularly scheduled individual and group interviews as well as short question-and-answer sessions. Adding together all of the press contact numbers—press conferences, short question-and-answer sessions, presidential interviews—President Clinton had an average of 200 a year (see pp. 24–25).[8] Eisenhower had an average of twenty-four such contacts with the press each year. In order to accommodate that degree of interaction, it was necessary to create an infrastructure to deal with the increased speaking commitment.

High Turnover Rate of Communications Advisers

The communications adviser's position has the highest turnover of any senior-level White House post. In addition to the natural pressures on those dealing with presidential communications, the job has certain rhythms to it depending on what the president needs at particular points during his tenure. Within an administration, communications directors often emphasize different aspects of the job as they see the needs. In looking at the list of who has held the post and how long their terms have been, shown in table 8, one sees the volatility of the job and the variety of backgrounds people bring to the position. One can also see, though, the importance of a background in presidential campaigns as well as service with the president and chief of staff. In the early years, newspaper experience was also important.

Today, the challenge of communications has become highly multifaceted, time-consuming, and crucial; the communications director has less job security and more inclination to move on than any other senior member of the White House staff. Other senior staff positions have shown much greater stability. During the lifespan of the 24 communications directors, there have been only 14 press secretaries, 19 chiefs of staff, 19 White House counsels, 15 domestic policy directors, and 14 national security advisers.

The high churn rate of communications directors reflects the multiple and often conflicting demands placed on this position as well as the challenging environment in which that person operates.[9] The environment includes several elements beyond the control of the office, including the lack of support from an outside constituency, the link to the president's approval rating, and the job's shifting responsibilities and routines within the entire White House apparatus for communications.

A press secretary has a group of outside constituents with whom he regularly deals: reporters. So, too, do senior White House staff members, including the heads of the Offices of Cabinet Affairs, Intergovernmental Affairs, and Political Affairs, who each develop supporters among departmental secretaries, governors, mayors, and party leaders at the state and local levels. The director of the public liaison office has a set of interest groups with whom he or she deals regularly. Having their own constituencies means that the directors of these offices have influential people outside the White House to call on for support if they find themselves in trouble inside the administration. The director of communications lacks such a constituency because he or she deals with a far-flung group of ever-changing media people and organizations.

George Stephanopoulos, who was given communications responsibilities in addition to policy ones when he accompanied President Clinton from the campaign trail into office, observed that his being relieved of his communications responsibilities after less than four months was no surprise: "By definition, if the president isn't doing well, it's a communications problem. That's always going to be a natural place to make

Table 8. Directors, Office of Communications, 1969–2006

President	Communications Director	Office Status and Title of Director	Years in Office	Primary Experience	Secondary Experience
Nixon	Herbert Klein	Director of communications for the Executive Branch; Office of Communications created by President Nixon, January 1969	January 20, 1969–July 1, 1973	Press secretary to Richard Nixon as vice president and presidential candidate	Editor, *San Diego Union*, 1959–1968
	Ken W. Clawson	Director of communications, Office of Communications	January 30–November 1974	Deputy director of communications for the executive branch, February 1972–1973	Reporter, *Washington Post*, 1966–1972
Ford	Gerald L. Warren	Deputy press secretary for information liaison, later director, Office of Communications	November 1974–August 15, 1975	Deputy press secretary, 1969–1975	City editor, assistant managing editor, *San Diego Union*, 1963–1968
	Margita E. White	Director, Office of Communications	August 15, 1975–September 22, 1976	Assistant press secretary, January–August 15, 1975	Assistant director, public information, U.S. Information Agency, 1973–1975
	David Gergen	Special counsel to the president for communications and director, Office of Communications, restructured the reemerging Office of Communications and shifted reporting level up one big notch from press secretary to Chief of Staff Richard Cheney	July 1976–January 20, 1977 as director, Office of Communications	Special counsel to the president for communications, April–July 1976; special assistant to Chief of Staff Richard Cheney, December 1975–April 1976	Consultant to Treasury Secretary William E. Simon, November 1974–December 1975; special assistant to president, speechwriting and research, 1973–November 1974

Carter	Unoccupied		January 1977–June 1978 and August 1979–January 1981		
	Gerald Rafshoon	Assistant to the President for Communications	July 1, 1978–August 14, 1979	Head of Rafshoon Communications, based in Atlanta, Georgia	Handled media for Carter's two winning gubernatorial campaigns
Reagan	Frank A. Ursomarso	Communications director, but ranked as Deputy Assistant, reported to the Assistant to the President David Gergen	March 27–September 15, 1981	Television production, Governor Ronald Reagan's presidential debates, 1976 and 1980	Advance man for Presidents Nixon and Ford 1973–1976; automobile business
	David Gergen	Director of communications at Assistant to the President level	January 21, 1981–January 15, 1984	Special counsel, Ford; Special assistant, Nixon, 1973–1974	See above
	Michael A. McManus Jr. (Acting Director)	Office of Communications; reported to Deputy Chief of Staff Michael Deaver	January 1984–February 1985	Arrangements for the 1983 G-7 Summit in Williamsburg, Virginia	Corporate law, Pfizer, and private law practice
	Patrick Buchanan	Assistant to the President and director, Office of Communications	February 6, 1985–March 1, 1987	Executive assistant to former Vice President Richard M. Nixon, 1966–1969; speechwriter and senior adviser to President Nixon, 1969–1974	Syndicated newspaper columnist, commentator, 1975–1985
	John Koehler	Assistant to the President and director, Office of Communications	March 1–13, 1987	Consultant to the U.S. Information Agency; transition from Chief of Staff Donald Regan to Chief of Staff Howard Baker	Associated Press executive and, previously, reporter

(continued)

Table 8 (*continued*)

President	Communications Director	Office Status and Title of Director	Years in Office	Primary Experience	Secondary Experience
Reagan	Thomas C. Griscom	Assistant to the president for communications and planning	April 2, 1987–July 16, 1988	Ogilvy and Mather Public Affairs, president and chief operating officer in 1987	Executive director of the National Republican Senatorial Committee, 1985–1986. Press secretary to Senator Howard Baker, 1978–1984
	Mari Maseng	Assistant to the president and director of communications and planning	July 1, 1988–January 30, 1989	Director, Office of Public Liaison, May 1986–July 1987; assistant secretary of transportation, public affairs, November 1983–April 1985	Speechwriting staff, January 1981–November 1983; vice president, Beatrice Companies, Chicago, Illinois
G.H.W. Bush	David Demarest	Assistant to the president for communications	January 21, 1989–August 23, 1992	Manager, George H. W. Bush presidential campaign, 1988	Assistant secretary of labor, public and intergovernmental affairs, 1987–1988
	Margaret Tutwiler	Communications director	August 23, 1992–January 21, 1993	Assistant secretary of state, public affairs, and spokesperson, 1989–1992	Assistant treasury secretary, public affairs; assistant to Chief of Staff James A. Baker III, and deputy assistant to the president, public affairs, 1981–1989
Clinton	George Stephanopoulos	Assistant to the president and director of communications	January 20–May 29, 1993	Senior political adviser, 1992 Clinton/Gore campaign	House Majority Leader Richard A. Gephardt's staffer; 1988, Dukakis presidential campaign

President	Name	Position	Dates		
	Mark D. Gearan	Assistant director to the president and director of communications and strategic planning	June 7, 1993–June 21, 1995	Deputy chief of staff; deputy to Transition Director Warren Christopher, 1992	Al Gore campaign manager, 1992; national headquarters press secretary, Dukakis-for-President
	Donald A. Baer	Assistant to the president and White House director of strategic planning and communications	August 14, 1995–July 31, 1997	Chief speechwriter, April 1994–August 1995	U.S. *News & World Report* writer-editor, 1987–1994; lawyer, magazine writer, New York City
	Ann Lewis	Assistant to the president and director of communications	July 31, 1997–March 10, 1999	Deputy campaign manager and director of communications, 1996 Clinton/Gore reelection campaign; vice president for public policy, Planned Parenthood Federation of America, 1994–1995	Assistant secretary of labor, public affairs, May 17, 1993
	Loretta M. Ucelli	Assistant to the president and director of communications	March 10, 1999–January 20, 2001	Associate administrator for communications, education and public affairs, Environmental Protection Agency, March 2, 1993–March 10, 1999	Director of communication, National Abortion Rights Action League, 1992–1993
G.W. Bush	Karen Hughes	Counselor to the president, managed the White House Offices of Communications, Media Affairs; also speechwriting, and Press Secretary	January 20, 2001–July 29, 2005	Communications director, 2000 Bush presidential campaign; 1994 and 1998 Bush gubernatorial campaigns	Director of communications, Texas Governor George W. Bush, 1995–1999; executive director, Republican Party of Texas, 1992–1994; TV news reporter, 1977–1984

(continued)

Table 8 (*continued*)

President	Communications Director	Office Status and Title of Director	Years in Office	Primary Experience	Secondary Experience
	Dan Bartlett	Assistant to the president for communications and White House communications director	October 2, 2001– January 5, 2005	Deputy assistant to the president and principal deputy to counselor Karen Hughes	Deputy to policy director, Governor's Office, Austin, Texas, 1994–1998; in 1998 reelection campaign
	Nicolle Devenish Wallace	Assistant to the president for communications—heads Office of Communications	January 5, 2005– June 30, 2006	Communications director, Bush/Cheney '04; previously, special assistant to the president and director of media affairs at the White House	Governor Jeb Bush's Press Secretary, 1999; communications director, Florida State Technology Office, 2000
	Kevin Sullivan	Assistant to the president for communications—now heads Office of Communications	July 24, 2006– present	Assistant secretary of education for communications and outreach; previously, NBC Universal and NBC Sports	Vice president for communications, Dallas Mavericks

a change."[10] The communications director is held responsible for how a president is doing, yet he or she has few resources with which to affect the basis for judging presidential performance. Stephanopoulos was held responsible when Clinton's job-performance ratings fell precipitously.

What most sets the Office of Communications apart is that whoever holds the communications portfolio is responsible for shaping what the office does. In the Clinton White House, for example, five different appointees were put in charge of communications, and they came up with at least three different ways of managing their responsibilities. Among Clinton's communications specialists were George Stephanopoulos, Mark Gearan, Don Baer, Ann Lewis, and Loretta Ucelli, all of whom served as communications directors, plus senior aides Sidney Blumenthal and David Gergen, for whom communications was central to their portfolios. Stephanopoulos and Gearan spent much of their time on tasks associated with the post of press secretary, such as talking to reporters. During much of the time that Gearan was handling communications, David Gergen was there. While Gergen had no communications title, Baer noted, "part of his portfolio was to work to bring a sense of coherence to the communications process." Baer himself, under the title of director of strategic planning and communications, was chosen to follow Gergen. Following Baer, Ann Lewis and then Loretta Ucelli took the official title of director of communications and focused on event planning. All of them approached the job differently in where they fit within the White House structure and what functions they emphasized.

During the early part of the Clinton administration, whoever handled the responsibilities of communications director also did the press work and served as primary spokesperson for the president and the administration. The emphasis was on the press work components of communications. As Baer explained, "Everybody, whether they were called communications director or press secretary, basically thought their job was to be press secretary and not to really be a communications director in any sense of laying down strategy, helping the various output arms of the public face of the White House to know what their role would be in the context of the larger strategy for public communications." Soon, however, people realized that nobody was in charge of strategy. Baer continued, "What most people spent their time doing was the care and feeding of the press rather than thinking about the strategic communications objectives of the White House and how best to push those out. So there was a desire to reorient that role somewhat more in the other direction."

When Erskine Bowles came in as deputy chief of staff, he assumed responsibility for some of the nuts-and-bolts offices charged with setting up events, such as the offices of advance and scheduling. "The whole purpose and idea was to try to get those units coordinating better because all of those are very important bits and pieces of what the larger strategic objectives of the White House would be," concluded Baer.[11]

In contrast to his predecessor, who tended to downplay and deinstitutionalize his communications operation, President George W. Bush has treated communications as a cornerstone of his presidency. Karen Hughes was granted the title of counselor to the president when she was chosen to run the office of communications. In the fall of 2002, when Karen Hughes left the White House but continued as an informal communications adviser from her home in Texas, Dan Bartlett inherited the title of director of communications. Two years later he received the title assistant to the president for communications. At the beginning of Bush's second term, Bartlett was made counselor to the president. Nicolle Devenish Wallace, fresh from success in her role running the Bush-Cheney campaign communications operation, was made director of communications.

Defining Relationships with the President

While the work of the press secretary is shaped by the precedents of his predecessors and the expectations of news organizations, the work of the communications director is defined by his relationships. The most important of these relationships are with the president and with his chief of staff because they define what it is the communications staff do.

Reagan media guru Michael Deaver, whose official title was deputy chief of staff, recalled that his work was defined by his relationships with the president and first lady. "I really sort of gained whatever control or power I had simply by my relationship," he said of his ties to the president and first lady. He controlled the schedules and travels of the first family and then ran the military office and all of the East Wing operations, which is where the first lady's organization is housed. He also had "an ad hoc seat on anything dealing with communications. When Gergen left, I took over officially the communications role."[12]

For David Demarest, who served as communications director for President George H. W. Bush, the job was greatly reduced. "I think the president saw me more as the guy that ran his speeches and his events," he recalled. "I don't think he saw that in terms of a communications message. I think that he saw the press as the vehicle for the communications message through Marlin and through his own interactions with the press."[13]

When President G. H. W. Bush decided that he wanted Press Secretary Marlin Fitzwater to handle his communications strategic planning as well as his press relations, Fitzwater did so despite his own misgivings over combining the two jobs. When members of the Clinton transition team visited him to discuss their plan to cut off reporters' access to the press secretary in the upper press office and their desire to combine the press and communications posts, Fitzwater discouraged them on both points: "I tried to explain in some detail why I thought that was a terrible idea, not only cutting them off but why they couldn't combine the two jobs. I had just gone through that. I had been forced to take the communications job over my objections and finally just got out of it six, eight months later because it was a total failure."[14] The press secretary and the communications director each has more tasks than he or she can accomplish. It is not possible for one person to successfully undertake both jobs.

Of all of the groups within the communications operation, the one that most relies on its relationship with the president is the speechwriters. To speechwriters it makes a great deal of difference who the president is, because some want to play a big role in crafting them, while others do not. Tony Snow, one of President George H. W. Bush's speechwriters and currently the press secretary for George W. Bush, said that the elder Bush regarded speechmaking as "a necessary evil. He didn't like giving speeches." President Bush had particular difficulty giving speeches where emotion was on the surface. "He was afraid to make emotional contact with the public in a way that Reagan did," Snow said. Thus, in 1991 when planning his speech to the nation about the riots in Los Angeles, he opted to avoid emotional issues: "We had a debate over the kind of speech to deliver after the L.A. riots, and he ended up doing a fairly straightforward law-and-order thing, rather than something to try to calm people's fear and to talk more personally, about unity and so on." To Snow's way of thinking, this president "did not have any sense of how language worked, and I think that's a reflection, ironically, of his both commendable and damnable humility."[15] Since he had little interest in communications, his communications operation was not a priority at any time during his administration.

In addition, communications staff had to work around President George H. W. Bush's communications difficulties in emotional situations. One such occasion was when he spoke in Norfolk, Virginia, to family members of the forty-seven sailors who died April 17, 1989, in an explosion on the USS *Iowa*. Associated Press reporter Terry Hunt, a pool reporter that day, recounted the difficulties the president had speaking to the family members of those who died. "There was [a] very emotional meeting with widows and . . . he was so overcome that he was smiling, which seemed inappropriate, but it was that he was so tense [and] overcome that he was trying to overcompensate," Hunt said. When the meeting was over, "instead of getting into his limousine, he walked from the hangar all the way back to Air Force One, and the photographers said that he was crying. When he was finally able to get out of the public eye, he just finally broke down because it was a terribly emotional thing. My point is that he wasn't as artful and able to show emotion like Reagan was."[16]

For President Reagan speeches were a top priority, so he spent time thinking about working on them. "All the way through the Reagan years, speechwriters were treated as special creatures, given a lot of access, considering their status, their rank in the White House," commented Mari Maseng Will, who worked as a speechwriter in the early years of the Reagan White House and as head of the Office of Communications at its end. During Reagan's first term, his speechwriters met with him on Fridays "to go over concepts, what he wanted to say." Then speechwriters would talk with the president's policy advisers followed by the writers proposing "what the speech should be, and then there would be a give-and-take." Reagan's support gave them a great deal of confidence in their role in the administration: "There was a funny saying in the Reagan White House among the speechwriters that they thought of themselves as the keepers of the Holy Grail. And there was that kind of enthusiasm and confidence."[17]

The differences in the speechmaking characteristics of Presidents George H. W. Bush and Ronald Reagan carried over into how the two presidents approached photography, which is an important element of communicating a president to the public. David Hume Kennerly, *Time* photographer during those years, spoke about the camera presence of Reagan and Bush. He found President Reagan "to be more 'up' when he was in front of the cameras than when he was behind the desk working," Kennerly said. "He had a stage presence." Reagan had a special energy when he was being photographed. "He was dynamic out in front of the camera, but his energy level was lower when he wasn't," Kennerly said. "For photographers, he was a great subject." Reagan was "really easy to get along with." President George H. W. Bush "liked the photographers personally, but, everything [being photographed] to him seemed to be kind of a bother. It took away from the serious business of being president."[18]

Whether it was speechcraft or photography, in the George W. Bush administration communications regained the pivotal position it had been given during the Reagan years. Karen Hughes was made counselor to the president, the highest-ranking position a communications staff member has held in any administration.

No matter who was directing communications in the George W. Bush White House during the first term, the speechwriters based their work on their understanding of the president. In an unusual move, there were three speechwriters who worked together on all of the president's major speeches and most of his minor ones. Indeed, they worked at the same computer, where for hours they would flesh out presidential speeches, said John McConnell. Mike Gerson, policy adviser and assistant to the president for speechwriting, led the group with Matthew Scully, special assistant to the president and senior speechwriter for the president, and McConnell, deputy assistant to the president and deputy director of presidential speechwriting. Because they wrote together for Bush during the 2000 campaign, the three of them came into the White House knowing their president very well. Having a sense of their man, they knew how to craft a speech that brought out the qualities they valued.

An example is the speech they wrote when President Bush unveiled the portrait of President Clinton. "We agreed that we work for a gracious man, and he is going to be gracious. It would be out of character for him to be reserved or pull back," said McConnell. "We wanted to do something nice and knew the president would too." That meant citing Clinton's virtues, such as his ability to "always see a better day." At the same time, they "wanted to see if we could get one of those Arkansas belly laughs out of him." They did so by having the president refer to Clinton's optimistic nature, which he would have to have to "give six months of your life running the McGovern campaign in Texas." The three speechwriters "delighted in picturing the president doing it," and Bush thoroughly enjoyed it as well.[19]

Relationship with the Chief of Staff

Effective communications requires the coordination of people and offices with political information and policy. The president's chief of staff is responsible for coordination at this level. Either the chief of staff handles the coordination himself, as Leon Panetta and James Baker did, or he assigns it to deputies. When Erskine Bowles was chief of staff, for example, he asked John Podesta, his deputy, to take responsibility for communications, and every morning Podesta followed their senior staff meeting with a meeting devoted to publicity.

Erskine Bowles chose to remain aloof from communications, although he occasionally offered general guidelines. When James Baker was Reagan's chief of staff, however, he spent a great deal of time explaining administration policy to journalists on a "background" basis—that is, imparting printable information without attribution. When Baker met with the chiefs who preceded him, he was given the following advice: "It's important for you to keep the press informed about what it is you're trying to do and continually spend time with them."[20] Michael Deaver, who served as Baker's deputy chief of staff, remembered: "He really was the senior spokesperson for the Reagan White House. It wasn't Speakes, it wasn't Gergen, it was Baker, and everybody knew it."[21]

James Baker did a lot of "background" interviews, but his successor could not understand why he did so. As Baker himself recalled, "When [Don] Regan replaced me as chief of staff, he said, 'I'm just amazed at the amount of time Jim Baker spent with the press.' Some people equated that with leaking. That's not leaking; that's spinning, which is what the chief of staff ought to be doing on background. Not up front [on the record], because the chief of staff is not elected."[22]

Today, a chief of staff is expected to be a regular presence on the Sunday television talk programs and sometimes on the morning news shows as well. Leon Panetta, who got used to appearing on such programs when he was chairman of the House Budget Committee, was the first of Clinton's chiefs of staff to become a regular television presence. His successor, Erskine Bowles, eschewed such appearances, but John Podesta returned to the Panetta model. Still, as little interest as Bowles personally had in communications issues, he knew that publicity was an important responsibility of the chief's office. On behalf of the current Bush administration, Chief of Staff Andrew Card did occasionally appear on Sunday interview programs, but he did not make a habit of it. Unlike many of his predecessors, he did not regularly talk "on background with reporters." Karl Rove, however, does spend a considerable amount of time talking with selected reporters on background and off the record.

Even more time-consuming is the job of orchestrating publicity rollouts. Some chiefs of staff get actively involved in the process, and others use a more hands-off approach. David Demarest described the difficulties the communications group under George H. W. Bush had dealing with outside groups and institutions. The root of the problem was Chief of Staff John Sununu, who wanted personal control over every aspect of legislative strategy or communications coordination. In this case, the chief of staff represented a block to coordination, not a facilitation of it. "Fred [McClure, Legislative Affairs Director] was about to set up a legislative strategy group, not a crazy idea, so that he would be able to pull all the elements together so that when President Bush wanted to move forward on some initiative we had a legislative strategy," noted Demarest. "Sununu said, 'No, I'm legislative strategy.' When I wanted to set up a communications strategy group, 'No, I'm communications.'"

To maneuver around Sununu, Demarest had to set up weekly events meetings: "But I pitched it as, 'This is simply to go over the next week's events, make sure that everybody from around the agencies and from within the White House knows what's going on.' So it was both informational to people, and it turned up a bunch of missing elements each week of what needed to happen. There'd be somebody from advance there, and there'd be somebody from policy, and somebody from the cabinet agencies, whatever. I made it kind of open to all."[23]

Most communications directors have no trouble working with other administration offices, agencies, and departments as they set up events, because these partners know they are likely to be affected by what happens. Don Baer, for example, worked with the Office of Intergovernmental Affairs on setting up an event that included an appearance by President Clinton at a meeting of the National Governors Association. The kinds of questions he asked prior to setting up the appearance were: "'What then does the president want to do when he's at the NGA? What does he want to say to the NGA?' It's a big, high-profile event opportunity. So you'd have to have a lot of work and negotiation with them over what the governors were willing to hear from him versus what we wanted to do and say there, all those kinds of things. It was complicated."[24]

Democrats and Republicans

In Democratic White Houses, the personal style of the president is an important aspect of the organization and operation of his staff, including that of his communications staff. More than anything else, its structure mirrors the degree that he wants to handle issues and situations that make their way into the Oval Office personally and the way that he is comfortable doing so.

Republican presidents establish a tone through business management principles while Democratic presidents tend to be more president-centered. The difference is most apparent in what it requires of a chief of staff, which can then influence what the communications operation does. "Jack Kennedy was his own Chief of Staff," recalled Theodore Sorensen, who worked as closely with him as any other staffer. And the same could be said of the early days of each of the other Democratic presidents who served after World War II.[25]

The partisan differences in White House management manifest themselves in communications most notably in the relationship of the Office of Communications to the Press Office. In Republican White Houses, both offices come under the supervision of an overall senior communications adviser. If there is no communications czar, then the Press Office is organizationally under the Office of Communications. The director of that office is the person responsible for presidential publicity. The persuasion operation is in charge of what information comes out of the Press Office.

While we have had only two Democratic administrations in the years since the Office of Communications was created, in both we see the communications operation with a smaller role than in Republican ones. In the Carter administration, there was a communications adviser heading the Office of Communications for a little over a year. The director, Gerald Rafshoon, did most of the tasks associated with the office, but he left and went to direct the reelection campaign. Even so, during his time in office, Press Secretary Jody Powell was the chief strategist on information and publicity issues. In the Clinton administration, the two offices operated separately, with each having a direct line in to the president and to the chief of staff. The Press Office worked at the direction of the press secretary, which meant that information policy was decided there rather than in an operation charged with selling the president's program.

Offense and Defense in the Bush Second Term: The Rapid Response Operation

Earlier we saw the way in which the Clinton White House operated to respond quickly to criticism or damaging events and scandals while the Bush White House openly eschewed such an operation. As Dan Bartlett said, his views changed in the second term when he realized they needed a hybrid operation that did long-term planning but would simultaneously be capable of responding to whatever was in the current news cycle.

Following the 2004 election, Nicolle Devenish Wallace, the communications director for the campaign, came back to the White House, where she had earlier served as head of the Media Affairs Office. She brought with her the concept of rapid response and the people who worked on the campaign's rapid response operation. "When we won reelection, and we looked at . . . how do we marry the best practices from the campaign, which obviously was successful, and the best practices from the White House, which obviously was very successful. We have made changes now," Wallace said. "And for the first time, we have a rapid response office."[26]

Housed in the Office of Communications, the rapid response unit is responsible for getting out information to a variety of selected audiences within the administration and on Capitol Hill as well as to Republican party officials, television and talk radio producers and hosts, and interest group allies. Sent by e-mail, the messages can quickly get into the news stream. "It is taking something good that is out there and distributing it in a different way," said Kevin Sullivan, who heads the Office of Communications. The information serves both offensive and defensive purposes, depending upon the need. The messages are "very helpful without question to administration staffers who work in the agencies, on the Hill, when they are dealing with reporters," said Sullivan. Individuals outside the White House find them useful as well. "Talk radio producers are one of the key groups," he said. "It provides questions for their hosts to ask sometimes that they might not have thought of. . . . For a radio host who doesn't have time to drill down into a military commission and know what it all means, you have a two-page document that explains what it all means."[27]

The basic activity of the rapid response operation is a set of e-mail messages carrying the administration's positive and defensive messages. As the news cycle has gotten even faster in Bush's second term, the need to infiltrate it is more pronounced than it was early in the administration, when Internet news traffic was relatively marginal. In the second term, newspapers, television networks, radio programs, and individuals have a variety of websites and blogs, all of which release information as soon as they get it. That puts pressure on officials in the White House and elsewhere to come up with a fast response.

The rapid response team sends out messages with both positive and negative themes. The goal of the positive messages is to have people who are important in the Washington and administration community see items they might otherwise have missed, especially ones that consolidate current information. Their negative messages are aimed at dousing fires that may be developing. "If we think something is misleading or inaccurate . . . the key is we want to get our response out before it becomes accepted, conventional wisdom," said Kevin Sullivan.[28]

In an environment where there is so much information available to people in the Washington community as well as elsewhere, there is a need for sources that synthesize information. Letting allies and others know what the president is saying and what their priorities and responses are, and doing so throughout the day, is important for keeping those people current. Chief of Staff Joshua Bolten said that White House staff have adapted to the profusion of information by having their own methods of synthesizing information, including within the administration. "We have adapted our mechanisms of coping," he said. "Along with the explosion of information sources, there have also been an explosion of ways of propagating and synthesizing information. E-mail is that. This is a White House that e-mails each other very heavily. We do physically get together. You know the place is a small place. It is easy for us to physically get together, but there is a lot of e-mailing of information back and forth. I think most of us pay attention to what the Press Office is putting out. 'In Case You Missed It' and things like that. And a lot of us rely on some of the synthesizing sources."[29]

Fourteen categories of e-mails are distributed to between 5,000 and 10,000 recipients.[30] The main groups a message goes to are, "first of all, everybody internally in the White House. It goes to the White House press corps as well as other national political reporters, it goes to contacts on Capitol Hill, and it goes to 'other interested parties' in Washington," said Rob Saliterman, who heads the rapid response unit and is responsible for developing the messages, along with his deputy, Nikki McArthur.[31] The Capitol Hill recipients are Republican communications people, and the "other interested parties" include surrogates who speak for the president and the administration as well as those associated with allied interest groups, bloggers, talk radio personalities and producers, and so on. In reality, the distribution is far broader because "other people will take them and push them out, depending on what the topic is. So they have a pretty good shelf life," said Sullivan.

Typically a page or two, the e-mail messages fit both offensive and defensive White House communications needs. "Rapid response by definition sounds like it's a defensive thing, but we look at it as a way of staying on offense," said Sullivan. "We're going to affirmatively, proactively, put something out. Because it is not always responding to something.

It is taking something good that is out there and distributing it in a different way."[32] There are nine basic categories of "offensive" messages, in which the administration tries to package information people might have missed.[33] These might include presidential speeches, snippets from Tony Snow's daily press briefing, briefings by administration officials, news articles, or op-ed pieces. The most frequently used categories are: "Morning Update," "Fact Sheet," "Straight to the Point," and "In Case You Missed It." During 2006, "Morning Update" was a daily message, and "Fact Sheet" came out frequently, but the frequency depended on whether there were presidential actions or initiatives calling for them on a particular day. There were twenty-six messages for "Straight to the Point" and thirty-eight for "In Case You Missed It."[34]

The "Morning Update" is a weekday daily sent at eight o'clock in the morning in time for people to see what the president's schedule is and read newspaper articles with pertinent information the White House wants to get out, including clips from interviews the president may have had with radio, television, or print journalists. The messages include links to articles, audio files of interviews, briefings, and press releases. The longest of the e-mails, it is broken up into three parts. First is the president's public schedule for the day. The second part, "From the Morning Headlines" has perhaps ten lines of quotations from several articles appearing that day. Third, "From the White House" has links to the previous day's briefing by the press secretary, personnel announcements, and presidential remarks. A second kind of positive e-mail message, "Fact Sheets," provides background information on presidential initiatives or facts on positive trends, such as an increase in the number of jobs. "Straight to the Point" has excerpts from presidential statements as they happen. Most come out within an hour of a presidential speech and less than ten minutes after the completed transcripts have been sent to reporters. In one week, of the three sent out, one was within twenty-three minutes and another within forty-two minutes of the conclusion of the president's remarks. The hourlong presidential press conference with Prime Minister Tony Blair took an hour and twenty minutes to get into excerpt form.[35] "The Briefing Breakdown" takes briefings by officials around the government, not just the press secretary, with an issue or issues related to a point the administration wants to make that day.

"In Case You Missed It" is a targeted message that has one topic, with either a full text or excerpts. In four messages released during a period of one week, for example, they contained the following information:

excerpts from Iraqi religious leader Abdul Aziz Al-Hakim's remarks to President Bush and the U.S. Institute for Peace; statements from Iraqi Prime Minister Nouri al-Maliki's press conference the previous day, arranged by topic; and an interview with U.S. soldiers in Iraq conducted by talk radio personality Sean Hannity.[36] Among the most numerous of the e-mail messages, in 2006 there were roughly thirty-eight "In Case You Missed It" messages distributed to their recipients. Deputy Press Secretary Dana Perino explained White House thinking about the messages: "It was a group effort to think of some ways to get the word out. 'In Case You Missed It' is a good one. It doesn't just go to reporters, it goes to communicators in the agencies, on the Hill. They're not necessarily reading all that we're reading or seeing all that we're seeing. If we see something that we think is good and interesting, we'll try to get it out there," she said.[37]

There are other more occasional e-mails—"By the Numbers," "What They're Saying"—that include information on polling ("8 of 10 Pharmacists, 7 of 10 Doctors Agree: Medicare Drug Benefit Helps Seniors Save") and statements by others about their initiatives ("Bipartisan Support for Gates").[38] The Medicare prescription drug program has its own e-mail message series ("Medicare Check-Up"), as does the economy ("Economy Watch"). A typical example of these messages might be the "Medicare Check-Up" containing a *Wall Street Journal* article, "Once Unloved, Medicare's Prescription-Drug Program Defies Critics, But Issues Remain."[39]

The five categories of defensive messages sent out by the rapid response team aim to correct a portrait officials regard as incomplete or attack a story viewed as inaccurate.[40] The group of messages includes the most frequently sent and important ones, "Setting the Record Straight," "The Rest of the Story," and, for its high impact, "Myth/Fact." If officials believe a story to be inaccurate, they will do a "Setting the Record Straight" pointing out its errors. In a May 10, 2006, message, "Setting the Record Straight: CBS News' Misleading Medicare Report," officials took apart a piece by correspondent Jim Axelrod. He was quoted as saying on the *CBS Evening News,* "Hoping to nail down at least one clear success story for Republicans to run on this fall, Mr. Bush wants to add another million seniors to the eight million already signed up." The heading for that segment was: "CBS News Misleadingly Reports That Only 8 Million Seniors Have Signed Up For Medicare Prescription Drug Coverage." The message went on to dispute the claim with short segments indicating that thirty-seven million seniors have prescription drug coverage, that others could be program participants without knowing it, and that the Department of Health and Human Services had signed up nine million seniors for Medicare prescription drug coverage. While these e-mail messages focus on facts, most often the difference between the articles and the White House response is a matter of interpretation and the relevance of the facts included.

The bulletins sometimes annoy the reporters singled out for dissection. Five months later, that particular "Setting the Record Straight" e-mail was still on Axelrod's mind. Howard Kurtz, media critic for the *Washington Post*, spoke with Axelrod: "CBS's Jim Axelrod recalls how Snow once issued a press release assailing a story Axelrod had done on Medicare eligibility. 'He basically sent out this report calling me a liar, and then showed up at the booth smiling, with a handshake, and we had a half-hour chat.' "[41] In reality, Tony Snow does not alone decide on the content of the messages, but Axelrod continued to smart from its sting.

"Setting the Record Straight" has targeted news organizations for their reporting involving the success status of a variety of administration policies and programs: Iraq, Medicare, the economy, the benefits of tax cuts, military recruitment, hurricane preparations, foreign policy, stem cell policy, climate change, national guard troops, and border security. In one four-day period, the e-mails addressed articles found in the *Washington Post*, the *New York Times*, *USA Today*, CBS News, and the Associated Press.[42]

When the White House sends out these messages, some news organizations take note of them. Perhaps the best example of an impact on a story in which the White House had adopted a defensive stance was the "Myth/Fact" e-mail distributed to extinguish the negative publicity coming from the book *State of Denial* by *Washington Post* editor Bob Woodward. The message singled out five aspects of Woodward's charges about the president's understanding and handling of the war in Iraq. Together, the "myths" included intelligence assessments, an alleged request by Paul Bremer for more troops in Iraq, Condoleezza Rice's response to a CIA warning about Al Qaeda, comments attributed to General John Abizaid concerning Secretary of Defense Donald Rumsfeld's credibility, and supposed efforts to remove Rumsfeld attributed to Chief of Staff Andrew Card and First Lady Laura Bush.[43]

The message was used in a variety of ways and in a variety of places. The *Washington Post* published excerpts from the book accompanied by a box with a Reuters story detailing the five myths in the White House release.[44] Tim Russert used the five myths when he asked Woodward about his book on *Meet the Press,* and Woodward brought them up himself on *Hardball with Chris Matthews* and *The Charlie Rose Show.* The myths were also discussed on the morning and evening network news broadcasts, for example *The NBC Nightly News* and *The Today Show.*

In addition to being used as part of a news story and as a basis for questioning, the defensive messages have an additional impact. Some correspondents are concerned that their reporting might be the subject of a "Setting the Record Straight" message. When Dana Perino calls reporters about a perceived inaccuracy, commented Kevin Sullivan, "There have been times when the reporter will say, 'You're not going to do a "Setting the Record Straight," are you?' "[45] Knowing that reporters can be sensitive to being singled out provides the White House with a possible lever in dealing with journalists—whether or not reporters regard it as such.

The decision to issue releases is made in the morning communications meeting, which includes approximately a dozen people working in the communications area. They are Dan Bartlett, who hosts the meeting; Tony Snow; Kevin Sullivan, communications director; Scott Sforza, director of television production; Jeanie Mamo, who heads the media affairs operation; Dana Perino, deputy press secretary; Tony Fratto or Scott Stanzel, the other deputy press secretaries; Susan Whitson, press secretary to Laura Bush; Gordon Johndroe, from the National Security Council; Rob Saliterman, who heads the rapid response unit; Eryn Witcher, who handles television; and Blain Rethmeier, responsible for policy communications. In that meeting, "We'll talk about the news of the day; what we are going to do today," said Sullivan. "The rapid response effort is a big part of the decisions that are made." While the unit wants to respond to what they feel is misleading or inaccurate as well as put out good news, staffers don't want to put out too many of them. "We don't want to be like a barking Chihuahua in the middle of the night where you are always yapping," said Sullivan. "You have to pick your spots."[46]

Once the decision is made to do one or more releases, Rob Saliterman and Nikki McArthur create them. They came to the White House from the 2004 campaign, where they worked on rapid response. Often the messages involve a repackaging of material that has already been released, such as a briefing, speech, or fact sheet. Such messages can be pushed out pretty quickly, while ones that include new material or selected items from other messages are subject to a slower release process.

Then the internal process involves sending the completed messages up a chain that includes the officials in the Press Office and the Office of Communications, the staff secretary, and a policy person if the messages deal with a policy issue. "If you have one person who makes a certain edit, then everyone else has to look at it to make sure they are okay with it. So you are dealing with a lot of moving parts, especially for the various economic ones we have done. You have to have CEA and NEC approve it. If CEA has one change, then you have to go back to NEC and make sure they are okay with it, and if they have another change, you have to go back to CEA," said Saliterman.[47]

The messages have succeeded in getting White House information into the fast-moving news cycle. In both offensive and defensive initiatives, the rapid response operation has gotten the attention of news organizations and insinuated the White House version of events into ongoing stories. While their efforts have gotten the president's words and explanations to the public through a variety of channels, there are limits to how much the messages can accomplish. There is no guarantee that the public will like what it hears in those messages, nor that anyone will change his or her mind. But at least the White House gets presidential words and thinking to the audiences the president and his staff want to reach.

Responsibilities of the Communications Director

Whatever the inclinations of the president and his chief of staff, the strengths of the publicity adviser, and the nature of the political environment, the communications director takes responsibility for message development and implementation and, when reelection looms, for campaign coordination as well. Even if one of those roles is emphasized, the others cannot afford to be overlooked. One way or another, each of these three tasks must be performed.

The message management role is twofold: developing and coordinating a message, sometimes even standing in for the president to deliver it, and framing and elaborating positions on issues of the president's concern. The implementation role belongs to those directors who are focused on carrying out message assignments rather than being the creator of them. The campaign coordination role begins with developing an overall reelection strategy and coordinating it with campaign officials. But it also extends to the role that communications directors play in managing the legacy campaign that gears up as a president approaches the end of his tenure.

Shaping and Selling the President's Message

The communications director must be able to centralize the collection and distribution of information and use it to explain and to defend the president's policies and actions. At the same time, he or she must establish and enforce standards of consistency and message discipline. When focused on this message role, the director has time for little else.

Nixon's first director and his deputy, Herb Klein and Ken Clawson, initially used the office to develop themes for administration communications but later shifted to defending the president. They proceeded in different ways. Klein appeared on television programs such as *The Phil Donahue Show* to discuss the president and his programs. He also met individually with reporters he knew from his various tours of duty with Nixon as a senator and as vice president. Because of his years as an editor at the *San Diego Union*, Klein had credibility with reporters, which made them seek him out as a source of information. Ken Clawson, on the other hand, pleaded the president's case in private sessions with groups of reporters. Dubbed "Cocktails with Clawson," the sessions were used to portray information in its most favorable light.[48]

Opprobrium attached itself to the Office of Communications when it was revealed during the Watergate episode and the subsequent impeachment hearings that it had been used to spread disinformation. Charles Colson and Jeb Stuart Magruder, deputy directors from Nixon's first term, served time in jail for their role in Watergate. As a result, until the arrival of the Reagan administration, communications staff erred on the side of caution when called upon to make a case for the president. The communications directors who served under President Ford were particularly conscious of the need to avoid using their position for blatant presidential promotion. In the Carter administration, everyone knew that there was only one spokesman for the president—Press Secretary Jody Powell, and Powell alone worked on and off the record, in public and in private, to present the president's views.

As part of its effort to restore the authority and influence of the presidency, the Reagan White House centralized its communications operations. The director of the Office of Communications worked closely with the chief of staff or the president himself to determine exactly what the administration wanted to convey to the public and how.

Here is how Tom Griscom, Reagan's longest-serving communications director, described his role in the Reagan White House: "There was a model to learn from, and the model was the first years of his administration." During those early years, the communications director's bailiwick included "speechwriters, scheduling, anything that affected an external environment." But that model slipped into a job that "spread out all over the place." When he assumed control, "we collapsed it back in, so my responsibilities as the organization's director . . . were all the speechwriters, scheduling speeches, press office, the outreach groups within the White House, the political shop, all that stuff got rolled together." Here is how Griscom fit in with others at the top level: "We broke it down this way. . . . Senator Baker was the counsel to the president, chief of staff. [Kenneth] Duberstein was the deputy, [and] worried about day to day," he said. "My job was to worry about what we are doing tomorrow. All those pieces that were affected down the road then got put into the responsibility of the communications director."[49]

David Gergen was the first communications director to emphasize development of the presidential message. Initially, Gergen served in the Nixon White House as a speechwriter and then in the Ford administration as head of the Office of Communications. By the time he returned for White House service in the Reagan administration, the memory of Watergate was not as fresh or raw as when Gergen headed communications efforts in the Ford administration. In that incarnation, he oversaw the process of weaving the themes of Ford's presidency into its campaign for reelection. Emphasizing that President Ford was a known quantity because he was in office, Gergen developed publicity emphasizing Ford's official performance.

Always at ease with reporters, Gergen had spent the Carter years at the American Enterprise Institute, where he established a journal called *Public Opinion*. Familiar with the needs of news organizations and reporters who covered a White House, he was a particularly good fit in an administration that was concerned with establishing the grandeur and authority of the presidency. He was comfortable talking about policy, but defining and projecting a presidential image were also within his ken. He used the period prior to Reagan's inauguration working on a 100-day plan that would guide administration communications efforts for the months to come. Michael Deaver applauded the plan because it "set the bones for the way the communication plan would work for a year."[50]

Clinton's communications directors, chiefly George Stephanopoulos, Mark Gearan, Don Baer, and Ann Lewis, also emphasized the message management role. Moreover, unlike Gergen, four of Clinton's five advisers

regularly appeared on television to explain presidential actions and policies. They became regular fixtures on the morning network news programs. While Stephanopoulos had a higher profile than the others and
was the most comfortable speaking about presidential matters, all of them
spent a lot of time explaining the president's positions. Loretta Ucelli was
the lone communications adviser who did not appear publicly to explain
the president's priorities.

George W. Bush's communications team began in the background but
gradually increased its visibility in order to explain the president's thinking. Karen Hughes was just as frequently quoted but not as often seen on
television as her predecessors in the Clinton administration. The root of
this difference partly lay in the Bush philosophy of making news on his
own terms, which meant appearing publicly when there was any advantage to doing so. President Bush sought less publicity as his administration began than President Clinton did. The same was true of his senior
staff, including the communications aides. Establishing consistency and
discipline in message matters is a communications director's responsibility. There has to be one message at a time, and it must be carefully
crafted. Often this need calls for controlling the president himself.

President Clinton proved to be a challenge when his message managers were trying to capitalize on the aura of his office. Public forums
sometimes proved to be his undoing. His willingness in 1994 to respond
to a young questioner on MTV who inquired about his underwear pref-
erences attested to his intractability. Not until Leon Panetta became his
chief of staff and Mike McCurry his press secretary did message discipline come to the Clinton presidency.

For President George W. Bush, by way of contrast, message discipline
was the signature of his candidacy, his presidency, and his White House
staff. His communications team knew that the time it invested in message development would pay off. In addition to focusing on a limited
number of items, his staff curbed or removed those who would not adhere to the party line, such as National Economic Council Director Larry
Lindsey and Secretary of the Treasury Paul O'Neill. Both made comments
requiring cleanup efforts by the communications team. Lindsey, for example, told the *Wall Street Journal* that the Iraq War might cost upwards
of $200 billion when the administration line was only $50 billion. Early
in his days at Treasury, Secretary O'Neill questioned the wisdom of a tax
cut, an initiative central to the Bush presidency.

While most communications chiefs focus on explaining their presidents in a manner that does not make the messenger the issue, Patrick Buchanan, who worked as communications director for Ronald Reagan, handled the job of message development in a completely different way. His hallmark was his personal advocacy of conservative stands on issues rather than explanation of the president's thinking and policies. He regularly wrote articles that appeared on the opinion page of the *Washington Post* and other newspapers. His topics were "hot button" issues, such as aid to the Contras and support for Oliver North when he testified before Congress.

With a vote on Contra aid in the House of Representatives close at hand, Buchanan wrote the following in a *Washington Post* opinion piece: "With the vote on contra aid, the Democratic party will reveal whether it stands with Ronald Reagan and the resistance—or Daniel Ortega and the communists."[51] Statements like this—it was but one of many—served to divide rather than to integrate communications efforts during Ronald Reagan's second term. In this case, Buchanan's comments met with a strong response from the Democratic majority in Congress. White House reporter Lou Cannon reported the fallout from the Buchanan editorial: "One key White House strategist said that this part of the plan worked, but that Buchanan's statements and writings angered a core of Democrats who had solidly supported contra aid in the past and resented the implied questioning of their patriotism."[52]

Along with key senior staff, the job of the communications adviser is to identify and to prioritize a presidency's defining issues and then to orchestrate their progress through the public domain. Good presidential interpreters act as explainers of the president's thinking, not of their own. These two ways of promoting messages produce different responses. While Gergen's consensus-driven policy explanations both drew on and reinforced agreement throughout the Reagan administration, Buchanan's lone-wolf advocacy sowed division in the White House. His sharp op-ed pieces made life more difficult for White House staffers whose jobs involved piecing together coalitions made up of disparate groups, including Democrats. Gergen's approach resulted in stories that were generally favorable to the president as well as to David Gergen himself, while Buchanan served his own brand of conservatism.

Success at message management is ultimately judged by what communications efforts have done to further the public's understanding of a president and his policies. In most administrations, evaluation is an ongoing ad hoc process that relies on qualitative rather than quantitative measurements. "You can come in with the knowledge base, we got good coverage in the *Washington Post* today," noted Karl Rove. "So you can, on some basis, say 'That's good coverage or bad coverage,' based on what we expect of it. That article was good in the *Dallas Morning News*, but we could have done better." Rove observed that it was more difficult to gauge success by looking at international coverage, where the press is more opinionated. "How many minutes of our response to their propaganda do we get on there? I think it may be like fine art: you know whether you're getting it, or you're not. Are you getting about as much as you can? Can you do better?"

During the 2000 campaign, Rove had an assessment operation run out of the University of Texas under the direction of political science professor Daron Shaw: "It was a very useful measure. You could at least tell early September, mid-September, things were bad. All the coverage began to turn in October. You could see it, hear it in the content analysis reports on we're 'winning the week,' or not 'winning the week.'"[53] In the White House, however, the Bush team lacked a comparable quantitative apparatus for evaluating their communications efforts.

When President Bush travels, the White House gets a report from the Office of Media Affairs on the local response to his visit. "Media Affairs will look at how much media did the president get on a trip to this state, and what kind of effect did it have, how many hours was it in local television," said Karen Hughes. "We'll get reports like that."[54]

Implementers of Strategy

The communications director who is an implementer of strategies is someone chosen to carry into effect the strategies he or she may have participated in developing but did not design. Several communications directors, including Frank Ursomarso and Michael McManus in the Reagan years, emphasized implementing communications strategies designed by others, especially those developed by Michael Deaver.

Until the end of the Ford years, when David Gergen revived the office, the people who exercised functions that were associated with the Office of Communications in the Nixon years operated out of the Press Office. In the wake of Watergate, the profile of the office was lowered by having its functions and personnel subsumed under the Press Office. The excesses of the Nixon White House, which extended to illegal activities undertaken by some who had worked in the Office of Communications, were still raw. No one in the Ford White House wanted to antagonize the public further by elevating an outfit charged with creating and selling presidential messages. Not until the end of that administration, when David Gergen came in, did this effort begin anew.

After Ronald Reagan defeated Jimmy Carter, who had been faulted for being a weak leader because he had communicated so poorly, the stage was set for the position of communications director to be strengthened. As both a senior adviser and a member of the troika running the White House, Deputy Chief of Staff Michael Deaver was keeper of the presidential image. He knew in what forums Ronald Reagan excelled and under what circumstances he performed poorly. He showcased the president with events that emphasized his strong qualities and stayed away from ones that highlighted his weak points.

As the senior staff member focused on communications (in spite of his title of deputy chief of staff), Deaver had the authority to implement communications strategies, but he preferred to do so through his deputy Michael McManus, who was acting director of communications during the closing months of the 1984 campaign. Deaver was the manager and McManus the implementer. "If you look at the early Reagan period, I would still call Mike Deaver the communications director," said Tom Griscom, who later served in the post when Howard Baker was chief of staff.[55]

In the Clinton White House, Don Baer was an implementer. "You can argue, now, that, really, Dick Morris is the communications director, but he's not," said George Stephanopoulos. Stephanopoulos went on to explain that Baer was less influential than some of his predecessors because "we've had a somewhat different situation in that we've always relied so heavily on outside political consultants." The same was true when David Gergen was in the White House. "When Gergen came in, he was communications director, but he didn't want the title," Stephanopoulos recalled. "So Mark [Gearan] had the title, he implemented things, but Dave was the strategist."[56]

Any communications director who is primarily an implementer is not someone who ends up with a high profile. Yet he or she must do the same basic event planning that a communications director who is primarily a strategist must oversee. For Loretta Ucelli, who served as an implementation-focused communications director during the final two years of the Clinton administration, her role was not to develop policy priorities or the timing but to coordinate the resources necessary for moving forward: "About a week to ten days, sometimes if we're really on top of our game

two weeks out, my office pulls together a meeting with a representative
from almost every office in the White House, from the policy people to
OMB to public liaison, the DPC [Domestic Policy Council]." If the president is going to announce his prescription drug plan, for example, there
is a variety of questions to answer and then staging to be done. The questions include, "What are the elements that have to be part of that? Who's
with him? At that point the substance is pretty much down, but what are
the most important pieces of that substance? Who was with the president? What is the president's message? What's our strategy for getting it
up to the Hill? What's our strategy for getting it to constituency organizations? Who are our best 'validators' on it? How do we get those 'validators' out there? Press-wise, do we want to do op-eds? Do we want to do
interviews two days out? Do we want people to go around briefing specific
constituencies about it? All of that will come out, and a plan is developed
for each event or announcement along those lines. Who is the greatest
opposition? How do we deal with that opposition? What paper do we put
out that day? What does that paper say? Who is going to brief on it? All
these elements are figured out in one of these meetings and then from
that point each office kind of goes off and does its thing."[57] Answering
these questions in order to assemble the necessary resources is the heart
of what a communications director does to implement policies developed
elsewhere in the White House.

When a president chooses not to develop a central message, the communications director spends time responding to the needs of others, including shaping the staff operation. David Demarest, who worked in both
the Reagan and Bush administrations, served as communications director for most of President George H. W. Bush's term. While the Reagan
team was concerned with shaping the future message, the Bush White
House approached it very differently. "The election of 1988 was not about
change. It was about continuity plus certain tempering goals, where Bush
was talking about trying to smooth out the rough edges of conservatism,"
said Demarest. "Our communications apparatus here reflected that, and
the way that it was manifested was not to do the line of the day. Not to
devote a lot of time and energy to try to dictate to the media what they
were going to cover that day," he said. Members of the media, he said, did
not like the constraints of the Reagan a-line-a-day approach, nor did they
respond well to the approach of the Bush White House. "Contrarily, with
us, they complained that you are not telling us what the key issue is today.
We would say, 'It's not for us to choose between which is more important,

a decision that we made regarding a trade issue or an education event,'"
Demarest said. Instead, the Bush White House staff told reporters: "You
have to decide what you think is the lead and if you can't decide what is
the lead, maybe it is because both are important and one should not be
suborned to the other." The result was that "we would do multiple events
in a day, public events, with the president that were on different subjects.
Our view was that that would create, in a sense, a mosaic that, over time,
would accrue to the president's advantage as a strong leader, a compas-
sionate leader, a leader who has a grasp of a lot of different issues that
were of concern to the public."

The result of this "communications salad" approach was that the public failed to associate President Bush with any particular policies. "If you
look at polling data of the summer [of 1992], there were plenty of people
who didn't know what President Bush stood for," Demarest said.[58] They
didn't have any better idea when the fall election arrived. The Bush lais-
sez-faire approach toward communications will stand as a striking example to future administrations of an approach to avoid.

Managing Electoral and Legacy Campaigns

The communications director plays a key role at the end of a presidential
term by explaining who the president has been and what he has done
for the country. End-game communications directors are essentially
"closers," who come in for one big inning. These final innings play a big
role in defining a presidency for posterity. The stakes are enormous—
whether a presidency is rewarded with a second term or not, there is still
the president's image in history to consider. At the end of the first term,
communications directors set the stage for the reelection campaign. At
the end of the second term, they begin the legacy campaign to define their
administration for posterity.

David Gergen, appointed in the Ford administration, was the first
communications director to assume a formal campaign role. Specifically,
his job was to integrate the official duties of the president into the election
campaign. He worked on strategy development with James Baker, the
director of the President Ford Committee, and with White House Chief
of Staff Richard Cheney. Gergen was the one who put in play the White
House communications component of their election strategy. Their basic
idea was to show the president doing his job. In campaign mode, President Ford often met with groups in the Rose Garden, where he would
demonstrate his command of facts and use the backdrop of the White

House and the West Wing to show how well he was handling his responsibilities. His poll numbers rose dramatically in the course of this campaign—a fact often obscured by his electoral loss to Jimmy Carter—which shows how successful their communications strategy was.

Since communicating that the candidate can handle the office is a key to success in any presidential election campaign, it is logical that the responsibility for integrating the campaign with the execution of his duties should fall to the communications director. This responsibility can be handled in a variety of ways, however.

Gerald Rafshoon, who arrived in the Carter White House during the summer of 1978 and left a year later, set up a communications operation for Carter's reelection campaign while he was in the White House. When he was ready to integrate Carter's images as working president with his performance as a candidate for reelection, he moved his base of operations to the campaign headquarters and tapped his White House resources from there. He then worked out of campaign headquarters as he integrated the presidential and campaign images. The same was true of Karen Hughes, who left the White House in 2002 but worked with the 2004 campaign staff first from her home base and then on the road with the reelection team. With Gergen for Ford and Margaret Tutwiler for George H. W. Bush, the opposite was true. They ran their presidential campaign from the White House.

In three of these cases—Ford, Carter, and George H. W. Bush—the president lost his bid for reelection. Consequently, the tenure of their campaign-managing communications directors ended abruptly. But they were not held personally responsible for the election outcomes in the way that communications directors are often blamed for publicity failures in legislative or policy matters.

At the end of a first term, the communications director gets immersed in an electoral campaign. At the end of the second term, the campaign is for historical status. Since Ronald Reagan and Bill Clinton are the only full two-term presidents to rely on the Office of Communications, they are the only ones who can shed light on a legacy campaign.

President Clinton remained involved in policymaking until he walked out of the residence door of the White House on the morning of Bush's inauguration. Much to the dismay of his supporters, including some on the White House staff, he took no time at the end of his administration to look back on what they had done, nor did he have others shape and preserve their legacy. At the end of his administration, his communications team was trying to keep up with the flood of rumors related to his executive orders on environment and his pardons. Their operation was set in response mode.

For a full-fledged legacy campaign, which requires the certain termination of a second term, the only examples are Ronald Reagan and Dwight Eisenhower. Though Eisenhower precedes the creation of the Office of Communications, Press Secretary James Hagerty developed the kind of end-game communications plan similar to the one played out at the end of Reagan's second term. He worked on it as President Eisenhower rounded out his seventh year in office. Hagerty suggested to the president that he spend his last year heralding peace on the road. The world trip was billed under the heading "A Man of Peace." Eisenhower toured eleven countries and covered 22,000 miles during his final year, punctuating the impression of his presidency he wanted to leave with the world.[59]

During the final year of Ronald Reagan's administration, Tom Griscom and then Mari Maseng devoted their communications operations to establishing their president's place in history. In a sense, the legacy campaign began too early. It had already become the driving force of Reagan's second term. In Griscom's view, this is why the administration ran into unexpected policy problems. Iran-Contra happened because there was not the same drive in the second term as his first. "Everybody would say the second term was to create his legacy, and legacy includes foreign policy," he noted. But "I don't think that the president of the United States runs on foreign policy. That's not the connection you are going to hand out to the voters." Without "core conditions that were driving him," the administration lost its way. If there is no focus, "then you get into all kinds of mischief."[60] By the end of the term with the 1986 tax reform bill and the beginning of the collapse of the Soviet Union, they had a legacy with some successes to discuss from the second term as well as the first.

Griscom and then Maseng worked off a plan to focus on the achievements of the administration. They listed and explained its accomplishments. They created a context for the inevitable summings-up. "For the last year of the Reagan presidency, we had a long-range plan that was a year long, and it had about six issue areas, many of which overlapped," recalled Maseng. They used overarching issues such as family values and education to organize details and target audiences. They defined "five key constituencies that we were going to speak to, and it was plotted out, who we were going to speak to, when, and about which subject, and how each of those things was going to be reinforced, and how there was only going to be one message for the day, and what that was going to be. We would not trample on that, and not allow the media to choose what was going to be the public's view of the president that day. We would choose, we would decide."[61] Their strategy generated much approval and little ill will, for few opponents care to criticize when a beloved president is playing out his final string.

Defending the President

Having a strong communications organization allows the team to defend the president when bad news is on the horizon. "You have to be strongly proactive and not let it wash over you in a big wave," said a Reagan staffer, explaining how carefully they had worked to minimize bad publicity. The Press Office dealt with breaking news stories. The long-range planning operations tackled developments that had the potential to generate criticism of the president. A member of the second group recalled the care with which the possible veto of an ethics-in-government bill was handled: "We met with [the White House Office of] Legislative Affairs on the question of legislation coming in, and a veto was a dynamic issue while the presidential campaign was on," the aide said about possible actions in 1984.[62] Another tricky issue was Reagan's veto of legislation that would have required plants to give a three-month advance notice to its employees before closing down its operations.[63] "That was a case of minimizing press coverage," the aide said. "A straight case."

A White House staff member involved in developing and executing communications plans in the Reagan administration described three basic damage control strategies: timing, argumentation, and spokespeople. In the plant closing case, the staffer said timing meant "release it after everyone's deadline so you force it to a second-day story." You make sure it is a day "when the readership is not strong," such as a Saturday. Put together bad news with good news. You consider "what else you are offering at the same time. If you know, you can pair it with something to offset it." Then you work on putting forward spokespeople to argue the issue. "Develop your strongest argument with your strongest people," the aide recommended. But sometimes it is best to say little. "Some part of it is not to say anything," said this person. "It is harder to keep it going if no one speaks, if no one is available for talk shows."[64]

Not surprisingly, a communications operation with an effective damage control operation anticipates problems and protects a president from negative fallout far better than one with no such operation. The Reagan administration was particularly adept at damage control. The Carter administration was maladroit because for so much of the president's time in office there was no communications office.

Often President Carter personally put forward (and then was directly criticized for) initiatives while in similar circumstances in the Reagan administration lesser officials took the heat for the president. A Carter official discussed that administration's failure to have others take criticism as Reagan administration officials had for their president. "It occurred to me when I watched Mr. Watt [James Watt, Reagan's first secretary of the interior] beaten around the head by [House Interior Committee Chairman] Morris Udall that Carter stood there and took the blow by blow by blow to the body and head for every one of those water projects that he announced—and that he could have let somebody else do that," observed Carter White House aide Robert Beckel. "We could have let [Secretary of the Interior] Cecil Andrus do that or somebody else."[65] But they did not. So President Carter took the heat for the cut water projects, the dropped tax rebates, and every other unpopular action his administration took.

Administration

With approximately fifty people serving in the communications operation, there has to be someone to give it direction and to coordinate the units. No matter how broad a range of responsibilities the communications director has, administration is a core aspect of the job. In recent years, direction and coordination involve either a large hierarchical structure, as is true in the George W. Bush administration, or a top-heavy one, with several senior staff doing communications, as was the case in the Clinton administration. The Bush model is a classic Republican operation, with fairly clean lines of responsibility and one person clearly in charge and all others given designated responsibilities.

The responsibility for administration grew as the staff operation developed to match the increased workload of presidential public appearances. The dramatic difference described earlier in the book in the public availability of Presidents Eisenhower and Clinton was reflected in equally dramatic differences in staffing and workload in their administrations. During Eisenhower's two terms, Press Secretary James Hagerty was a one-shop communications operation. Advocating for the president, coordinating his public relations efforts with those of other governmental units, and establishing his administration's official record were all within his ken. When others in the White House worked on publicity-related matters, as the speechwriters did, they were always expected to have Hagerty approve what they did.

With one deputy press secretary, two secretaries, an official stenographer, and two career employees responsible for printing work, Hagerty was able to handle all of President Eisenhower's public relations. His extra help consisted of two speechwriters housed in a separate unit and television consultant Robert Montgomery. Chart 1 shows the White House communications operation during Hagerty's tenure.

Forty years later, presidential publicity required a large, centrally controlled communications apparatus. President George W. Bush made it the responsibility of one of his most influential campaign advisers, Karen Hughes, giving her the prestigious position of counselor to the president. She oversaw a staff of fifty White House employees in addition to ten to twenty professionals responsible for outsourced products, such as the White House News Summary and transcripts of briefings and speeches. The homey speechwriting and press operation of Hagerty's day had become a multifaceted bureaucracy. Its makeup required an organization chart that defined the titles and responsibilities of all but its most senior officials in fairly specific terms.

The hierarchy was clear: Karen Hughes was in charge, and others report directly to her. In addition, she oversaw the full sweep of communications offices. The number of units reporting to her was greater than was the case with those designated as communications advisers in earlier administrations. But the units themselves were preexisting ones that appear across administrations, no matter who is president or what party he represents. The units reporting to her included speechwriting, media affairs, communications, and press. While there were others involved in communications issues, especially Karl Rove, all of the basic units devoted to publicity reported to her.

At a comparable point in the Clinton administration, the communications setup featured a different blend. There was no one communications adviser handling all communications units. Instead, there were several people within the communications area reporting to Chief of Staff Leon Panetta, who of course was responsible for many other aspects as well.

The pieces of the communications pie were divided with Mark Gearan handling strategic planning and research, Don Baer heading speechwriting, David Dreyer in charge of media affairs, and George Stephanopoulos

Chart 1. President Dwight D. Eisenhower, White House Press Office, 1958

Source: Author interview with William Ewald, deputy speechwriter, May 24, 2003; Stephen Hess, speechwriter, April 21, 2003; William Hopkins, executive clerk, April 17, 2003.

Note: A speechwriter and a television consultant both reported to Chief of Staff Sherman Adams and coordinated with Press Secretary James Hagerty.

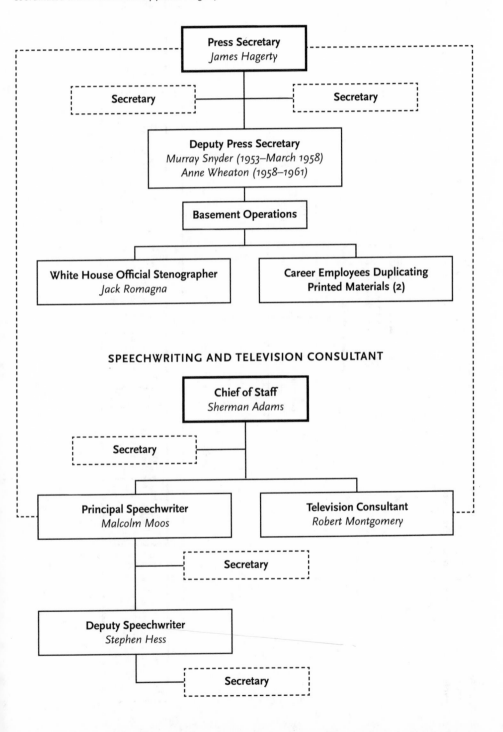

Chart 2. President George W. Bush, White House Counselor's Office, July 2002

Source: BNA, Daily Report for Executives, "White House Phone Book," number 140, July 22, 2002.

Note: The stenographic work transcribing the president's sessions with reporters and those of his press secretary is now done by a private firm, Diversified Reporting. A regular team of five stenographers do the work Jack Romagna did during his tenure.

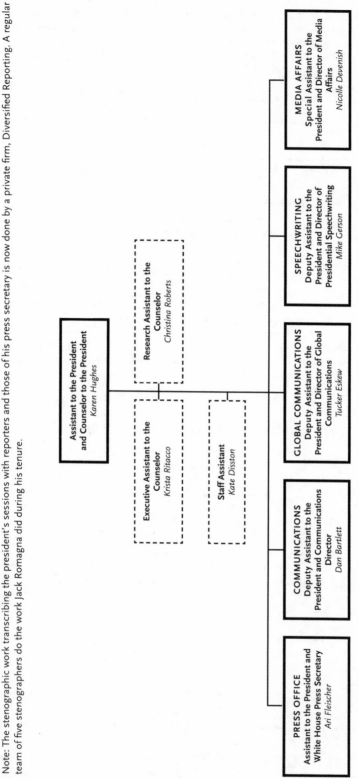

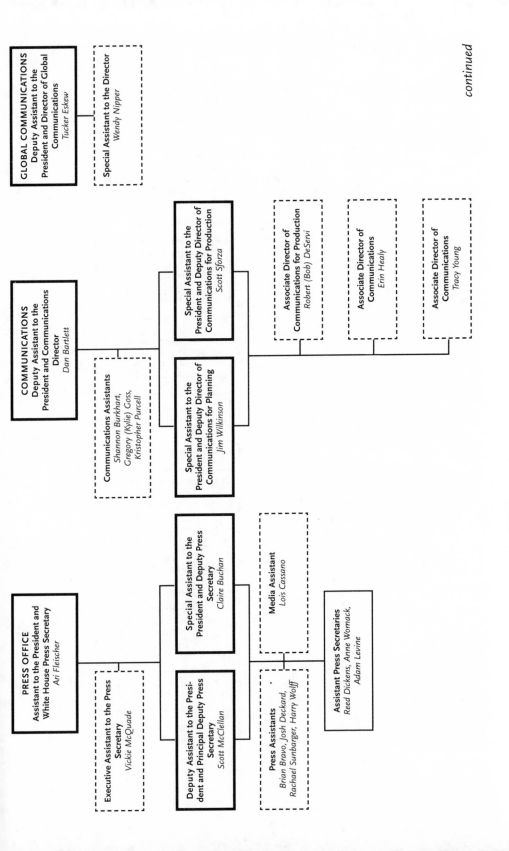

GLOBAL COMMUNICATIONS
Deputy Assistant to the
President and Director of Global
Communications
Tucker Eskew

Special Assistant to the Director
Wendy Nipper

COMMUNICATIONS
Deputy Assistant to the
President and Communications
Director
Dan Bartlett

Communications Assistants
*Shannon Burkhart,
Gregory (Kylie) Goss,
Kristopher Purcell*

Special Assistant to the
President and Deputy Director of
Communications for Production
Scott Sforza

Special Assistant to the
President and Deputy Director of
Communications for Planning
Jim Wilkinson

Associate Director of
Communications for Production
Robert (Bob) DeServi

Associate Director of
Communications
Erin Healy

Associate Director of
Communications
Tracy Young

PRESS OFFICE
Assistant to the President and
White House Press Secretary
Ari Fleischer

Executive Assistant to the Press
Secretary
Vickie McQuade

Special Assistant to the
President and Deputy Press
Secretary
Claire Buchan

Deputy Assistant to the Presi-
dent and Principal Deputy Press
Secretary
Scott McClellan

Media Assistant
Lois Cassano

Press Assistants
*Brian Bravo, Josh Deckard,
Rachael Sunbarger, Harry Wolff*

Assistant Press Secretaries
*Reed Dickens, Anne Womack,
Adam Levine*

continued

Chart 2. *continued*

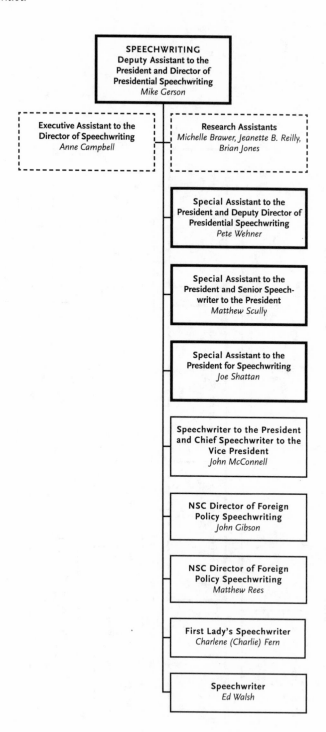

SPEECHWRITING
Deputy Assistant to the
President and Director of
Presidential Speechwriting
Mike Gerson

Executive Assistant to the
Director of Speechwriting
Anne Campbell

Research Assistants
*Michelle Brawer, Jeanette B. Reilly,
Brian Jones*

Special Assistant to the
President and Deputy Director of
Presidential Speechwriting
Pete Wehner

Special Assistant to the
President and Senior Speech-
writer to the President
Matthew Scully

Special Assistant to the
President for Speechwriting
Joe Shattan

Speechwriter to the President
and Chief Speechwriter to the
Vice President
John McConnell

NSC Director of Foreign
Policy Speechwriting
John Gibson

NSC Director of Foreign
Policy Speechwriting
Matthew Rees

First Lady's Speechwriter
Charlene (Charlie) Fern

Speechwriter
Ed Walsh

Chart 2. *continued*

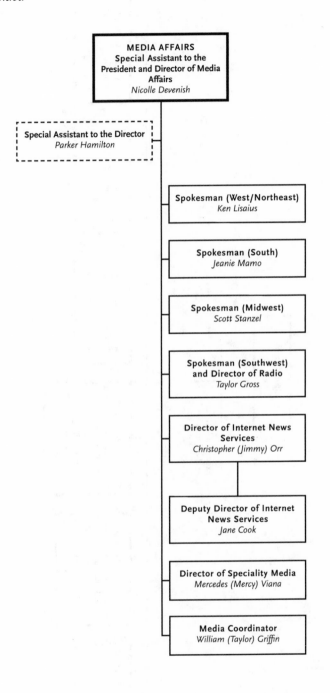

MEDIA AFFAIRS
Special Assistant to the
President and Director of Media
Affairs
Nicolle Devenish

Special Assistant to the Director
Parker Hamilton

Spokesman (West/Northeast)
Ken Lisaius

Spokesman (South)
Jeanie Mamo

Spokesman (Midwest)
Scott Stanzel

Spokesman (Southwest)
and Director of Radio
Taylor Gross

Director of Internet News
Services
Christopher (Jimmy) Orr

Deputy Director of Internet
News Services
Jane Cook

Director of Speciality Media
Mercedes (Mercy) Viana

Media Coordinator
William (Taylor) Griffin

Chart 3. President William Clinton, White House Office of Communications in the Office of the Chief of Staff, Fall 1994

Source: White House Interview Program (whitehousetransitionproject.org). Based on data in *The Capital Source*, Fall 1994, National Journal Group Inc., Washington, D.C.

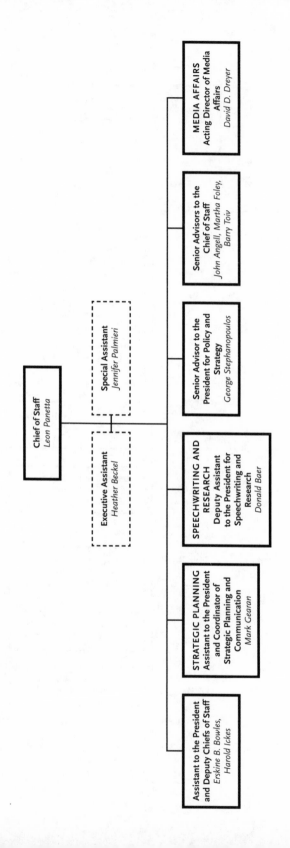

Chief of Staff
Leon Panetta

Executive Assistant
Heather Beckel

Special Assistant
Jennifer Palmieri

Assistant to the President and Deputy Chiefs of Staff
Erskine B. Bowles, Harold Ickes

STRATEGIC PLANNING
Assistant to the President and Coordinator of Strategic Planning and Communication
Mark Gearan

SPEECHWRITING AND RESEARCH
Deputy Assistant to the President for Speechwriting and Research
Donald Baer

Senior Advisor to the President for Policy and Strategy
George Stephanopoulos

Senior Advisors to the Chief of Staff
John Angell, Martha Foley, Barry Toiv

MEDIA AFFAIRS
Acting Director of Media Affairs
David D. Dreyer

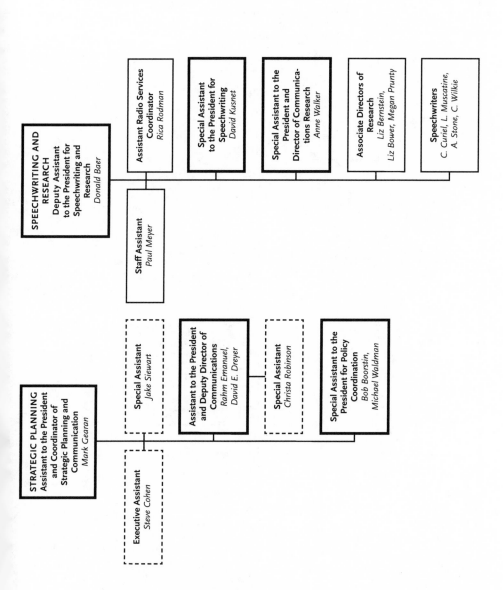

continued

SPEECHWRITING AND RESEARCH
Deputy Assistant to the President for Speechwriting and Research
Donald Baer

Assistant Radio Services Coordinator
Rica Rodman

Staff Assistant
Paul Meyer

Special Assistant to the President for Speechwriting
David Kusnet

Special Assistant to the President and Director of Communications Research
Anne Walker

Associate Directors of Research
Liz Bernstein, Liz Bower, Megan Prunty

Speechwriters
C. Curiel, L. Muscatine, A. Stone, C. Wilkie

STRATEGIC PLANNING
Assistant to the President and Coordinator of Strategic Planning and Communication
Mark Gearan

Special Assistant
Jake Siewart

Executive Assistant
Steve Cohen

Assistant to the President and Deputy Director of Communications
Rahm Emanuel, David E. Dreyer

Special Assistant
Christa Robinson

Special Assistant to the President for Policy Coordination
Bob Boorstin, Michael Waldman

Chart 3. *continued*

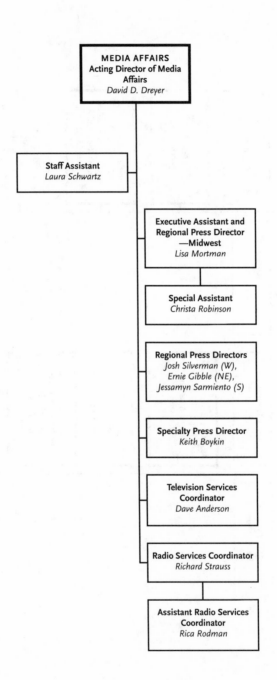

in his position of policy and strategy. The press secretary reported directly to the chief of staff as well. Administrative tasks were divided according to their individual bailiwicks. In short, Clinton had a far different model than the one used by the current Bush administration.

Late in the Clinton administration, a different model came into play. Loretta Ucelli had the title director of communications, but, muddying the waters, Sidney Blumenthal worked on communications issues as well. Both Ucelli and Blumenthal held the rank of assistant to the president.

In Blumenthal's case, he worked alone, with no staff reporting to him. Ucelli headed the basic communications office, with speechwriting under its purview. But she did not have either media affairs or the Press Office within her orbit.

Coordination

The better the communications operation is able to coordinate resources inside and outside of government, the more likely it will achieve the stated goals. A good manager can plan ahead and stage better events in a more efficient manner than would otherwise be possible if planning is left to the last minute. Staging events is expensive. "The further out you can predict what you're going to be doing, the more you can drive down costs, the more you can predict schedules, personnel, whatever it may be," said Dan Bartlett, who at the time was serving as director of the Office of Communications. "Particularly for the folks on my side of the job. We're in charge of the picture of events and things like that. If we have a good idea further out, we don't have to rush projects to get banners or get backdrops." In the end, effective planning "makes it more economical from a budget standpoint."

Particularly in the days and months following the September 11 attacks, the staff members were concerned with their presidential presentations because the stakes were very high, with so many people following Bush on television. Bartlett explained that "we spent a lot more time making sure that that environment we put him in looked well, and that's very expensive." He explained how the money can add up: "We spoke in an international televised event from Atlanta to talk about homeland security. There were ten thousand people in that hall, and we lit the entire arena. Lighting for that alone is $75,000."

It takes good management and time for staff to appreciate and to learn how to leverage the resources of others: "You don't think about those things during the course of a campaign, but you do in the sense of when

Chart 4. President William Clinton, White House Office of Communications, Fall 1999

Source: White House Interview Program (whitehousetransitionproject.org). Based on data in *The Capital Source*, Fall 1994. National Journal Group Inc., Washington, D.C.

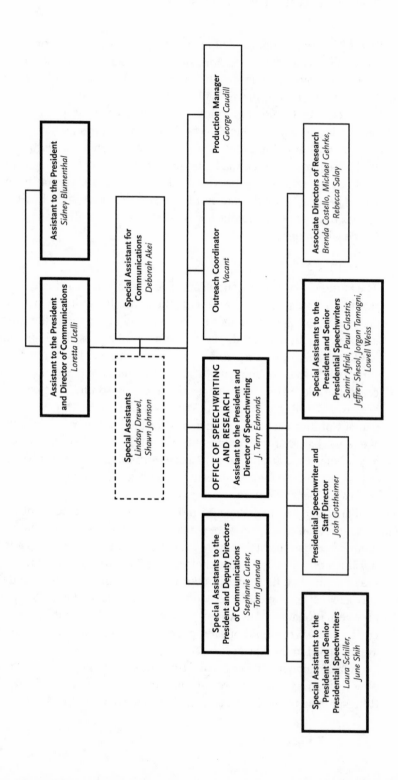

you're on a budget that the Congress controls." In 2002, Bartlett spoke about what they needed to do in order to increase their efficiency in presenting the president: "From a standpoint of what we have continued to do and what we need, frankly what we need to do a better job of is finding existing events that we can go and speak to—the national XYZ association on this or that, the American Medical Association—go to an event, fly to an event, do that, as opposed to trying to create your own event, which requires more resources."[66]

A White House communication operation that coordinates all of the affected offices and devotes considerable resources to planning presidential publicity has a leg up on staying on top of events and shaping how reporters portray them. Marion Blakey, who headed the Office of Public Affairs in the Reagan White House, explained the success of that administration: "This office's most basic role is to coordinate our spokesmen all over the government and to provide them with information on our policies and achievements. From the ambassador in Mozambique to the undersecretary of commerce, we make sure they have the same information and are all singing from the same choir book."[67]

In a hierarchically organized and well-managed administration, it is clear that the programs the president wants and the timing of his agenda are more important than the wishes or interests of any one of his department secretaries. This principle governs publicity initiatives at every level. "One of the things you learn in an agency is you avoid running into White House stories. White House stories are on page one," said a Reagan White House staff member with departmental experience. "You only want the A section."[68]

Being less hierarchical and more participatory, Democratic administrations are less likely to control or coordinate with cabinet secretaries. Secretary of Health, Education, and Welfare Joseph Califano was the rogue elephant of the Carter administration, seeking media attention any day of the week rather than on one designated day, rarely consulting with his superiors in the White House. In the Kennedy and Johnson eras, cabinet secretaries had been more constrained. But even then they rarely coordinated with the White House like they did during the Reagan years. The Califano figure in the Clinton administration was Secretary of Labor Robert Reich, who thought nothing of giving speeches conflicting with the president's themes—even when President Clinton was making news himself. In August 1995, for example, as the president was in Hawaii to mark the fiftieth anniversary of the dropping of the atomic bomb, Secretary of Labor Reich gave a pessimistic speech questioning the health of the economy.[69]

Placing value on planning mechanisms gives a president and his staff a leg up on keeping ahead of events. Richard Moe, chief of staff to Vice President Walter Mondale in the Carter administration, described the problem this way: "There is such a tendency to become a reactive force in the White House. There are so many issues bubbling up and coming in through the windows from all directions that need to be dealt with urgently that there is little time and no resources to look ahead and try to anticipate and do the necessary planning. . . . I guess you'd have to be in the White House to feel the dynamic of it. You just feel the walls and ceilings caving in on you daily. It's something that's always got to be done today or tomorrow or next week. I mean next week is long-range planning in the White House."[70] At least it was in the Carter White House.

Coordination: Selling the Nomination of Robert Bork to the Supreme Court

One of the most difficult tasks of the communications operation is to coordinate publicity among units of the national government and with outside supporters as well. All of this is done in a context of opposition criticism of the president's plans. The Reagan administration provides a good illustration of how difficult it is to sell a program. In the case of the nomination of Robert Bork to the Supreme Court, the Reagan communications operation went all-out in support of the nominee in meetings with news organizations, publicity plans for the president and others in the administration, and supporting material in favor of the nominee's appointment. Yet a combination of factors was important. For example, Bork's critics operated as a coalition combining their communications efforts to outflank the administration. They proved nimble in responding to administration efforts on Bork's behalf while the White House operation adopted a plan and stuck with it. Even when opponents came out earlier than the Reagan communications team had anticipated, the White House stuck with its original plan. The case also demonstrates what can happen when political events weaken the president and a high-profile nominee proves difficult to manage.

This case is significant because many in Washington still remember the communications campaign to this day—it still comes up frequently when the White House makes controversial nominations. The Bork case took place in 1987, but in many ways it is timeless. It demonstrates the limitations of a White House when a president is politically wounded and when its staff operations are slow to respond to changing circumstances. Both of these situations repeat themselves in most administrations. With all of the resources the White House has at its disposal, one would assume that the president and his staff would be able to use them in a successful publicity campaign to achieve their policy goals. Even a major publicity effort can go awry if the goal of the campaign is not shared by others whose support the president needs.

Major White House publicity campaigns require the energies of the president, his senior staff, and top officers of the administration. Such efforts usually concern issues or events at the heart of the president's agenda. But President Reagan's nomination of Judge Robert Bork to the United States Supreme Court also required a full-fledged White House effort in which senior staff, administration officials, and outside allies worked together. Despite the sizeable resources available to them to sell the nomination, they were not able to prevail. The Bork battle demonstrates the difficulties a president and his staff can have in identifying, coordinating, and using their vast resources. It also demonstrates the potential sophistication of opponents to presidential initiatives.

Reagan's senior staff knew that the Bork nomination would be a hard sell, requiring the coordination of resources from both inside and outside the administration. What they failed to anticipate was that its message-driven communications operation would have a difficult time responding to the tactics of its critics. The White House staff failed to assess the importance of the growing opposition to the Bork nomination and to rework its communications plan.

The nomination process began with a public announcement by President Reagan. On July 1, 1987, he came to the White House Briefing Room to announce the nomination of Judge Robert J. Bork to fill the vacancy left by the resignation of Justice Lewis Powell. To pave the way for Bork's Senate confirmation, the president's staff moved forward with a plan based on their prior experience. In the cases of Reagan's Supreme Court appointments of Sandra Day O'Connor and Antonin Scalia and of Reagan's elevation of Justice William Rehnquist to Chief Justice, questions were raised at the committee level, but all easily won Senate confirmation. On the Senate floor, O'Connor was confirmed by a unanimous vote of all senators, Scalia by a vote of 98-0. The vote on Rehnquist's promotion was 65-33 in a Republican-controlled Senate.

From statements by his critics even prior to Reagan's announcement,

White House staff members were aware that Bork, who had a very conservative record at the federal district and circuit court of appeals, had a wider and stronger array of opponents than any of the earlier nominees. The timetable they scheduled for Robert Bork was similar to the one they had used in 1986 for William Rehnquist: nomination in early July, with hearings and a vote in late September.

Working with that timetable, the confirmation plan had three basic components. First, it called for using surrogates rather than President Reagan himself to sell the nomination in the pre-hearing period, when they were developing and presenting their case for the nominee. From the start of the Senate Judiciary Committee hearings until the vote on the Senate floor a little over a month later, the president would be more engaged in the issue, but only close to the committee and floor votes. Second, the plan anticipated presenting the nominee in terms they defined—as a mainstream jurist—and overshadowing the criticisms leveled by opponents. Third, it involved selling the nomination outside Washington during the summer, as the Washington press would not be interested in the nomination until September.

A Limited Role for the President

After November 1986, when the Iran-Contra scandal broke, President Reagan had all but dropped from sight. In July 1987, the House of Representatives and the Senate were conducting joint hearings into the Iran-Contra case, and the president was reluctant to appear in any setting that might force him to face questions from reporters. Oliver North and John Poindexter gave widely watched and discussed testimony on television through much of July. In mid-August the president addressed the American people with an apology for the breaches of law associated with Iran-Contra. His public opinion ratings had already dropped to an uncharacteristically low level, with just over 50 percent of the American public approving of his performance. Reagan was not in a good position to lend support to his embattled Supreme Court nominee.

President Reagan only intermittently discussed the nomination in public during the period between July 1, when he made the announcement, and September 15, when Bork's nomination hearings began. He used his July 4 radio address to make some remarks about the Bork nomination.[71] He mentioned the Bork nomination as part of his remaining agenda in his August 15 address to the nation on the Iran-Contra issue, and on August 28 he spoke about the nomination to law enforcement officers in Los Angeles. He also answered a couple of reporters' questions on the Bork nomination at that law enforcement session.

President Reagan increased his public presence once September arrived, but he did not consistently press for Bork during the three weeks between the start of the hearings and the Senate Judiciary Committee vote on October 6. He spoke of the nomination in a September 19 radio address and then reserved all of his effort for the final week before the committee vote. He made remarks at a White House briefing on September 30 and then answered reporters' questions on October 2 and 6 as well as devoting his October 3 radio address to the nomination.

After the Judiciary Committee members voted against the Bork nomination, events overtook the president and reduced his presence as Bork's advocate. Two days after the Senate Judiciary Committee vote, fifty-one senators announced their opposition to Bork. His nomination was viewed as all but dead. But the president devoted his October 10 radio address to the nomination and addressed the nation on the subject of Bork on October 14. Then on October 17, Nancy Reagan had breast cancer surgery, and coincidentally the stock market declined sharply.

In Reagan's place, White House officials took the lead in selling the nomination to the public with help from allies in the private sector. Those who presented the case for the nominee included members of the White House staff, especially Chief of Staff Howard Baker, members of the administration, and well-known political and community leaders. They communicated via television and radio appearances, opinion articles in newspapers, and private meetings with influential people in news organizations. They met with senators and with allies in interest groups.

Chief of Staff Howard Baker, who had once been Senate majority leader, was the principal White House advocate, arguing the case on television, on the radio, in interviews with print reporters and organizations, in private meetings with representatives of selected communities, and in phone calls with Republican and Democratic members of the Judiciary Committee.[72] The work Baker did for Bork from early July to mid-September included nine speeches to groups ranging from the NAACP to the American Farm Bureau, and twenty-two television presentations, including appearances on *Meet the Press, Face the Nation,* and *The Today Show.* In addition, Baker made himself available for interviews with *Time, Newsweek, US News and World Report,* the *Wall Street Journal,* and the *Washington Times.* Baker also met with the editorial boards of the *Washington Times,* the *New York Times,* the *Los Angeles Times,* and *USA Today.*

Throughout this publicity blitz, Baker worked with his long-time Senate aide, Tom Griscom, who headed the Office of Communications. With the help of the Office of Media Liaison and Broadcast Relations and the Office of Public Affairs, the Office of Communications developed the communications plan and oversaw its implementation. Griscom's operation also cooperated with the Press Office, the White House Counsel's Office, the Office of Political Affairs, the Office of Public Liaison, the Office of Cabinet Affairs, and the Office of Legislative Affairs. In the end, the whole top layer of the White House senior staff devoted time to the Bork nomination.

The Communications Plan: Focus, Timing, and the Chief of Staff

The second component of the confirmation plan was presenting the nominee from the White House perspective rather than letting him be defined by his critics. The materials the White House sent out were short pieces describing Judge Bork's views on a variety of subjects. These "advocacy materials" included "talking points" and "issue briefs"; Tom Gibson, director of the Office of Public Liaison, called them "one-pagers" on specific issues, such as Bork's views on the First Amendment, civil rights, and abortion. They also had one-pagers devoted to Bork's qualifications and his judicial philosophy.[73] The initial installment, which consisted of fifteen pages of briefing materials, was sent out at the end of July. Updates on Bork on crime and civil rights appeared in early and late September.[74] The distribution list was broad. The information was sent to "800 Administration spokesmen (including ambassadors and members of boards and commissions) and approximately 2,500 editorial writers and columnists."[75] The Office of Media Liaison sent materials to the people on its list, and other White House outreach offices—political affairs, public liaison, intergovernmental affairs—did likewise.

The third component of the confirmation plan was timeline and focus. When President Reagan announced the nomination, there was no plan in place. In plotting their strategy for getting Bork approved, the office had a timeline and a focus. It used the period from mid-July to early September to lay the groundwork for the confirmation hearings. When that period was over, the White House staff regrouped to develop strategies for the confirmation hearings themselves.

Describing the initial media strategy, Elizabeth Board, head of the Office of Media Liaison and Broadcast Relations, noted, "As the national media will show little interest in the Bork nomination before September, August will be the ideal time to make our case in the local media. Through interviews, editorials, and dissemination of facts, perhaps we can set a few minds before the national media has a chance to make their pitch."[76] As it was, the five-week rollout featured a variety of media, including weekly television, radio, and opinion pieces in newspapers. The staff members held to their plan even though their initial assessment that the Washington media would not pay attention to the nomination was incorrect.

The Office of Media Relations sent out opinion pieces, which were generally published as opinion articles in newspapers around the country. The common theme was that Judge Bork was a mainstream jurist.[77] Reflecting on their work, Board said that they "placed" twenty articles under the signature of administration officials during the five weeks they pushed for his nomination.[78] For example, they placed editorials under the signatures of such administration officials as Clarence Thomas, at the time the head of the Equal Employment Opportunity Commission.[79] Second were the radio interviews, which averaged fifteen a week for five weeks, according to Board. Together with Communications Director Tom Griscom, Board worked on selecting media markets to target. "We chose the major markets and the areas where we thought we would have a chance," she said. The South was one of the areas they chose for their television interviews, their third strategy. The operation focused on five states: Alabama, Louisiana, North Carolina, Illinois, and Arizona. During the month of August, they did TV interviews in the major cities and media markets each week and also placed opinion articles in the newspapers covering those cities. They contacted local bureaus and arranged for them to do live satellite interviews with White House staff members.

Print media were also not forgotten in the Bork campaign. "We have 200 different lists," Board said. "Ethnic lists, editorial writers, labor issues, business writers, blacks, women; many special interests." She continued, "On Bork, we mailed to law enforcement, crime, aging, and youth."[80] Their records showed that they also used their lists of African-American radio and print news organizations, business, veterans, and women's groups to send specific "issue briefs."

In addition to mailing information to groups, they brought in groups through the Office of Public Liaison. "We did constituent groups through the Office of Public Liaison discussing the importance of the judiciary," commented Marion Blakey, who later headed the Office of Public Affairs for the administration.[81]

Critics Define the Nominee

While the three-pronged White House initiative was under way, there was a surprise. Robert Bork's critics were not holding their fire until September, as anticipated. Nor were their materials general overviews. Rather, they included in-depth discussions of his record on the bench as well as his writings.

While the White House was touting the Bork nomination outside Washington, his critics were continually releasing critiques. First came an analysis of Bork's record based on research by two Columbia law students in an article scheduled for publication in the *Columbia Law Review.* Their conclusions, released July 27, went to the heart of the White House strategy to define him as a mainstream jurist. "President Reagan's judicial appointees have not been much more conservative than those of other recent Republican Presidents, but Judge Robert H. Bork's voting patterns show him to be far more conservative than the average Reagan appointee," concluded the account of the study that appeared in the *New York Times.*[82]

Next, on August 6, Ralph Nader's Public Citizen Litigation Group released a study critical of Bork's record. The theme of the attendant criticism was that Judge Bork was the enemy of the underdog. The Nader study concluded, "Where anybody but a business interest challenged executive action, Judge Bork exercised judicial restraint either by refusing to decide the case or by deferring to the executive on the merits. However, when business interests challenged executive action on statutory or constitutional grounds, Judge Bork was a judicial activist, favoring the business interest in every split decision in which he participated."

In contrast to the White House promotional materials, which consisted of 15 pages, Public Citizen offered 149 pages analyzing more than 400 cases and 144 opinions that Bork signed after 1982, when he became a judge on the United States Court of Appeals for the District of Columbia. The *New York Times* article reporting the study included an administration response: "A Justice Department spokesman dismissed the study, conducted by the Public Citizen Litigation Group, as being full of distortions. 'Through a variety of mathematical acrobatics, they lay out a record which simply doesn't accurately represent his record,' said Patrick Korten, the spokesman."[83] But the White House and Bork himself avoided entering the fray.

The opposition continued to mount. On August 17, the AFL-CIO weighed in with a thirty-two-page memorandum. Laurence Gold, the organization's counsel and Walter A. Kamiat, a Washington lawyer, stated that Bork was not fit to sit on the Supreme Court, as he "has never shown the least concern for working people, minorities, the poor or for individuals seeking the protection of the law to vindicate their political and civil rights. The causes that have engaged him are those of businessmen, of property owners and of the executive branch of government."[84]

Now came more studies. On August 18, the National Women's Law Center released a report calling the nominee's views "a clear and present danger to the principles of equality." This study held that Bork was "a judicial activist who supports reversing many Supreme Court decisions that establish key rights of women and who seizes every opportunity to advance his positions."[85] It concluded that "Judge Bork's views reflect America of the 18th and 19th century, where under the law women stood behind men—not by their side."[86]

Not far behind, on August 31, was the American Civil Liberties Union, with its forty-seven-page report on Judge Bork's civil liberties record. This study concluded that Judge Bork's "conception of the Court's role is radically different from most, if not all, of the Justices who have sat on the Court in the past 40 years." It added, "We do not believe it is possible to locate Judge Bork within the broad range of acceptable judicial thought consistent with a commitment to liberty and democracy, and the institutions designed to protect and assure both."[87]

On September 3, the Democratic-controlled Senate Judiciary Committee issued a report written by consultants that attacked not only Bork's record but also the White House briefing materials released in July. "Among the omissions are clear examples of Judge Bork's advocacy and implementation of conservative activism, which demonstrate that he is not the apostle of judicial restraint and moderation described in the White House position paper," the consultants wrote. They said that if Bork were confirmed to the Court, he "would cement a five-vote majority for undoing much of the social progress of the last three decades."[88]

Each of the hefty and detailed reports was released in Washington and New York and then was quickly picked up by the national press. Since the White House was committed to its strategy of focusing on the local press, the studies were refuted in only the most cursory way.

The White House Seeks to Reverse the Damage

By September 8, White House Counsel A. B. Culvahouse saw that Bork had already been defined by his critics as unrepresentative of mainstream judicial thinking. Even critics on the White House staff joined in. In his early September memorandum to Chief of Staff Howard Baker, Culvahouse complained that "the brand-new Newsweek distressingly quotes a senior White House aide as saying that Bork is a 'right wing zealot,'—which statement is *very unhelpful.*" Culvahouse continued, "The White House Briefing Book has been overwhelmed by these opponents' studies. More than one reporter has advised me that the only pro-Bork piece they have is the White House Briefing Book and that their desks are literally stacked with opponents' studies." He was particularly concerned by the focus of the critical studies: "All of these studies give scant or no attention to his four-year record as Solicitor General of the United States. Rather, these studies concentrate upon the provocative statements and comments made by Judge Bork in articles, magazines, speeches and other forums outside of his record as Solicitor General and as a Judge."[89] A few days later, the Justice Department released a 213-page report that concluded that these earlier studies used "arbitrary and misleading methodology, highly selective use of evidence and a distressing tendency towards inflammatory mischaracterization." The report said the studies "should be dismissed for the propaganda that they are."[90]

Shortly before the mid-October vote, Tom Korologos, who was promoting the nomination for the White House, cited the unpopularity of Bork's civil rights record in the black community: "We played catch-up on that all month." In the end, Bork's nomination was voted down because there was no strong group of advocates for him, with the result that senators were being asked to risk their own political futures by voting to confirm him—for little gain. "A senator has far more to lose on voting for Bork than voting against him," said conservative Republican political consultant Ralph Reed. "Six months from now, he's another lawyer or judge who got turned down. He has no line of constituents behind him."[91]

While the Reagan communications team invested a great deal of effort promoting Judge Bork's nomination to the Supreme Court, that effort was doomed from the beginning. Part of the problem was the absence of a president willing and able to play a personal role in selling his nominee. But the communications plan also contained a fatal flaw. While the White

House can deal with the local press, a strategy that relies on that is no substitute for providing substantial information to the national media and especially its sophisticated bellwethers, the *Washington Post* and the *New York Times*. In the Bork case, the White House communications team did not alter its communications plan when it turned out that major news organizations were indeed covering events related to the Bork nomination. In addition, assertions by interest groups were left unattended, so their information became integrated into the Bork nomination story.

Communications were only part of the problem. The nominee had a long paper trail of incendiary statements, and the White House never gave any thought to counteracting them until it was too late. Nor did the staff show the nominee how he was coming across. In retrospect, Tom Korologos said much later, he should have said to Bork, "'OK, now shut up and listen to me. Here's how we're gonna do it. Here's how you answer this.'" Instead, he said, Bork "scared all of us into thinking that he was so good that he would be brilliant in the hearing. And that brilliance just didn't come through. And it finally did us in."

As for Bork, he faults his political handlers as much as he does the length of his record. "It's true that I was unprepared for what you call a political knife fight, but so were all my advisers," he commented. "You really can't overlook the effect of that political campaign. Full-page ads, radio and television ads with Gregory Peck. There was no answer from my side at all."[92] No matter how you look at it, communications was crucial to the outcome.

In the thirty-six years since the Office of Communications was created, the unit has become an important office in the development, implementation, and coordination of communications plans. The environment in which the White House now operates is a more sophisticated one than was the case when the office was first created. Today, campaigns for passage of legislation and for confirmation of judicial nominees routinely involve a communications component. Even with these efforts, success is often difficult to achieve. What the White House communications operations can do is provide a coordinated effort to get an issue to the public on the president's terms, explain his argument. What they can't do is assure victory.

5

The Press Secretary to the President

The press secretary is the White House staff member responsible for creating and disseminating the official record of a president's statements, announcements, reactions, and explanations.[1] Unlike the communications chief, who often speaks on an anonymous attribution basis, the press secretary speaks on the record and is the one person whose statements are regarded as representing the thoughts and words of the president.

Because he or she speaks for the president, the press secretary must be credible. What makes a press secretary a credible spokesman is hewing to a set of tacit understandings. Ron Nessen, press secretary to President Ford, discussed the basics of the job. "I think most press secretaries, no matter what their background is, come to understand that the same set of rules always apply year after year, administration after administration: Tell the truth, don't lie, don't cover up, put out the bad news yourself, put it out as soon as possible, put your own explanation on it, all those things," he said.[2] As easy at that sounds, sticking to it is another matter, Nessen pointed out: "But a lot of times other members of the staff don't want to do that; they don't understand it." What makes the job difficult is getting the staff and the president to provide accurate information and then to agree to release it.

The difficulties press secretaries have in acquiring the truth and putting it out to the press corps can be seen in an experience of Scott McClellan, George W. Bush's second press secretary. The failure of senior White House staff members to tell him the truth in response to his request for information about leaks to columnist Robert Novak ultimately led to McClellan losing his job. On July 6, 2003, an opinion piece by former ambassador Joseph C. Wilson IV appeared in the *New York Times* claiming that President Bush's assertion in his 2003 State of the Union message that Saddam Hussein had sought yellowcake uranium from Niger was based on inaccurate information.[3] He based his conclusion on a visit to Niger he made at the direction of the CIA. Shortly after the Wilson piece appeared, Robert Novak wrote in a *Washington Post* column that Wilson's trip had been at the suggestion of his wife: "Wilson never worked for the CIA, but his wife, Valerie Plame, is an Agency operative on weapons of mass destruction. Two senior administration officials told me Wilson's wife suggested sending him to Niger to investigate the Italian report." Divulging the name of an undercover operative is a crime. Thus, there was great interest in who leaked her name and status.[4]

Reporters soon asked McClellan, who had recently become press secretary, about the possibility that the leak had come from administration officials, specifically Karl Rove. McClellan said that Rove was not the source of the leak about Plame to Novak. "You said this morning, 'The President knows' that Karl Rove wasn't involved. How does he know that?" McClellan responded: "I've made it very clear that it was a ridiculous suggestion in the first place. . . . I've said that it's not true. And I have spoken with Karl Rove." A few minutes later, McClellan elaborated on the accusation that Rove was the leaker. McClellan said, "I've made it clear that it simply is not true, and I'm speaking on behalf of the White House when I say that."[5] In July 2005, it came out that Rove and Vice President Cheney's chief of staff, Lewis Libby, about whom reporters had also queried McClellan as a possible source for the leak about Plame's CIA undercover identity, had indeed been sources for Robert Novak's column about Valerie Plame, as was Deputy Secretary of State Richard Armitage. When it came out that the information McClellan had given from the podium was inaccurate, it compromised him. A press secretary must be credible. If he isn't credible, it is only a matter of time before a president must find someone else to fill the post.

"It's the toughest job in the country because the president has me to explain what he says and I don't have anyone to explain what I say," noted Reagan Press Secretary Larry Speakes, quoting an observation by veteran White House correspondent Helen Thomas about his job.[6] The press secretary is out in public on his own. As the official spokesperson for an administration, he or she is the one expected to deliver authoritative information to many audiences, including the general public, the president's special publics in Washington, and the governments of nations around the globe. When people look to the president for comment, it is the press secretary who most often presents it. While the president may be seen making formal presentations in official settings, the press secretary is responsible for speaking on his behalf to individual reporters and their news organizations. As such, he must please the White House staff and the press even as he pleases and protects his boss. In an era in which the press secretary is the public face of the White House on a daily basis through his televised briefing, he is especially vulnerable when the president is low in the polls. In the Clinton administration it was communications director George Stephanopoulos who lost his post when the president's poll numbers sank early in his term. In the Bush administration, it was press secretary Scott McClellan who was replaced when President Bush's job approval numbers fell into the 35 percent range and stayed there.

Environment in Which the Press Secretary Operates

Three givens shape the organization, routines, and responsibilities of the White House Press Office and the press secretary who heads it and his or her ability to succeed in providing authoritative information that is responsive to his constituents' needs. First, the press secretary has one boss but three major constituencies, and they often have expectations of him and his office that contradict one another. He must respond and satisfy the needs of the president, the White House staff, and reporters and their news organizations.

Second, reporters and White House officials need each other in order to do their jobs. Journalists require help from the White House in order to obtain the information they need to cover this beat. By the same token, White House officials need news organizations in order to get presidential messages conveyed to the audiences they want to reach. The resulting cooperation is built on tacit understandings. And this cooperation is enhanced by physical proximity. The Press Office lies within fifty feet of the Oval Office. Reporters and television crews are there every day from before dawn to ten o'clock at night—longer if events require it. Those living in close quarters learn to get along.

Third, the press secretary's job is shaped by expectations and traditions resulting from the long history of the position. It is the oldest continuing staff office in the White House.[7] Since 1929, when President Hoover appointed George Akerson to handle press matters, presidents have found this role essential. The tempo of the news cycle has quickened, but the need for information remains the same. Reporters want facts and opinions that are accurate, timely, and relevant to their news needs.

What has changed the most is the professional experience required of press secretaries. Early on, they tended to be former reporters selected because of their familiarity with the working press. Over time, greater value was attached to their experience in presidential campaigns and their service as public affairs specialists in government agencies.

Cooperation among Officials and Reporters

Perhaps the governing factor in the environment within which the Press Office functions is the cooperative character of the relationship between White House officials and reporters. Their public grumbling may mask it, but reporters and officials cooperate with each other far more than they fight.

The daily briefing epitomizes the symbiotic relationship between news organizations and the White House. Each side needs the other: reporters must have information for their stories, and the White House must have publicity for its programs. Reporters may publicly complain about the amount of information they are receiving at the briefings, but they ask the questions they want answered and have found ways to make sure that the White House will answer them, one way or another.

Establishing relationships of trust is the foundation for everything else. Reporters must believe what the White House is telling them before they will report it. This is how Roman Popadiuk, who served as deputy press secretary in the George W. Bush White House, described the rapport that he developed with the reporters on his watch. "I operated under the personal notion of full disclosure," Popadiuk said. His goal was "to have the reporter have, without giving away state secrets or things of that nature, as much information as possible, because I felt that made a better story for us, built a trust with the reporter and me personally . . . and as a result of that, gave me more credibility in the future with that reporter, if I needed something deleted I could argue." "So I always operated on the notion to have the parameters as wide as possible. . . . It seems logical to do business that way because, first of all, you're building your credibility, you're building trust, and you have something in the bank for the future. Many times I've had to tell a reporter, 'Don't do that,' 'Don't print that,' 'You've got to help me out on this one,' and they say, 'Okay, we'll take care of you.' "[8]

To facilitate cooperation, the press secretary must have a general understanding of how the press works. Larry Speakes recalled, "I tried to make it my business to understand how the press worked, what they needed, when they needed it, and to get our order in early if we had something to get in that first lineup of stories."[9]

For the Carter White House, as it was for the Clinton White House sixteen years later, the big determinant of cooperation was prior experience and reputation in Washington, D.C. Past relationships with members of the Washington community, including reporters, were—and remain—important for two reasons. First, it helps a president's credibility if reporters have a sense of who he is and what drives him. They will be hesitant to report a story that does not seem to fit in with a president's known persona. Second, reporters can also be helpful to those coming in who may not be familiar with White House operations.

Cooperation tends to be a two-way street. For the White House, reporters can be an important source of intelligence about undercurrents in Washington. Larry Speakes believed it necessary to "establish that two-way street, between the press [and the White House]—because you learned a lot from the press. They called you and said, 'I hear this is going on,' you were getting information that was valuable inside the White House; something is brewing out there that you needed to prepare for."[10]

The federal investigation into the leak of the name of CIA operative Valerie Plame brought to the surface some of the information-sharing practices of reporters and White House officials. Karl Rove said that he got information about Plame from two reporters, one of whom was columnist Robert Novak. He then passed that information to Matt Cooper of *Time*. Lewis Libby testified to a grand jury that he had received information about Valerie Plame from Tim Russert, NBC bureau chief and *Meet the Press* moderator. Russert denies that he provided such information, though he did indicate that he had spoken with Libby. Cooper testified that he had brought up the subject of Joseph Wilson's wife in a conversation with Libby.[11]

Along with cooperation, tension is a major part of the rhythm of the relationship between the White House and news organizations. Some of this tension results from the unwillingness of the president or the White House to respond to the queries of reporters. Press Secretary Mike McCurry believes that it cost President Clinton a lot when the White House did not respond to the questions about fundraising that reporters posed at the end of the 1996 campaign. "I think, in retrospect, people didn't realize how much damage we were doing to Clinton's prospect of having a successful second term, because they were creating such ill will with the press by basically being quite obvious about the fact we were not going to deal with the press's agenda, period; we were only going to be putting on the events that we were putting on, and trying to drive the storyline in the direction we wanted to drive it," McCurry later said. They did cover the events, but the atmosphere was contentious because reporters were interested in campaign finance and fundraising issues: "What happened was—you could probably even get some reporters to be candid about this—they decided they would get even in 1997. They basically said, 'Clinton skated through this election, dodged the issues, he essentially ran unopposed because Dole was such a weak candidate, we're going to make him address these questions he should have addressed in 1996.' I think that's what drove the storyline in the White House in 1997."[12]

A major aspect of the tension between the White House and reporters is the difference in the perspective of what constitutes news. Most White House staffers who have dealt directly with reporters do not think that they are biased in a partisan way. Rather, they blame them for being more interested in conflict and in personalities than in issues. "Ideological inclinations? I don't see the White House press as one way or the other," said Jody Powell, press secretary under Carter. "In most cases there wasn't any impression that reporters were struggling mightily to keep deeply held views from their reporting. Tension wasn't there, because the feeling wasn't there. There was an absence of feeling about issues—at what point does it indicate an absence of something else?"[13]

While Powell feared that reporters' lack of interest in issues reflected a journalistic lack of substance, President Carter likewise faulted reporters for their interest in petty politics. In the third year of his presidency, he told a group of reporters whom he met in an informal session: "I would like for you all as people who relay Washington events to the world to take a look at the substantive questions I have to face as president and quit dealing almost exclusively with personalities, and whose feelings got hurt, and whether an administration employee who is a contact of yours thinks he might lose his job because he has to have a fitness report. That really is the important thing."[14]

Ground Rules for the Release of Information

While these three constituencies often have competing interests, each has hewed faithfully to a common set of rules relating to the release of information. The overarching rule holds that there are four basic classifications of information: "on the record," "off the record," "background," and "deep background."

Officially released information, as in the case of information announced at the press secretary's afternoon briefing, is "on the record," no matter where it is released. In fact, most information coming from the Press Office is "on the record." Even then, there are sometimes restrictions accompanying the release. If, for example, a reporter has an exclusive interview with the president, the timing of the release of the interview is determined by the news organization, not the White House.

The timing of the release of information is frequently an issue. President Bush's Saturday radio address is taped on Friday and given to reporters on an "embargoed" basis, which means that reporters may not report on the information until Saturday, when the radio address goes on the air. Embargoing texts is a useful device for both reporters and officials. When the president gives a major address, such as the State of the Union, reporters will receive the text on an embargoed basis. Often they receive it several hours beforehand in order for them to digest it, which enables them to report knowledgeably on it when the president delivers it.

The next two classifications of information are "background" and "deep background." Information given "on background" allows reporters to reveal the information but not its source. If the official providing the information is the chief of staff, for example, the reporters might refer to the source in their articles as "a senior White House official." If, on the other hand, the chief of staff were to provide the same information on a "deep background" basis, the designation might have to be the less specific "according to an administration source." The more sensitive the information, the greater the distance officials are likely to seek. Sometimes White House officials do interviews on background; if reporters want a particular item on the record, the official or staff member in question will consider the request. Negotiation is a regular aspect of the interviews reporters conduct with White House officials.

"Off the record" is the opposite of "on the record." It means that the reporters present must avoid using the information in their reporting. Off-the-record disclosures are used sparingly—in this sense, the White House, regardless of party affiliation, is far more transparent than it was twenty-five years ago. Today, more information is on the record, with official transcripts provided even for brief presidential chats accompanying a photo session of the president when he meets with dignitaries in the Oval Office. Briefings that were once off the record and limited to a small number of people, such as prior to a presidential trip, are now held in the Briefing Room and are done on at least a "background" basis.

As it is, even "off the record" information rarely stays that way any more, because information usually travels well beyond the limited number of people a president or high official gives it to. Most reporters, for example, will report off-the-record information to their news bureaus, and they sometimes share it with their close colleagues. Since those not present are not covered by the "off the record" rule, it rarely takes long for such comments to surface.

In March 1999, when President Clinton held two dinner sessions with reporters during a trip to Guatemala, it took less than three days for his remarks about the first lady's earning capacity to find their way into the *New York Daily News*. "President Clinton believes the First Lady could rake in '$20 million' if she kisses off a New York Senate run, but he will back her either way," wrote White House correspondent Ken Bazinet. "During at least one gathering, the President also hinted that his wife's decision-making on a Senate bid is on a faster track than her aides have indicated."[15] Bazinet, who broke this story for the *Daily News,* was not present at the dinners, but he was told of Clinton's comments by reporters who were. As much as the White House could complain, there was no violation of the off-the-record ground rule.

In discussions with White House officials on the release of information about Joseph Wilson's wife, CIA operative Valerie Plame, the ground rules were particularly tricky. In his conversations with *Time* reporter Matt Cooper, Karl Rove sought broad cover. In notes he sent to his editor, Cooper related that the information he received from Rove was to be held on "double super secret background." In an appearance on NBC's *Meet the Press,* Cooper later said that the designation was "a play on a reference to the film 'Animal House,' in which John Belushi's wild Delta House fraternity is placed on 'double secret probation.' "[16]

In addition to wanting to distance oneself from the release of certain kinds of information, deep background and off-the-record sessions are useful in instances where the staff wants reporters to get a sense of the thinking of a staff member or the president himself without any one person being quoted on any specific item. Such sessions are useful, Dan Bartlett said, because reporters "can get a sense of [the president's] thinking, get a sense of what he thinks is important. And sometimes if you do that on camera or if you do it in an on-the-record type format, just by human nature, you're going to be more cautious, you're going . . . to think through your answers a little bit more. You have a public answer, it's going to be a little bit different than what you may do in a private conversation." In 2004 the communications staff arranged a presidential session with correspondents for the five networks. "It didn't contain a lot of things that they could rush out to the front lawn and use as a hard news event," Bartlett said. "But what it gave them is some context to a lot of different issues in case they did come up, whether it be North Korea or this or that. And they had had some background information from the president that could illuminate their thinking and help enrich their reporting."[17]

Since it was a presidential conversation restricted to television network correspondents, reporters for other organizations who later found out about the session did not feel similarly constrained about writing about what was said. Mike Allen of the *Washington Post* wrote about the session and the president's thoughts, particularly those dealing with the presidential election.[18] Knowing the article was coming the next day, Bartlett and Scott McClellan both talked to Allen and his editor to see if they could halt the piece: "Both Scott and myself complained to his editor . . . who was overseeing the story, saying that this was going to hinder our ability to do this in the future and it would actually influence our decision as to whether the *Washington Post* would be able to participate."[19] The piece ran. Such sessions are useful for both the president and for reporters but almost always become public, especially in an election year. In fact, the *Post* has participated in similar sessions since the story ran.

Who Serves as Press Secretary

In the seventy-eight years since President Hoover created the position of press secretary, all thirteen administrations have had someone in that post from the beginning to the end of the president's tenure. The same cannot be said for any of the other major senior staff positions—not even chief of staff.

While not all of them have had the formal title of press secretary— Larry Speakes, for example, was referred to as the principal deputy press secretary—all were responsible for the same basic tasks and services. They may have delegated functions, and they may have viewed them in a different light, but the office has consistently been characterized by the same fundamental tasks of gathering information, packaging, consulting, and establishing the official record.

The job is challenging, but press secretaries have also had greater longevity than other heads of White House offices. While senior staffers usually serve around two years, most press secretaries serve longer. Since 1953, five of the ten administrations have had the same press secretary for the full administration. James Hagerty, Pierre Salinger, Ron Ziegler, Jody Powell, and Marlin Fitzwater all stayed for an entire presidency. In fact, after President Kennedy was assassinated, Salinger stayed on for several months into the Johnson administration, and Fitzwater, who began as Reagan's press secretary in 1987, stayed all the way through the George H. W. Bush administration. While Jake Siewert came in for the final four months of the second term, and Mike McCurry served 3.75 years, Clinton's other press secretaries served an average of two years. In the future, there may be a new pattern resulting from the strains of regular televised briefings and increased visibility. In the sixth year of the George W. Bush administration, Tony Snow became the third presidential press secretary of the administration.

The position of press secretary has endured, and its basic responsibilities have remained the same. Yet the kinds of experience considered to be desirable professional background have changed over time, as table 9 shows. The four kinds of professionals who have served as press secretaries are reporters who covered the president, campaign professionals who helped elect a president, public affairs specialists with experience in state or federal government positions, and White House staffers.

Theodore Joslin (Hoover), Stephen Early (Franklin Roosevelt), Charles Ross and Joseph Short (Truman)—all were chosen for the job because of their backgrounds as newsmen, although some of them knew or had previously worked for the presidents they served. The last newsmen to become press secretaries were Pierre Salinger (Kennedy) and Jerald ter-Horst and Ron Nessen (Ford).

Beginning with Roger Tubby in the Truman administration, some press secretaries had served in government affairs positions in agencies or the White House. Tubby had served as a press aide in the State Department before becoming an assistant to Press Secretary Joe Short. James Hagerty (Eisenhower) had been press secretary for Governor Dewey of New York and continued in that role when Dewey ran for president in 1944 and 1948. Two other press secretaries also began as spokesmen for governors. George Christian came into the position for President Johnson after having served as spokesperson for Governor John Connally of Texas. Once in the White House, Christian spent a year working as an aide in the National Security Council before becoming press secretary. Jody Powell served as spokesperson for Governor Jimmy Carter before taking over the same role in Washington.

Several press secretaries did press work in Congress before their stints in the White House. Pierre Salinger worked in Kennedy's Senate office during the runup to his presidential campaign. George Reedy helped Lyndon Johnson in the Senate before handling media for Johnson

Table 9. Presidential Press Secretaries, 1929–2006

President	Press Secretary	Years in Office	Primary Experiences	Secondary Experiences
Hoover	George Akerson	March 4, 1929–February 5, 1931	Government public information officer, Department of Agriculture and 1928 campaign press staffer for Hoover	Reporter, *Minneapolis Tribune*
	Theodore G. Joslin	March 16, 1931–March 4, 1933	Washington reporter, Boston *Evening Transcript*	
Roosevelt	Stephen T. Early	March 4, 1933–March 24, 1945	Reporter, Associated Press and United Press and Paramount Newsreel Company	Advance work for Roosevelt in 1920 campaign
	Jonathan Daniels	March 24–April 12, 1945	Administrative assistant to President Roosevelt, 1943–1945	Assistant director, Office of Civil Defense, 1942; editor, *Raleigh News and Observer*, 1933–1942
Truman	Charles Ross	May 15, 1945–December 5, 1950	Editorial page editor, *St. Louis Post-Dispatch*	Harry Truman childhood friend
	Joseph H. Short Jr.	December 18, 1950–September 18, 1952	Washington correspondent, *Baltimore Sun*	
	Roger Tubby	December 18, 1952–January 20, 1953	Deputy press secretary	Press officer, State Department
Eisenhower	James C. Hagerty	January 20, 1953–January 20, 1961	Press secretary to Governor Dewey, 1942–1959, and campaign press secretary for 1952 Eisenhower campaign	Reporter, *New York Times*
Kennedy / Johnson	Pierre Salinger	January 20, 1961–March 19, 1964	Press secretary for Senator John F. Kennedy and 1960 campaign	Reporter, *San Francisco Chronicle and Collier's*

President	Press Secretary	Dates		
Johnson	George Reedy	March 19, 1964–July 8, 1965	Aide to Vice President Johnson, 1961–1964; aide to Senator Lyndon Johnson, 1951–1961	Reporter, United Press
	Bill Moyers	July 8, 1965–January 1, 1967	Associate director and deputy director, Peace Corps	Staff assistant to Senator Lyndon Johnson
	George Christian	February 1, 1967–January 20, 1969	Staff assistant in National Security Council	Press secretary to Governor John Connally and Texas politician Price Daniel
Nixon	Ronald Ziegler	January 20, 1969–August 9, 1974	Assistant to Herb Klein in 1968 presidential campaign	J. Walter Thompson advertising agency, working for H. R. Haldeman
Ford	Jerald terHorst	August 9–September 8, 1974	Reporter, *Detroit Free Press*	
	Ron Nessen	September 20, 1974–January 20, 1977	NBC reporter, covered Gerald Ford as president and vice president	Covered White House for United Press International
Carter	Jody Powell	January 20, 1977–January 20, 1981	Press secretary to Governor Carter, 1971–1975, and 1980 presidential campaign	
Reagan	James Brady	January 20–March 30, 1981	Assistant to Senator William Roth (R-DE)	Worked in the Nixon and Ford administrations
	Larry Speakes	March 30, 1981–February 1, 1987	Assistant press secretary to Jerald terHorst and Ron Nessen in the Ford administration; press aide to Nixon lawyer James St. Clair during Watergate	Press secretary to Senator James Eastland (D-MS)

(continued)

Table 9 (continued)

President	Press Secretary	Years in Office	Primary Experiences	Secondary Experiences
Reagan / G.H.W. Bush	Marlin Fitzwater	February 2, 1987–January 20, 1993	Assistant press secretary, 1983–1985; press secretary to Vice President Bush, 1985–February 1987	Press aide for Appalachian Regional Commission, Department of Transportation, Environmental Protection Agency, and Treasury Department
Clinton	Dee Dee Myers	January 20, 1993–December 31, 1994	Press secretary for 2000 Clinton presidential campaign	Democratic campaigns in California
	Mike McCurry	January 5, 1995–October 1, 1998	Spokesperson at State Department	Press aide to Senators Harrison Williams, Daniel P. Moynihan, and worked for the Democratic National Committee and on the presidential campaigns of Senator Robert Kerrey, Governor Bruce Babbitt
	Joe Lockhart	October 2, 1998–September 9, 2000	Deputy press secretary, 1997–1998; 1996 campaign spokesperson at the Democratic National Committee	Television producer for NBC
	Jake Siewert	October 1, 2000–January 20, 2001	Assistant and deputy press secretary under Lockhart and economic aide under Gene Sperling	

President	Press Secretary	Dates		
G. W. Bush	Ari Fleischer	January 20, 2001–July 14, 2003	Campaign press aide 2000 campaign	Press secretary to Representative Bill Archer (R-CA), chairman, House Ways and Means Committee and to Senator Pete Domenici (R-NM)
	Scott McClellan	July 15, 2003–May 10, 2006	Principal deputy press secretary under Ari Fleischer	1980 presidential campaign
	Tony Snow	May 10, 2006–present	Fox radio and television host, "Fox News Sunday"	Chief White House speechwriter for President George H. W. Bush; columnist, Detroit News

Sources: At his April 17, 1945, press conference, President Truman announced that J. Leonard Reinsch "is going to help me with press and radio affairs" but he was not named as press secretary. At his April 20 press conference, Truman announced Reinsch would be returning to work for Governor Cox of Georgia; There is a notation in Tubby's file that he received an increase in salary commensurate with the press secretary position, but no documentation of having the position. Carol Martin, archivist, Harry S Truman Library, telephone discussion, September 2005; James Brady, after being severely wounded in an assassination attempt on the president, retained the title of press secretary throughout the Reagan administration.

when he was vice president under Kennedy. Mike McCurry worked for several senators, including Harrison Williams (D-NJ), Daniel P. Moynihan (D-NY), and Bob Kerrey (D-NE). Ari Fleischer was press secretary for Senator Pete Domenici (R-NM) and Representative Bill Thomas (R-CA), chairman of the House Ways and Means Committee.

Interestingly, the first press secretary, George Akerson, came to the White House after having served as Secretary Hoover's press and appointments person in the Department of Commerce.[20] Presidents Reagan, Clinton, and both Bushes also chose press secretaries with public affairs backgrounds in the federal government. Marlin Fitzwater, Mike McCurry, and Ari Fleischer had each served as government spokesmen before coming to the White House. When McCurry and Fleischer left their positions, they were followed by people who had worked as their deputies, Joe Lockhart and then Jake Siewert in the Clinton press office, Scott McClellan in the G. W. Bush operation.

An increasing number of press secretaries have also had a substantial campaign background with the president they accompanied into the White House. While Steve Early worked for a brief time for Franklin Roosevelt when he was working for the 1920 nomination, he returned to a newsroom until joining the White House staff in 1933. James Hagerty worked in the 1952 campaign prior to joining the White House, as did Pierre Salinger for Kennedy, Jody Powell for Carter, Dee Dee Myers and Joe Lockhart for Clinton, and Ari Fleischer and Scott McClellan for George W. Bush.

Tony Snow represents an entirely new trend in press secretaries. Rather than a public affairs background or a campaign position with the administration, Snow comes from television and radio, where he did opinion broadcasting. He also was a columnist for the *Detroit News*. He did not know the president, but he had worked for President George H. W. Bush as his chief speechwriter. What Snow brought to the post was knowledge of the needs of news organizations as well as a polished delivery at the televised daily briefing. With his ease before the camera and his sense of how to control the room during a briefing, Snow brought order to the daily session and a more effective daily voice and face. What has not changed is the amount of presidential information reporters receive.

Tony Snow suited the needs of the White House in a variety of ways. When asked what White House officials wanted from their new press secretary, Dan Bartlett cited several of Snow's qualities: "Obviously, his communications skills honed over many years doing live television. Both

Josh Bolten and I recognized that he had a lot of interests and understanding of policy both on the foreign and domestic [sides]," he said. Both of those are important qualities for the briefings a press secretary conducts. "We were in a position where we had to have somebody who could hit the ground running. Not have somebody with training wheels for six months." Snow satisfied that need because he had a "reservoir of understanding of issues, having been in Washington and dealing with these issues, which was very helpful." He would also be able to have a fast startup because he could fit in easily with White House staff. "People who knew him also understood while he was on one hand a celebrity with all the status that comes with that, . . . he is not a person who has an ego, he is a good colleague to work with internally in the White House structure. And that has proven to be the case." Adding to his knowledge was his credibility within the Washington community, as he is "well respected here from both sides of the aisle." All together, "it is a huge asset for us to have somebody who is not only known and credible in the minds of the public and the media but also is effective in delivering a message."[21]

So popular was Snow that many requests came into the White House for him to speak at fundraising events during the 2006 congressional election season. He appeared at approximately twenty events, eighteen were fundraisers (although there were two where he simply spoke to volunteers) and which, he said as he began the appearances, he planned to treat as "pure advocacy," not as partisanship. He said that he did not plan to talk about Democrats but rather wanted to "explain Bush."[22] He saw the fundraising appearances as "new territory" for a press secretary, but it was not one that he chose: the White House senior staff had asked him to do the fundraisers. Snow was not, in fact, the first press secretary to make fundraising appearances. Mike McCurry made a couple of appearances for friends running for office in 1996, but did not do so on government time.[23] From Bartlett's point of view, the fundraising role was a sign of the ways in which the press secretary's job has changed. "I think that is more reflective of the evolution of the press secretary job," he said. It has moved from "closed huddles in the press secretary's office to live broadcasts of press briefings. I think it has adapted with the times."[24]

Having a well-known figure with an opinion background as press secretary led to some rough moments. In the press secretary's position, one has to leave behind one's own views and represent only those of the president. That can be difficult to do, as Tony Snow demonstrated in his discussion from the podium of President Bush's views on the issue of federal funding of stem cell research. It was an issue Snow had previously discussed on his radio program prior to coming into the White House.[25] When the Senate was considering stem cell legislation, Snow told reporters in a televised briefing, "The president believes strongly that for the purpose of research it's inappropriate for the federal government to finance something that many people consider murder. He's one of them. ... The simple answer is he thinks murder's wrong."[26]

The following Sunday, Chief of Staff Josh Bolten appeared on the NBC news interview program *Meet the Press*. Tim Russert asked Bolten a series of tough questions related to Snow's comment on the reasonable premise that the president now believed stem cell research to be murder, including, "Then if the president believes it is human life, how can he allow private stem cell research to go forward ... if, in fact, that is murder?" Bolten responded, "It's a very ... difficult balance. I mean, the president recognizes that there are millions of Americans who don't recognize that as a human life, and that the promise of that research for the saving of life is so important that they, that they want that to go forward."[27]

Josh Bolten was clearly not willing to assign the same views to the president that Snow had in his briefing. The day after the *Meet the Press* interview, Snow apologized in his briefing for putting Bolten in the position he did: "I overstepped my brief there, and so I created a little trouble for Josh Bolten in the interview. And I feel bad about it. I think there's concern. The President has said that he believes that this is the destruction of human life."[28] Snow said about the flap, "That was a pretty good slap in the face." He said, "I did step over the line. You have got to make sure, and I remind myself of this every day before I go to the podium, having spent many years in policy and in opinion, I am not the president. I speak for the president."[29]

The problems Snow had reflecting the president's position on the stem cell issue came about in part because Josh Bolten and Dan Bartlett wanted a situation where Snow would be viewed as unscripted. In 2006, when reporters were regularly questioning the accuracy of the information coming from the White House, they decided that it was time to bring in a new press secretary. The press secretary is the most visible White House official and, as such, is closely associated with the amount and quality of the information provided to reporters. As Chief of Staff Josh Bolten described the move to bring in Tony Snow, "We had developed a reputation for being closed and scripted. . . . I thought as I came in that one of the changes I could make is change that impression, however inaccurate it might have been, the most visible way was a new press secretary, to fill the press secretary job with a person like Tony, who is clearly not a scripted person. Who understands the policies and has his own sort of interesting take and articulation on it that nobody can write for him. It is him spontaneously. So my direction to him was, 'Let that happen.' Now, I also said, 'Stay—try to color within the lines here, be studious about the policy here and you'll find very good support. Any time you want to dig in to what policy is, you will find people here to help you do that. Be studious about that so you are not freelancing. But, otherwise, let Tony Snow be Tony Snow. Because I think that is good for the president and good for the White House, and I think for the most part, it has been."[30] Bolten knew Snow well from their time in the George H. W. Bush administration.

What the professional backgrounds of recent press secretaries reveal is that modern presidents believe that familiarity with government and political savvy are essential to the job. They need the background it takes to understand their president's goals and policies, but they also need established relationships with campaign reporters who will follow the president once he comes into office. Increasingly, they need the partisan experience they will have to tap in order to engage in successful political combat from the podium.

Before 1953, when press conferences went on the record, press secretaries did not engage in the kind of political sparring they sometimes do in televised briefings today. In an earlier time, press secretaries could backtrack on a misstated point or keep it off the record. Today there can be no off-the-record or background status for any utterance in a press secretary's briefings. Press secretaries need to be experienced in handling public affairs. Their expertise must range from understanding how to get information from government officials to appreciating the resonance of their chosen words. In a televised world, there is no easy way to restate a misstatement.

The Twenty-Four-Hour News Day

Both McCurry and Fitzwater tended to end their work day well after eight o'clock in the evening. Fleischer and McClellan got out only slightly earlier. After their final staff meeting, each returned calls and, in the case of Fleischer and McClellan, who served after the mid-1990s, wrote e-mails. Their days differed, however, in the degree to which the twenty-four-hour news cycle affected them.

By the 1980s, news was being broadcast twenty-four hours a day, and the press secretary had to develop a system to respond to it. The first priority of this new system was coverage. Press deputies were assigned full coverage, twenty-four hours a day, seven days a week. "You go to a twenty-four-hour White House staff," explained Mike McCurry. It began in late Reagan or early Bush, "when the importance of steering the story hour by hour through the wires or CNN became a reality, because people were watching twenty-four-hour news reporting all day long," he said.[31]

Marlin Fitzwater described how the twenty-four-hour duty shift worked, emphasizing its challenges. Those at the deputy and assistant level in the Press Office were assigned to rotations: "Everybody was a duty officer, since it was such a horrible job, basically staying awake all night long," Fitzwater said. "In that five o'clock meeting we'd talk about issues. If it was one of my younger people who had overnight duty, I'd say, 'If you get a call tonight that Marines have been killed in the barracks in Frankfurt or something, call me. Don't start out on your own.'"

During the night, Fitzwater might get calls from the Situation Room about important developments: "If I'd get a call in the middle of the night saying there was a plane shot down in Iraq or something, then I'd call my duty officer, and we'd work out what he's going to say." Reporters would then deal with the duty officer: "But they also knew they'd get a statement, and they knew that by talking to him they could get confirmation of things and they knew that I was involved. They knew that if it was anything really big, I wouldn't let them just sit through the night. I'd do a call-out or something."[32]

The Clinton White House continued the full-coverage system with duty shifts. Their rotation system was similar to the one observed in both Bush administrations. "First of all, you don't sleep soundly, you have to wake up in no time flat," commented Dawn Alexander, who served as deputy press secretary from 1993 to 1995. "If you don't know the answer, say that you don't know the answer—but you'll get it. To me, that was like a cardinal rule. That is one that you can really say, because the news changes so fast. The other thing is that you had to appreciate the fact that whatever you said, you represented the White House, and that could affect incredible things around the world."[33] The same duty system is in practice in the current administration. Scott McClellan described how they set up the rotation system of duty officers early in their tenure: "We switch every day. The main thing is it's important for the duty officer to know who to call and have all the numbers at their disposal."[34]

The twenty-four-hour news cycle altered the president's communication operation substantively as well as structurally. In this ongoing, ever-moving system, there is no new news, so to speak. "The president never makes an announcement that is news," observed McCurry. "He always 'as expected announced today that,' because the only way to get any coverage is to put it out the night before, so that people wake up saying, 'The president today is going to do x, y, or z.' What his day is about is already known, because the shelf life of an announcement is short, and you never get to carry through in more than one news cycle."[35]

Marlin Fitzwater described how the situation evolved after the Clinton administration took over: "The Clinton people have a much more sophisticated and comprehensive communications operation than was true in the Reagan and Bush administrations. It reflects the twenty-four-hour news cycle," said Fitzwater. "It requires coordination and lines of the day." Fitzwater pointed out that before the growth of cable television, the networks' evening news was what mattered. In those days, 20 million people a night watched the network news. But in the latter part of the Clinton administration, when there was a growth in the number of cable networks, things changed. "What we learned during "Monica" [the Lewinsky scandal] is that 200,000 watching Chris Matthews or Geraldo Rivera is enough, because those people who are watching it are the news junkies, the ones who get the buzz going." It doesn't matter how many people are watching, but *who* is watching. During the impeachment proceedings in 1999, Fitzwater observed, "after it was over each day, all of the people appeared on MSNBC, CNBC, Fox, and talked to each other on their shows." There was no comparable system to exploit during Fitzwater's days in the Reagan and Bush White Houses. It was the Clinton administration that understood what was happening and made the needed adjustments. "The White House has made itself a part of that system," Fitzwater concluded.[36]

McCurry's deputy, Barry Toiv, explained how the Clinton press operations responded in 1996 to the relatively sudden presence of five networks at the White House. The acceleration of the pace at which news moves ended up reshaping the White House news day. "It's very easy to get something injected into the bloodstream now," said Toiv. "Now you have CNN and the others blasting away all day long, and as soon as something happens here, that's it." The ever-present CNN gives the White House opportunities throughout the day. "If you want to get into a story that's ongoing, someone can do an interview with CNN or talk to a CNN reporter or one of the others. CNN is still the more prominent, although MSNBC has the advantage of being hooked in to NBC," Toiv indicated.

The White House can target a message during the day by making use of the technology of the ever-present television camera. For economic news, for example, the White House can use CNBC and CNNfn. CNBC is a particularly good television spot during the day because "they'll take a Bob Rubin or a Gene Sperling or a Larry Summers—people like that— because their viewers want to see what these people have to say every day. So those are good places to get a certain message out to a certain audience," Toiv indicated. On the weekends and at night, there are other opportunities too for administration spokespeople.[37]

The Press Secretary's Changing Portfolio

In recent years, the job of salesmanship has been added to the portfolio of the press secretary, a development about which Mike McCurry remains quite ambivalent: "Now there is a persuasion function that is located in the office, too, and that is the one I'm increasingly ambivalent about. Is part of the job of that office to participate in the selling of the program? . . . I think that's where you drift over to spin, and you drift over to argumentation and opinion-based communicating. I think that's a little more problematic."

In McCurry's view, this development raises serious questions about the difference between the duties of the Press Office and the role of communications. "I'm not sure that's a legitimate function of that office. I've even thought of going so far as to separating the political function out of that office entirely. We really changed the nature of the office of the press secretary and the person in the [press secretary's role] a lot, but if you had a career government employee, or if you had some sense that this is the public information office, and we don't do politics here, you have to go to the DNC, or you have to go to the president's political operation in order to get political commentary, the result would be it wouldn't be a job I would be as interested in having."

McCurry went on to suggest how the position might be broken up in order to have the sales function performed by one person and the hard information offered by someone else. "It's interesting. Clinton had an opportunity—they might have tried something like that if they had a Stephanopoulos in the position as chief policy/communications person and a press secretary junior. The press secretary could be the person who handled the flow of information, the detail work of government, presenting all the information necessary just to get the hard news right. Then you could bring in another official to talk about the background to the whole thing and the purpose, and how it fits with the whole program. If I was waving a wand to change the way things worked, I think I would put much more premium on the flow of hard-core, factual information. People are definitely hungry for that."[38]

In both the Jimmy Carter and George H. W. Bush administrations, the press secretaries got high marks because of the hard information of McCurry's conception. There was no communications office trying to persuade Press Secretary Powell to reduce or redirect the flow of information. There was a communications office in the George H. W. Bush administration, but the president and the chief of staff did not emphasize it for most of Bush's years in office. Fitzwater remarked, "Jody and I always get credit for being great press secretaries, but one of the reasons was because we had such poor communications shops that we were just pure news guys basically. We just went out and told it the way it was."[39]

While it may have worked well for the press secretaries and was probably the most common ground shared by these two administrations of different parties, the fact remains that both presidents lost their bids for reelection. Clearly there are costs to confining one's press secretary to the role of delivering information. Just as clearly, there are political benefits to using each day's televised briefing as a vehicle for advocacy, salesmanship, and persuasion.

Responsibilities of the Press Secretary

The press secretary has three basic functions that can be characterized as information conduit, constituencies' representative, and manager of the Press Office. While some press secretaries were once involved in communications planning, today almost no press secretary has the time to do more than coordinate with the other offices that are handling the planning.

The press secretary's role as information conduit requires him or her to provide presidential information to reporters on a regular basis, in settings both formal and informal. In addition to the two daily briefings of reporters, there are the many phone calls with reporters. Reporters can also drop by the press secretary's office to discuss a particular matter. The press secretary spends a certain amount of time explaining the president's public relations to others on the White House staff. He or she also negotiates between White House staffers and reporters. Having three constituencies requires him to represent each to the other two.

As the head of an office that in many administrations stretches between two buildings and includes approximately thirty people, the press
secretary must also devote time and resources to manage his office. With
the arrival of the twenty-four-hour news day, the longstanding schedule of
daily meetings is now supplemented with the requirement that he or she
be available to answer questions throughout the day. During the night
and on weekends, deputies respond. While the communications office
handles the events at which the president speaks, the press secretary is
responsible for organizing presidential press conferences and overseeing
the chief executive's short question-and-answer sessions with reporters.

Information Conduit

The press secretary's success depends upon the quality of the information he or she provides to the president, White House staff members,
and reporters. Yet each of these three constituencies assesses the quality
of the press secretary through the prism of its own values. The president
wants the press secretary to build support for himself and his programs.
The White House staff expects the same but wants the press secretary
to be the administration's point man for criticism and blame. Reporters
want the press secretary to provide the accurate information they need to
do their jobs.

Satisfying Reporters versus Accommodating White House Priorities

Whatever their news organization, reporters tend to seek similar kinds of
information. Bill Plante, who has covered presidential campaigns since
1968 and the White House since 1981, maintains that this is as true over
time as it is in the present. "I don't think that the kind of information that
we have gotten has changed that much," he observed. "When you cover
the White House, you are looking for the story as well as keeping an eye
on what the scheduled appearances of the president are and what he is
scheduled to do and say."

In looking for information, reporters also continue to query the president and the press secretary in similar ways. Plante continued, "You are
trying to coerce more news out of the press secretary at the briefing, or
out of the president, by asking questions when you get to see him, and
then you talk to the staff to get their take on what is going on and try to
develop something from them." The big change that has accompanied
today's age of continuous news output is the reporter's need to release in-

formation throughout the day. "We did that the same way when I started covering full-time in 1981 as we do today," recalled Plante. "But there is a lot more attention paid in getting it out. Whether on radio, or on the morning broadcasts, or just making it available, getting it fed back to the bureau and turning it around and fed out."[40]

Reporters judge press secretaries both by the quality of their information and the access they have. Some measure up and others don't, even within the same administration. Veteran White House correspondent Terry Hunt of Associated Press offered a picture of a good press secretary that many reporters could agree on. "Be accessible, be honest, open, be quotable, be forthright," he said. "We frequently need a preview of what the president is going to do as we write two cycles of stories a day and we are always trying to leap ahead. Just basically do your job, by providing information on what the president is going to do and what he is thinking."

No matter how much reporters liked Dee Dee Myers personally, her lack of access to the big decision-makers in the Clinton White House limited her usefulness to them. "It was clear that she didn't have the access, she didn't have that inner knowledge that you can get by being part of the circle," said Hunt in 1996. On the other hand, "McCurry is an insider. First of all, he is well established. He has been around Washington for twenty years or more. He knows what works and what doesn't work." That type of knowledge gives a press secretary credibility in an administration. "I think he is part of the decision-making process here." Marlin Fitzwater also "had that edge," said Hunt. Being close to decision-making "gives you a distinct advantage when you are giving a briefing when you know what the president thinks."[41]

Given their different priorities, the president and his staff have different views of what makes a press secretary successful. White House officials believe that they have a right to choose what information they release rather than meeting an information agenda tendered by reporters. And those administrations that are most successful in crafting and sustaining a positive agenda are the ones that succeed in releasing information on their terms. Helen Thomas cited the manner in which the Reagan White House handled releasing information. "Every day they work on a story of the day and how to shape it," she said. "They don't believe in a right to know but people's right to know some things at some times." That is no different from what administrations prior to Reagan tried to do, observed Thomas, who began her coverage of presidents with John F. Kennedy in

1961. "But every administration has tried to manage the news, and some do it better than others." About the Reagan administration, she said in 1985, "they do it the best. They work at it every day, and very little slips through the cracks. Most of the time they are on top. They are successful because they work at it. They plan the day. They follow their scenario. One story a day, if that."[42]

Though Thomas's basic observations are as true today as they were in 1985, today White House officials now have to come up with more than one story daily in order to accommodate the rolling deadlines of most news organizations. What Thomas called the central communications priority of the Reagan White House—getting on television—was also the goal of the Clinton and George W. Bush administrations. As Terry Hunt put it, "What can get me on television?" This emphasis on television is reflected in the energy the press secretary puts into getting airtime. "They construct events and backgrounds and appearances to make an appealing picture to television so that the television producers find it difficult to resist putting it on the air," continued Hunt. During the George H. W. Bush's administration, "if it was six o'clock and Leslie Stahl [of CBS] wanted to see Marlin Fitzwater . . . that door flew open, because he wanted to have whatever the story was, he wanted to have his imprint or offer his rebuttal to whatever she was going to put on. If a wire reporter or a newspaper reporter was standing outside, she [Stahl] went in ahead of us."[43]

Today this quest for time on television dominates each weekday. The Press Office provides information and supplies officials for appearances on the morning network news shows. Throughout the day it accommodates news programs run by cable news organizations, such as CNN, Fox News, CNBC, and MSNBC, by allowing cameras and reporters to locate on the North Lawn of the White House. In the evening it supplies what is necessary for the network news programs and, to round out the day, ABC's *Nightline.* Today's communications priorities are summed up by technology: television news organizations have at least sixteen cameras located near the driveway, each ready to handle any breaking news in addition to their regular news spots.

To fulfill his role as information conduit, the press secretary must have his White House associates supply information to news organizations, either in person or through some other direct means. He encourages White House staff members to brief groups of reporters. He and his deputies arrange for particular staffers to speak with individual reporters working on stories related to that official's expertise. Shortly before he became press secretary, Deputy Press Secretary Scott McClellan spoke about putting together reporters and officials on a particular issue, such as Medicare: "One thing I have tried to do more and more over time . . . [is] put together the reporter on background with Doug Badger on Medicare, since he's our lead policy person inside the White House on this."[44] But the most important figure a press secretary can present to reporters is the president himself.

Both to encourage these dealings with reporters and to prepare his associates for them, the press secretary and his deputies gather and assess information for the president and his staff members. Newspapers are one of their important sources. "There's news to us in every single newspaper you pick up, to every one in this office. And it doesn't matter how high or low you are," said Joe Lockhart, who served as press secretary for most of Clinton's last two years in office. "I guarantee that if they asked Mike [McCurry, press secretary at the time] after he reads the paper in the morning every day, in every story, there is one thing that he didn't know. Because this is a big place, a big sprawling place, and someone may try to tell you something, and you're not listening, or they're going ahead and doing something for the wrong reasons."

Reading the newspapers is a way for the Press Office to gauge what is going to be carried on the evening television news. "The way to reach television is the *New York Times*," Lockhart said. As a former network television producer, Lockhart is familiar with the rhythms of television news: "Every television executive in America wakes up in the morning and reads the *New York Times*. They will deny this up and down, but I have seen it so many different times in so many different ways. They'll have a story days before the *Times* has it" and yet hold it back.[45] The story only becomes legitimated when it is carried by the *Times* and then television will carry it.

In recent years, as more information has been issued on the record, a press secretary's duties include getting the president to respond to reporters' queries in on-the-record sessions. Those sessions include press conferences, short question-and-answer sessions, and individual and group interviews.

Overseeing the Official Paper Flow

The gaggle and the briefing occasion the preponderance of official statements for an administration. But throughout each day, the press secretary must issue official statements on behalf of the administration, supply background information about new initiatives, provide schedules of presidential appearances and arrangements, and distribute transcripts of official information sessions.

In addition, on most days, the Press Office issues perhaps fifteen releases pertaining to nominations and appointments made by the president, background information on upcoming trips and events scheduled by the White House, and transcripts of remarks made by the president in the Oval Office and elsewhere. When the president stages an event in the East Room to introduce a policy, for example, there will be fact sheets to identify attendees and their interests and to explain the touted policy.

Prior to a presidential trip or a visit by a head of state, one or more White House officials may come to the Briefing Room with background or on-the-record information for reporters. Remarks made at ensuing public sessions are always transcribed and distributed to reporters. The Press Office shows its sensitivity to the short news cycle by moving quickly. Since the Kennedy administration, the White House has arranged for a private transcribing firm to be present at all public presidential events for the purpose of complete transcription. The White House Communications Agency operates the recording equipment.

As late as the Clinton administration, Press Office releases made available in plastic bins in the hallway behind the Briefing Room were the main source of information for a substantial number of the reporters covering the White House. Beginning in the George W. Bush administration, e-mail became the favored vehicle for sending information to reporters and within the administration. On a normal day in the George W. Bush administration, reporters will electronically receive a batch of appointment announcements, briefing transcripts, pool reports, fact sheets, schedules, and briefing materials associated with events. For a state dinner, for example, there are menus, descriptions of the china, flower arrangements; in the pool reports there will also be descriptions of the participants to supplement what a particular reporter could see of the event itself.

Leaders of groups coming into the White House for a presidential event and invited dignitaries and members of Congress often speak with reporters following a meeting with the chief executive. Generally, they appear at the "stakeout" set up outside of the West Wing entrance, a clutch of microphones that permits reporters to question selected interviewees about their meeting with the president. The "stakeout" is run by reporters, not by the White House, although the press secretary has a hookup in his office that allows him to hear what is said there. The Press Office facilitates the "stakeout" through a "mult" [slang for "multiple feed," referring to the sound system's ability to convey sound to several points at once], but it does not generate transcripts of comments offered at the stakeout.

Supplying Accurate Information

Whether in the gaggle, the briefing, or individual sessions with reporters, providing accurate information is the greatest challenge a press secretary faces. He must be creative in finding ways to acquire the facts he needs. And he must learn how to check his facts. The latter was foremost in the mind of Marlin Fitzwater when he took over as Ronald Reagan's press secretary: "I would have liked to have asked somebody about how you cover the government. If you find information is bad, how do you check it out with State and CIA?" So the press secretary must continually ask himself, "What is the best way for me to check out the veracity of information?" That question gets to "the most crucial job in my area, the integrity of information. I developed a very, I thought, sophisticated, but at least kind of intricate, beat system for putting my staff in various places around the government to check out information." The process of acquiring solid information is difficult, Fitzwater concluded: "It's just a constant struggle to stay atop the information flow."

Getting information from worlds of foreign policy and defense poses different challenges than getting information from the domestic arena. According to Fitzwater, "The other phenomenon is that domestic agencies are so anxious to be a part of the White House, because they so seldom get their nose in the door, that when you ask them for something, they'll usually fall all over themselves giving it to you. State, Defense, and CIA are the kings, the princes, and princesses of government, and they want to protect their information and so forth. But if you call the Interior Department, they can't wait to get over to you."

For Fitzwater, learning about specific topics meant dealing directly with department specialists, not public information officers. "I think because I was a line bureaucrat myself, I would always ask who's the specialist on this and often would call them for specific stuff," he recalled. "The public affairs assistant secretary was always good at policies, and what's the secretary thinking, and those kinds of issues, but the kinds of information I often needed were the nuts and bolts things like, 'Okay, we've got a new education proposal here but tell me how many kids in America get Pell grants? How many new schools are there every year? How much money do we spend on new construction?' Those kinds of things."

Another challenge was the time pressure. "The one thing that departments never understand about the White House—again, this goes back to the differences—is the time factor. In a White House, almost everything you need, you need that day, probably within two or three hours. Departments have a terrible time responding like that, because they all have clearance processes and all that business," he commented. "The quickest way to circumvent that is to call up somebody and ask them specific questions. They'll say, 'Let me get you a paper on that.' 'No. Don't get me a paper. Just tell me this one thing: how many schools were built?'" What Fitzwater wanted was specific facts: "I only need about three facts or five facts to make my case; I don't need the whole thing. That's always the toughest part. So what you have to do is go down the food chain far enough until you find the person who knows those kinds of answers. The irony is, of course, the more technical information you need, the lower you have to go."[46]

During a crisis, the press secretary might have his staff fan out among the agencies to troll for information or identify someone from the agency to come into the White House. Larry Speakes described how the Reagan administration operated after the U.S. action in Grenada, when the Press Office was caught without accurate information. "We learned from that [Grenada] that when crisis occurred—the Gaddafi stuff, the Challenger— that the minute something like that occurred we would send somebody from our office to the Defense Department or to NASA," he recalled. And the agency would send somebody from their office to the White House. They would come in early in the morning and stay all day. "The deal that that gave us was, first of all, someone that was fairly knowledgeable about the subject from that department and knew the details, but also knew, if we had a question, and we couldn't answer it, they knew who to go to in the Defense Department or NASA or wherever. That really served us well to be able to have that immediate exchange and have those people on hand."

During some of the crises, officials from dispatched agencies spent several days in the Press Office answering questions. When the Challenger exploded, NASA had someone there for almost a week. Speakes indicated that when Libya provoked a crisis by shooting at U.S. naval ships, a Defense Department specialist sent to the Press Office was able to respond to reporters' queries in the briefing. "They asked what kind of firepower it had," Speakes recalled about the reporters. "So he's sitting there with a book of the profiles of all the foreign ships and handed it to me, and I'm able to tell them how many guns it's got on it, how much armament, how many people, length, width, and all that. It really helped to be more knowledgeable on that subject." Sometimes, such as when a Russian seaman jumped ship in New Orleans during the Reagan administration, several departments are involved. Each had representatives at the ready to answer queries, many of them jurisdictional ones.[47]

The most difficult situations that involve digging for accurate information come when a scandal is involved. In scandal situations, according to Fitzwater, the press secretary gets few offers of help. "It was amazing to me how many times you'd have a little scandal story come up, and nobody would even say anything about it," he remembered. During the Monica Lewinsky scandal, he noted, White House staffers said that the issue was not even discussed in meetings. "It may seem strange to the outside world, but I know that phenomenon well. The more disastrous the story, the more silence." And: "the more troublesome the story, the more willing they were to let me deal with it myself. On the really nasty stuff, you never had the chief of staff come down and say, 'Here's how to work that out,' or 'Here's a good way to phrase that.' They would run from it like it was poison."[48]

All press secretaries have to deal with scandals at some point during their presidencies. A key consideration is how much information to acquire and what should be brought into the Briefing Room. Mike McCurry worked early in the Monica Lewinsky scandal to have the lawyers take it over and move it out of the Briefing Room so that he could speak about other subjects during his briefings. One of the reasons to adopt that strategy is that it is dangerous to discuss the facts of a breaking scandal without getting caught up in it. Getting through those days is difficult, as Mc-Curry commented: "I'm pretty much a realist. I've just about danced as many dances as you can dance up there until the act starts to wear a little thin." As the scandal was unfolding, McCurry was aware of the expressed warnings of his predecessor, Marlin Fitzwater. Said McCurry: "I see him [Fitzwater] quoted a lot talking about my performance, saying that it's not so much that you get through the first couple of days. It's the corrosive effect, and the problem of getting just one more step out into the swamp, and you start sinking deeper and deeper into it. I'm very conscious of that." He sought to be careful what statements he made from the podium. "I'm not going to position myself out there as stalwart defender. And I haven't. Correct me if I am wrong, but I have not been out there giving the ringing defense of Bill Clinton."[49] While the scandal lasted for the remainder of McCurry's tenure, his position did not change.

Acquiring Presidential Information

Reporters want information about the president, and they want it from a press secretary who meets with the president every day. On October 2, 2000, Press Secretary Jake Siewert held his first gaggle. Helen Thomas asked him about his arrangements to meet with the president. Would they meet daily? He responded that he had the same kind of access provided to Mike McCurry and Joe Lockhart when they held the post. Would that be daily access, she queried. Finally, Siewert indicated that he would be meeting daily with the president.[50]

From the viewpoint of reporters, daily meetings with the president are crucial to getting information that reflects presidential thinking, rather than that of the press secretary. Marlin Fitzwater understood this. When he talked to George H. W. Bush about becoming his press secretary, he described what he needed to do the job. "I told him I expected the same kind of relationship that I had with President Reagan, which was access to every meeting. Certainly open access to the Oval Office," he said. "When I said 'every meeting,' I meant every National Security Council meeting, top secret meetings, everything." He remembered that Bush's response was, "Fine." According to Fitzwater, the president lived up to their agreement: "I tried to go to every meeting. No matter what it was, I would go to it. And that was helpful because it's truly the only way to know what's going on and get the feel for the president's thinking and how he might react."[51]

Ari Fleischer met daily with the president, usually before or after the gaggle. "Depending on what's in the news, before I gaggle, or I'll gaggle and pretty much right after the gaggle, I'll go see the president and tell him where I see the news going that day." While Fleischer was allowed into most presidential meetings, he was not part of personnel matters or intelligence briefings. Fleischer said that President Bush talked to him about the job on election day: "First he talked to me about how much access I'd have, which is exactly what he's done. It's a lot. He stressed that he knew the job was a tightrope, that I'd have to serve him, also the White House staff, as well as the press." In terms of the information he would not get, Fleischer said, "There are issues that not everybody knows about. That really applied, what he said in that case, to personnel . . . and intelligence matters, of course."[52]

Scott McClellan met regularly with President Bush in the morning, soon after McClellan came into the White House. "Depending on the day, it's not unusual for me to walk over to the Oval and try to catch the president," McClellan said. "I'll maybe bounce a couple of things off him, issues that I know, questions that are going to come up that I'm going to get asked, and I maybe want to get his thoughts."[53] Tony Snow said that when he speaks with President Bush, he gets from him "the voice, the policy, the context" of the issues and initiatives Snow speaks about at his briefings.[54]

Mike McCurry met with President Clinton, both individually and with groups of other staff members. Among the things he would do in meetings would be to discuss possible answers to questions, and his staff would also make suggestions. "We invariably, most days, had an opportunity to talk to him, and I would get some sense of how he wanted to answer certain questions," McCurry recalled. "Often we'd just say there's no reason for you to get into this, so if you don't want to take a question, you can just not take a question." On most occasions, though, Clinton would have a public event and simply take reporters' questions himself. "Most days, for most of the time I was at the White House, he'd have some kind of event that would be a photo opportunity, he'd get the big question on the news of the day and we would have addressed it. So that was then in the can by the time of my briefing . . . that's often helpful to me to go over there and get his thoughts."

In situations where the president had already spoken, the press secretary's role was to flesh out his response: "So you had the president shaping the answer or shaping the story, and I was doing the background news around it by the time the briefing came. Occasionally it would happen that we had practiced how he was going to answer a certain question but it didn't come up in the photo opportunity." Developed answers, however, rarely went to waste: "So when the press raised it with me, I gave the answer Clinton would have given if he had been asked. That happened a lot. That was the utility of really hearing him talk it through."[55]

Constituency Representative

The press secretary can only be effective if he or she has the trust of all three constituents: the president, the press, and the White House staff.

In relationships in which various sides have big stakes, the participants are wary of one another. Because few people who come into work in the White House have experience dealing with news organizations, the press secretary often has to smooth the way for reporters. At the same time, the press secretary is responsible for determining what information is appropriate for White House staffers to release. Unauthorized contacts can result in leaks of information. Presidents usually get upset when unauthorized information appears in the news. Often their response is to have the press secretary track down leaks.

Nonetheless, nurturing the press is an essential part of the press secretary's job. Mike McCurry considered it his top priority when he took the job. "My assessment, when I got here in 1995, was that it was such a poisonous relationship, and there was such a sense of 'You people really don't like us,' that I had to affect the culture of the relationship or the personal dimension of the relationship," he recalled. He placed an emphasis on "being responsive, and being more respectful of the press as an institution."[56] And he dealt with the creature comfort and access issues about which reporters were disturbed.

One of the changes from Fleischer's practices that Press Secretary Scott McClellan brought to his job was regularly going back to the press area to meet with reporters in the late afternoons. Around 4:30 p.m. once every two or three weeks he used to go back by the Associated Press booth and talk to anyone who wanted to engage in conversation. He'd ask, "What's going on?" and it usually did not take long for a group of reporters to ask questions or talk about a brewing issue. After he finished up there, he would go down to the basement press area and cruise down the aisles to the Fox and CNN booths to see what is on reporters' minds. If there was a particularly contentious briefing or a series of them, McClellan was likely to come back to speak with reporters. He did so in mid-July after reporters had sharply questioned him about the truth of his unequivocal 2003 statements that Karl Rove was not involved in releasing information on Joseph Wilson's wife. After three days of tough questions, including several questioning his truthfulness, McClellan made his rounds of the press area.

Getting reporters to like the president or his press representatives has limited utility. McCurry cited the relationship with reporters that Senator Bob Dole had when he ran for president against Clinton in 1996: "The press corps traveling with him, they came to know him, really had a huge amount of affection for him, which is something they never professed for Clinton under any circumstances. But it did absolutely no good for him."

In the end, though, in order to establish a good relationship with reporters, what counted were the leaks and the stories provided them. "I think ultimately it all boils down to whether you give them good copy," McCurry said. "And the days that are bare around here, when you give them a good story, the story that you want to give them that's got some sizzle to it, you basically have a very happy harvest at the end of the day when you watch the networks." On the other hand, "if they can't get on the air, or can't get on the front page, they're ornery about it."

In dealing with reporters for elite news organizations that emphasize White House reporting, press secretaries sometimes have special sets of relationships. Such was the case with Mike McCurry and Ann Devroy of the *Washington Post*. McCurry remembered Devroy told him when he came to the White House, "'You've got to understand one thing, that there are only two or three people I count on to be "ground zero," which is, after all the spin, after all the one faction trying to do in the other faction, I need to know what's really going on,'" she told him. "She counted on George [Stephanopoulos] in that role and she came to count on me after I got here. We would tell her straight what was going on and wouldn't try to hoodwink her or spin her on something. We would tell her 'Here's what the deal is; here's what we're saying about it.'"

An important reason for establishing such a relationship was that it organized the many requests for information coming from *Post* reporters. As the newspaper following White House activities at the closest range, there were more requests for information coming from the *Post* than from any other news organization. McCurry said, "I was talking to [*Washington Post* managing editor] Len Downie one day and was telling him, 'You have to understand the *Post* is "ground zero" for us too.' The *Post* is a very complicated place. . . . They are coming at you with a combination of a dozen different storylines they were pursuing." Devroy was important to McCurry in sorting out priorities: "Devroy always gave you a sense of what mattered to them, what was going to be treated significantly by the paper, what was going to be treated less significantly." As good as their relationship was, it did not prevent bad stories from coming his way: "You always knew where you stood. . . . It was the perfect expression of the adversarial relationship retaining some amicability. I would count her as a friend, but I wouldn't count it as a plus in public relations terms. It wouldn't prevent her from writing an article if I had screwed up, she would be the first in print."[57]

Marlin Fitzwater had a similar relationship with Devroy: "You knew that she had not one source, two sources, but a whole line of sources. Part of it was she worked for the *Washington Post,* and they have the most resources. But she was relentless in gathering information. That made her authoritative in herself." She was able to bore deeper into the Reagan, George H. W. Bush and Clinton administrations than any other reporter. Because of that, she got quick responses from press secretaries: "She was very good at not taking no for an answer. She was a great interviewer. She would ask five or six questions, and you thought she had exhausted everything, but then she would come at you with more questions. I told Presidents Reagan and Bush, 'You can't help but give her information. If you pick up the phone and talk to her, you are going to give her the information she wants. She knows how to prod and pry.'"

At the same time, she was willing to hold off if a press secretary told her that she didn't have the story nailed down. Fitzwater recalled, "She did have a special fairness about her. She was willing to back off a piece of information if you convinced her it needed more checking. You knew she would get to the bottom of a story. If you asked her to check, you would know she would do it."[58] Establishing such a relationship turned out well for the White House as well as the reporter. The press secretary did not get blindsided by a story with unfamiliar charges, and the *Washington Post* got information in her stories it could count on.

Fending for the President and the White House Staff

The better the ongoing daily relationships between the Press Office and reporters, the better it can serve the White House when there is trouble. Roman Popadiuk, the NSC press person in the George H. W. Bush administration, explained how it works. Once a professional rapport is established, a reporter might bring a story to a Press Office staffer to ascertain certain themes or facts. The staffer cannot tell him what to add to his story, but on the other hand, he can say, "'You might want to work on that second paragraph,' or 'Search around a little more on that paragraph.' That's exactly how we would say it sometimes," said Popadiuk. "'You could either add to a story,' which I didn't mind at times, saying, 'You forgot some points here' or 'Your story would be fuller,' or negative, saying, 'This is really off the wall, and I'll tell you why.' So it worked both ways."[59]

The press secretary must maintain cooperative relationships with reporters in order to protect the president and his White House staff. Both expect press secretaries to sound an alarm when they hear about impending troubles from reporters. Ann Devroy had no qualms about letting press secretaries know what she was working on so that the White House could provide a response. She did not want to blindside the press secretaries with whom she worked. "I always tell them what I'm doing. I don't believe in gotcha journalism, when you pick up something in the morning and are shocked and surprised," she said. "I think it's a matter of fairness. A press secretary is really in trouble if he's sitting there inside the White House, and it's a surprise to him when the *Post*, the *Times* have a big White House story that he didn't know about."

It hurts a press secretary to lose credibility with his own troops. "Everyone looks at him and says, 'Hey, what kind of press secretary are you, they didn't call you, they think that they can do something like this without even calling you?'" Devroy explained. The cooperative working relationship is essential for both reporters and press secretaries, as each trolls for information. "One of their functions is not only to give out information but to get information," she noted. "They patrol the press to find out what's moving that thing. That's what good press secretaries do: 'What's on your mind?' 'What are you working on?'"[60]

Sometimes the press secretary serves as in-house constituent by trying to unravel a story to which a staff member objects. When Ari Fleischer was George W. Bush's press secretary, he got involved in the administration's reaction to a *Washington Post* piece about the role that National Security Adviser Condoleezza Rice had played for the administration in a court case dealing with affirmative action in higher education. The article, which appeared in January 2003, stated, "National security adviser Condoleezza Rice took a rare central role in a domestic debate within the White House and helped persuade President Bush to publicly condemn race-conscious admissions policies at the University of Michigan, administration officials said yesterday."

The piece laid out what she had supposedly said during the debate: "Rice, the first female national security adviser, told Bush that she worked to increase the number of African American faculty members at Stanford but that she was 'absolutely opposed to quotas,' a senior administration official said. . . . Officials described Rice as one of the prime movers behind Bush's announcement on Wednesday that he would urge the Supreme Court to strike down Michigan's affirmative action program."[61]

Rice, upset by the article, talked to Fleischer about it. That morning, he telephoned April Ryan, White House correspondent for the American Urban Radio Networks, a group of African-American radio stations, reaching her at the doctor's office with her one-year-old daughter. Fleischer told her that the *Post* piece was incorrect and that Rice wanted to address it in an interview with her. Ryan had a telephone interview with Rice and then aired the story. In no time, Ryan's story was on the Associated Press, and the following day, the *Washington Post* carried this development. "In an interview yesterday with American Urban Radio Networks, Rice said she agrees with affirmative action 'if it does not lead to quotas and if people work hard at it to look at the total individual,'" the *Post* reported. "'It is hard to talk about life experiences, or the experiences of an individual, without recognizing that race is part of that,' she said. Rice told the radio network she has been 'a supporter of affirmative action that is not quota-based and does not seek to make race the only factor.'"[62]

Ryan was not the only reporter to whom Fleischer had spoken. The Associated Press carried another story explaining Rice's anger about the piece and summarizing her discussion about it with President Bush. This story noted that "advisers" had told reporters that Rice was "stung" by the original *Post* story. It continued, "Rice discussed the article with Bush, who urged her to go public with her differences, officials said. Her statement quickly led to speculation that there were sharp differences between Rice and Bush. The adviser made a series of calls to reporters in an effort to dispute such talk."[63]

In short order, Fleischer created such a ruckus about the piece that Mike Getler, ombudsman for the *Washington Post,* wrote a critique of the article's shortcomings. "This was a fascinating, behind-the-scenes look at a different role on a touchy issue for one of the White House's, and the country's, most recognizable figures. Yet there was no indication in the story, by White House reporter Mike Allen and legal affairs reporter Charles Lane, that anyone had asked Rice, or even her aides, whether the portrait of her being painted by the administration officials was accurate. There wasn't even a line saying the paper had tried to reach her, if that was the case. This is pretty fundamental stuff."[64]

Part of the effectiveness of a press secretary comes from the relationship he or she has with the president. The president needs to be willing to listen to the press secretary and accept his counsel. There is an excellent example from the Truman years of the services a press secretary can perform for a president. Press Secretary Charles Ross's value to President Truman became evident after Ross's death. On the morning of December 6, 1950, Truman wrote a letter to *Washington Post* music critic Paul Hume. The evening before, Margaret Truman, the president's daughter, had performed in a concert at Constitution Hall. Hume wrote in the morning paper: "Miss Truman is a unique American phenomenon with a pleasant voice of little size and fair quality. She is extremely attractive on stage," and then added, "Yet Miss Truman cannot sing very well. She is flat a good deal of the time—more so last night than at any time we have heard her in past years."[65] Truman's response was sharp: "I've just read your lousy review of Margaret's concert. Some day I hope to meet you. When that happens you'll need a new nose, a lot of beefsteak for black eyes and perhaps a supporter below."[66]

Truman frequently wrote letters to news organizations, and, as often as he could, Ross intercepted them to avoid unbecoming publicity. The 10,000 letters that resulted from his letter to Hume attested to the costs of Ross's death. Sooner or later, most presidents need a Charlie Ross.

Running the Press Office

The central task of the Press Office has always been the acquisition and delivery of information. As the person who heads the office, the press secretary is responsible for setting up an operation that acquires the kind of information he needs to provide reporters and the public. For the last four decades, the press secretary's administrative role has called for presiding over approximately four daily staff meetings while representing the Press Office in additional White House sessions.

More than anything else, the press secretary's day revolves around the news needs of the gaggle and the daily briefing. While different press secretaries have relied on different information-gathering practices, they have all spent their days preparing to dispense this information. Inevitably, this preparation involves a meeting with the president himself.

The Daily Drill

Mike McCurry's description of a typical day, set forth below, is representative of what other press secretaries describe, as illustrated by occasional comparisons with the routines followed by Marlin Fitzwater, Ari Fleischer, and Scott McClellan. Together their experiences build a portrait of a typical day in the Clinton and Bush years.

Meeting in the Chief's Office: 7:30 a.m. The first of the press secretary's daily meetings usually brings the press secretary together with the president's chief of staff, the chief's deputies, the communications director, the domestic policy chief, and, if foreign policy was in the news, the national security adviser. Officials who have issues in play are the ones who meet to plan the day. Mike McCurry remembers that Chief of Staff Leon Panetta "used to call it the management meeting, because the idea was— the way he kept some people out and other people in, was the senior managers at the White House had to be present, which was a clever way of excluding some people who thought they were important enough to be senior staff. So that was the real meeting at 7:30."[67]

McCurry described the session as follows: "The first meeting was a very candid assessment of what are we going to do today, and how are we going to get through the day, and how is this shaping up and how is that shaping up." While Chief of Staff Andrew Card has a small meeting prior to the senior staff meeting, the press secretary is not included in that session.

Senior Staff Meeting: 8:00 a.m. The senior staff meeting that followed "was the expanded universe of people who were serious players in one way or another." The purpose of this meeting differed from the meeting it followed every morning, as the first was a decision meeting and the second an information one.

As McCurry explained, the senior staff meeting was for "Leon or Leon's designee to really give the marching orders to the entire staff, sometimes based on what had just been decided at the 7:30 meeting. He'd come in and sort of describe 'Here's what we're going to do today, here's how we're going to do it, and here are the assignments for everyone.'" Following the chief of staff's opening, they would "go around the table, and everyone could report in on whatever issues they were dealing with. So it [was about] making sure the rest of the organization knew what your operation was up to that day, and then making sure that the entire staff had some sense of what the primary purpose of the day was."

Marlin Fitzwater, who attended senior staff meetings during the Reagan and the George H. W. Bush administrations, explained why his contributions were unique among the staff. Each morning, when he came into the office, he wrote a "little memo of the stories that I thought we would have to respond to that day. My role at the staff meeting would be always the same: 'Marlin, what do we have to deal with today?' Everybody's got my memo around the table. 'These are the issues. If any of you want to add anything to any of these, or give me any advice, come do it as soon as possible, because I'm going to have to come up with an-swers.'"[68] By letting everyone know what stories he expected to deal with on a particular day, he gave other senior staffers an opportunity to offer their views, thus putting the burden on them for responses. If they had nothing to offer, then they had no reason to complain if they disliked what he said on their behalf during the briefing.

Communications Meeting: 8:30 a.m. When John Podesta became Clin-ton's deputy chief of staff, he arranged for the first two staff meetings to be followed by one devoted to communications. McCurry described its participants and purposes: "That communications meeting really did become kind of the way in which the public relations, public affairs, con-gressional affairs people then intersected with the legal team," he said. "That was what it really was in 1998. Now prior to that, when Podesta first had it, he had everyone who had some responsibility for communi-cations, a communications function. We all kind of got together and just went through, 'What's the message of the day and how are we going to deliver it, who's going to do what.' That was usually a pretty good meet-ing, and we usually came out of that with a good sense of who was going to have what assignments."

Meeting with Press Office Staff: 9:00 a.m. "I went back and had a staff meeting with my staff so the press staff would know, this was what they were going to have to do today, and I could report on other things that they needed to know about. It was a way of keeping my team wired in." Now the press secretary is ready for the gaggle, which took fifteen or twenty minutes most days and was attended by a couple of dozen report-ers from television, radio, and the wire services.

The Gaggle: 9:30 a.m. The first daily exchange of information between the White House and reporters is an informal one that suits the needs of both sides. Picture it as a crowd of around thirty reporters standing around the press secretary's desk for some fast give-and-take. The press secretary uses the session to give reporters the president's schedule and to take care of technical details of the coverage of his events, while letting them know what message the White House wants to emphasize that day. Reporters fish for a sense of how the White House feels about events that may have taken place overnight and about reports that have appeared in the morning papers and on morning newscasts. McCurry assigned a staff person to take notes so that the staff could use them to parcel out assignments following the gaggle. The gaggle is discussed in detail in the following chapter.

Post-Gaggle Meeting: 9:45 a.m. After the gaggle, the press secretary begins preparing for the daily news briefing by assigning members of his staff to obtain various bits of information. Those six or seven people who have titles at the deputy and assistant level are assigned information tasks. The gaggle orients them by letting them know what issues are on reporters' minds. To McCurry's way of thinking, "We had kind of the scratch-and-scrounge part of the day, where you run around and look for the information I needed, or read whatever I needed to read or study, and get on top of an issue. One part of that was to read the news summary much more thoroughly, to really go through all the different stories. Ninety percent of the information about a given thing was coming from the press, not coming from inside the government. I would go down and read the intelligence down in the security room or in the Situation Room. I would generally talk to Clinton. I'd go and see Panetta and then Bowles, and sort of go through my briefing book, sometimes with George [Stephanopoulos], later with Rahm [Emanuel] or others, and say, 'Here are the key questions today.' When we needed to do that with Clinton, we'd go in and see Clinton."

Morning Meeting with the President: Between 10:00 a.m. and 11:00 a.m. Sometimes, but not always, McCurry and the president met alone. McCurry recalled that if Clinton had to "sign a proclamation in the Roosevelt Room, there's going to be a photo opportunity. We'd take that same group, Panetta, Ickes, Bowles, McCurry, Stephanopoulos, sometimes Rahm, sometimes Don Baer, sometimes other people." Once the group was assembled, they would discuss possible scenarios for the "photo op." Based on what McCurry had been asked in the gaggle, he would anticipate questions the president was likely to get: "Here is what they're going to ask you. Clinton's usual response is 'What do I say?' He wanted to hear how someone else was going to propose that he answer it, even though he generally knew what he was going to give as the answer. He would usually say, 'What I'd rather say is. . . .' Sometimes, if it was something he accepted the premise of the answer, he'd go over it and say, 'Let me get it right.' "

While prepping the president, the two of them discussed how much detail he should use in a response: "If he wanted to kind of go chapter and verse on something, and we didn't want him to do that because we wanted to save it for later, or we didn't want him to be the primary person carrying a message, we'd talk about how he could minimize an answer when it was necessary." If the president does not use answers they have worked out for a given topic, then McCurry can use them in his briefing.

The prep group also discusses the stance and tone they want to convey. "Then there were times when it was really tonal quality. If the suggestion was that I go out and mix it up a little bit with the Republicans, or Gingrich, on a certain issue, I wanted to make sure I had clearance from the president on that. He more often dialed me back rather than torqued me up. It was rather interesting, but he was juggling all these conversations that he was having with Gingrich, and he always wanted to be very careful about how much we frontally assaulted the Republicans, and came at it from different angles sometimes."

Conference Call: 11:00 a.m. The conference call connects public information officers from the State and Defense Departments, the Joint Chiefs of Staff, the Central Intelligence Agency, and the United States mission at the United Nations. When Joe Lockhart replaced Mike McCurry as press secretary, he asked the State Department to take the lead on the call, because "they have a much wider brief. They sort of go around the world. The Pentagon will chime in, we'll chime in."[69] The call can take up to an hour. In the G. W. Bush administration, this session is much briefer, lasting around fifteen minutes and confined to the State and Defense Departments and the CIA.[70]

This conference call is followed by a staff meeting in which the deputy and assistant press secretaries report on what they have found to be on the minds of reporters. Lockhart continued, "That's generally the best guide for what's going to get asked. Whatever Barry [Toiv], Amy [Weiss], Jim [Kennedy], David [Leavey], and P. J. [Crowley] are getting is going to be what's going to come up at the briefing." These were all deputies who responded to reporters' queries throughout the day.

In the G. W. Bush White House, the deputy press secretaries were assigned departments to cover through conference calls with their counterparts. Scott McClellan explained how he and Claire Buchan operated as deputies. "Claire and I have daily conference calls with our counterparts in the cabinet agencies [Claire's at 10:15, Scott's at 10:30], and part of that is, every day, just staying on top of gathering information and making sure everybody knows what's going on and what issues may be coming up that day," he said. "Or things that we need their help with in terms of getting information. So I'll deal with Justice, HHS, EPA on environmental issues, Interior. HUD, housing issues. Labor. Veterans Affairs. So there are probably like eight or nine people."[71] After touching base with their departments, they reported to Press Secretary Ari Fleischer, prior to his afternoon briefing.

The Briefing: 1:00 p.m. The most important event in the press secretary's day is the daily briefing. Running approximately thirty minutes in the George W. Bush administration and between thirty and sixty minutes under Clinton, the session is held most days when the president is in town. When he is traveling, daily briefings are fit into the president's travel schedule. The format and dynamics of this crucial information-sharing event are covered in the next chapter.

Afternoon Calls and Appointments: 3:00–6:00 p.m. The press secretary spends most of his afternoons talking on the telephone with reporters and news organizations and doing one-on-one interviews. On Thursday afternoons he generally does one session each with reporters from the major newsweeklies, *Time, Newsweek,* and *US News and World Report.* Every recent administration has followed this tradition. The information they get, commonly referred to as "tick-tock," provides context and color for the stories they must produce for their Saturday deadline.

Here is how Marlin Fitzwater described a typical afternoon: "If I'm in meetings with the president, I would always go back in between to see if there's anybody who's trying to get to me. They come and go. It's just a constant stream of people, usually after lunch, between 1:00 and 5:00. It might be reporters who need new quotes for a story update or one question or two questions for a story they were working on. Once a week you'd meet with the newsmagazines to get in the tick-tock business that they want. And every day about 4:30 or 5:00, each of the networks would call just to get an update: 'Anything new happening?' 'Anything I need to worry about?' 'Anything I need to alert my desk to?' 'We're running a piece tonight on this.' 'Here's our view.' They usually tell you what they're doing."[72]

End of the Day: 6:00 p.m. on. The end of the day generally finds the press secretary with Press Office staff. Several other press secretaries followed

Fitzwater's routine.[73] "That was a locked-door session. No outside guests, no other offices. The rule was, this was the meeting before we all go home in which we hear every complaint, every gripe. Everybody is mad at everybody. We let it all [out], we deal with it. We deal with our problems. My admonition at the beginning was always, 'Look. I know how much abuse you have to take down here during the day, in the Lower Press Office especially,'" Fitzwater remembered.[74] He would joke with the young staffers who had to deal with the likes of Naomi Nover, an eccentric woman in the press corps who sometimes wielded an umbrella or her purse to get what she wanted.[75] "'Not only that, but mad press calling you. Everything is going wrong. By the end of the day you're going to hate the press, you're going to hate yourself, you're going to hate the person at the desk next to you because of something they've done to you. You're going to think the president is stupid, and you're going to hate me.' I said, 'All that's fine. But you've got to conceal it.'" He concluded, "You come back in here at five o'clock, and you can cuss and swear and call people names, call the president a bum or me a bum, whatever you want to do. But we're going to deal with it, get it out, and start over the next day."[76]

A president and his White House staff members have a stake in an effective presidential press secretary. The quality of presidential communications depends on the press secretary's ability to gather accurate information, to give it out to reporters in a timely way, and to be responsive to the queries the White House receives from reporters. While the press secretary does not have the time to work on long-term strategy, he or she is crucial in gathering and disseminating authentic information. In order to be valuable, he or she needs to bring together three constituents: the president, the White House staff, and reporters. With each suspicious of the intentions of the others, the press secretary is the one who can ensure good relationships among them.

While at one time the press secretary focused on providing information and establishing the official record of an administration, today he is part of a communications team that makes use of a wide range of resources to sell the president and his program. With the daily afternoon briefing now televised, the administration can use the press secretary's forum to make swift contact with governments around the world as well as with critics and allies here in the United States.

6

The Gaggle and the Daily Briefing

Following the practice of his predecessors, on most weekdays when the president was in town, Press Secretary Scott McClellan engaged in two public briefing sessions with reporters. While only one source of information among many and far from the only occasion for news-related give-and-take for journalists, these meetings are still important information exchanges for both participants. At the midpoint of the Clinton administration, for example, Associated Press senior correspondent Terry Hunt estimated that he got 40 percent of his information from the two sessions.[1] Both sides learn from these sessions, although the briefings have become less important in some ways as the news cycle has accelerated. For Terry Hunt, though, the two sessions remain important. In August 2006, Hunt said that the 40 percent figure "is somewhat higher, as we are more reliant on the two sessions because of the difficulty in reaching officials by phone."[2]

The first of the two daily sessions is a fifteen-minute morning briefing, informally known as "the gaggle," which through at least two administrations was held in the office of the press secretary at approximately 9:30 a.m. Shortly after September 11, 2001, Press Secretary Ari Fleischer moved the gaggle to the Briefing Room, where it remains. A formal televised session known as "the briefing" or "the daily briefing" is held in the James S. Brady Briefing Room around 12:30 p.m., generally lasting about thirty minutes. In 1999, President Clinton dedicated the room to President Reagan's press secretary who was wounded in an assassination attempt in 1981. While the whole press area underwent reconstruction in 2006 and 2007, the James Brady Briefing Room today occupies the same space that it had in earlier years.

In addition to the daily gaggle and the televised afternoon briefing, there are also specialty briefings to supply supporting information. These sessions can take place in the Briefing Room, via a conference call, or in a staff member's office. The gaggle and the daily briefing have occurred in approximately the same numbers, though in a different form, during the last four administrations, but the frequency and the ground rules for specialty briefings in recent administrations have varied.

While these information sessions differ in substantial ways from comparable sessions held sixty years ago, the routine of two daily news briefings conducted by the president's press secretary has been followed by most administrations since the press post was created. The Nixon, Ford, and Carter administrations held only one daily briefing session. When Ari Fleischer became George W. Bush's press secretary on January 20, 2001, he inherited a set of routines, expectations, and tacit understandings that had been developed very gradually over the course of a century. The reporters he faced were generally the same people who had been there on January 19, when Jake Siewert presided over his final gaggle and daily briefing for Clinton. As press secretaries soon find, the continuities in rules, practices, and reporters covering the institution remain fairly constant within and between administrations.

The Gaggle: Information Curtain Raiser

Referring to its mutually beneficial nature, Joe Lockhart noted that the gaggle represents "a starting point for both of us." Emphasizing its benefits for the White House, he continued, "We get a chance to throw out the schedule, make sure everybody knows [what's going on]. It's sort of a last chance to get everyone interested in whatever the event of the day is and then to lay down whatever tracks we want on stories that are developing, or have developed overnight, react to things in the paper, either knock down a story early or try to pump up a story."[3]

Mark Knoller, who has covered the White House for CBS Radio on and off since the Ford administration, spoke of its usefulness for news organizations: "You get some reaction to things that will be happening that day. You get the rundown of the schedule, some advance word on what the president will be doing. Sometimes that will produce news and I file on that."[4]

The Changing Rhythms of the White House News Day

The gaggle has a fairly short history. No one can definitively pinpoint when the term was first used to refer to the morning session in the press secretary's office, but reporters and officials regularly used it in the Clinton administration. The phrase "to gaggle" is derived from the noise of squawking geese. Either way, it fits a session where reporters are clustered around the press secretary's desk to gather information and pelt him with questions.

The informal session began late in the Reagan administration when Marlin Fitzwater replaced the early morning full-scale briefing held by Larry Speakes with a more informal session in which he revealed details about the president's day. Originally, it was intended to accommodate the need of the wire services, radio, and television for logistical information. Slowly but surely it has evolved into a meeting in which the White House delivers its message of the day and responds to events and stories that have developed overnight, this in part because of the news needs of cable networks and online versions of newspapers. These trends began toward the end of the Clinton administration. Fitzwater noted back in 1999, "The gaggle is more important to them [the Clinton White House] because the fact is that cable systems are going in the morning. When I was there you didn't have television until 6:00 p.m., so the morning was the wires, which was for them the president's schedule."[5] As cable television news shows proliferated and the mid-1990s growth of the Internet ushered in continually updated online versions of newspapers and magazines, the gaggle became the important event for all forms of media it is today.

From Hoover through Johnson, two briefings a day were held in the press secretary's office. There was no formal room dedicated to briefings where all interested parties could gather. The twice-daily briefings were intended to accommodate the needs of the morning and evening newspapers as well as the wire service. The Nixon administration judged two briefings to be one too many. By that time, evening newspapers were gradually going out of business. The administration preferred to work with the rhythms of morning papers and evening newscasts. Jerald ter-Horst and Ron Nessen under Ford and Jody Powell under Carter followed this precedent. In the Reagan administration, Larry Speakes added an early morning session, but Marlin Fitzwater believed there was not enough news to justify two full-scale briefings a day.

While serving as press secretary for Presidents Reagan and George H. W. Bush, Fitzwater developed the gaggle into a regular daily session but used it to supply primarily wire service reporters with the president's schedule. The format was even less formal than is currently the case, although it had devolved somewhat from a more elaborate form. James Brady used to hold a daily session in his office to provide wire service reporters with the president's schedule for that day. "Speakes did it at nine every morning, and invited everyone in until his office got full," noted Fitzwater. "Then when it got too large to hold in his office, he moved it to the Briefing Room."

Once Speakes moved the session into the more formal quarters, he was essentially briefing twice a day. "Truth was that he didn't have enough to say and got into arguments and fights with the press," Fitzwater believed. So when Fitzwater took over, he cancelled the 9:00 a.m. briefing and held a smaller, more informal session in his office. He still attracted a lot of reporters because "when you give out news tips at nine o'clock, then everyone wants to come." In an effort to "limit membership," he tried moving this session into the adjacent hallway. "I talked to them when I came in from the senior staff meeting and then gave out the president's schedule and then escaped into my office."

From his own experience with the format of the gaggle, he maintains, "the lesson is, the only thing you have you can control is yourself," he said. "You can't say, 'I will only take three questions' or 'I will just give it to the wires.'" Consequently, he opted for the strategy of not being available to provide anything more than the presidential schedule. He admits, however, that with today's endless appetite for news, with so many more news organizations and multiple forms of media, his former strategy would have failed: "I wouldn't have been successful in limiting it in today's circumstances, because there are so many news shows in the morning."[6]

The gaggle became firmly established as a daily information session during Mike McCurry's tenure as press secretary. It differs from the daily briefing in two ways. First, the issues addressed in it are less complicated than those tackled in the briefing. Second, the answers given to questions are far less formal and mature.

Nonetheless, the gaggle, like the daily briefing, plays the important integrating role of assembling information from throughout the White House in one central place. Because the press secretary must be familiar with all of the president's activities, plans, and policy stances as well as everything else that may be happening in the White House, every shop in the White House is responsible for updating the press secretary as he prepares for his two daily sessions with reporters. The press secretary reciprocates by distributing summaries in order to let each White House office know what other offices are thinking. So preparing for the gaggle and the daily briefing is also a routine for distilling, integrating, and disseminating information throughout the White House.

First and foremost, the success of this effort depends on the press secretary having a full range of staffers to check in with him whenever necessary. According to Joe Lockhart, "Everybody around the building is on notice that if it's an issue they're concerned about, they need to brief the press secretary, or the press secretary will make it up, causing problems for the policy people. . . . It's mutually assured destruction. It's not because they want to do it. It's because they have to do it. You don't want to roll the dice and have somebody making it up."

Even then, staffers with information to report understand that the gaggle is less important than the daily briefing. "For the gaggle, sort of the accepted rule is, if you just want to swing by—if Chris Jennings [deputy for domestic policy] on health policy just wants to swing by and say, 'Here's what you should say,' that's fine with me," said Lockhart. The press secretary can then take some notes and "if it gets complicated and detailed, I'll kick it to one o'clock." For the daily briefing, however, preparing the press secretary is a more formal obligation: "For the briefing you need to do a piece of paper."[7]

When Ari Fleischer became George W. Bush's press secretary, he too held a fifteen-minute morning session in his office. Not until after September 11 did he opt for more formality and greater control by moving it to the Briefing Room. Like Marlin Fitzwater, he had found it difficult to avoid taking more questions when everyone was in his office. Fleischer lamented, "You get ten people in here who say, 'Just one more minute,' all of them want another five or ten. I can't get people out of my office. And I don't have the time in the day to do that. The gaggle is supposed to be fifteen minutes, and the gaggle has become just a second briefing. It's a serious session."[8]

From the time Mike McCurry did the job for Clinton through the early Bush days until September 11, there was a simple routine to the morning session. As 9:15 approached, reporters assembled outside the two doors of the press secretary's office. Some stood in the hallway that connects the press secretary's office to the Oval Office, about fifty feet away. Others waited in a narrow interior hallway near the desks of the assistants to the press secretary. By the time one of those assistants opened the two doors to give them entry, about thirty reporters were ready to crowd in.

While today's gaggles are held in the Briefing Room, the ground rules remain fairly similar. Reporters place their tape recorders on the podium in front of the press secretary as the session begins. No television cameras are allowed to roll, no photographs can be taken, and tape recorders may be used only for the purpose of quoting the press secretary's remarks accurately—not for playing his voice on the air. The one camera allowed to operate is perched on the ceiling of the Briefing Room. It televises every session throughout the White House residence, the West Wing, and the Eisenhower Executive Office Building. This innovation arrived early in the Clinton administration. The White House Communications Agency is responsible for the operation of this internal system, which covers both daily briefing sessions and any specialty sessions held in this room. This agency also splices segments of the evening network news into a tape that is broadcast internally on the following day, usually around midday.

The gaggle's question-and-answer session lasts for fifteen minutes and typically includes questions from a dozen or more reporters. While the White House creates a transcript of the session, it is only available to those in the administration—it does not circulate to reporters. "If the gaggle starts to circulate, the people who come out every day are disenfranchised," explained Fleischer in early 2001. By withholding the transcript from reporters who were not present, the White House is encouraging people to attend. "I think the gaggle is a White House press corps event in this office, and I think that's good for the press and good for the White House."[9] The White House benefits when a substantial number of reporters are present because the press secretary can learn what is on their minds, what issues reporters believe are cooking that day.

During the Clinton years, the gaggle lasted somewhat longer, permitting around forty answers from the press secretary to many more queries called out by reporters, often simultaneously. In four fairly typical sessions, McCurry responded from 26 to 46 times.[10] In a 1996 session in which reporters asked about the White House security office's illegal accumulation of FBI files on Republicans, leadership questions at the United Nations, and a possible settlement in the Paula Jones case, much more time was needed to dispose of reporters' queries.[11] In that session, McCurry gave approximately seventy-five responses to reporters ranging from detailed answers to telling the reporter he would mention the issue at his daily briefing. Many of McCurry's sessions lasted closer to twenty-five minutes than the fifteen assigned in his schedule.

In contrast, on three consecutive July days in 2005 when Scott McClellan was responding to questions on Karl Rove as an information leaker, he answered an average of twenty-three questions in each session, and none of the sessions lasted the full fifteen minutes.[12] The McClellan sessions were smaller than the ones McCurry held and convened earlier in the morning. The second of the three July 2005 sessions, for example, was convened at 8:39 a.m. Early sessions generally draw smaller groups of reporters, sometimes as few as fifteen.

While there may be as many as thirty questions in a gaggle when there is breaking news, those queries come from a fairly consistent group of reporters. In looking at some of the basic elements of the gaggle in the Bush era, an average of ten reporters ask questions in what is almost always a fifteen-minute session, no longer and no shorter. But the number of reporters can vary depending upon how early the gaggle is held and how hot the day's issues are.

The reporters at the gaggle tend to be ones from media with rolling deadlines. These are the wire services—particularly Associated Press and Reuters—radio, and television, including CNN and Fox News and the three networks. No matter how early the gaggle is convened, representatives of those news organizations are always present. Newspaper and magazine reporters are much less likely to attend, and when they do, it is mostly to sample the atmosphere rather than to get substantive information for a particular story. Generally, information presented in the gaggle concerns short-term schedules and immediate allocations of resources, including time. It is not a place for important policy announcements. Even formal statements tend to come at the 2:30 p.m. daily briefing, unless there is an overnight development of a breaking story that requires an immediate response.

Orienting Reporters

"The gaggle is the primary indicator of the day's direction," recalled Mark Felsenthal, who covered the White House for the Bureau of National Affairs, a group of business dailies. "It serves as the road map for the day. It generates two or three story directions that I am either going to have to follow up on or monitor through the course of a day."[13]

Having a "road map for the day" helps reporters budget their time and choose the resources they will use to produce their stories. "A more practical use is the guidance for the day, so you know where you are going to be and what you will need," said Ken Bazinet, who at the time reported on the White House for United Press International.

In an important way, the gaggle represents the end of the preceding news day. For the wire services, the gaggle occurs at the end of the p.m. news cycle. "Within that news cycle comes the gaggle," continued Bazinet. "That cycle is intricate, because you have to match the stories the metropolitan newspapers are printing, particularly the *New York Times,* the *Washington Post,* and others on a catch-as-catch-can basis, including the *Los Angeles Times,* the *Boston Globe,* and the *Wall Street Journal.*"[14] The gaggle permits wire service reporters to get the administration's response to stories appearing in the morning in newspapers and on television. Afterward, Press Office staff goes to work preparing for the formal afternoon briefing.

The White House operates with an accurate view of how the gaggle benefits reporters covering the president, and it does its best to serve them accordingly. "I think they use it to get a sense of what we're selling on any given day, and then what they can expect our first line of defense to be, on whatever they think is the main story," said Lockhart.[15]

Educating Press Officers

In addition to introducing their messages for the day, the Press Office uses the early morning gaggle to take its measure of the press corps and to learn what reporters are thinking. When they read reporters accurately, they have a sense of what to expect at that day's daily briefing. There are a number of reporters who are known to preview their briefing questions in the gaggle.

This early-warning system is important: because the daily briefing is televised, missteps there are far more costly. One reporter who asks questions in a particular policy area recalls that when she first came to the White House and asked her policy questions in the briefing, a Press Office deputy told her the routine: ask your questions in the gaggle—and only then in the daily briefing.[16]

Being able to predict what questions someone will ask in press briefings or press conferences makes an enormous difference to the officials responsible for those sessions. Press Secretary Ari Fleischer identified the gaggle as the second of three warning systems that prepared him for his day: "I've found that there are three warning systems about where the press is going that day, what the news is. One is the morning papers. Two is the gaggle. The third is to think like a reporter yourself, to know what questions you're going to get, because this is what reporters think about. I think every press secretary has to have radar antennae that allow them to think like a reporter so they know what the storyline of the day could be."[17] In short, the gaggle permits each side to sniff out the other.

The gaggle can be very useful for the indications it provides of issues on which the press secretary needs to get up to speed. The press secretary often gives incomplete and tentative answers in the gaggle, only to realize that a more comprehensive answer is needed. The day following the congressional testimony of Michael Brown, former director of the Federal Emergency Management Administration, in the wake of the 2005 Gulf Coast hurricane and flooding catastrophe, McClellan gave a brief answer in the gaggle to a question relating to the gutting of FEMA during the Bush administration. Note the differences in McClellan's response in the two sessions to the same basic question. In the morning gaggle, Peter Maer, CBS Radio, asked McClellan:

Q: So has FEMA been emaciated over the past three years?

MR. MCCLELLAN: As you know, Congress and the President made a decision to create the Department of Homeland Security in the aftermath of September 11th. And as part of that, they merged some 22 agencies under one umbrella so that we could focus our resources on making sure that we were prepared—fully prepared for terrorist attacks and fully prepared to respond to catastrophic events. And we support Secretary Chertoff's leadership and his efforts, and that's the way I would talk about it.

Q: I mean, here you have the guy that the President put in charge of FEMA, and he says that over the past three years under this administration's watch, that agency, that important agency was, in his words, "emaciated."

MR. MCCLELLAN: You have his—you have his comments from yesterday.

Q: Right. And I'm asking you—

MR. MCCLELLAN: And I'm expressing our views.

Q: But I don't think you answered the question, Scott. I mean—

MR. MCCLELLAN: Well, I think you have to talk about the overall picture, and that's what I was doing.[18]

Contrast this with McClellan's response three hours later at the briefing to the same question posed based on Brown's testimony that FEMA had been "emaciated" over the course of the administration. Based on the questions asked at the gaggle about FEMA, McClellan put together a mature answer for the briefing as a result of information he and his staff had pulled together in the interim.

Q: Thank you. Following up on what you just said about lessons learned, and you've repeatedly said you want to fix what went wrong. To what extent did

Mr. Brown advance that goal of fixing what went wrong or learning lessons when he said that FEMA had been emaciated by this administration over the past three years?

MR. MCCLELLAN: Well, the hearings are just getting underway, so this is part of Congress moving forward on their responsibility to look at these issues and to help us learn the facts, and to help us apply the lessons learned, and so that yesterday was just—really the process getting underway. And so we look forward to seeing what others have to say, and we look forward to learning what all the facts are.

Q: Is that an accurate statement, though, that he made, Scott, about FEMA being emaciated?

MR. MCCLELLAN: Well, let me point out the record and the facts. And Secretary Chertoff actually spoke about the steps that we've been taking to bolster our preparedness and our response efforts.

Under this administration the core FEMA budget has increased from $693 million in '01 to over $1 billion in '05. That's for the core FEMA programs, minus the disaster relief funds. Now from year to year, some of that budget is going to vary, depending on the different levels of disasters that occur. But just from fiscal year '04 to fiscal year '06, we have increased the overall budget by some 13 percent. So I think it's important to look at the record and look at the steps that we've taken.

The core full-time work force at FEMA has grown by approximately 23 percent, from 1,907 full-time individuals to—that was in fiscal '01 to 2,350, I believe, today.

Now, again, the overall budget will vary from year to year because of the disasters that occur, the different levels of disasters that occur. But it's not enough just to look at this in the context of FEMA. You have to look at it in the overall preparedness efforts. First responder funding under this administration has dramatically increased from some $464 million in '01 to $4 billion per year in fiscal year 2005. Close to $15 billion has been sent to state and local first responders under this President. And you also have to look at the massive investments that have been made in public health systems in the aftermath of September 11th, as well.

Secretary Chertoff talked at length yesterday about some of these issues. He talked about the new structure and strategy he was putting in place to revamp and bolster our preparedness work. I would encourage you to look at that speech. He talked about how they are focused on the full range of our capabilities to prevent, protect against and respond to acts of terror or other disasters. And he's outlined a plan for improvement. And what he intends to do is really take the Department's existing preparedness efforts and integrate them into a single directorate of preparedness.

Now, FEMA will continue to report directly to the Secretary with enhanced capabilities. It has a historic and vital mission to support response and recovery, and it must continue to be strengthened to enable it to work well in support of state and local officials.[19]

In addition to giving the press secretary an opportunity to develop mature answers to questions he learns are on reporters' minds, the gaggle also provides the White House with a forum in which to test-market new initiatives. "It is also useful, to very useful, for us to know what the press is interested in, and you can generally at the end of the gaggle say, 'Okay, whatever we're selling today, they're not buying,'" said Lockhart. "Most days we don't change post-gaggle, but there is a rare occasion where we realize that we have to sharpen up the language or be a little tighter in focus or more expansive, including some things."[20]

When there is an initiative the president and his staff want to highlight, the gaggle is the place to begin the process of information distribution. In a typical gaggle held during the summer of 1996, Press Secretary McCurry previewed and laid out the line for the day by describing a speech the president would deliver to the American Nursing Association later in the day. "We will take the most significant step yet to reform welfare as we know it by issuing directives today that will greatly enhance the capacity of our welfare system to collect payments from those who should rightfully take responsibility for parenting a child in this world, principally fathers," said McCurry. To buttress their case, handouts were in the works and would be distributed when ready: "There will be a lot of paper that we will be able to give to you. I'd like to give that out before the president's remarks this morning, so that you can start looking through it, because it is pretty weighty."[21]

Prior to the gaggle, senior members of the Press Office discuss issues and questions arising from news stories that appeared overnight on the wire services, radio, and television and found a place in the morning newspapers. If there is a story that needs knocking down, the press secretary will handle it in the gaggle. Because wire service, radio, and television reporters attend the gaggle, it is a good vehicle for getting a message into the news stream quickly. All of these reporters have the capacity to go live—if necessary, immediately.

On July 18, 1996, the morning after the TWA plane went down over Long Island Sound, McCurry quickly let people know what the facts of the case appeared to be, how the president was told of the crash and his response, and what the president was doing to discover the reason for the plane crash. McCurry led off the morning gaggle with a rundown on each point. As soon as he was finished with the short version of the facts, several of the reporters present left to file their stories without waiting for the question-and-answer part of the session. Ten minutes later or so, when the gaggle was over, the television in the Lower Press Office, continually tuned to CNN, showed Wolf Blitzer on the North Lawn of the White House wrapping up his account of what McCurry had just said.

McCurry himself learned to use the gaggle to do things that might be too harsh or risky to do in the daily briefing. When he wanted to castigate a newspaper or magazine, for example, he could deliver a strong message in the gaggle that would not be associated with the president's voice, face, or even, in visible form anyway, his press secretary.

When leaks of testimony given by White House officials during their appearances before the grand jury convened by Special Prosecutor Kenneth Starr began to circulate in the press, McCurry became the point man delivering White House criticism. On February 6, 1998, for example, the day President Clinton was to hold a joint press conference with British Prime Minister Tony Blair, McCurry used that morning's gaggle to deliver stiff criticism of these leaks. "This is the second day in a row that there is an alleged leak of grand jury testimony," he said. "Two days, two sets of testimony. . . . This is a very dangerous environment now."[22] Reporters quickly understood that they had been given a strong message of the displeasure of the White House over the leaks, and several wire reporters left to file their stories before the gaggle was concluded.

Even when he uses the gaggle to deliver criticism, the press secretary can engage in good-humored banter with reporters, as a reminder that they have common interests as insiders. Even in the Bush administration, the gaggle retains its informal tone and serves to reinforce camaraderie rather than antagonism.

In the days when no transcript was made and the contents of this information were restricted to reporters and Press Office officials alone, press secretaries were freer to discuss subjects they could not bring up in the televised daily briefing. On March 14, 1994, when President Clinton was going to Florida to play golf with Greg Norman, McCurry got into a private conversation with reporters that threw some light on his relationship with the president. A reporter asked him if he would be accompanying the president to Florida. McCurry responded that he was not. Did he not want to play golf with the president? No, he responded. Don't you want to be the president's friend? posed another reporter. No, I'm at the White House to do a job. McCurry was shrewdly reminding reporters of their links, but such banter might have caused him problems if it had been televised.[23]

Negotiating Ground Rules for Coverage

When the gaggle was held in the press secretary's office and, just as important, when there was no transcript of the session circulating around the White House, the morning session was an informal one. Reporters felt much freer when they came into his office and spoke with him than they did in the Bush years when they met with him in a formal session in the Press Room and a transcript was sent around the administration. At the September 4, 1996, gaggle, McCurry told reporters the president wouldn't say anything newsworthy to high school "presidential scholars." "He'll talk about the Fellows program. Not terribly newsworthy, but those of you [interested in local news], you guys will want to get the list of who they are and where they are from." There are issues one can discuss among colleagues in the gaggle that one cannot in the briefing. Shortly after the Monica Lewinsky scandal broke, news organizations put pressure on their reporters to track down the issue in an aggressive manner, but White House reporters felt uncomfortable about asking the president about his sex life. Following the candid revelations published in the *Washington Post* on January 21, 1998, White House correspondents wondered what line the questioning would take when Prime Minister Tony Blair visited President Clinton and the two of them held a joint news conference. Recognizing how small-minded their questioning about Lewinsky might appear and feeling uncomfortable with the whole subject, the president of the White House Correspondents' Association, Laurence McQuillan of Reuters, asked Press Secretary McCurry whether there was some way of holding a session in which reporters could ask the president about Lewinsky, a solution that would permit them to devote their attention to international issues when Blair and Clinton appeared together.[24] McCurry replied that he saw no way to work out such an arrangement.

He reminded them that they had tried to deal with the controversial fund-raising issues by holding a short question-and-answer session with the president on his trip to Latin America. As McCurry anticipated, reporters brought up the Lewinsky issue in the joint press conference that was to be devoted to foreign policy questions.

These negotiations over the ground rules for the Lewinsky scandal were an attempt to reach an informal agreement between partners in an ongoing professional relationship. The attempt was important for both sides, even though they were unable to avoid what reporters found a distasteful public discussion of the president's personal life for most of 1998.

In the gaggle reporters sometimes try to see what changes can be made in the day's ground rules to provide them with information they seek. When they want to negotiate ground rules for covering an event, they try to negotiate privately or in the gaggle, rather than the daily briefing.

More routinely, reporters ask the press secretary if he can get a change in White House briefing plans to accommodate their needs and if he will give them a sense of how newsworthy an event might be. On one occasion, McCurry told reporters that a State Department spokesperson would brief them about a bombing. "Will that be on camera then?" asked a reporter. "We'll let you know. I am working on it. I'm leaning on them, leaning on them, we'll see," responded McCurry.[25]

The Afternoon Briefing: Information with Politics

The press secretary's daily news briefing has several basic elements. It is another information-sharing session that benefits both the White House and the press. The White House puts forth messages it wishes to publicize and responds to queries about the president's intentions, actions, and policies. Both the kinds of questions it gets and which reporters are asking them provide the press secretary with a reading of the subjects that interest news organizations and the assessments that reporters are making of public opinion.

The challenge for the presiding press secretary is to accomplish several different objectives in thirty to forty minutes. These goals generally include announcements of new policy, responses to the actions and criticisms of others, satisfaction of the information-seeking agendas of reporters, and comments on breaking news. This is how Mike McCurry discussed the range of briefing needs. "The problem with the format and the problem with the job is that you have to wear different hats at different moments. Sometimes you have to be giving a formal declaration of

U.S. policy, particularly when it's a question of foreign policy and that has to be read in just the right way and has to be communicated in a way in which it's the government speaking," he began. "There are other times when you're sort of being political and doing combat with the other team. There are other times when you're just getting raw information in front of reporters so they can do the primal function of reporting the news."[26]

Though less so than in the gaggle, recent press secretaries have also had to fend off fallout from the short news cycle felt in the daily briefing. The gaggle remains the first information-sharing opportunity of the day, just as it was in earlier times. Rarely does the press secretary release information before the gaggle. But a lot of information now goes out by e-mail, and White House officials, including the press secretary, frequently appear on the morning television programs with the White House response to an issue or event. All of this takes place prior to the briefing.

Because the rapid-fire twenty-four-hour news cycle requires the White House to issue a continuous stream of information rather than the two-a-day releases of yesteryear, the content of the early afternoon briefing is also different. The briefing is no longer the source of news it once was. During most of the century, the press secretary's daily briefing has been a primary source of news stories. Those days are over. "Most days we don't have announcements. The briefing has changed," observed Joe Lockhart. "It's a completely different thing than it used to be, with twenty-four-hour news services. It used to be that you made news in the briefing, that you announced things. You announced policy." There were breaks so that reporters could file hot stories and then return to their seats for the remainder of the briefing. "We don't do that anymore. It's now news happens and nothing holds. The briefing is more of a. . . . People know what your policy is, and it's a chance to poke some holes in it, or what your announcements are, because they've seen it on CNN."[27] As a result, the briefing has moved from being an activator of policy to a reactive forum in which reporters ask questions about policies that have already been revealed or announced.

Moreover, because less briefing time is spent making news, more time is spent on critique. The briefing has become a venue in which policies are criticized and in which the press secretary is prodded to make remarks about how others have responded to presidential initiatives. When the agenda shifts to critique, discussions between officials and reporters can quickly turn acrimonious.

Built-In Tensions and the Resulting Resolution

More than half a century ago, Leo Rosten, in his book about Washington correspondents, wrote about the tensions inherent in operating between national officials and reporters. "The newspaperman, motivated by the ancient values of journalism, is interested in precisely that type of news which the official is least eager to reveal," he noted. "In the final analysis, the press conference reduced itself to a contest between reporters skilled in ferreting and officials adept in straddling."[28] The same is true of the daily briefing, which still finds reporters "ferreting" and officials "straddling."

The press secretary's daily briefings are staged events in which he or she is rarely surprised by questions or thrown off his prepared scenario, and he or she almost never provides a response that was not intended. At the same time, briefing reporters is a tough assignment, which sometimes leads to raised voices and charges that the White House is holding back information reporters regard as essential to their work. The more familiar the press secretary is with internal White House maneuverings and the more he or she knows about the president's thinking about matters likely to come up at briefing sessions, the more likely he or she is to have a successful day at the podium. In addition, it helps for him or her to be well versed in the intricacies of administration policy and to have at least one major policy area to fall back on when he or she needs relief from questions he or she wants to avoid. Ari Fleischer could filibuster on tax and budget issues, while Mike McCurry used foreign policy to cool down a room hot with scandal talk.

The atmosphere in the room gets its hottest when the press secretary's earlier assurances come into question. Take the case of Press Secretary Scott McClellan defending his previous statements that Karl Rove had played no role in revealing the identity of CIA agent Valerie Plame. On September 16, 2003, McClellan called such charges "totally ridiculous."[29] At the October 10, 2003, briefing, reporters questioned him about it in more detail.[30] They sought to pin down the press secretary from a variety of angles on the Rove matter:

> Q: Scott, earlier this week you told us that neither Karl Rove, Elliot Abrams nor Lewis Libby disclosed any classified information with regard to the leak. I wondered if you could tell us more specifically whether any of them told any reporter that Valerie Plame worked for the CIA?

MR. MCCLELLAN: Those individuals—I talked—I spoke with those individuals, as I pointed out, and those individuals assured me they were not involved in this. And that's where it stands.

Q: So none of them told any reporter that Valerie Plame worked for the CIA?

MR. MCCLELLAN: They assured me that they were not involved in this.

Q: Can I follow up on that?

Q: They were not involved in what?

MR. MCCLELLAN: The leaking of classified information.

Q: Did you undertake that on your own volition, or were you instructed to go to these—

MR. MCCLELLAN: I spoke to those individuals myself.

It took a year and ten months for this issue to resurface in the Briefing Room. When *Time* correspondent Matthew Cooper revealed that he had testified before a grand jury that Karl Rove had been one of his sources, White House correspondents confronted McClellan at his daily briefing on July 11, 2005. NBC White House Correspondent David Gregory sharply questioned McClellan:

MR. MCCLELLAN: And if you will recall, I said that as part of helping the investigators move forward on the investigation we're not going to get into commenting on it. That was something I stated back near that time, as well.

Q: Scott, I mean, just—I mean, this is ridiculous. The notion that you're going to stand before us after having commented with that level of detail and tell people watching this that somehow you decided not to talk. You've got a public record out there. Do you stand by your remarks from that podium, or not?

MR. MCCLELLAN: And again, David, I'm well aware, like you, of what was previously said, and I will be glad to talk about it at the appropriate time. The appropriate time is when the investigation—

Q: Why are you choosing when it's appropriate and when it's inappropriate?

MR. MCCLELLAN: If you'll let me finish—

Q: No, you're not finishing—you're not saying anything. You stood at that podium and said that Karl Rove was not involved. And now we find out that he spoke out about Joseph Wilson's wife. So don't you owe the American public a fuller explanation? Was he involved, or was he not? Because, contrary to what you told the American people, he did, indeed, talk about his wife, didn't he?

MR. MCCLELLAN: David, there will be a time to talk about this, but now is not the time to talk about it.

Q: Do you think people will accept that, what you're saying today?

MR. MCCLELLAN: Again, I've responded to the question.[31]

While David Gregory may have had the harshest tone of the press secretary's questioners, Dana Milbank of the *Washington Post* questioned McClellan's credibility even more directly:

Q: Scott, I think you're barraged today in part because we—it is now clear that 21 months ago, you were up at this podium saying something that we now know to be demonstratively false. Now, are you concerned that in not setting the record straight today that this could undermine the credibility of the other things you say from the podium?

MR. MCCLELLAN: Again, I'm going to be happy to talk about this at the appropriate time. Dana, you all—you and everybody in this room, or most people in this room, I should say, know me very well and they know the type of person that I am. And I'm confident in our relationship that we have. But I will be glad to talk about this at the appropriate time, and that's once the investigation is complete. I'm not going to get into commenting based on reports or anything of that nature.[32]

McClellan faced two sessions a day of this for the better part of two weeks. Not until President Bush nominated Judge John Roberts for a Supreme Court vacancy on July 19, 2005, did the focus of the twice-daily briefing sessions change.

Contention at this level is as inevitable as it is distasteful. After all, the White House intends the briefing to provide reporters with information favorable to the president and his policies. Reporters and their news organizations succeed by exploring undersides and exposing secrets. The opposing goals of the two parties mean that there will always be tension underlying the surface bonhomie.

Terry Hunt, senior White House correspondent for the Associated

Press and a veteran front-row observer of the daily briefing, emphasized the challenge of the job of briefing reporters about contentious issues. "People who go out there and dance on that high wire every day and not fall off are remarkable," he said. "It's a tough job, coming out here, and standing before thirty or forty people [whose] job is to pick at what you say. . . . You come up with some information you want to present, and then they are going to pick it apart and look for the flaws in it."

Hunt points out that "not everybody can do it. I've seen people here who have been disasters. Deputy press secretaries who, when the principal is not here, come up and try to do it. You see them up there with trembling hands and sweat pouring down their face. I think that anybody who gets up there and does that job well is extraordinary."[33]

Perhaps the biggest challenge is for a press secretary to shape the tone and the direction of a briefing. Marlin Fitzwater always came to the daily briefing armed to reduce its inherent risks. His strategy was to learn five things about each of the five biggest issues. He would conclude each of his prep sessions with his staff by reviewing each of the top issues he would face. He recalled, "And at the end of that meeting were always the top five issues. I always felt that if I could get the top five issues on the minds of the press corps, and if I knew five facts about each one of them, I was smarter than they were. I could get through any briefing with that advantage. The worst case is when you go out and you don't get a subject they're interested in or you're just unprepared." He would assign each member of his staff a different issue. The guidance he sought "was basically a half page of background that tells me what the issue was and a half page that tells me what to say."[34]

When an issue is hot or when the press secretary needs help, the staff gets behind their chief. NSC press aide James Fetig discussed how he would slip information to McCurry when he was briefing at the podium. He noted that if a staff person was watching the briefing and noticed that McCurry needed information or made an error, he would be paged to supply the correct information. "That was an interesting way of slipping [in information] so that the question could be answered in real time before the briefing closed, or if you made a mistake they would send down the correction. Maybe he used the wrong word, or 'misdescribed' something, so he could correct it right there in the same briefing. So you didn't have a bad news story result, or one that would mislead or cause a problem."[35] Correcting mistakes as quickly as possible instills confidence in those conducting the briefings.

Setup and Protocol

At one time all of the press secretary's briefings were held in his office. There was no Briefing Room, no press area over the swimming pool.[36] Until the Nixon administration, reporters were housed in the West Wing near the lobby, an area that today is home to the office of the national security adviser.

As the number of journalists covering the White House increased, there was a need for better accommodations. In 1969 the Briefing Room was created adjacent to the West Wing by putting a floor over the swimming pool. Behind it, booths were built for sets of wire service, television, and radio reporters. Print reporters were assigned desk space. When cable television came to the White House, each network received space in the basement, where the soundproof radio booths were located.

In 1981, at the beginning of the Reagan administration, old green leather couches and randomly placed chairs in the Briefing Room were replaced with forty-eight theater-style seats arranged in eight rows of six each. The communications priorities of the White House were reflected in the seating assignments. Television and the wires come first. As the press secretary sees it from the raised podium, the seats starting from the right are reserved for the following news organizations: NBC, the Associated Press, CBS, Helen Thomas, ABC, and Reuters.

Helen Thomas covered the White House for United Press International from 1961 to 2000. At that time, she left to work for Hearst Newspapers; in honor of her seniority, the plaque on the chair was changed from "U.P.I." to "Helen Thomas." Behind the wire services and the television networks come the leading newspapers and cable television networks. The second row, starting with the press secretary's right, has seats assigned to the following: *Wall Street Journal*, Fox News, *Los Angeles Times*, CNN, *Washington Post*, and the *New York Times*.

There are three and sometimes four more rows of reporters who get called on, but the press secretary almost never reaches the two back rows when he or she looks for questioners. Nor does the wire service reporter look to the back of the room for every person with a hand up. He does make certain, though, that all of the regular reporters get their questions in before he signals the press secretary that it is time to call it a wrap. When he is present, Steve Holland of Reuters signals to the press secretary when the time has come to end the session. That it is a press person who by tradition calls an end to briefing relates to the purpose of the briefing. It is supposed to be a session informing reporters, so journalists are the ones who get to determine when they have received sufficient information from that briefing. (The press secretary does in fact wait for the signal. One day, a briefing run by Tony Snow lasted more than an hour because the only wire service reporter present was unaware of the rules: "By tradition, you get the senior wire service reporter to say 'thank you' to put an end to it. You're always hoping they will say 'thank you' before you get to that [outlandish questions]. Sometimes they do, sometimes they don't. I had to take the highly unusual step in one case of putting an end to a briefing after an hour and fifteen minutes because one of the junior Reuters people didn't know to say 'thank you.' "[37] Snow held to the rule as long as he realistically could.)

While representatives from news organizations warranting seats in the first two rows are almost always there, occupants of the remaining seats are less faithful. Often reporters without assigned seats will take any seat that happens to be vacant. Protocol requires that the usurper relinquish the seat if its rightful owner finally shows up.

Those sitting in the front two rows of the Briefing Room dominate the daily briefing. Table 10 indicates the percentage of his time that the Press Secretary Scott McClellan spent in selected briefings in 2005 answering questions from reporters in the first two rows and then from the remaining six rows.

Journalists who come into the daily briefing represent a mixture of reporters regularly assigned to cover the White House and ones who are only there for that day's session. Those assigned to cover the White House have "hard" passes. Reporters receive them following a request from their news bureau that they be credentialed to cover the White House on a daily basis. The Secret Service conducts a background investigation of each of the reporters after the Press Office passes the names on. The number of hard passes held fairly steady from the Reagan administration through the early months of the George W. Bush administration. During those twenty years, the number hovered at around 1700. Since September 11, 2001, hard passes are restricted to those who regularly come to the White House. In renewing passes, the Press Office and the Secret Service check how often the reporters have entered the White House in order to establish the need for such a credential. Now there are approximately 800 hard pass holders. Reporters without a hard pass must get their news organization to call them in for the day.

Everyone in the Briefing Room, officials and reporters alike, is quite

Table 10. Percentage of Press Secretary Time Spent
Responding to Reporters in Selected Daily Briefings, 2005

2005	% of Total Q&A Minutes	% of Reporters Recognized
Row 1	32.0	29.7
Rows 1 and 2	61.7	57.2
Rows 3–8	38.3	42.8

Source: Author's notes. Percentage figures are tabulated for each briefing and then averaged in the selected categories for the group of nineteen briefings.

aware that it is being televised. Televising the briefing influences not only the language people use but also the way they deport themselves and the messages they send.

With its transcript circulating almost immediately, the daily briefing has taken on increased importance. Yet on most days, fewer reporters now attend than before. Thanks to television, they watch the session in their offices, where they do not have to wait around for the session to start, which is frequently much later than the scheduled time. Thanks, too, to the Federal News Service and the Press Office, transcripts are available from both sources. Reporters who choose to watch or read from elsewhere, however, miss the opportunity to ask questions of their own, of course. Nor can they take advantage of the give and take that often takes place as they accompany briefers into the hallways and their offices.

How a reporter asks a question also affects the prevailing atmosphere. It is difficult to get it just right. Once, when a reporter for a major news organization new to the briefing asked questions of Press Secretary McCurry that one veteran of the beat regarded as too soft, the experienced reporter took the correspondent aside, reminded him the briefings were on television, and told him that his questions were making them look like "ass kissers."[38]

Self-Serving Strategies and Angles

Many reporters believe that a televised briefing requires them to show the company flag seriously. "Another aspect of the briefing is the public representation of your news organization," said one reporter. "To some extent, reporters feel it is important to be there and show their face and show the seriousness of their news organization with their questions.

By showing my face, asking questions, I become a force to be reckoned with."[39]

Occupying the seat assigned to their news organization is another aspect of "being present." One journalist remembers his wife's surprise when he told her about booting a pregnant woman from his seat.[40] The principle of holding company territory outweighs questions of etiquette. Even if a reporter arrives late, he or she almost always makes a point of claiming his or her own assigned seat over just any seat in the back. There is prestige attached to the placement of the seats, and daily attendance is important to hold a news organization's location. Neither reporters nor White House officials regard seating placement as a casual matter. One of the biggest issues the White House Correspondents Association has had to deal with in its representation of reporters is their recommendation for changes in seat assignments. Reporters do not take a shift to the back rows lightly.

Some reporters use the televised briefing to grab air time for favored issues. There have always been reporters who have come to the Briefing Room to ask on-the-record questions dealing with the special niche their news organization represents. Now that the daily briefings are televised, this practice has increased. Early in the Monica Lewinsky scandal, aware that all of the cable networks and some of the traditional ones were televising the briefing, reporters flocked to the Briefing Room with agendas extending far beyond the news of the day. On January 21, 1998, Miguel Sandoval, who writes on issues relating to Cuba, engaged in the following exchange with Mike McCurry. Sandoval, not among the 34,396 national and regional journalists listed in the *News Media Yellow Book,* is unlikely to attract the spotlight unless he insinuates himself into someone else's stage.[41]

> Q: Mike, on another development, the 15th of February will be the centennial of the sinking of the Maine in Havana—yesterday the Pope was there and explained that the embargo is hindering the population of Cuba, mainly the women and people of African descent, who in 1779, 1,100—Cubans came here under the order of—
>
> MR. MCCURRY: What's the question? That's enough. Please pose your question . . .
>
> Q: —the women of Havana sold their jewelry and made a give [sic] of $1.3 million to George Washington and they make—

MR. MCCURRY: Please pose the question.

Q: —is now an opportunity to consider the right to become—aware in 1988 and—whether the United States—

MR. MCCURRY: Okay, I think this is yet another example of why these things should not be on live television. [Laughter][42]

Other reporters have self-serving routines of their own. Television reporters sometimes pose questions that will give them video clips suitable for stories scheduled for their evening news programs. They are seeking images as well as information. Thanks to his heated exchange with Scott McClellan about Karl Rove, for example, David Gregory's day at work merited coverage on the *NBC Nightly News* that evening. Such confrontations usually end up on MSNBC news programs as well as the *Nightly News*. Thus, interesting video with their White House correspondents included gets used in a variety of places.

Reporters for major newspapers will press the press secretary to get administration views and policy explanations on the record. Wire service reporters tend to be more interested in responses to late-breaking stories. Radio reporters need sound for the stories they are working on, so they will use the briefing to get a clip of the press secretary speaking on the subject of their story.

For most reporters, phrasing the question is a matter of shaping a query in such a way that it will bring out the information one is seeking. Radio reporter Mark Knoller characterized his approach to questions, which is one shared by many: "I think that you get a better response if it is a clever question, or if it is a question that is encased with humor, but can still be pointed. Our job is not to piss them off. Our job is to elicit information."[43]

Journalists with assigned seats in the first two rows of the Briefing Room can easily get a response from the press secretary by visiting him in his office or phoning him. They can get to other senior staff. They get call-backs. As a result, they often use the daily briefing to pursue issues not related to stories they are working on.

Reporters working for foreign newspapers usually ask questions related to America's dealings with their country. Raghubir Goyal, White House correspondent for *India Globe* and *Asia Today*, almost always asks questions about the administration's stances vis-à-vis Pakistan and, to a lesser extent, issues related to India. The exception to this general practice is the *Financial Times*, which covers the American presidency as its own beat.

There are, of course, also American reporters whose interests are limited to particular issues or their own slants in reporting. Russell Mokhiber, who has a newsletter devoted to corporate corruption issues called "Corporate Crime Reporter," surfaces at the daily briefing when his interests are in play. More regular in his attendance, but less predictable in just what he might ask, is Les Kinsolving, who has a talk radio program on Baltimore's WCBM. Kinsolving focuses on getting sound bites from the press secretary on issues related to conservative causes, particularly ones with a sexual angle, such as homosexuality, that are often unrelated to the news of the day. So obsessed is he with his own issues that, in the old briefing room, after getting the answers to his questions, he would unplug his recording equipment, located near the podium, by crawling on his hands and knees to the platform while Scott McClellan was still answering questions just a few feet away.

Reporters in the middle rows tend to be the ones who ask questions about particular realms of policy. Alex Keto of Dow Jones and Paula Cruickshank, who reports for a financial information service called CCH, are predictably interested in issues related to trade, taxes, currencies, and budgets. April Ryan, representing American Urban Radio Networks, closely follows presidential initiatives related to race.

Routinely Dispensing Facts

However much it occasions self-serving agendas, the daily briefing fulfills its primary obligation when it dispenses official information on behalf of the president. As a matter of routine, the press secretary announces events on the chief executive's schedule, upcoming visitors, and travel plans. Rarely controversial, these "housekeeping" matters permit reporters and their news organizations to plan their coverage of upcoming events. Ari Fleischer began his daily briefings with routine rundowns of George W. Bush's schedules and appointments, and his successors have done the same.

Sometimes the briefing begins with a policy announcement. Marlin Fitzwater often started with a statement of some sort, even if it meant having to do a lot of reaching. "I always tried to do a statement on something because I wanted something that was news that I could give them even if it wasn't real news. I always tried to read a brief statement at the top of the briefing. Sometimes it was just State Department guidance. I'd just take it and rewrite it a little bit for an issue that was in the paper that morning," he recalled. Using a State Department guidance had a special advantage: "I wouldn't have to get it approved by anybody, get clearance by anybody, because it was official State Department policy. I knew it was okay with the president. I was doing it as a spokesman so it allowed everybody to write a story off of that to say the president today reiterated his concern about Cyprus." By providing reporters with some shred of news right off the bat, this tactic was a smart way to make the routine briefing seem less bland. "It got the briefings off on a good start. It was news; it was substantive and it was real. And it was good for the president."[44]

With a great deal of news released earlier in the day or saved for a presidential appearance, Joe Lockhart often opted not to begin his briefing with a formal statement. Nonetheless, "I generally try to do announcements at the top, because people are paying attention at the top. Most days we don't have announcements." As a result, "then it's just whatever people in the room want."[45] The initiative shifts to the reporters present, starting with the lineup of heavyweights in the front row.

Political Jousting

Most reporters treat covering the White House as a political beat. This is partly because they have no substantive area of specialization. Moreover, since most new initiatives are now introduced elsewhere, the briefing is used for follow-up purposes. Once a new initiative has been reported on in the *Washington Post,* the *New York Times,* the *Wall Street Journal,* and *USA Today,* members of Congress, leaders of interest groups, and officials from relevant agencies respond to the initiative. Reporters can use the briefing to query the press secretary about the reaction to these responses.

While the press secretary might provide reporters with a further explanation of new policy or some analysis of how the administration's views compare with those of outspoken members of Congress, he or she does not volunteer these views. The tendency is to wait for reporters to ask about a policy before offering new material. If briefing papers have been prepared for something that does not come up, the information is simply saved for another day.

Many press secretaries experience a great deal of political combat on the way to their jobs. A veteran of many political wars in campaigning as well as governing, McCurry enjoyed jousting with reporters, when required. After observing McCurry's performance during the 1996 reelection campaign, veteran ABC White House correspondent Brit Hume concluded that he "is deliberately briefing the way he does because he is a combative, bare knuckled political spokesman."

Hume contrasted McCurry's style at the Briefing Room podium with the way he handled his previous job as spokesman for the State Department. The sense you had "when he was speaking [there] was that he was speaking for the Secretary of State, yes, but in a large sense for the institution and the State Department and for the U.S. government. You don't have that sense here. He is speaking for the president and the Clinton White House, not for the United States government." Hume would challenge McCurry because "there are times when things are coming just so much over the top that you are obliged to challenge it."[46] On one occasion when McCurry admitted to having "his mouth work faster than his mind," he related his certainty that if Brit Hume had been in the Briefing Room, Hume would have challenged him.[47]

The combative political cast the daily briefing has today reflects the partisanship that now surrounds every elected official in Washington. While the daily White House briefing might once have had what Hume called "a certain kind of neutrality about it, a certain official standing," it has become another arena for ongoing political combat.

Scandal-Related Jousting

When scandal breaks, the Briefing Room is a combat zone whether the president is a Democrat or a Republican. Now that these sessions are televised, the intensity of scandal-related combat has increased. During the Lewinsky scandal, television reporters dominated the daily briefing. With their assigned seats up front, the television reporters were difficult to ignore. The correspondents for CBS, NBC, ABC, CNN, and Fox asked the great majority of the questions.

July 28, 1998, was an important day for the Lewinsky scandal because it was revealed before the daily briefing that Monica Lewinsky's lawyers had reached an immunity deal with Kenneth Starr. On that day, television reporters for the networks asked two-thirds of the ninety-two questions posed. Sam Donaldson of ABC and Scott Pelley of CBS asked sixteen and seventeen, respectively. Of the remainder, radio reporters asked about a third, while journalists representing newspapers and magazines posed 22.7 percent of the questions.

As the Lewinsky scandal unfolded, television reporters used the briefing to portray themselves and their broadcasts as watchdogs for the public. "There's not a huge space up there on that podium, but all the networks have got to have their camera crews up there to do the reverse shot, getting their correspondents asking the tough, hard-nosed questions so they can get the response," noted Mike McCurry, who assumed the role of presidential guardian. The pictures were used regularly by the network as the images for the scandal stories they featured.

As the days wore on, McCurry did his best to avoid serving as a prop for network correspondents seeking to build their cases against Clinton. "One of my little head games that I play for fun is to see if I can figure out a way to screw up when I know that Scott Pelley summons up all this mock bravado to ask the tough question," recalled McCurry. "I'll say, 'Let me come back to this, Scott. On that other point. . . .' Sort of break the train so they can't use it without doing violence to the sequences of the back and forth."[48] By not providing Pelley with an answer until after questions from other reporters, McCurry denied Pelley the footage he wanted, showing Pelley posing a heated question followed directly by McCurry providing an answer. McCurry became accustomed to giving other reporters similarly deferred responses. While breaking up the picture for television and the sound for radio, this technique also provided McCurry with extra time to think.

Signaling and Coordinating Insiders

The president and his staff also use the daily briefing to let those in the administration know what their priorities are and where they stand with official policy. In every administration, officials in the departments and agencies watch the televised briefing to learn from the press secretary as well as from reporters. It is the most immediate way for them to get a sense of what the White House is up to.

McCurry began a practice that was continued by his successor, Joe Lockhart. "We take all the guidance after the briefing, put it in a little packet, and send it around to everybody in the building, so that everybody knows what we're saying about any issues that could possibly come up in the briefing," said Lockhart.[49] Consequently, all of the materials assembled before the daily briefing contribute to overall coordination by letting White House staffers know what is being said in their name, what issues are bubbling to the surface, and what positions the White House is taking.

Deputy Press Secretary Mary Ellen Glynn recalled that the briefing book, which ran anywhere from twenty pages to about fifty, "is very help-

ful to all of us [because it forms] our written record. It is not so much for
Mike necessarily, but for the rest of the building, because after he is done
with his briefing, we take those sheets of guidance out, Xerox them, and
distribute them around so that anybody else that may be talking. . . . If you
are Leon Panetta, you are talking a lot on the Hill. . . . The Public Liaison
folks who are talking to constituency groups, they have that little package
and everybody knows" what the White House is thinking.[50]

Thus, the briefing serves integrating and coordinating functions that
extend far beyond what it does for an administration in the public relations wars. The briefing book embodies the manner in which the press
secretary serves the entire White House staff in addition to the president
and reporters.

Additional Briefings and Information

In all recent administrations, officials have regularly come into the Briefing Room or into Room 450 in the Eisenhower Executive Office Building
(a 250-seat theater-style briefing room across West Executive from the
West Wing) to deliver various specialized briefings. They have briefed
reporters on the budget, economic reports, pending presidential trips,
new policy initiatives, or scandal-related matters. In addition, beginning
under the George W. Bush administration, officials have begun the practice of briefing reporters in conference calls, where reporters queue up to
ask questions after entering a prearranged code.

Briefings on specific topics are important for two reasons. First, they
publicize information about issues and events that are important to the
administration. When the president is to travel abroad, for example, the
national security adviser usually briefs reporters about the purposes of
the trip. Specialized briefing sessions also fill in gaps left by the daily
briefing, especially when attention is on economic policy issues.

On January 22, 1998, for example, the day after news of Monica Lewinsky's involvement with the president broke in the *Washington Post* and
on ABC News, McCurry's forty-four-minute briefing was consumed by
questions about it. Of the 121 questions posed, only seventeen dealt with
other issues, and eight of those were about Yassir Arafat's visit and meetings with the president, which was taking place at the time.

Yet if one looks at the other briefings held on that day in the White
House, it is evident that the policy track was still operating in the White
House. Secretary of State Madeleine Albright came into the Briefing
Room late in the afternoon and gave a rundown of the meeting between

Clinton and Arafat. In that fifteen-minute session, eighteen questions were asked of Secretary Albright, and none of them were about the Lewinsky issue.[51] White House news releases issued that day covered the signing of an accord about a border dispute between Ecuador and Peru, the president's reaction to the apprehension of a war criminal from the Balkan conflict, and a presidential report on Albanian emigration policies to the speaker of the House and the president of the Senate.

Generally, whenever the president presents a policy initiative, signs a bill into law, or prepares for a trip or for an official visit from a head of state, officials familiar with these developments will produce background papers for the journalists writing about them. Whenever officials conduct specialized briefings and distribute handouts to reporters, the information coming from them influences the content of the gaggle and the daily briefing. For example, having been prepped ahead of time, and with the details committed to paper, reporters have no need to ask the press secretary about who will be participating in an event, how you spell their names, and what their titles and backgrounds are. That information has already been sent by e-mail, distributed via handouts, and placed in bins located in an area between the Briefing Room and the "cubbies" and booths where reporters work.

When briefings are held in the White House or when the president speaks, transcripts of every session, no matter how brief, are distributed in an e-mail and placed in those bins, usually within the hour. In addition to those transcripts, the Press Office routinely supplies reporters with detailed weekly and daily schedules for the president, background information on scheduled events, announcements of appointments, background data about nominees, and copies of presidential messages and letters sent to the speaker of the House and the secretary of the Senate.

Everyone on the White House e-mail list for reporters also receives pool reports written by the print pool representative covering the president at events where there is room for only a small number to accompany him and his party, which is very common on trips. At the beginning of each month, reporters are given the rotation schedule for the newspaper and radio organizations regularly covering the White House. The April 2007 rotation schedule had thirty-one print organizations, five television networks, nine radio organizations, and two magazine photographers.[52] When an event requiring a pool takes place, such as a brief statement by the president in the Oval Office, those representing the news organizations for that day in the five categories go in. Then the person representing newspapers writes a report to all other reporters on the White House correspondents list. The report gives information on who was present at the meeting, how they were dressed, what took place while the reporter was there. A separate transcript is put out to the same group of recipients, so the pool report will only have the highlights of what was said.

On a normal day, the Press Office may e-mail fifteen releases and stock the bins with a total of forty pages. All are meant to serve as backup information giving facts the White House wants to highlight, including the impact of major initiatives and facts about how programs would work. Their goal is to provide sufficient information for reporters to understand what the issues are and how the president's initiative will respond to the needs of the situation.

With a constant stream of news, the White House press staff in the Clinton administration opted to give out information in additional ways, including in sessions with policy specialists held in the Briefing Room. While the Bush administration also holds briefings with policy specialists, they do so out of the Briefing Room. Following a practice they used in the 2000 campaign, the Bush staff often use conference calls to brief reporters about some set of facts they want to alert reporters to. Reporters are informed by e-mail that a conference call will take place at a certain hour with instructions on how to log on. When they log on, they give their name and news organization and then indicate that they want to ask a question. This is done before the conference call takes place. They are often used as a complement to a presidential speech. For example, when President Bush gave a speech on energy on the morning of April 25, 2006, the Press Office followed it up with a one-page fact sheet on the president's initiative called "President Bush's Four-Part Plan to Confront High Gasoline Prices." Fifteen minutes later, the director of the National Economic Council, Al Hubbard, held a conference call with reporters to explain the plan.

The advantage to the administration is that such briefings take less time to put together and can be done at any time of day. In fact, such briefings have been held in the evening as well. That way, if they have some initiative they would rather downplay but still want to explain, they can do so after the network evening news programs.

7

Presidential Press Conferences

Press conferences and short question-and-answer sessions represent the best examples of presidential communications in unscripted forums. Presidents and their staffs go to great lengths to control public situations where a chief executive appears. They do not like surprises. Yet, at the same time, presidents need to demonstrate that they can answer hard questions about their policies and motivations. Because presidents do not answer questions from officials in other branches of government, there is no public questioning of a chief executive in any official setting. By tradition, that role has been filled by reporters acting for the public. How presidents and their staffs adjust to reporters' queries under different sets of conditions demonstrates the ability of the White House to respond to changing times and rules. It also shows how enduring such forums have been in the face of presidential discomfort in environments where they don't control the setting.

Presidents may joke about the sessions, but it is clear that they don't look forward to press conferences. Before every Thanksgiving holiday, it is traditional for the president of the United States to host a gathering in the Rose Garden at which he grants a pardon to a turkey. Before performing this ritual in 2002, George W. Bush made a joke about the apparent anxiety of the turkey. "He looks a little nervous, doesn't he," he asked his audience of youngsters, parents, and teachers. "He probably thinks he's going to have a press conference."[1]

In 1953, President Eisenhower made the same point more starkly: "I will mount the usual weekly cross and let you drive the nails."[2] As president-elect, Eisenhower considered avoiding news conferences. Like presidents before and after him, Eisenhower believed that most reporters were rude in their questioning. On behalf of the American Society of Newspaper Editors, concerned the presidential press conference was in danger of being cut back or cancelled, James Russell Wiggins, editor of the *Washington Post,* went to see the president-elect. The president expressed concern about the conduct of the press. "Eisenhower told me that he thought press behavior at Truman's press conferences seemed unpleasant and often rude to President Truman and disrespectful of the presidency. He said the president was questioned as though he were a person suspected of a crime or a witness in a criminal proceeding," Wiggins recollected in 1998. In touting the benefits of press conferences to President Eisenhower, Wiggins stressed two points: helping citizens to understand policy and the front-page coverage the sessions guarantee a president. As government has grown, it has become more difficult for people to understand the government's actions. Press conferences are an educational tool, Wiggins argued to Eisenhower. And they guarantee him front-page coverage in the nation's newspapers.[3]

President Eisenhower and his successors have grumbled about their treatment at the hands of reporters, but they have continued to hold press conferences. On November 8, 2006, President Bush held one in the East Room, more than ninety-three years after President Woodrow Wilson gave the first formal news conference there in 1913. The intervening years have been accompanied by an explosion in communications technology, growth in the size and importance of the presidency in our national political system, and enormous changes in the scope, reach, and the public face of government.

Yet some things have not changed in the years separating Presidents Wilson and Bush. In their conferences, both men answered questions from reporters on a broad range of topics, and the reporters came in on an equal-access basis—that is, all credentialed reporters could attend, not just those hand-picked by the president. The fourteen presidents serving in the years between Presidents Wilson and Bush also held such conferences, where they met with reporters to answer their queries.

The bottom line is that the presidential press conference endures even after dramatic changes in the ways that such a forum exists in the environment within which presidents and reporters must do their respective jobs. The two basic elements of the press conference mentioned above, a broad range of topics and a large number of reporters participating, have remained. At the same time, many developments have affected the format of press conferences, the frequency with which they are held, and the ground rules under which their participants operate. The changing shape of the presidential press conference illustrates how the essence of democratic institutions can endure even as their specific characteristics evolve.

Why Do Presidents Hold Press Conferences?

If they have other ways to communicate with the public and if they don't particularly like press conferences, why do presidents continue to hold them? In the first place, they do it because press conferences have come to be regarded as part of the foundation of democratic government. Elected officials are expected to show that they are responsible to the public by explaining their policies in response to hard questions posed by those outside government. But presidents have also come to see that they can build popular support for themselves and their policies by performing well in such challenging forums. The press conference provides opportunities for winning friends and allies among pundits as well as publics.

Democratic Tradition

When President Bush welcomed President Hamid Karzai of Afghanistan to the United States in a Rose Garden meeting in 2004, each made a few remarks before President Bush welcomed questions from invited reporters. "We'll answer some questions, in the tradition of democratic societies," said President Bush.[4] To further illustrate his belief in the tie between democracy and an inquiring press, he reiterated the point to reporters later the same year in an Oval Office meeting with Iraqi interim president Ghazi Al-Yawer. After the two leaders made statements about their meeting, President Bush said to the assembled press, "We'll answer a couple of questions in the spirit of democracy."[5]

In fact, both the White House and reporters understand that the president needs to answer queries in public that are posed not only by people not in his employ but also by professionals perceived to be knowledgeable and tough in their questioning. When Dan Bartlett, senior White House communications adviser, was asked why the president and his staff decided to hold a press conference prior to the Iraq War, he responded, "During the Iraq debate, there was a point when the public needed to see him questioned about what we were doing and why. And that was part of the communications objective. Yes, this president has taken and answered the tough questions about what we're doing."[6] As it was, the White House staff had scheduled a press conference in part because they knew it would be perceived as a challenging forum.

Presidents and their staffs have accepted the press as a legitimate vehicle for public scrutiny even while disagreeing on exactly what role the
press is supposed to play in our society. Helen Thomas, who has covered
Washington since 1943 and is considered the dean of the White House
press corps, represents the conventional wisdom among reporters about
their place in the American political system: "I think you can't have a
democracy without the press corps, a very active one, and have press conferences. We're the only forum in our society where the president can
be questioned on a regular basis, Otherwise he can rule by edict and live
like a king."[7]

USA Today reporter Susan Page explained the importance of press
conferences in terms of reporters acting as surrogates for the public: "We
don't have a parliamentary system where a president has to subject himself the way the prime minister does, to hectoring. Where a president
has to subject himself to questions from the opposition party. The closest
thing we have is a news conference where reporters are standing in for
the public."

By way of contrast, White House officials are quick to dismiss the
idea that the press should be regarded as a representative of the public. White House Chief of Staff Andrew Card commented to a reporter,
"They [reporters] don't represent the public any more than other people
do. In our democracy, the people who represent the people stood for election. I don't believe you have a check-and-balance function."[8] This clash
of viewpoints is bound to—and does—result in very different ideas about
the kinds of information a White House is obliged to provide to reporters. Nonetheless, both sides are aware how much they have to gain from
press conferences.

Dominate the News and Galvanize Supporters

Press conferences provide good publicity for presidents because they permit the public to see him in a more engaging event than a set speech.
"The value of a press conference is, it helps you dominate the news for
some period of time," observed former Reagan chief of staff James Baker.
"It gets the president front and center. It gives you a very, very broad gauge
way to get your message out, and it gives you the opportunity to present
the president in a good light." In Baker's view, press conferences are not
nearly as difficult for presidents to handle as they anticipate. "Generally
speaking, anybody who has been elected president is going to be able to
handle a press conference quite well," Baker said. "That's going to be the

rule of thumb. Otherwise, they wouldn't be there. They wouldn't have gotten there."[9]

Presidents can also use press conferences to help them govern. In this case their audience is less the public at large than the chief executive's committed supporters inside and outside of government. President Clinton held a press conference on December 16, 1996, to describe what he envisioned for his second term. A little more than a year later, Mike McCurry recalled the responsible senior staff as saying, " 'We have to have a big press conference at the end of the year to kind of get people ginned up and excited about what lies ahead, in the year ahead, and then really come out of the box in January with an activist strategy to put the president's agenda out there.' And that worked. It seems like a long time ago now. It worked exceedingly well."[10] As with Clinton's December 1996 conference, the impact of a press conference goes beyond a president's coalition of supporters. A successful press conference, commented David Gergen, "galvanizes all operations."[11] Those in the Congress and bureaucracy can hear the president's priorities firsthand. They also can see where their priorities fit into his agenda, so they can move ahead as a team.

Press conferences can be a useful device for updating people on the progress of a presidency. Rather than dealing with achievements one event at a time, a solo press conference can be useful as an opportunity to consolidate what a president views as his achievements and his vision of where he wants to take his presidency. Scott McClellan described them as a useful place for a president "to sum up a lot of the things that we've accomplished. . . . We've achieved some really great things here, but maybe it hasn't gotten the kind of attention where people know what we've done." So the president comes out "to highlight some of that."[12]

In fact, President Bush has sometimes held a press conference in late summer for the purpose of discussing his legislative accomplishments before retreating to his ranch for a vacation. By then the Congress has adjourned for its summer recess, allowing the president to spotlight their joint achievements. He held such a session with the press in the Rose Garden on July 30, 2003, in which he stressed his accomplishments. He held more wide-ranging sessions of this kind following the 2002 congressional elections and the 2004 presidential contest.

Refine Policy Decisions

White House staffers appreciate the role press conferences play as an action-forcing mechanism from the president down to the department and

agency levels. In most administrations, senior staff members use preparations for all presidential interchanges with reporters to confront policy.
John Podesta explained that the press conferences have a way of "forcing
the staff to work through a policy process that forces us to commit ourselves to a particular answer. Not to waffle." Thus, preparing for a press
conference is "in and of itself a relatively valuable exercise."[13]

McCurry discussed how it worked in the Clinton administration. In
sending out questions for review to people in the administration, staff
members asked for agency responses and provided them to the president:
"You usually get some kind of warmed-over pabulum, and that wouldn't
be good enough for the president. So you'd say, 'Here's the answer' and
he'd say, 'Well, that's no good. We have to make a decision. Call so-and-so
and find out why we're not doing something on that.'" Action resulted
from the search for answers. "Sometimes it would lead to change in policy or sharper definition of policy. So they had the kind of effect of forcing
the government and the bureaucracy and the White House to come to
grips with issues that had been kind of languishing for a while."[14]

Reporters Hold in High Value

Because a president's staff members are concerned about his relationship with the press, they look for signs that reporters are restless when it
has been a long time since the last solo press conference. Reporters pressure for solo press conferences because they get to hear from the president in a response that does not come pre-varnished by his staff. They see
no substitute for such sessions. During the impeachment vote and subsequent impeachment trial of President Clinton, he generally took no more
than three questions in joint press conferences or in short question-and-
answer sessions. He also avoided solo sessions. Reporters complained to
Press Secretary Joe Lockhart, both in the informal setting of his morning
gaggle and in the daily briefing.

Early in March 1999, Don Fulsom of UPI Radio surprised Lockhart
by inquiring if the president would be holding a press conference on
April 30. Lockhart said he did not keep the schedule that far in advance
and then inquired about the reason for his interest. Fulsom noted that
April 30 would mark the one-year anniversary of President Clinton's last
press conference—and Fulsom was not the only one pressing for a press
conference. The president held one on March 19.

The press secretary is traditionally more interested in lobbying for
press conferences than are others on the staff. Scott McClellan some-

times argued for such sessions because he knew that reporters were pressuring him for them. You do one when "it's time to do one," McClellan said. "I mean, the press has an expectation to do one."[15] On the other hand, Assistant to the President Mary Matalin was skeptical of this view. "You don't do a press conference to do a press conference. You don't give a speech just to give a speech," she said. "It's not a box-checking thing."[16]

Patterns of Presidential Press Conferences

From Wilson on, press conferences have been a regular, if not always successful, fixture of presidential public relations.[17] A president established the forum, but news organizations have been interested in seeing them continue, no matter who serves as president or what he says or does.

Wilson warranted the unusual attention of reporters because he was a wartime leader. His successors, Warren Harding and Calvin Coolidge, dealt with no comparable crises, yet reporters continued to request news conferences because the presidency had come to be regarded, by both public and news organizations alike, as a continuing fount of important information.[18] By the end of Coolidge's presidency, the press conference had become institutionalized. President Hoover did not enjoy them the way Coolidge seemed to, but he met with reporters all the same. Many of Hoover's sessions, though, were truncated ones with little interaction between the president and reporters.

It remained for Franklin Roosevelt to turn the press conference into a compelling event. He did so by explaining his policies and unfolding events. During the Roosevelt and Truman years, press conferences continued to operate under the off-the-record rules that had governed them since their start in the Wilson administration. The Harding-Hoover era requirement that reporters submit their questions in advance was abandoned. This rule change altered the dynamics of the sessions, for it allowed them to become forums in which presidents could talk about their own agendas in addition to those of reporters.

The Roosevelt administration was a policy furnace, and its chief executive enjoyed talking with reporters because he believed that news organizations could help him inform the public about what he was doing. His explanations of the budget provide an example of his approach to press conferences. When President Roosevelt was ready to send his budget message to the Congress, he met with reporters to brief them about its contents. He told them what he thought was important about his product. His first press conference on a budget was held on January 5, 1934.

He began by suggesting what the resulting stories should emphasize. "In regard to the Message, I suppose if I were writing your stories for you, I would say it is the most brutally frank Budget Message ever sent in. In other words, I am not mincing words or trying to hide anything," he said. His budget director was out of town, so he personally briefed reporters for approximately an hour. He likened a similar session, held on January 4, 1936, to a "class" with himself as the "professor," an analogy he occasionally used in his press conferences.[19]

Roosevelt's press sessions were so popular that administration figures attended them, as did out-of-town editors and visiting foreign dignitaries. Truman's were not the magnet Roosevelt's were, but they remained important sources of information for reporters. There was an ebb and flow to the number of sessions each president held, but from Woodrow Wilson through Harry Truman, off-the-record press conferences became a primary news source for White House correspondents.

Presidents and their staffs also found them useful, in part because they did retain some control over what the president spoke about. If he did not want something published, he could retract an unwise statement or refashion it into one he preferred. A good example is the characterization of Senator Joseph McCarthy that President Truman tendered in the press conference held March 30, 1950: "I think the greatest asset that the Kremlin has is Senator McCarthy." A reporter let him know how controversial his statement was: "Brother, will that hit page one tomorrow!" Truman swiftly revamped his statement: "The greatest asset that the Kremlin has is the partisan attempt in the Senate to sabotage the bipartisan foreign policy of the United States." With this modified quote, he was able to backtrack without harming himself. Once press conferences went on the record, there was no way to undo damaging statements. Table 11 demonstrates the consistent importance of the presidential press conference.[20] Note, however, the sharp drop in their frequency following the Truman administration.

Dramatic changes transformed presidential press conferences during the Eisenhower administration. After December 16, 1953, they were on the record. Beginning on January 19, 1955, they were also televised for broadcast in the evening. These developments changed a low-risk exercise into a high-risk performance. As a result, presidents and their staffs began searching for ways both to reduce their vulnerability and to influence public opinion directly.

Once press conferences were on the record, presidents and their staffs

Table 11. Presidential Press Conferences, 1913–2007

President	Total	Months in Office	Press Conferences Per Month	Press Conferences Per Year
Wilson 3/4/13 to 3/4/21	159	96	1.7	19.9
Harding 3/4/21 to 8/2/23	No transcripts	29		
Coolidge 8/3/23 to 3/4/29	521	67	7.8	93.3
Hoover 3/4/29 to 3/4/33	268	48	5.6	67.0
Roosevelt 3/4/33 to 4/12/45	1,020	145½	7.0	84.1
Truman 4/12/45 to 1/20/53	324	94½	3.4	41.1
Eisenhower 1/20/53 to 1/20/61	193	96	2.0	24.1
Kennedy 1/20/61 to 11/22/63	65	34	1.9	22.9
Johnson 11/22/63 to 1/20/69	135	62	2.2	26.1
Nixon 1/20/69 to 8/9/74	39	66	0.6	7.1
Ford 8/9/74 to 1/20/77	40	30	1.3	16.0
Carter 1/20/77 to 1/20/81	59	48	1.2	14.8
Reagan 1/20/81 to 1/20/89	46	96	0.5	5.8
G. H. W. Bush 1/20/89 to 1/20/93	143	48	3.0	35.8
Clinton 1/20/93 to 1/20/01	193	96	2.0	24.1
G. W. Bush 1/20/01 to 1/20/07	151	72	2.1	25.2

Sources: Unless otherwise noted, the presidential press conference information comes from *The Public Papers of the Presidents of the United States.* There are a series of volumes for Presidents Hoover, Truman, Eisenhower, Kennedy, Johnson, Nixon, Ford, Carter, Reagan, George H. W. Bush, and Clinton. President George H. W. Bush had a press conference not contained in the *Public Papers,* which was held at Kennebunkport, Maine, on August 16, 1991. The tran-

(continued)

Table 11 *(continued)*

script is in files in the Bush Library. Information for President George W. Bush comes from *The Weekly Compilation of Presidential Documents* published by the National Archives and Records Administration. The press conference transcripts of President Calvin Coolidge are found at the Forbes Library in Northampton, Massachusetts. Woodrow Wilson held only two press conferences in his second term, so his percentages may lead to a false impression of how frequent they were for his first term: 3.3 per month and 39.0 per year. The press conference numbers differ in some respects from earlier lists. The Wilson figures include the press conferences found in Volume 50, "The Complete Press Conferences, 1913–1919," edited by Robert C. Hildebrand (Princeton, NJ: Princeton University Press, 1985) as part of *The Papers of Woodrow Wilson* as well as two other press conferences found in volume 39 and one each in volumes 40 and 61 in the series, the particular volume edited by Arthur Link as well as one short one found in the Princeton University Library files of Charles Swem, White House stenographer during the Wilson years. The conferences on January 26, June 22, July 13, 1914, January 8, 1917, and June 27, 1919, were not in the Hildebrand volume, and the short session on November 13, 1913, was found in the Charles Swem files. The Roosevelt numbers vary from the standard number of 998, which comes from the numbering done by the stenographers at the time. The last conference was numbered 998. That figure includes two press conferences from 1934—numbers 138 and 139—that did not take place. The stenographer went on vacation for three conferences, but only one was held. The error was not discovered until some time later, and a decision was made to retain the numbering as it was. I have added 22 press conferences that were listed as "A" or "B" by the transcribers. By year, the ones I have added include the following. For 1933, I include 14A and 14B and 49A. The first two are sessions held in the president's office at the behest of the president with Prime Minister Ramsay MacDonald of Great Britain. While the two sessions do not both involve regular questions and answers as later develops, these are the first two sessions where the president brought reporters to talk to a foreign leader. They establish an enduring pattern calling for joint press conferences with foreign leaders to have a different format from his regular solo sessions with reporters. They are shorter in length and usually involve statements from one or both foreign leaders. Included in the 1933 count is a short session on September 6 [49A], which probably took place shortly after the conclusion of an earlier one. In 1934, in addition to numbers 138 and 139, which did not take place, we can add 129A and 161A, which are not really different from regular press conferences. Others falling into the general press conference categories include 193B, 530A, and 703A. Additionally, I have added sessions with business editors as they were counted into the 998 total in the later years. From 1941 on, sessions 744, 858, 903, and 956 with business editors were counted as regular sessions as were ones with the American Society of Newspaper Editors (879) and the Negro Newspaper Publishers Association (933). I have included such sessions in the early years of Roosevelt's presidency when they were noted with an "A" or "B." The session with such groups include the following ones counted in these numbers: 98A, 193A, 275A, 360A, 448A, 449A, 452A, 452B, 540A, 557A, 614A, 636A, and 652A. There are others in the totals including 485A where Press Secretary Steve Early was instructed by an ailing President Roosevelt to conduct the press conference in his place. It turned out to be an experiment not repeated. Also in the totals are 356A with a Canadian official and 399A held in Canada responding to reporters from that country. Introduction by Jonathan Daniels, *Complete Presidential Press Conferences of Franklin D. Roosevelt* (New York: Da Capo Press, 1972); The Truman press conferences include in their numbering a series of sessions much like those with President Roosevelt. While the text of several of the sessions was not included in *Public Papers of the Presidents of the United States*, the numbers remain. Thus, cumulative totals for President Truman include all of the sessions designated as press conferences. Those include numbers 11, 39, 61, 103 (American Society of Newspaper Editors), 13 (Association of Radio News Analysts), 36 (Editors and Publishers of Gannett Newspapers), 42, 81 (National Conference of Business Paper Editors), 51 (Negro Newspaper Publishers Association), 52 (editors of monthly magazines of Standard Railroad Labor Organizations), and 73

(continued)

Table 11 *(continued)*

(editors and executives of the McGraw-Hill Publishing Company). Later in his presidency, sessions with these groups were included in *Public Papers* as press conferences, including numbers 121 and 177 with the National Conference of Business Paper Editors, 179 with the American Society of Newspaper Editors, 124 with the National Conference of Editorial Writers, 202 with the Association of Radio Analysts. Also included in the totals (though the text was not) are 109, which was a joint press conference held in Canada with Prime Minister Mackenzie King, and 82, where he corrected a previously made statement but did not take questions. That session was similar in its lack of questions to 114, where he simply thanked reporters for the courtesies they extended to him when his mother died. He did not take questions. In *Public Papers*, 114 is included with text as well as its number; The press conference on December 16, 1953, was the first to allow direct quotation of the whole press conference. The press conference held on January 19, 1955, was the first to be televised, although it was not broadcast live; August 30, 1963, President Kennedy had a "special news conference" in Hyannis Port, Massachusetts. I have added it to the 64 press conferences designated with numbers. President Nixon had two sessions titled "Unscheduled News Conference" on March 21 and July 20, 1970. I have added them to the 37 numbered press conferences. October 21, 1974, President Ford had a "News Conference of the President and President Echeverría of Mexico" in Tubac, Arizona. I have added it to the 39 press conferences designated with numbers. President George H. W. Bush had a press conference not contained in *Public Papers*, held at Kennebunkport, Maine, on August 16, 1991. The transcript is in files in the Bush Library.

adapted to the heightened risk of error and embarrassment by making changes in the press conference itself and then by developing alternate forums where the chief executive could respond to reporters' queries.

In refashioning the press conference format, chief executives and their communications teams developed three strategies to diminish the potential negative impact from the event. They reduced the frequency and regularity of traditional press conferences. They varied press conference settings in order to reflect the importance of what the president was going to say. This included developing certain settings to dramatize the event and certain other settings for more low-key sessions. Then they reshaped this forum from an occasion where the president faced reporters alone to one where he appeared together with others. Gradually, the presidential press conference was transformed into a diplomatic tool by bringing foreign leaders onto the White House stage to answer questions alongside the president.

In addition to altering the press conference itself, presidents and staff members developed publicity strategies to provide them with alternate ways to respond to reporters' queries. They developed short question-and-answer sessions as vehicles for answering reporters' queries on a fairly regular basis and increased the number of one-on-one and group interviews they did with domestic and foreign reporters. Not all of these changes were made at the same time.

Changes in Frequency, Setting, and Format

When press conferences were off the record, presidents did not worry, as they later did, about the difficulties of commenting on unfolding events, especially during a crisis. The president and his staff controlled the release of information. If they did not want something the president said to leave the room, it did not leave the room. Reporters respected the rules governing information.

When press conferences went on the record, presidents had to respond to questions on world crises still under way and policy initiatives stuck in Congress. Earlier, chief executives were free to discuss closely held strategies and people if they liked, but not once the sessions became part of the official record. Presidents became sensitive to the timing of the sessions. Sometimes they wanted to avoid an issue, and other times they used the press conference setting to confront one. It is difficult to find a "good time" to hold a press conference in a fast-paced news world because there is always a crisis or event occurring that the president may not want to talk about just then.

Abruptly, presidents reduced the frequency of press conferences. Instead of once a week, as was Truman's practice, Eisenhower held his press conferences twice a month. While President Truman had an average of 41.1 press conferences a year, President Eisenhower averaged 24.1. Press conferences became less frequent in the Nixon and Reagan years, with 7.1 and 5.8 per year, respectively. Presidents George H. W. Bush, Bill Clinton, and George W. Bush have held press conferences more frequently than did Presidents Nixon and Reagan, but a large portion of their sessions were joint press conferences with foreign leaders, not solo sessions. President George H. W. Bush held an average of 35.8 press conferences a year, President Clinton 24.1, and President George W. Bush 25.2.

While President Eisenhower reduced the frequency of his press conference appearances, he held them on a regular basis. Eisenhower held press conferences in 85.4% of the months in his eight years in office. Reagan, by way of contrast, held press conferences in only 46.9% of his months in office. One of the reasons President Reagan held relatively few press conferences was that he invested so much in the ones he chose to have. Instead of low-key morning or afternoon sessions held in the Indian Treaty Room in the Eisenhower Executive Office Building, he opted to hold 67.4% of his conferences as evening events in the East Room. Carried live on the three major networks, they attracted a large audience. Reagan's polished performance was a match for the pomp and polish of the East Room décor. So what if his answers were sometimes muddled and error-prone—the public enjoyed watching the spectacle of the president speaking in the East Room at night.

His successors have shied away from such formal extravaganzas except when a national moment promises to draw an audience looking to the president for guidance. President George W. Bush has held four sessions of this kind. All dealt with war issues the public expected him to address. George H. W. Bush held two in his four years, while Clinton held four evening East Room sessions in eight years.

One of the ways in which presidents adjusted to the advent of on-the-record sessions was to reduce their exposure to a wide assortment of questions. What was traditionally a session in which the president appeared alone to answer questions is now usually a joint one. The practice of joint press conferences began when the president appeared with important domestic advisers, especially budget officials. Presidents Roosevelt, Truman, and Johnson regularly held such sessions. Now it has become common for the chief executive to hold joint press conferences with foreign heads of state. Instead of answering questions from perhaps fifteen reporters, as in a solo session, in a joint session the president and his visitor answer questions only from two or three reporters apiece.

As shown in table 12, joint appearances were occasionally held prior to the George H. W. Bush administration, although not often with foreign leaders. President Truman liked to hold press conferences with budget aides as well as an occasional visiting foreign official. In 1946, for example, he had others participate in seven of his press conferences.[21] Presidents Eisenhower and Kennedy refrained from this practice. But Lyndon Johnson resurrected it. In sixteen of his 135 press conferences, he had officials alongside him who answered some of the questions. Budget Director Charles Schultze would deal with budget details. Secretary of Defense Robert McNamara handled some Vietnam questions in joint sessions with President Johnson.[22] President Johnson also held joint sessions with state officials, including governors.

Presidents Nixon, Carter, and Reagan avoided inviting other officials to their press conferences. They sometimes had foreign leaders join in short question-and-answer sessions, but not press conferences. President Ford developed the current trend by appearing with a foreign head of

Table 12. Presidential Press Conferences by Term: Joint and Solo Press Sessions, 1913–2007

President	Total	Solo	Joint	Joint as % Total	% Months Press Conferences Held	% Months Solo Sessions Held
Wilson 3/4/13 to 3/4/17	157	157	0	0	62.5	62.5
Wilson 3/4/17 to 3/4/21	2	2	0	0	4.2	4.2
Harding 3/4/21 to 8/2/23	No transcript record					
Coolidge 8/3/23 to 3/4/25	130	130	0	0	100.0	100.0
Coolidge 3/4/25 to 3/4/29	391	391	0	0	100.0	100.0
Hoover 3/4/29 to 3/4/33	268	267	1	0.4	95.8	95.8
Roosevelt 3/4/33 to 1/20/37	344	332	11	3.2	97.8	97.8
Roosevelt 1/20/37 to 1/20/41	389	377	10	2.6	100.0	100.0
Roosevelt 1/20/41 to 1/20/45	279	267	12	4.3	100.0	100.0
Roosevelt 1/20/45 to 4/12/45	8	8	0	0	100.0	100.0
Truman 4/12/45 to 1/20/49	165	157	8	4.8	97.8	97.8
Truman 1/20/49 to 1/20/53	159	154	5	3.1	97.9	97.9
Eisenhower 1/20/53 to 1/20/57	99	98	1	1.0	83.3	83.3
Eisenhower 1/20/57 to 1/20/61	94	94	0	0	87.5	87.5
Kennedy 1/20/61 to 11/22/63	65	65	0	0	97.1	97.1
Johnson 11/22/63 to 1/20/65	36	35	1	2.8	100.0	100.0
Johnson 1/20/65 to 1/20/69	99	83	15	15.3	89.6	85.4

Table 12 (*continued*)

President	Total	Solo	Joint	Joint as % Total	% Months Press Conferences Held	% Months Solo Sessions Held
Nixon 1/20/69 to 1/20/73	30	30	0	0	56.3	56.3
Nixon 1/20/73 to 8/9/74	9	9	0	0	36.8	36.8
Ford 8/9/74 to 1/20/77	40	39	1	2.5	72.4	72.4
Carter 1/20/77 to 1/20/81	59	59	0	0	75.0	75.0
Reagan 1/20/81 to 1/20/85	27	27	0	0	54.2	54.2
Reagan 1/20/85 to 1/20/89	19	19	0	0	39.6	39.6
G. H. W. Bush 1/20/89 to 1/20/93	143	84	59	41.3	89.6	85.4
Clinton 1/20/93 to 1/20/97	133	44	89	66.9	93.8	66.7
Clinton 1/20/97 to 1/20/01	60	18	42	70.0	75.0	37.5
G. W. Bush 1/20/01 to 1/20/05	89	17	72	80.9	79.2	33.3
G. W. Bush 1/20/05 to 1/20/07	62	18	44	71.0	91.7	66.7

Source: In both the Roosevelt and Johnson administrations there were press conferences with no transcripts, so the totals for those presidents are slightly higher than the combined total of listed solo and joint sessions. For Franklin Roosevelt, there are three press conferences for which there are no transcripts: one in his first term, no. 41, held August 7, 1933, and two in his second, nos. 473 and 474, held July and August 1938. For President Johnson, the transcript is missing for no. 48, which was held on August 19, 1965. President George H. W. Bush had a press conference not contained in *Public Papers*, which was held at Kennebunkport, Maine, on August 16, 1991. The transcript is in files in the Bush Library.

state. On October 21, 1974, in Tubac, Arizona, he appeared before the press with President Luis Echeverría of Mexico. The format was closer to today's joint press conferences, with reporters posing questions on any subject to both leaders in a shorter session, than to solo press conferences.

Beginning with the administration of President George H. W. Bush, presidents have made joint press conferences with foreign leaders a staple of a White House visit by a head of state, or of a presidential trip abroad. Joint sessions now account for over half of all press conferences a president holds. Of the three most recent presidents, joint press conferences account for 41.3 percent of those held by President George H. W. Bush, 67.9 percent of President Clinton's sessions, and 76.8 percent of those held by President George W. Bush.

This kind of joint press conference is an adaptation to the needs of reporters, foreign leaders, and the president. Before the joint appearance was made standard operating procedure by President George H. W. Bush, a scrum of reporters often met with visiting leaders or their surrogates. Each leader, or more generally their surrogates, would respond to reporters' questions about the meeting. These sessions with reporters did not draw public attention, as they were not usually televised; this was before the advent of cable television.

The joint press conference gives the White House control over both the extent a president is questioned by reporters and the range of responses available to a foreign leader when addressing reporters about his or her meeting with the president. As Marlin Fitzwater said, "Both parties were more careful when standing next to each other; it minimizes discrepancies."[23] The joint press conference afforded certain advantages: both leaders could count on its happening, descriptions of the meeting from different parties would not conflict, and reporters would get an opportunity to query the president himself, rather than an anonymous senior official, about the meeting as well as about other subjects.

Since it is easier to control the format when time is shared with another and both leaders have statements of several minutes to begin the sessions, the president can focus on a few queries secure in the knowledge that he will not be grilled repeatedly on one subject. During the scandals of his second term, President Clinton could regularly avoid answering the full number of queries posed in a regular press conference. In a February 1999 press conference with President Jerry Rawlings of Ghana, for example, President Clinton answered only three questions, all posed by wire service reporters from the Associated Press, United Press

International, and Reuters. Whether they occur in the United States or abroad, the sessions are divided equally between the two leaders.

With reporters divided up according to their country, the leaders alternate calling on reporters. That reduces the number of questions the president has to answer from the White House press corps. By calling on the wire services, President Clinton was sure that he would get not only scandal-related questions. At least one if not two of the wire reporters will ask about policy, especially foreign policy. Rarely do wire reporters have the same political edge in their questions that is true with some other reporters, particularly those representing the television networks.

The president and his staff were well aware of reporters' disquiet over the limitation. In the press conference with Rawlings, a Ghanaian reporter complained that American correspondents did not pose queries about Africa. President Clinton responded: "It's my fault because I don't let them ask me enough questions on other occasions, so I'm forcing them to use this opportunity to pepper me."[24]

Additional Venues for Meeting with Reporters

Ever since television has become the primary vehicle for presidential communications, thus putting press conferences on the record, the trend has been for presidents to hold fewer sessions in which they stand alone and respond to reporters' queries for a televised half hour or so. Instead they hold brief question-and-answer sessions. These sessions are similar to joint press conferences in that not many questions are asked. Yet they are different because only a small number of reporters are invited to each session, and there is no assembled audience brought together in advance, as at a joint press conference. Even if the president calls on three reporters in a joint press conference, the whole press corps is present for the session.

In some short question-and-answer sessions, the president takes anywhere from one to five or six questions from a pool of reporters invited into the Oval Office (or some similar setting) at the beginning of a president's meeting with congressional leaders, members of the Cabinet, or a visiting head of state. The reporters' questions generally deal with just an issue or two, the identity of which the president typically will have been alerted to and briefed on beforehand. Wire service reporters representing the Associated Press and Reuters are usually the ones invited to pose the questions, and they tend to be interested in the hot topic of the moment.

Table 13. Short Question-and-Answer Sessions, 1989–2007

President	Total	Months in Office	Average per month
G. H. W. Bush 1/20/89 to 1/20/93	331	48	6.9
Clinton 1/20/93 to 1/20/01	1,042	96	10.9
G. W. Bush 1/20/01 to 1/20/07	430	72	6.0

Source: "Exchanges with Reporters," Weekly Compilation of Presidential Documents.

    Short question-and-answer sessions are a fairly recent development in the president-press relationship. When the president met regularly with reporters in solo press conferences, there was little need for such sessions. Reporters knew they would have an opportunity to question the president extensively, even if it was only a couple of times a month. The transcribed short question-and-answer sessions date from the Nixon period, when press conferences became infrequent. Reporters wanted answers to questions, and the White House did not want to provide them in a press conference setting. The short session with a pool of reporters was a way to release some of the pressure building up among reporters for a press conference. As cable television grew, so too did the number of short question-and-answer sessions—cable networks became a ready outlet for them.

    Short sessions for a pool of reporters set in a restricted space are relatively easy to plan. Generally, in 2007 each of the major wire services is represented (Associated Press, Reuters, Bloomberg) plus one reporter representing the television networks (ABC, CBS, NBC, CNN, and Fox) and one reporter each representing the major print publications and radio. Since the president will generally take no more than two or three questions from familiar figures, their focus is easy to anticipate. On August 23, 2005, for example, President Bush took four questions from reporters during a vacation at the Tamarack Resort in Donnelly, Idaho. Standing in a forest clearing with Idaho governor (later secretary of the interior) Dirk Kempthorne at his side, Bush made a statement and answered reporters' questions for twelve minutes. With war protester Cindy Sheehan camped outside of his Crawford ranch, it was not difficult to anticipate the first question. The Associated Press correspondent asked about Sheehan, and

Table 14. Reporter Interviews with President Bush, January 20, 2001–January 20, 2007

Year	Total	Print	Television	Roundtable
2001	49	21	18	10
2002	34	11	19	4
2003	45	7	26	12
2004	69	34	31	4
2005: to 1/20	12	5	6	1
First Term	209	78	100	31
2005 1/20 to 12/30	33	9	18	6
2006–1/20/07	63	22	34	7
2001–1/20/07	305	109	154	44

Source: Internal White House figures.

then the Reuters reporter asked a question about the unfolding Israeli withdrawal of the settlements in Gaza. A Bloomberg reporter and a Fox reporter asked about the roles of the Sunnis and women in the development of the Iraqi constitution, respectively. All of the questions were on hot topics and therefore predictable.

In addition to press conferences and short question-and-answer sessions, presidents began conducting face-to-face interviews with individual reporters and specially selected groups of reporters. Until recently, journalists tended to object to such singling out of individuals and groups on the grounds that it was unfair to everyone else. But those exercises in presidential discretion have become standard practice, as we shall see.

Complete counts of presidential interviews are difficult to come by, because the interviews are regarded as the property of the news organizations, not of the White House. The White House does make a transcript, but it provides it solely to those reporters who attended the session. It is not distributed to the whole White House press corps unless the attending news organizations consent.

Table 14 presents internal White House figures with a breakdown of the interviews President Bush conducted in six years. The numbers are divided into three types of interviews, which include both interviews with a single reporter and ones with a group from the same news organization. The three types of interview sessions are print, television, and round tables. Interviews with reporters from print publications include those with U.S. and foreign newspapers and magazines. Television interviews consist of all of the five television networks, plus many from abroad. Generally, the president does an interview with one television news organization at a time, although several reporters from that network might participate. Round tables are interview sessions with a group of reporters. Often the groups are based on state, region, or country. Before going on vacation in the summer of 2005, for example, President Bush had an interview with five reporters from Texas print publications.

A president will also do round tables with reporters before he travels abroad. Before he left for the G-8 summit in Scotland and a stop in Denmark in July 2005, President Bush did interviews with the Danish Broadcasting Corporation, ITV of London, the London *Times*, and a round table with reporters from several European countries. The interviews serve as a lead-in to presidential visits in the United States or abroad to appear prior to his arrival.

As these totals suggest, television has become the dominant medium for interviews as fully half of his interviews are television ones. Here, as elsewhere, pictures have become more important than words.

President Clinton observed the same practices, although he had a large number of radio interviews in addition to the print and television ones. He had approximately 189 interviews with reporters during his first term though these figures contain only some of the print interviews in which the president participated.[25]

The Rhythms of a Press Conference

At 2:00 p.m. on April 30, 1998, President Clinton strode down the red carpet in Cross Hall into the East Room and took his place at the podium in front of approximately 175 reporters and perhaps 25 staff members. Anticipation was high on both sides. This would be the president's first solo press conference since the surfacing of the Monica Lewinsky case in January. If he was to be successful in responding to reporters' questions, he would have to demonstrate that he was focused on his job as president and be convincing in his responses about his behavior with the intern.

Everyone in the room knew that he was in for a rough ride, but he and his staff calculated that he could no longer avoid reporters. At the same time, his staff knew that any solo press conference would require a lot of work with him beforehand. They would have to blunt any possible angry outbursts. Preparation keyed to his personal and policy issues would be necessary if he was to have a successful session with reporters.

As unusual as the central topic of this particular press conference was, the fifty-seven-minute session still demonstrates the rhythms of most solo press conferences, including what it takes to prepare for one. In particular, it illustrates the pecking order of news organizations covering the White House, the variety of questions posed, the way a president can work the room, and the lengthy preparation for such sessions with the whole senior staff. Some of the patterns are unique to a specific president, but most practices get passed from one chief executive to another.

Even if he has a scandal to deal with when he holds a solo press conference, a president has strong factors working in his favor. He gets to call on the reporters he wants to recognize, and he can do so in the order of his choosing. His staff prepare in advance a list of questions they believe may be asked, and senior staff members also prepare possible responses, which they discuss with the president in preparatory sessions.

But even with all of those advantages, when he walks out to that podium, he is alone. No one else can answer for him.

Preparing the President

It is very important for the president to avoid any element of surprise when he meets reporters in a public arena to answer their questions. Generally, the press secretary can anticipate almost all of the questions that will be posed and use them in the prep session to get the president ready. McCurry explained, "After press conferences I would grade myself on the prep session that I ran [based] on what percentage of the questions did the president have an answer for. It was very rare that we didn't have like—out of twenty-one, twenty-two questions, we might miss one or two, but generally we got most of them. Generally even the ones we didn't specifically prepare for, he had a pretty good answer for."[26]

There were four ways for him to anticipate questions he might receive, beginning with a list compiled by McCurry based on questions reporters have asked at recent gaggles and briefings. The questions that come up in the gaggle and in the briefing are a primary indicator of the subjects reporters will ask about when they get the chance. There are approximately thirty-five reporters who come to the White House on a regular basis for gaggles and briefings. They form the nucleus of those who even have a chance to ask a question at press conferences. Of the twenty-nine reporters who questioned Clinton on that day, all but four of them regularly attended briefings and asked questions. There may be 150 people in the reporters' section at an East Room press conference, but when a president is picking out people to call on, he works from a short list of known reporters.

The press secretary sometimes knows just what questions a particular reporter will ask, given the opportunity. In the morning gaggle the day of Clinton's press conference, McCurry joked to the assembled reporters that he would see to it that anyone who wanted to give him a question they planned to ask would be called on. "We got takers," McCurry said.[27] At the end of the gaggle, one reporter was seen slipping McCurry a piece of paper.[28] Later on that day, she was one of the people on whom the president called. To be fair, McCurry indicated that she was not the only one to provide him with a question. "You'd always get like three or four people who would say, 'I'm not going to be so shameless as to play your game, but I am really interested in this, and as long as the questions have been vetted on the other topics, if he wants to talk about so-and-so and has something interesting to say, I'd be prepared to get in to that subject.'" That is the way reporters phrased it. "It's predictable. It's people who are working on some project that's not necessarily connected to the news of the day. That was useful. Clinton would not always respond to that. I'd tell him, 'So-and-so may ask a question about this if you get to a point where you want to get into that subject.' He sometimes would call on the person, and sometimes he wouldn't."[29]

While some may be surprised that reporters would tip their hand in this way, the tradition goes back to the time when press conferences were held on a regular schedule. Press Secretary James Hagerty on many occasions noted in his diary what questions reporters indicated they would ask the president in the press conference scheduled for the following day. Wire service reporters regularly offered advance notice in the Eisenhower and Kennedy years.[30] Advance notice by reporters fell out of favor during the Nixon years—but it did not disappear altogether.

A president's staff members also look at what issues are hot with reporters in the news publications that the president will most likely call on. Thinking through the questions allows them to consider the direction the president might take with a conventional question. John Podesta said, "We do think about what the expected, conventional pack journalism questions will be and think about how you can use these as a jumping-off point to make a different point."[31]

In most administrations, the preparation for a solo press conference is very arduous. The stakes for a televised East Room event are much higher than for a regular afternoon session. If the president has not held a press conference for some time, the importance of the session escalates accordingly.

For Clinton, press conference preparation was basically a verbal exercise held the day of the session. McCurry commented, "We always did same-day. We sometimes tried to do a little preparation the night before, but we always ended up having to go back and do a refresher on the same questions the next day, so it was kind of a waste of time." The staff provided Clinton with a briefing book, but it was not a major part of the preparations. McCurry recounted, "Sometimes there was evidence that he had looked at it, but sometimes ample evidence that he hadn't looked at it once prior to the briefing. He was very good about looking at a piece of paper and saying, 'Okay,' and you'd talk to him while he was reading. He could read and listen to you simultaneously. And then he'd put it down and he'd usually have a pretty good sense of the answer."

For this session, staff preparation with the president focused on policy issues and personal questions he might get from reporters. It was an intense session led by McCurry, with segments devoted to different areas. "We would sit in the Cabinet Room and beat the crap out of it for five straight hours," he commented about the preparations for such sessions. As willing as McCurry was to let colleagues participate in press arrangements, press conference preparations were a different matter: "It was the one thing I would not let anybody else mess around with. I sat right across from him, Gore sat next to him, and then Panetta, then Bowles sat on the other side. I sat opposite and ran the damn thing." When Bowles replaced Panetta as chief of staff, he sat next to the president, as he did on this occasion.

The drill was to go through the policy areas as expressed in question form: "We went through all the questions. I would bring in the foreign policy people. [National security adviser Sandy] Berger would do foreign policy stuff. Berger was very insistent that he come in and go through his stuff. He had a set way that he liked to prepare things. I would defer to him on that. We would call them in and then call in various other teams of people to brief him on domestic issues, social issues, scandal issues, political issues. We kind of went through the whole milieu."[32]

Deputy Chief of Staff Harold Ickes explained the speed with which they could go through issues with President Clinton. "You listen to him and then say here's a nuance," Ickes remembered. "First of all, you're dealing with somebody who is very smart and a very quick study. He would listen. He would do an answer, and people would chime in very quickly and say, 'Why don't you try this, why don't you try that, why don't you try that.' He would listen to that and sometimes rework an answer in his head without being questioned again, or sometimes [he would] ask to be asked the question again so he could work it through."[33]

Preparing President Clinton for answering questions relating to the Lewinsky scandal was a two-step process. First the assembled group asked the toughest, harshest questions so that Clinton could work out his anger at what he considered to be his critics' attempts to embarrass him. Joe Lockhart explained how he worked on the president's anger when he was press secretary: "The president, like any human being, has got a temper. The trick in some of these sessions is to get him to vent his anger at me and not in front of the camera. So there is a little baiting that goes on. I ask a question with an edge that even a reporter, I don't think, will ask. There have been many times when he has sort of answered in a way that would be unhelpful for cameras."[34]

Shortly after the April 30 press conference, Deputy Press Secretary Lockhart explained staff thinking about scandal questions. "The majority of these questions, from the Travel Office to Monica Lewinsky, are bullshit. They have nothing to do with the way this government is run, the way this country is run. It has nothing to do with what people in this country are concerned about, but they're part of the game. And we need to make sure that we don't let this game trip us up." Their approach was to avoid answering scandal-related questions in such a way that made news in its own right: "What you do with these questions is you develop sort of a benign answer which is an answer that just sort of leaves someone feeling like, 'Well, what can I do with that, because it's not important.' It's not like we're saying, . . . 'This is defense policy and we're just not going to tell you what our policy is because we think it should be a secret.' We've made a judgment that this is not a serious effort at newsgathering."[35]

While five hours were set aside, not all of the time was always used. The timing depended upon the completion of the questions and the president's energy reserves. "And he got to the point where you could only try his patience so much," recalled McCurry. "I always had it about right, because I used to pretend we had about another hour's worth of work when we were essentially done, and then he'd say, 'You're going to wear me down; I'm going to be exhausted by the time I ever get out there.' I'd say, 'Okay. Let's take a break. You can go have lunch or do what you want to do.' He'd usually go and have lunch and sometimes sneak in a quick nap, take a shower, come back, and be ready to go. I think he always did pretty good in these things."[36] Shortly after the session, President Clinton walked out into the East Room ready to give his statement and provide thought-out responses.

The Questioners and Their Questions

When Clinton looked down on his podium, his statement was accompanied by a chart that the Press Office staff had worked up to show him who was facing him and what organization each attendee represented. But Clinton himself made real-time decisions about who to call on. During the press conference, Clinton could be seen making check marks on the chart as he called on those individuals. He knew where he wanted to go.

McCurry's list followed a long tradition of recognizing the more prestigious press outlets. The slate was dominated by the major news organizations, with wire services and television selected in that order. According to tradition, Clinton began with one of the American wire services, United Press International, and reserved his second question for another, Associated Press. Reuters got the third.

With the first question, President Clinton got a taste of what was to come. After delivering a statement about "an American economic renaissance" and NATO expansion, he turned to Helen Thomas of United Press International, the dean of the White House press corps. "You get the first question," he said. "You may not like it," she told him, laughing. "I never expected to," he responded. Thomas then asked about the president's previous denials on the subject of Lewinsky. When she followed up by asking if he felt the special prosecutor was "out to get you," Clinton responded, "I think modestly observant people are fully capable of drawing their own conclusions to the latter question." Throughout the session, he took aim at his critics and provided little information about his personal relationship with Lewinsky.[37] Thomas's scandal-related questions were followed by policy questions from the other two wire service reporters, Terry Hunt of Associated Press and Steve Holland of Reuters. They asked about the stock market gains and sanctions against Iraq relating to their weapons programs, respectively.

Terry Hunt explained his approach to asking questions at press conferences: "You come to this job with the idea you are not there to promote yourself or embarrass the president. And you try to get his views on

Chart 5. Presidential Press Conference, East Room, The White House, April 30, 1998

ANSA Alejandro Rodrigo	Audio-Video News Connie Lawn	TV Asahi Yokio Kashiyami	Tribune Lisa Leigh	Congress Daily Keith Koffler	Talk Radio News Service Ellen Ratner	Arkansas Democrat Gazette Terry Lemmons	Scripps Howard Ann McFeattor	Christian Science Monitor Skip Thurman	Bloomberg Radio Tina Stage
	Aviation Week Paul Mann	WTTG Jan Smith	BNA Mark Felsenthal	ARD	New York Post Deborah Orin	FOX 2 Julie Kurtz	Chicago Sun Times	CNN 2 Eileen O'Connor	Trude Feldman
		Sarah McClendon	Cox Bob Deans	Dallas Morning News Bob Hillman	VOA Deborah Tate	Boston Globe Brian McGrory	Baltimore Sun Carl Cannon	Washington Times Warren Strobel	Bloomberg News Dina Temple-Raston
			Washington Post 3 Mary McGrory	Houston Chronicle Nancy Mathis	AFP Gretchen Cook	Newsweek Karen Breslau	Los Angeles Times Liz Shogren	USA Today Mimi Hall	New York Daily News Kathy Kiely
				FOX 1 Wendell Goler	New York Times James Bennet	CBS 1 Scott Pelley	Washington Post 1 John Harris	ABC 1 Sam Donaldson	AP Terry Hunt

UPI Radio Don Fulsom	San Francisco Chronicle Mark Sandalow	Newhouse	Media General	WTOP Radio Dave McConnell	ABC Radio Ann Compton	National Journal Alexis	St. Louis Post Dispatch	Market News Service Kevin Kastner	Seattle Post Michael Paulson
Irish Echo Susan Garraty	ABC 2	Copley George Condon	McClatchy Muriel Dobbin	NBC 2 David Bloom	Gannett Chuck Raasch	Standard News Radio Greg Clugston	CNBC	CCH Paula Cruikshank	
CBS Radio Mark Knoller	NPR Mara Liasson	CNN-Radio Noticias Jacobo Goldstein	CBS 2 Bill Plante	AP Radio Mark Smith	Washington Post 2 Peter Baker	American Urban Radio April Ryan	Business Week Rick Dunham		
Time Jan Branegan	Wall Street Journal Jackie Calmes	NBC-Mutual Radio Peter Maer	Knight Ridder Steve Thomma	Chicago Tribune Roger Simon	Hearst Stewart Powell	Newsday Bill Douglas			
UPI Helen Thomas	NBC 1 Claire Shipman	Reuters Steve Holland	CNN 1 Wolf Blitzer	US News & World Report Ken Walsh					

PODIUM

something he hasn't spoken on. Candidly, get him to make news."[38] Most likely, Hunt guessed that he would have more luck getting a response from Clinton on the rise in the stock market than he would if he sought to follow up on Thomas's Lewinsky question.

While Clinton often moved from the wires to the five television networks in solo sessions, as President George W. Bush regularly does, President Clinton did not do so on this occasion. Television was very important in driving the Lewinsky story, and it was unlikely the network reporters would ask about anything else. Knowing that, Clinton did not recognize television reporters consecutively but rather spaced them out. After the wires President Clinton called on two television reporters, Sam Donaldson of ABC and then Wolf Blitzer of CNN, before seeking relief. Both television reporters asked Lewinsky-related questions; now it was time for policy. He called on two reporters he anticipated would not ask scandal questions, and each delivered. One of the reporters, Trude Feldman, almost always asks about the Middle East. On this occasion, she asked about Russian strategy in dealing with Middle East issues.

Then it was back to television and another round of scandal questions, beginning with Claire Shipman of NBC. By this time, the president's anger was beginning to rise. When Shipman asked him about the legal expenses facing many of his staff members, he lashed out at Independent Counsel Kenneth Starr. "There are all these people who have been hauled through this, who under the governing statute, can never get their legal bills reimbursed—so that you have—the independent counsel not only has an unlimited budget and can go on forever—10, 20, 30, 40, 50 years, spend $40 million dollars today, $100 million tomorrow—."[39] Now it was time for some policy relief by selecting Kenneth Walsh of *US News and World Report*, who asked about a compromise on a bill to curb tobacco use by teenagers.

President Clinton called on only one reporter from each news organization, with the exception of CBS. The observed practice in calling on reporters for the networks and the major newspapers is to recognize the reporter who is placed in the "first" seat. If a news organization rates two reporters, then one is assigned by his or her news organization to the "first" or "second" seat. As the words imply, the first seat is close to the front while the second one is farther back. Presidents rarely call on the reporter in the designated second seat. In the case of CBS, Scott Pelley was selected by his news organization to sit in the front-row seat reserved for CBS. As a snub to Pelley, who was particularly critical of the president in the press secretary's daily briefing, President Clinton called on Bill Plante, who was sitting in the back and also Mark Knoller, CBS radio reporter.

Only later did he call on Pelley who focused on unanswered questions about the president's relationship with the intern. "But, respectfully, there has been no explanation for her dozens of visits to the White House after her employment here ended; no explanation for the Secret Service concern about her behavior in the West Wing; no explanation about the extraordinary effort by your secretary and your closest friends to find her a job. Sir, could you now give us some better sense of what appears to be an extraordinary relationship that you had with this woman, and fulfill your promise to the American people of more [information], rather than less, sooner rather than later?" By this point in the press conference, President Clinton knew that he was close to the end. He had no trouble holding back his anger and telling Pelley, "I have nothing else to say. I have been advised—and I think it's good advice under the circumstances—but I just don't have anything else to say about that."

For the remainder of the press conference, President Clinton worked the room by recognizing reporters from a mixture of elite and foreign news organizations. He could anticipate that most major American news organizations would have their reporters ask scandal-related questions. As with Pelley, he left the *Washington Post* and the *New York Times* to the end of the conference. He correctly guessed that he would get questions related to the scandal from their reporters. After taking those three reporters as well as one from the Fox correspondent, he wound up his conference with reporters representing organizations interested in specific domestic issues and ones concerned with foreign policy issues related to particular countries. He called on two African-American reporters who asked about his race initiative and needle exchange programs. Then he went to a Hungarian reporter and two Latin American ones, each of whom posed questions related to the countries they cover.

All in all, the president took a group of questions almost evenly divided between politics and policy. Of the twenty-nine reporters the president recognized, fifteen asked questions on politics and fourteen on policy. Almost all of the politics questions dealt with Monica Lewinsky, but the policy ones were divided with nine about domestic policy and five on foreign policy.

As much as Clinton might have enjoyed responding to the policy queries, news organizations focused on his responses to the Lewinsky questions. They emphasized scandal and its impact on his leadership and on his administration. At the same time, national newspapers, such as the *Washington Post*, the *New York Times*, and *USA Today*, carried excerpts of the press conference, including parts of his opening statement and his responses to a variety of policy questions. In addition, his statements on the economy were used in economic articles, and his foreign and domestic policy points were included in articles on NATO, the Middle East, and tobacco legislation under consideration in the Congress.

While the session may have been rocky when it came to personal issues, Clinton provided his audience with information on what was going on in government and what he was doing on major issues facing the government. McCurry's judgment was that it had gone fairly well. "The president does understand that meeting regularly with the press is a function of the presidency and he should do it," McCurry told Susan Page of *USA Today*. "I was grateful all the questions didn't end up being about scandal. If it had been, I would have called time on it earlier, but I thought it was going reasonably well."[40]

When Eisenhower was president, press conferences represented a big bite of the presidential publicity apple. Of all of Eisenhower's speech and press conference appearances, press conferences were approximately 40 percent of the total. In the Clinton years, press conferences themselves represented less than a third of the president's appearances. But if you include the short question-and-answer sessions, then the sessions with reporters represent the same amount as in the Eisenhower years, 40 percent.

With alternative ways for presidents to meet with reporters, chief executives have been less interested than they once were in holding the solo press conferences that many reporters prefer. What reporters have received in the last twenty-five years, though, is an increase in their opportunities to pose a limited number of questions to a president. Today, a president answers one or more questions from reporters several times a week. Reporters for the wire services, radio, and television are pleased with those opportunities to get the president on the record—and on camera—with responses to unfolding events and issues. What they have lost is the traditional press conference, where reporters could explore the president's thinking on a variety of topics for a half-hour or more. From the public's perspective, they see the president respond to reporters quite frequently.

Marlin Fitzwater, press secretary to Presidents Reagan and George H. W. Bush, mused about a televised solo East Room press conference given by President Clinton on March 19, 1999. "One of the things that struck me about the president's press conference is how their relevance has changed," he said. "That press conference was held for the press corps. It was like a private thing between the president and the people in the room." The press corps put increasing pressure on the White House for the president to hold a session with the president alone answering questions rather than posing together with another head of state. Clinton's last such solo conference had been held on April 30, 1998, almost a year earlier. "No one in the country realized he hadn't been giving press conferences," Fitzwater observed. "They saw him appearing before people every night."

Today presidents have many choices in how they communicate with the public, and the press conference is merely one item of many in their publicity grab bag. "The presidential press conference has been overtaken," Fitzwater indicated, by the alternative opportunities a president now has to communicate with the public through speeches and other exchanges with reporters.[41] Presidents Clinton, and now George W. Bush found other ways to communicate with their constituents, including with those within the Washington political community.

At the same time, the solo press conference is not about to go away. Many reporters prefer it as a way to explore the president's thinking. It is a session where the president is vulnerable. He has no set text he can use, nor can he rely on aides to come up with his answers for him. He must be able to advocate for his policies—and for himself.

8

Managing the Message

Several presidents have solved the puzzle posed at the beginning of the book calling on chief executives and their staff to figure out ways to reach the public regularly and activate support for their initiatives and goals through independent news organizations. Though the press is not part of the government, presidents and their White House communications staff have developed ways of using the press to carry the chief executive's messages to the general public and to particular groups they want to target. But it is not easy to establish an effective communications system and, once created, to maintain its success. As we saw with Presidents Clinton and Bush, creating an effective system requires the right people, resources, and strategies to advocate for the president, to explain his policies, to defend his actions and ideas, and to coordinate publicity inside and outside of the government.

Since the end of World War II, eleven presidents who have served full first terms have been reelected. Presidents Eisenhower, Nixon, Reagan, Clinton, and George W. Bush represented different political views and parties, but did have one thing in common: at some point during their first term in office, all of them developed effective communications operations. In each case, the president and his staff understood the importance of helping others realize what their priorities were and how they were achieving them. They also had substantial challenges in their second terms that tested the strength of those operations.

Two of the remaining seven presidents who served full first terms sought a second one and lost. What Republican George H. W. Bush and Democrat Jimmy Carter had in common was minimal interest in presidential communications as an integral aspect of their presidency. Neither ever created a communications apparatus capable of integrating policy initiatives with plans to sell them to the Washington community and the public. Even with those presidents who were able to win reelection, though, the chief executives and their staffs had difficulty winning the support of the public and members of the Washington community on specific initiatives. In spite of the large numbers of personnel and organizational resources available to them, presidents have difficulty getting their constituents inside and outside of Washington to respond to them in the ways they wish.

In summing up this book, there are four areas where we can view trends and developments in the area of White House communications. First are the basic elements of an effective presidential communications operation. There are at least five elements important to the ability of a presidential communications operation to accomplish its goals. Second are the benefits that a good communications operation buys for a president. Third, there are considerable limits to what a White House communications operation can do for a president. And fourth, we can understand the nature of the institution of the presidency by studying its communications operation.

The Elements of an Effective Presidential Communications Operation

In order to establish a communications operation that advocates, explains, defends, and coordinates on behalf of their president, there are some basic elements related to how effectively it carries out the above four areas. Those elements include what an administration is trying to sell, the communications savvy of the president himself, the organizational components of the communications operation; all are important to the ability of a president and his communications team to perform the basic functions. The organization needs central control, an infrastructure that meets the continuing news needs of reporters, and a communications staff that understands reporters' routines.

Policies with Public Support

In his first year in office, President George W. Bush signed into law two of his policy priorities. During the 2000 presidential campaign, Bush spoke about a half dozen issues that formed his legislative priorities. Among them were education reform and tax cuts. During his first year, he won congressional support for his "No Child Left Behind" education reform bill, which featured student testing and performance-based analysis of schools. He also succeeded with his tax reform plan to eliminate the estate tax and to provide tax cuts to people in most income categories. Dur-

ing the campaign he discussed both education and tax reform with specific ideas of what he wanted to see enacted by Congress. Both proposals
were popular with voters, both before and after the election.

It is hard to sell illusions. Good communications operations have to
be grounded in solid policies and effective performances. No matter how
good a presidential communications team, if a policy or its implementers
are weak or absent, it will be difficult to make it appear otherwise.

In the case of Hurricane Katrina, the federal government's disaster
plans and organizational resources were inadequate for confronting the
problems spawned by the hurricane. President Bush's apparent slowness
in responding to Hurricane Katrina mirrored the demonstrably slow response by federal government agencies tasked with disaster planning, as
broadcast far and wide by news media. Context also counts. Since billions
have been spent on homeland security since September 11, 2001, both
the Washington community and the public were surprised and dismayed
that the federal government's capacity for handling a domestic disaster
was so poor. There was no way to portray the federal government's handling of the hurricane as successful. Thanks to extensive media coverage,
too many people saw that it was not.

So too were the reforms in Social Security a hard sell for the George
W. Bush administration in 2005. The president, his cabinet officers, and
his agency heads went on the road from March to May in a high-profile
campaign, "60 Cities in 60 Days," to sell his twin ideas: that the Social
Security system was in a perilous state and that personal retirement accounts would benefit the public. That campaign was a renewed effort
to build on his administration's actions following his 2005 State of the
Union message in which he discussed his proposal. The more the president spoke about the issue, the more the public disapproved. In early
February, a CNN / USA Today / Gallup poll found 44% approval, 50% disapproval, and 6% unsure with respect to George W. Bush's approach to
addressing the Social Security system. By late July, the approval number
had dropped to 29%, the disapproval number had risen to 62%, and unsure stood at 9%.

After five months in Washington and on the road discussing the
problems of Social Security and the importance of personal retirement
accounts, the public was less likely to support the president's account
plan. People responding to an ABC News / Washington Post poll showed
greater concern about personal retirement accounts after the president's
tour than before he began it. When asked whether they would support or

oppose a plan in which people could invest some of their Social Security contributions in the stock market, in mid-March 56% supported the idea, with 41% opposed and 3% unsure. By early June, support had dropped to 48% while those opposed had increased to 49% and unsure had fallen to 2%.[1] The public simply was not buying personal retirement accounts.

A President Adept at Communications

Communications operations reflect the president they serve. The White House staff is not a complement to a president but a reflection of him. If the president is adept at communications, his apparatus reflects it. If he is uninterested in communications, that, too, will be reflected in the staff operation.

President Reagan's decades of experience in show business equipped him for his extraordinary success as a presidential communicator. James Baker recalled, "We had a president who loved communicating. That was his medium. He was terrific. Boy, was he good. So it was sort of easy for us."[2] President George H. W. Bush had little experience as a performer, was ambivalent about public relations, and invested low resources in developing communications plans for his programs. At one point, he asked Press Secretary Marlin Fitzwater to run his communications operation as well as the Press Office. John Sununu, Bush's chief of staff, was equally uninterested in communications. So it was difficult for other members of the White House staff to develop and implement public relations initiatives.

When the president was preparing to introduce a cooperative venture with Latin American countries, "Enterprise for the Americas," Sununu insisted that no news come out beforehand. His restriction extended to advance preparation of reporters in the White House press corps as well as journalists in involved countries. When the subject of this impending event came up in a senior staff meeting, Fitzwater asked, "How can we just do that today? Why isn't there some buildup to this? Haven't we told the countries that we're going to have the ambassadors over here? We should have them supporting this and putting out statements in support of it and talking to the press in the driveway. And what about Congress? There must be committees who love this, who want to join us, committee chairmen."

Sununu was adamant. He told the staff, "No. I'm not going to have this leak. I'm telling you right now: we're going to do it at ten o'clock."[3] The chief of staff had his way, and no groundwork was laid for this initiative. The result was lackluster stories in the press. The *New York Times* reported the next day about the policy announcement, "The initiative was presented in vague terms that made it difficult to assess its potential impact on trade, industrial development or debt reduction in the hemisphere."[4]

Control at the Top

Whether the president is a Democrat or a Republican, successful communications operations have been controlled at a central point, where the chief of staff or another senior staff member has a view of all the elements of a chief executive's presidency, including the status of his initiatives, his political strengths and weaknesses, and his goals. There are different ways of centralizing such operations. All but one of them calls for coordinating communications at the senior staff level. Generally, the chief coordinating official is the chief of staff. The chief alone controls all of the essential levers for information-gathering, policymaking, and implementation. No other member of the White House staff has access to all of the elements needed to make communications work.

Chiefs of staff interested in centralizing their administration's communications have followed three models. In the first model, the chief coordinates White House communications personally or through deputies but also deals directly with reporters. When James Baker was Reagan's chief of staff, he made a point of having deputies who were experienced in communications, but he would also make his administration's case personally. He recalls Richard Cheney, who had served as President Ford's chief of staff, telling him: "Be sure you spend a lot of time with the press giving them your spin, why you're doing these things. Talk to them. But always do it invisibly."[5] Both Michael Deaver and David Gergen, responsible for the hands-on management of Reagan's operations, reported to Baker. Clinton Chief of Staff Leon Panetta followed Baker's model. He, too, coordinated White House communications through his deputies and would also often talk to reporters personally.

The second model for centralized control of communication has the chief of staff working through deputies but spending little time briefing reporters. Erskine Bowles, who served in the Clinton administration, had deputies responsible for press contacts, but he avoided public media presentations and briefings with reporters. Bowles put Deputy Chief of Staff John Podesta in charge of communications. When Podesta replaced him as chief, he reverted to the first model by taking responsibility not only for coordinating communications but also for making the administration case on Sunday news programs and elsewhere.

The third model for centralizing communications has an appointed communications adviser oversee the coordination of information. President George W. Bush opted for this model when he made Karen Hughes responsible for coordinating all of his publicity. During the remainder of Andrew Card's tenure as chief of staff, Dan Bartlett was responsible for all communications units. Under Josh Bolten, Bartlett's portfolio remains the same.

Where there is a central communications adviser, the chief of staff tends to avoid interfering with that role. Andrew Card occasionally appeared on Sunday news programs and did some traditional Thursday briefings with journalists from *Time, Newsweek,* and *US News and World Report,* but he was not an explainer of policy unless he was involved in the policymaking process himself, as he was with transportation issues. This model is most similar to that of Press Secretary James Hagerty in the Eisenhower administration. While serving as press secretary, Hagerty also performed functions similar to those that a communications adviser would perform today. Eisenhower's chief of staff, Sherman Adams, left both the briefing of reporters and the development of communications plans to Hagerty.

The alternative to one of these centralized communications models has neither the chief of staff nor a communications adviser taking responsibility for the public presentation of a presidency. In the Carter administration and in part of the George H. W. Bush administration, there was no chief communications officer. Instead the press secretary was expected to perform communications functions on an ad hoc basis.

As these two administrations demonstrate, however, there is no substitute for having some sort of official in charge of communications. The press secretary spends too much time on daily operations to plan ahead effectively. If there is no one to oversee the planning and implementation of communications, those jobs tend to end up haphazard or undone.

An Available Publicity Infrastructure

Administrations tend to centralize their communications operations in different ways, but the infrastructure of publicity offices has grown more similar over time. President Clinton had a centralized communications structure operating out of his chief of staff's office, while President George W. Bush has centralized his with a communications czar. Yet both of these structures incorporate permanent White House units. In every recent administration, the Press Office has handled daily press matters, the Office of Communications has served as a planning vehicle, the Office of Media Affairs has worked with news organizations at the regional, state, and local levels, with special offices overseeing photography and speechwriting. President Carter did not have an Office of Communications during some years in his term in office, but he did have all of the other functions represented. President George H. W. Bush had an Office of Communications, though it was not active in the way it has been in the last two administrations.

Who reports to whom can vary from one administration to another, but where to go for what remains the same. Each cog in the White House publicity apparatus has a group of constituents who depend on what these units do for them. If an incoming White House team wanted to eliminate any of these publicity offices, there would be a well-orchestrated campaign to save it.

Staffers Familiar with the Routines of News Organizations

The kinds of stories that news editors assign and news reporters write are fairly predictable. They deal with conflict, disaster, policy setbacks, personal turnarounds, and reversals of political fortune. After all, the word *news* implies something new.

Even so, a clever presidential communications operation can get the news media to channel and to sustain its focus. The Reagan White House made focus the primary objective of its publicity effort. In 1981, when Reagan arrived in the capital, the issue the public found most pressing was the economy. By having President Reagan devote the vast majority of his public remarks to this subject, then segueing to a succession of specific planks in his economic plan, such as his tax cut program, the administration succeeded in keeping the press focused on his economic plans. Administrations ever since, particularly that of George W. Bush, have copied the Reagan administration's strategy of focusing attention on one issue at a time. While events often overtake plans, acting on the basis of strategies and schedules planned in advance remains the best bet for getting the press to follow a lead.

Hiring staffers who are aware of the routines of news organizations is the best way to anticipate what reporters are likely to do, and when. Increasingly, knowing the routines of news organizations has competed with loyalty and experience demonstrated in a campaign as a prerequisite for work on presidential publicity. The Clinton administration had a rough start when it arrived in the White House because its communications team was unfamiliar with the routines of news organizations. Press Secretary Dee Dee Myers and communications director George Stephanopoulos split the job of briefing the press, in public as well as in private. It was a system that did not work, as there can be only one official spokesperson for the president. But President Clinton learned that appointees familiar with the routines of news organizations were the most appropriate people to handle the press. His communications operation improved markedly when his second wave of picks included two of the savviest press veterans in Washington: David Gergen and Mike McCurry.

What a Good Communications Operation Buys a President

The benefits of a skilled publicity operation range from effective organization to the efficient acquisition and allocation of resources. Benefits can be personal as well as institutional. And they include what does not happen as well as what does.

The Opportunity to Reach the Public on His Terms

While it is easier for the president than for any other official to get the attention of the American public, of other government officials, and of world leaders, he still has to compete for publicity. Members of Congress and leaders of interest groups try to define the president and his ideas as they want people to see them. The most sophisticated of his critics know how to insinuate themselves and their own ideas into news stories about him.

By coming in with a clear slate of items to discuss and a plan of how to do it, President Bush made certain that his critics did not get the opportunity to define him before he set forth who he was and what his agenda would be. His critics did begin to make gains, but it took several months for them to do so, and then their efforts proved fleeting after September 11.

When Eisenhower was in the White House, the challenge of getting and keeping public attention was much less difficult than it is today. Interest groups were far more inclined to influence the inner workings of Congress and the executive branch than to challenge the president in print. Often groups felt that they could operate more effectively without publicity. Today, interest groups spend a great deal of money on communications operations. When President George W. Bush traveled the country to defend personal retirement accounts as a facet of his plan for

Social Security reform, he faced a barrage of television commercials produced by the American Association of Retired Persons and MoveOn.org,
a group sponsored by billionaire George Soros.

Arriving in the White House with a communications operation that
is already up and running makes it possible to take immediate advantage of publicity opportunities. A campaign platform is not the same as a
governing agenda. When a president takes over the White House, he has
the public's attention, but he cannot use it as an opportunity to convey
what he wants to do until he has a well-schooled publicity effort in place.
In President George W. Bush's case, he was ready and able to discuss his
agenda when his term began.

During the first two months of his administration, Bush and his staff
focused on one issue a week, and the press followed suit. By focusing on
what they wanted to talk about, they channeled the attention of everyone
else. Education was the subject for the first week, followed by increased
funding for the military, creating a network of faith-based organizations
to help carry out certain government programs, and tax cuts. During the
first week, President Bush spoke in the East Room of the White House
about his "No Child Left Behind" initiative. As with his other issues, he
spoke in town but traveled outside of Washington as well. By planning
the subjects and locations of his speeches well in advance, he took advantage of the opportunities for publicity afforded every new president and
limited his risks of making mistakes.

During his administration, President George W. Bush has, more than
any other recent president, focused on the agenda he wants to discuss.
Through this discipline, his administration has been drawn off of their
topics less frequently than has been the case when policy divisions in
other administrations have dominated reporting from the White House.
"They have been much more focused on the substance of the policy that
they're trying to deliver to the American people, and less discussion
around the theatrics or the infrastructure or the process behind the curtain," observed Mike McCurry.[6]

Fewer Mistakes

Even as George W. Bush was campaigning for the presidency, well before
the transition that followed his election, Karl Rove studied earlier transitions with an eye to learning what mistakes to avoid and how to lay the
groundwork for an effective tenure in office. Rove knew that his candidate had treated communications as a vital component of his politics and

his governance. "We did take a look at the seven [presidential transitions], essentially [John F.] Kennedy forward," he recalled. "We actually looked at the first 180 days and tried to draw lessons about not only the things that happened in the first 180 days, but what were the things that allowed them to then move on to have a successful period after that. We looked also at the structures of the offices and examined those, but our starting point was really the President [George W. Bush]'s office in Texas, and then the campaign where there had been this close integration between policy and politics and publicity—communications."[7]

Rove's research confirmed Bush's view that publicity gaffes made early, when the public's attention is high, can be very costly. During his own first press conference, President Clinton focused his opening statement so heavily on the issue of gays in the military that it drew attention to this issue and then it was difficult for him and his team to shift its focus to programs they wanted to highlight.[8] When an administration has mapped out its publicity plans in detail, there is less chance of its "speaker-in-chief" being led or thrown off track.

Advance Warning of Political and Communications Problems

Problems often surface in the Briefing Room or in conversations reporters have with officials. Sometimes, the warning comes in the form of reporters' questions, which are asked because news organizations regarded the issue as an important question—this was very much the case with persistent questions about President Bush's State of the Union address claim that Iraq had sought yellowcake uranium. Some reporters raised the issue of the accuracy of the presidential claim in the press secretary's gaggles and briefings before the White House responded to it adequately. During the interim, the White House watched its bad publicity over the issue mount.

An area where President Clinton received a great deal of bad publicity was his series of meetings in the White House with contributors to his 1996 reelection campaign. If communications staff had chased down the information reporters had sought about possible sessions with contributors, one scandal might have not occurred. "Had I been a little more inquiring and been a little more emphatic about trying to get information for reporters, I would have dug harder in uncovering all these sessions that Bill Clinton was having with his contributors, including some who had no business being in the White House in the first place," said Mike McCurry. If McCurry had asked questions about suspicious events on the president's calendar or the identity of the attendees, "me asking those questions probably could have stopped from happening one of the crises that I would argue was the most debilitating scandal that impacted the Clinton presidency. . . . It was the campaign finance questions that really tarnished the impact of his election in 1996."[9]

Reporters can share White House information in another valuable way. Veteran *Washington Post* correspondent Ann Devroy remembered the mistakes the Clinton staff made in the early days of their administration. In part, she believed, their problems could have been avoided by talking to press people who knew the rhythms of White House operations. Citing the 1993 firing of White House Travel Office personnel, Devroy explained exactly how veteran reporters could have been useful to the new staff members. "The press could have warned them, had they had any kind of working relationship, that they were going to get themselves into deep doo-doo if they did this," she said. Firing the long-serving White House personnel "was so stupid, because they could have said that we are going to save money, and we are going to do this, and we are going to transfer these people to other places. Instead, they walk up and accuse them all of being crooks, and not only did they do that publicly, but people from the White House were calling people here, at the *Post* and elsewhere I know, to directly accuse those people of being criminals and of stealing."[10] After operating in the dark, President Clinton had to deal with fallout from this issue for years to come. The issue could easily have been avoided.

Supplementary Resources

Coordinating with communications strategies within a number of departments makes it easier for the White House to leverage the resources available for particular publicity campaigns. Department secretaries can serve as effective surrogates for the president on issues important to the administration. Agencies have resources of their own to contribute to particular campaigns.

When President Bush was ready to sign the farm bill, the Department of Agriculture provided him with a 6:30 a.m. live radio feed to farmers via Farm Radio. Dan Bartlett commented, "There, the Department of Agriculture used its resources. They just called in a feed to WHCA [White House Communications Agency], and they had the bridge over there, which Farm Radio stations throughout the country could call in and link up to. So we used their communications apparatus to execute that communications." Once the broadcast took place, the Department of Agriculture could estimate how many stations took the feed: "There is a service that tracks the ratings of radio markets, and then we can tell through the Department of Agriculture how many of them picked up the feed live, how many took tape feeds of it, et cetera. Our estimation, I think, was probably a half million homes, farm homes, that that morning listened to it."

While presidential campaigns tend to have the latest costly communications technology, the same is not true of the White House. If a president and his staff want to keep up their speaking schedule and reach particular parts of the country, they have to come up with creative ways to share the costs. Here is how Dan Bartlett explained the issue of resources: "Planning the schedule helps husband our resources for bigger events. The other thing is, particularly after 9/11, the president was so much on, and so many people were watching him, and so many people were tuning into network live coverage of things, that we spent a lot more time making sure that the environment we put him in looked well, and that's very expensive." When he spoke from Atlanta about homeland security in October 2001, the scene was set for an international audience. "There were ten thousand people in that hall, and we lit the entire arena. Lighting for that alone is $75,000. You don't think about those things during the course of a campaign, but you do . . . when you're on a budget that the Congress controls."[11]

The Limits of Presidential Communications Operations

White House communications operations provide the president with personnel, resources, and strategies as he seeks to develop, articulate, and reach his policy and political goals. We have seen the time and energy an administration puts into thinking about communications issues and acting on them. Yet there are limits to what a communications operation can do for a president. Among the limits are ones related to the president himself, his staff, his policies, and the public. Some presidents produce and perform for top-flight communications operations. Others allow their publicity efforts to drift. How a communications apparatus is structured depends on a president's choices, including how he organizes his staff. How it operates depends on the ability and desire of the president and his staff to explain his administration's policies and goals. It also depends on the interest the public has in hearing what the president has to say.

A President's Personal Style

The emphasis of an administration in part mirrors a president's personal style. For the most part, the chief executive's personal style is a strength. It usually helps presidents get elected, after all. Yet a president's personal style can also be a limitation in how an administration operates. President George W. Bush is known for his management style emphasizing long-range planning. While his ability to set out goals and plans and stick to them has been a personal strength and an administrative one as well, it has also caused him problems. Once he makes plans, he and his team find it difficult to switch to another course of action.

President Bush was late in responding to Hurricane Katrina, which happened in part because he was enjoying a long-planned vacation in Crawford, Texas. His communications and administrative staffs were taking the same weeks off as well. When asked about antiwar protester Cindy Sheehan, who had camped out near his Crawford ranch during August 2005, Bush replied, "I think it's important for me to be thoughtful and sensitive to those who have got something to say." Sheehan, whose son died in Iraq serving in the U.S. military, wanted the president to talk to her about the Iraq War. "But I think it's also important for me to go on with my life, to keep a balanced life. I think the people want the president to be in a position to make good, crisp decisions and to stay healthy. And part of my being is to be outside exercising. So I'm mindful of what goes on around me. On the other hand, I'm also mindful that I've got a life to live, and will do so."[12] He was sticking to his carefully planned schedule—as he was when Hurricane Katrina hit two weeks later.

As the hurricane gained strength, government officials issued warnings to residents in its potential path. Saturday, August 27, Bush declared a state of emergency in Louisiana from his Crawford ranch and authorized the Federal Emergency Management Administration (FEMA) to provide aid. On Sunday, August 28, the day before the hurricane struck, he tucked a few comments on the emergency into longer remarks about the Iraqi constitution. He had two Medicare speeches scheduled in Arizona and California on Monday and then a speech about the war on terrorism on Tuesday in San Diego. All three sets of planned remarks incorporated remarks at the beginning of the speeches dealing with the hurricane. But referring to the unfolding crisis exclusively in such tacked-on remarks made him seem strangely out of touch.

The situation on the ground in the hurricane zone was grave. Soon after the hurricane struck New Orleans, its levees were breached and serious flooding ensued. Gulf Coast towns in Mississippi and Alabama were also hit very hard. Still the president stuck with his schedule. Not until he was flying back to Washington on Wednesday did he get even a glimpse of the affected area—and that view he got from his plane at 1,700 feet. By this time, New Orleans was flooded, people were stranded on their rooftops, conditions at the Superdome and the convention center, where evacuees had been sheltered, were unsanitary and unsafe, and, except for the Coast Guard, the federal government agencies had little presence.

With the president out of Washington, Michael Chertoff, secretary of homeland security, as overseer of the department in which FEMA is housed, was in charge of handling the federal response to the effects of this hurricane. In a news conference in Washington, he declared that he was "extremely pleased with the response" of the federal government. But he had yet to visit the affected areas. So his comments gave the impression that even the administration officials who had remained in Washington were remote and out of touch. All of this was being shown on television, to an audience swelled with viewers entirely free to watch television because, like the president, they too were on summer vacations. Two additional elements of President Bush's personal style made it difficult for him and his staff to alter the perception that he was out of touch and disengaged: his reputation for not following the news and his well-known reluctance to fire, or even criticize, officials working for him.

President Bush often made a point of describing himself as someone who neither read newspapers nor watched television, although insiders, including his wife, have noted that he does do some of both in addition to relying on others, including her, to fill him in. Because he was traveling during those first days of the hurricane, he saw little more than snippets of the television coverage. When an article in *Newsweek* reported that communications adviser Dan Bartlett had made a DVD of news broadcasts to show the president as he traveled to the Gulf for the first time, the impression of an out-of-touch president was cemented.[13]

By the latter part of the week, officials in both parties were critical of the way federal officials and their agencies had handled both the preparation for and the consequences of Hurricane Katrina. But Bush believed it bad for team morale to criticize in public those who were working for him. "A lot of people are working hard to help those who've been affected, and I want to thank the people for their efforts." Immediately following this praise, he said, "The results are not acceptable."[14] But he did not specify why the results were unacceptable or who was at fault. Critics of the federal government effort singled out FEMA. Later the same day, Bush stood next to the director of FEMA, Michael Brown, and said, "Brownie, you are doing a heck of a job."[15] The scene was widely seen as evidence of a president who had lost touch with the realities of one of the most devastating natural disasters in the history of the United States.

Smooth communications operations are hard to come by, because they must handle short-term, nuts-and-bolts emergencies as well as long-term, policy-oriented campaigns. Each poses different demands on the lifestyle and governing style of a president.

Hurdles in Altering Established Presidential Reputations

There is usually a context to a presidency. The chief executive comes into office with a reputation in terms of his leadership and his personal style. Once they are established, reputations and images are difficult to alter. Sometimes a president's communications team can make some headway in altering a negative image, but most often this is not possible. President George H. W. Bush provides an example of the difficulty of turning around an image once formed. Viewed as a patrician from a long line of wealthy political and financial leaders, Bush was also seen as a person who was not in touch with the average citizen. News stories emphasizing those points were difficult for his staff to counter. One example makes the point.

When Bush was traveling around the country at the beginning of the reelection campaign in February 1992, he went to an exhibit at the convention of the National Grocers Association. An article in the *New York Times* by Andrew Rosenthal described his encounter with a grocery store scanner in the following way: "As President Bush travels the country in search of re-election, he seems unable to escape a central problem: This career politician, who has lived the cloistered life of a top Washington bureaucrat for decades, is having trouble presenting himself to the electorate as a man in touch with middle-class life. Today, for instance, he emerged from 11 years in Washington's choicest executive mansions to confront the modern supermarket." Rosenthal added, "Then he grabbed a quart of milk, a light bulb and a bag of candy and ran them over an electronic scanner. The look of wonder flickered across his face again as he saw the item and price registered on the cash register screen. 'This is for checking out?' asked Mr. Bush. 'I just took a tour through the exhibits here,' he told the grocers later. 'Amazed by some of the technology.' "[16]

White House staff later maintained the machine that so amazed the president was not an ordinary scanner.[17] But contemporaneously, his staff was not able to counter the impression the president was confronting the same things that housewives saw every day. As a response that day, Press Secretary Marlin Fitzwater "told reporters that Bush had seen this [older] technology at work before. At least once. In Kennebunkport, Maine."[18] Fitzwater explained: "I had made the case that Bush could never have seen the new scanner technology before because NCR told us it was experimental and had not been sold. Then the press asked if the president had ever seen checkout scanners before, implying he had never been to a grocery store. I replied that he had been to the grocery in Kennebunkport, where they presumably had the older technology."[19]

It did not take long for an image to take hold. The second- and third-day articles bore titles such as "President Bush, Checkout-Challenged" and "Message for Rip Van Bush; A Primer on the Technology Thing."[20]

The Problem of Simultaneously Listening and Advocating

One of the byproducts of a communications operation geared toward action is the difficulty in listening while selling the president's ideas. Operations focused on an agenda require the president and his staff to have a sense of their mission, to articulate it, to repeat it, and to adhere to it. They want to discuss their issues and not to spend time responding to the agendas of others, particularly their critics. In doing so, those same people can fail to listen to alternate interpretations held by others or items worth putting on their agenda.

Both the Reagan and the George W. Bush administrations developed exceptionally well-run communications operations. By the same token, each had difficulty getting those operations to change course. The Reagan administration's communications plan for promoting the nomination of Robert Bork to the Supreme Court relied on fielding short press releases and interviews to local news organizations. The premise of this strategy was that the elite national media would have little interest in covering the nomination during the summer months. Even when it turned out that the *New York Times* and the *Washington Post* were in fact very interested in covering the Bork nomination, Reagan's communications team stuck with their original plans. Analyses of Bork's long and controversial legal record contained in stories coming out of Washington and New York went uncountered. The opposition succeeded in defining the nature of both the debate and the nominee. Admittedly, the nominee did prove a difficult person to sell to the public and to the Senate.

The George W. Bush administration took months to add corporate responsibility to its slate of pressing issues. While President Bush discussed it repeatedly in his campaign speech in 2004, it was a long time before he and his staff viewed it as a salient issue when it surfaced in 2001. It took several months after the Enron collapse in December 2001 and the corporate fraud issues raised in the telecommunications field with the downfall of WorldCom, Global Crossing, and Qwest Communications International before the president highlighted the issue. It was not until July 9, 2002, that the president gave a major speech on the issue. The following month he held an August 13 conference in Waco, Texas, focusing on corporate responsibility as one of several key economic issues.

The Tendency to Communicate with One's Friends

Rare is the staff that is truly ecumenical in providing information to news organizations. Most place primary attention on those reporters and news organizations they know and ones they believe have a wide effect in the Washington community and among the public.

Communications staffers provide information to sources with whom they are comfortable. That puts a premium on contacts with reporters and organizations they know and reduces contacts with those they may not know, and thus not trust. White House staff work from a viewpoint of distrust for news organizations. One senior staff member explained the apprehension of staff in talking to reporters. Sometimes a particular item is pulled out of an interview in a manner, this staff member said, that characterizes the interviewee's sentiments in a way that is unfair: "So what tends to happen—and this requires a long history in this business—you develop your own sources. I know who my friends are in the press who I can trust, and they get better information. They get better contacts, they get better color."[21]

In reality, the more broadly a White House disseminates information and the more quickly and accurately it does so, the better the publicity they receive. The opposite holds true as well.

A measure of the difficulty the Bush White House has had letting in contrary viewpoints can be seen in the manner in which their allies communicated with them in the runup to the Iraq War. Two Republican supporters of the administration, James A. Baker III, who managed the

Florida recount for George W. Bush, and Brent Scowcroft, member of the administration's Foreign Intelligence Board, both wrote newspaper commentaries in the *New York Times* and *Wall Street Journal* to communicate their concern to the administration over the Iraq situation. They were not persuaded that they could reach the president in a traditional way, so they took a public strategy instead.

Reluctance to Admit Mistakes

Most administrations don't like to admit mistakes. A good staff operation can help an administration reduce the number of mistakes it makes, but once committed, errors are difficult to handle. Allowing mistakes to drift without correcting the record proves to be costly because the issues in question will remain in people's minds until they are dealt with. But most administrations learn the lesson the hard way, and then learn it many times over.

As we noted earlier, Ron Nessen said that in the White House the "same set of rules always apply year after year, administration after administration: Tell the truth, don't lie, don't cover up, put out the bad news yourself, put it out as soon as possible, put your own explanation on it, all those things." What he also found, though, was the difficulty of getting others to sign on to those rules, especially if mistakes were involved: "A lot of times, other members of the staff don't want to do that; they don't understand it. They're political strategists; they have a slightly different set of goals. Sometimes you have to fight that battle inside the White House, and sometimes the president is reluctant to do that."[22]

Communications and the Presidency

Studying White House communications operations teaches us valuable lessons about the presidency. Communications is a major activity of presidents and their staffs, so we can learn about the office of the presidency and the staff operations. Communications trends point to overall presidential patterns.

The White House Staff Reflects the President

No matter what administration it is, the White House staff structure reflects the president the staff serves. Of course, if a staff represents the president's strengths, it also reflects his weaknesses. It does not provide what he lacks. Those presidents who are good communicators spend their time and energy on publicity—as do their staffs. Those chief executives who are weak communicators choose to devote few staff resources to strengthen their own shortcomings. Instead, they focus resources on the areas they prefer to emphasize.

With his background in Hollywood image-making, President Reagan made certain that he had a publicity operation that would carry the messages and actions of his presidency to the American people as well as to specific publics inside and outside of government that he wanted to reach. He had Michael Deaver, who was close to him and to Nancy Reagan, handle issues and events related to his image on television and in person. Reagan created a White House staff structure in which communications was important to those at the top level as well as throughout the organization.

James Baker explained why staff reflect, rather than complement, a president. "I think the staff is always going to reflect the president's strengths and weaknesses because everything is derivative from him. There is no power that is not derivative from him." Thus, staff makes certain to respond to the president's interests. If he is not focused on a particular organizational area or policy, neither are they.

Baker said that staff reflect a president in more than the area of communications: "I think that's true on foreign policy. I think it's true in domestic policy. I think it's true generally." During the George H. W. Bush administration, "what a wonderful time it was to be secretary of state . . . because we had a president who understood foreign policy, he liked foreign policy, he devoted presidential time, resources, and attention to it, and he was good at it. And we were good at it, as a consequence. I think the same thing is true whether it's communications, whether it's campaigning, whether it's domestic policy, no matter what it is."[23]

On the other hand, President George H. W. Bush did not enjoy communications and developed a system that reflected his lack of interest in presidential publicity. He met with reporters and gave speeches, but he did not work on them as a coordinated whole. His most important communications staff member was Marlin Fitzwater, his press secretary, not his communications director.

White House Staff Are Often Risk Averse

In the first term, communications staff was reluctant to risk President Bush's popularity by having him or someone else in his administration make a communications mistake. Above all, they wanted to avoid putting him or his surrogates in a position of vulnerability. "I think staffers or administration people have the fear of making a mistake," Bartlett said. "And when you are making a mistake before the president is going before the people for reelection it has a different consequence than making a mistake when he is no longer running for reelection." The fear is that something will be used in a way the administration official may not have intended. In the "campaign environment things can be taken out of context or misconstrued or used against you in a way that somebody would fear it would be used in a politically harmful way to their boss. And obviously no one wants to be put in that precarious situation."[24] Such a case for the Bush team occurred early in the campaign season in February 2004.

The annual economic report prepared by the Council of Economic Advisers had been the centerpiece for a week of events highlighting how well the economy was doing—but not, alas, without its share of fallout. The report made mention of the sensitive issue of outsourcing of jobs by American corporations to other countries. In releasing the report, Gerald Mankiw, chairman of the CEA, told reporters, "outsourcing is just a new way of doing international trade." He explained, "More things are tradable than were tradable in the past and that's a good thing." Mankiw was an immediate target of criticism by Democrats but also by midwestern Republicans, such as Representative Donald Mazullo of Illinois, who called for his resignation: "I know the President cannot believe what this man has said. He ought to walk away, and return to his ivy-covered office at Harvard."[25] Others in the administration came to Mankiw's aid, which kept the issue in the news.[26]

Republicans and Democrats Are Developing Similar Communications Approaches

From Eisenhower through Carter, there were partisan differences in the way the White House was run. Republicans from Eisenhower to Nixon to Reagan organized their White House communications in a similar manner, with a sophisticated organization controlled by senior aides with a broad view of administration operations. Except for the Eisenhower administration, where Hagerty handled planning as well as daily press operations, the key communications figure in the Nixon and Reagan administrations was the director of communications, who organized planning. Of all the post–World War II Republicans, only President George H. W. Bush eschewed a long-range planning operation in favor of a daily press strategy controlled by Press Secretary Marlin Fitzwater.

Democrats during this time held to a different pattern, mainly in that

Presidents Kennedy, Johnson, and Carter, except later in his administration, did not have chiefs of staff who organized and managed White House operations. Instead their staff structures were loose ones, with several different key players in senior posts. For all of them, the press secretary was the most important official in the communications area.

President Clinton broke from the pattern once he opted for a strong central staff structure under Chief of Staff Leon Panetta. Even though the press secretary was still the key communications official, the chief of staff was a central figure and, to a lesser extent, the communications director. They saw planning as important, even if they felt that their ability to adapt to events and situations was crucial as well.

Future Democratic and Republican administrations will most likely adopt a strong staff system under the control of a chief of staff who values communications. If they learn from the lessons of what works from their predecessors, they will have a system that emphasizes planning, discipline, targeting audiences, and adaptability to changing circumstances.

Presidents and Their Staffs Treat Political and Policy Difficulties as Communications Problems

Fresh off of his 2004 reelection win, President Bush in one year met with strong resistance to his handling of Hurricane Katrina, his Social Security package, his plans for immigration reform, his failed nomination of Harriet Miers to the Supreme Court, and the administration-backed deal involving a Dubai company managing container terminals at several major U.S. ports. On top of this, throughout the year he faced increasing criticism of his handling of the war in Iraq. Having Republican control of both houses of Congress didn't bring about support for his policies. It did, however, bring calls for him to make changes in his communications team.

The response of an administration to the pressure of political and policy difficulties is often to assume their problems lie in communications. Presidents will change their communications staff and sometimes their chiefs of staff as well. Under the weight of the Iran-Contra scandal, President Reagan brought in a new chief of staff, former Senator Howard Baker, and a communications director, Tom Griscom. When his job approval numbers appeared stuck in the 30 percent range for the better part of a year, President George W. Bush opted to bring in Josh Bolten as his chief of staff and Tony Snow as his press secretary. After several months, his job approval numbers had hardly budged.

In reality, what presidents have are political and policy problems, not communications problems. The expectations of what presidential communications can deliver are much greater than what they can really do. Yet there is still much an effective communications operation can do for a president.

Presidents Adapt to Communications Opportunities

Presidents and their staffs have demonstrated the adaptability of the presidency to a changing environment in the important area of communications. When George B. Cortelyou served as an assistant secretary and then secretary to Presidents McKinley and Roosevelt, he was very aware of developing technology, especially photography. He made certain that his presidents were well covered by the new medium and that photographers were included when the president traveled. Twentieth-century presidents adjusted to radio, television, and the Internet. They and their staffs viewed technological change as an opportunity, not as a burden.

President Eisenhower included the new medium of television as a central part of his publicity plans. He and his advisers saw television as a method of reaching the public directly. Since his time, other presidents have worked with technological changes to accomplish the same goal: to reach an audience with minimal edits and interpretation by reporters and their news organizations.

In Eisenhower's day, reaching the public regularly occurred through his twice-monthly press conferences. Although they were presented on tape delay, the broadcasts gave a full picture of the president responding to a variety of questions. President Kennedy saw the advent of live news conferences carried in full by the networks as a regular feature of his effort to explain to the public his thinking and actions. For Presidents Nixon and Reagan, it was nighttime East Room news conferences at a time when there were three national networks (ABC was not a major news player in the 1950s and 1960s). A large audience stopped their routines and watched.

Today, getting to the public in as unfiltered a manner as possible still involves television, but now presidents can choose a combination of cable news networks and local ones and the Internet. No matter what the available technology is, presidents have developed ways to maximize their time with the public.

While the fast-paced news cycle makes it difficult for presidents to get ahead of the news to explain their case in their terms, both Clinton and

Bush managed to do so. In both cases, they talked about the subjects they wanted to discuss, and in both cases, the viewers understood their meaning. People may not have liked what both presidents had to say, but the public had the opportunity to listen to them many times.

In order to lead effectively, a president needs to be able to communicate with the public on important issues and events. While at one time the president could handle his own communications planning, it is no longer possible for him to do so. Today, effective presidential communications requires the chief executive to put together an organization capable of arranging his publicity. He needs to have an organization behind him that is capable of crafting messages for the public and then of managing those messages in a way that appeals to the public he is interested in reaching.

The technology that presidents use to get to the public has developed into many different forms. Even so, presidents continue to need news organizations. News organizations represent the vehicle for the president to reach the public on a daily basis with news of himself and his administration. For the press, the president is just as important as news organizations are for him. He is central to the concept of news their readers or viewers have. It is the need that each side has for the other that makes the presidential-press relationship an important feature of the modern presidency. It is a relationship that provides the president with his needed link to his supporters, whom he informs, encourages, and activates on behalf of himself and his programs.

Notes

Introduction

1. Press conferences, Calvin Coolidge Papers, Forbes Library, Northampton, Massachusetts.

2. George W. Bush, "Remarks to the Chamber of Commerce in Portland," March 23, 2001, Portland, Maine, *Weekly Compilation of Presidential Documents*. Available at www.gpo.gov/nara/nara003.html.

3. Jonathan Weisman and Bradley Graham, "Dubai Firm to Sell U.S. Port Operations," *Washington Post*, March 10, 2006, p. A1.

4. Michael McAuliff, "Chuck's Port-Deal Terror, Urges Prez to Nix 'Risky' Sale to Arab Biz," *New York Daily News*, February 14, 2006.

5. Sheryl Gay Stolberg, "How a Business Deal Became a Big Liability for Republicans in Congress," *New York Times*, February 26, 2006, p. 14.

6. Dan Bartlett, interview with the author, Washington, D.C., October 27, 2006.

7. "Interview with Reporters Aboard Air Force One" and "Remarks on Arrival from Golden, Colorado," February 21, 2006.

8. Dan Bartlett, interview with the author, Washington, D.C., October 27, 2006.

9. Paul Blaustein, "Dubai Firm Cleared to Buy Military Supplies," *Washington Post*, April 29, 2006, p. A6.

10. Michael Baruch Grossman and Martha Joynt Kumar, *Portraying the President: The White House and the News Media* (Baltimore: Johns Hopkins University Press, 1981).

11. Richard E. Neustadt, *Presidential Power: The Politics of Leadership* (New York: Wiley, 1960).

12. Richard Neustadt, "A Preachment from Retirement," in *Presidential Power: Forging the Presidency for the Twenty-First Century*, ed. Robert Y. Shapiro, Lawrence Jacobs, and Martha Joynt Kumar (New York: Columbia University Press, 2000), 465–66.

13. While the number of studies of the White House written from the viewpoint of staff regarding the choices they make and the reasons behind them is small, there are studies from other perspectives that were important for my work. There is a growing literature about White House operations written by political scientists interested in the dynamics of staff operations. Particularly important for me was the

groundwork established in Karen Hult and Charles Walcott's *Governing the White House: From Hoover through LBJ* (Lawrence: University Press of Kansas, 1995) and *Empowering the White House: Governance under Nixon, Ford, and Carter* (Lawrence: University Press of Kansas, 2004), John Burke's *The Institutional Presidency*, 2d ed. (Baltimore: Johns Hopkins University Press, 1992), and Bradley Patterson's *The White House Staff: Inside the West Wing and Beyond* (Washington, D.C.: Brookings Press, 2000).

Presidential decision-making studies are important because they provide a view of how chief executives and their staffs operate. In contemporary presidency studies, Roger Porter, who served as senior economic and domestic policy adviser in the George H. W. Bush administration and worked in the Reagan and Ford White Houses as well, went from academic life into presidential advising on economic policy and then returned to Harvard University, where he teaches the presidency course there. His *Presidential Decision Making: The Economic Policy Board* (New York: Cambridge University Press, 1982), based on his White House years in the Ford administration, adds to our knowledge with its view from inside the White House in an important area of presidential activity. So too does John Burke and Fred Greenstein's *How Presidents Test Reality: Decisions on Vietnam, 1954 and 1965* (New York: Russell Sage Foundation, 1991) tell us about presidential decision-making, in this case on Vietnam-related issues.

14. A separate literature focuses on the general relationship between the government and the media and on presidential leadership, which includes the chief executive's relationship with news organizations. In the area of government and the news media, a key work is Tim Cook's *Governing with the News: The News Media as a Political Institution* (Chicago: University of Chicago Press, 1998). While we often think of the relationship between government and the press as hostile, he showed another side of the partnership by emphasizing the ways in which news organizations and government officials benefited from the relationship in spite of the tensions.

In his *Presidential Leadership of Public Opinion* (Bloomington: Indiana University, 1965), Elmer Cornwell was one of the first political scientists to identify and write about the importance of presidential communications. He discussed how presidents used available resources to further their programs and how the chief unit at that time, the Press Office, was organized and operated. His work provided a good measure of how far White House communications organization had come since its nascent days in the Eisenhower administration. Among the important books on presidential leadership, those by George Edwards, including *At the Margins: Presidential Leadership of Congress* (New Haven: Yale University Press, 1989) and *On Deaf Ears: The Limits of the Bully Pulpit* (New Haven: Yale University Press, 2003), explain how difficult it is for presidents to change public opinion.

Samuel Kernell and Jeffrey Tulis have made important contributions to the study of presidential leadership in their classic works *Going Public: New Strategies of Presidential Leadership* (Washington, D.C.: Congressional Quarterly Press, 1986) and *The Rhetorical Presidency* (Princeton: Princeton University Press, 1987), respectively. Kernell discussed presidential strategies designed to create public support for a chief executive's initiatives, and Tulis traced the development of presidential rhetoric over the history of the presidency.

The difficulties presidents have in directing and activating public opinion is matched by their problems in establishing and controlling their own agenda. Shanto Iyengar wrote about the news media's role in determining what gets regarded as news. While the White House would like to determine what stories news organizations emphasize, the president and his staff have to work with the rhythms and routines of news organizations in order to exploit the process to their benefit. See Shanto Iyengar and Donald R. Kinder, *News That Matters: Television and American Opinion* (Chicago: University of Chicago Press, 1987); Shanto Iyengar, *Is Anyone Responsible? How Television Frames Political Issues* (Chicago: University of Chicago Press, 1991); Stephen Ansolabehere, Roy Behr, and Shanto Iyengar, *The Media Game: American Politics in the Television Age* (New York: Macmillan, 1993). Donald L. Shaw and Maxwell E. McCombs, eds., *The Emergence of American Political Issues: The Agenda-Setting Function of the Press* (St. Paul, Minn.: West, 1977) is also relevant.

Presidents and their staffs have responded to the agenda-setting routines of news organizations by creating organizational units that use their knowledge of the media to advance the president's case. Two important works that explain how White House organizations respond to news media routines are John Anthony Maltese's *Spin Control: The White House Office of Communications and the Management of Presidential News* (Chapel Hill: University of North Carolina Press, 1992) and the book I wrote with Michael Grossman, *Portraying the President: The White House and the News Media* (Baltimore: Johns Hopkins University Press, 1981). Maltese's book focuses on the early years of the Office of Communications, with emphasis on the formative Nixon and Reagan years; it is the focus on this relatively new body, also covered in this book, that makes it so valuable.

15. Developments in the way White House officials plan their communications can be tracked in the memoirs of those who have worked there. Each provides information on the rhythms of their White House years, making them useful in following the organization of White House units. For this study, the books by presidential press secretaries Marlin Fitzwater, Ron Nessen, Jody Powell, and Ari Fleischer provided valuable insights into the respective media operations headed by each author. See Ari Fleischer, *Taking Heat: The President, the Press, and My Years in the White House* (New York: William Morrow, 2005); Marlin Fitzwater, *Call the Briefing: Bush and Reagan, Sam and Helen: A Decade with the Presidents and the Press* (New York: Times Books, 1995); Jody Powell, *The Other Side of the Story* (New York: William Morrow, 1984); and Ron Nessen, *It Sure Looks Different from the Other Side* (New York: Simon and Schuster, 1978).

Two presidential communications advisers have also detailed what they have learned: Michael Deaver wrote about his years in the White House during Reagan's first term, and David Gergen expressed his views on presidential leadership based on his tenure in the Nixon, Ford, Reagan, and Clinton White Houses. See Michael K. Deaver, *Behind the Scenes: In Which the Author Talks about Ronald and Nancy Reagan* (New York: William Morrow, 1987), and David R. Gergen, *Eyewitness to Power: The Essence of Leadership, Nixon to Clinton* (New York: Simon and Schuster, 2000). In order to pull together information from all of the presidencies in which these press secretaries and communications directors served, I also interviewed each to isolate commonalities across administrations but also factors that differentiated them.

16. Stephen Ponder, *Managing the Press: Origins of the Media Presidency, 1897–1933* (New York: St. Martin's Press, 1999); Melvin Laracey, *Presidents and the People: The Partisan Story of Going Public* (College Station: Texas A&M University Press, 2002); Martha Joynt Kumar, "The White House Beat at the Century Mark," *The Harvard International Journal of Press/Politics* 2 (Summer 1997): 10–30, and "The White House Beat at the Century Mark: Reporters Establish Position to Cover the 'Elective Kingship,'" paper presented at the American Political Science Association convention, San Francisco, California, August 29–September 1, 1996.

17. Archivist John Ransom, discussing with the author information in the diary of President Hayes, Rutherford B. Hayes Presidential Center, November 30, 2006.

18. Kumar, "The White House Beat," 14.

19. Library of Congress, Manuscript Division, George Bruce Cortelyou Papers.

20. Cornwell, *Presidential Leadership of Public Opinion*, 48–57.

21. See Presidential Press Conferences in chapter 7, table 11.

22. Craig Allen, *Eisenhower and the Mass Media* (Chapel Hill: University of North Carolina, 1993).

Chapter 1. Creating an Effective Communication Operation

1. Mike McCurry, interview with the author, April 19, 2006. I conducted many of the interviews cited in this book for my Towson University course "The President, the Press, and Democratic Society," filmed at the Washington Center of the University of California. All of the interviews conducted in this program are available in audio format at www.ucdc.edu/aboutus/whstreaming.cfm.

2. Mike McCurry, interview with the author, "The President, the Press, and Democratic Society," University of California, Washington Center, March 7, 2005.

3. Dan Bartlett, interview with the author, "The President, the Press, and Democratic Society," University of California, Washington Center, March 8, 2004.

4. Mike McCurry, interview with the author, "The President, the Press, and Democratic Society," University of California, Washington Center, April 19, 2006.

5. Dan Bartlett, interview with the author, "The President, the Press, and Democratic Society," University of California, Washington Center, March 8, 2004.

6. These numbers are based on compilations made from the May 2005 edition of the internal White House Phone Book. Bureau of National Affairs, "Daily Report for Executives: White House Phone Directory," no. 116, June 17, 2005.

7. The operations in Karl Rove's orbit in his role as senior advisor are: Office of Strategic Initiatives, Intergovernmental Affairs, Political Affairs, Public Liaison, and Policy and Strategic Planning.

8. The offices that are included in the secondary communications and press offices are: Chief of Staff, Oval Office Operations, Advance, Cabinet Liaison, Scheduling, and Staff Secretary. In addition, both the Office of the Vice President and the Office of the First Lady have staff to perform support operations for communications, including scheduling, advance, and correspondence. Additional people work in Presidential Correspondence, the Travel Office, the White House Communications Agency, and there are also speech transcribers and military baggage handlers, who move television equipment on presidential trips.

9. Mike McCurry, interview with the author, "The President, the Press, and Democratic Society," University of California, Washington Center, March 1, 2004.

10. Frank Ahrens, "Hard News: Daily Newspapers Face Unprecedented Competition . . . Including from Their Own Online Offspring," *Washington Post*, February 20, 2005, p. F1.

11. For a discussion of the environment within which presidents operate, see Martin G. Wattenberg, "The Changing Presidential Media Environment," *Presidential Studies Quarterly* 34, no. 3 (September 2004): 557–72.

12. George C. Edwards III, *On Deaf Ears: The Limits of the Bully Pulpit* (New Haven: Yale University Press, 2003), 241.

13. Lisa Caruso, "What's in a Number," *National Journal*, March 25, 2006, 18–19.

14. Karl Rove, interview with the author, Washington, D.C., May 8, 2002.

15. Edwards, *On Deaf Ears*, 193.

16. Edwards, *On Deaf Ears*, 194.

17. Mike McCurry, interview with the author, Washington, D.C., April 7, 1999.

18. Karen Hughes, interview with the author, Washington, D.C., June 13, 2002.

19. Dan Bartlett, interview with the author, Washington, D.C., May 22, 2002.

20. Joe Lockhart, interview with the author, Washington, D.C., June 29, 1998.

21. Mary Matalin, interview with the author, Washington, D.C., October 3, 2002.

22. Karen Hughes, interview with the author, Washington, D.C., June 13, 2002.

23. Dan Bartlett, interview with the author, March 8, 2004. "The President, the Press, and Democratic Society," University of California, Washington Center.

24. For press perspective on the embeds program, see Terence Smith, "The Real-Time War: Hard Lessons," and other articles on the program in *Columbia Journalism Review*, May/June 2003.

25. Mike McCurry, interview with the author, "The President, the Press, and Democratic Society," University of California, Washington Center, March 1, 2004.

26. President George W. Bush, Interview with Al Arabiya, May 5, 2004; President George W. Bush, Interview with Al-Ahram, May 6, 2004. Both interviews can be found on the website of The American Presidency Project, Public Papers of the Presidents of the United States at www.presidency.ucsb.edu/ws.

27. President George W. Bush, interview with foreign journalists, July 10, 2006. Interview can be found on the website of the American Presidency Project, *Public Papers of the Presidents of the United States*. Available at www.presidency.ucsb.edu/ws.

28. E-mail sent to White House correspondents from the Democratic National Committee Communications Director Shripal Shah, March 28, 2006.

29. "Talking Points: Not Playing with a New Deck of Cards," Center for American Progress, March 28, 2006. A half hour later, a more extensive e-mail entitled "Progress Report: Meet the New Chief" provided biographical information and specifics about the administration's budget deficits.

30. Stephen Labaton, "Politics: The Fund-Raisers: Indonesian Magnate and Clinton Talked Policy, White House Says," *New York Times*, November 5, 1996.

31. Mike McCurry, interview with the author, Washington, D.C., April 7, 1999.

32. Ari Fleischer, interview with the author, Washington, D.C., July 11, 2002.

33. Terry Moran, conversation with the author, May 2005.

34. "White House News Summary," December 3, 2003, produced for the Office of the White House Press Secretary by the Bulletin News Network. The issue was 175 pages long, which is consistent with the length of other issues of the summary.

35. Lawrence R. Jacobs and Robert Y. Shapiro, *Politicians Don't Pander* (Chicago: University of Chicago Press, 2000).

36. Lawrence R. Jacobs and Melanie Burns, "The Second Face of the Public Presidency: Presidential Polling and the Shift from Policy to Personality Polling," *Presidential Studies Quarterly* 34, no. 3 (September 2004): 537.

37. Mary Matalin, interview with the author, Washington, D.C., October 3, 2002.

38. Ari Fleischer, interview with the author, Washington, D.C., July 11, 2002.

39. See www.strengtheningsocialsecurity.gov/60stops/.

40. Andrew Card, interview with the author, Washington, D.C., November 30, 2001.

41. Dan Bartlett, interview with the author, Washington, D.C., May 22, 2002.

Chapter 2. The Communications Operation of President Bill Clinton

1. For an analysis of the Clinton transition, see John Burke, *Presidential Transitions: From Politics to Practice* (Boulder, Colo.: Lynne Rienner, 2000), chs. 7, 8. It is the authoritative book on presidential transitions from Presidents Carter through Clinton.

2. David Gergen, interview with the author, Washington, D.C., September 27, 1995.

3. For a description of his days in the Clinton White House, see Gergen, *Eyewitness to Power*, 251–342.

4. Mark Knoller, interview with the author, Washington, D.C., June 6, 1996.

5. *Washington Post*, April 27, 1993, p. 1.

6. "Clinton Administration Accomplishments and Actions: First 100 Days," April 1993. Distributed by the Office of Media Liaison through its White House computer network. "The First 100 Days, Administration of President Bill Clinton, January 20 – April 30," dys100.txt, January 20–April 30, 1993.

7. Ann Devroy, "President Discounts Panetta's Doubts," *Washington Post*, April 28, 1993, p. 1.

8. "Remarks in the 'CBS This Morning' Town Meeting," May 27, 1993, http://www.presidency.ucsb.edu/ws/index/php for all presidential speeches.

9. "Remarks by the President in Question and Answer Session during 1993 Newspaper Association of America Annual Convention," Boston, Massachusetts, April 26, 1993.

10. Gergen, *Eyewitness to Power*, 265.

11. Sidney Blumenthal, "Dave," *New Yorker*, June 28, 1993, 36–41.

12. Burt Solomon, "A One-Man Band," *National Journal*, April 24, 1993, 970.

13. Background interviews.

14. Bill Clinton, *My Life* (New York: Alfred A. Knopf, 2004), 467.

15. John Podesta, interview with the author, Washington, D.C., July 12, 2001.

16. "Remarks by the President to Weather Forecasters," Office of the Press Secretary, White House, October 1, 1997.

17. Interviews with White House officials who served when Clinton gave the global warming speech indicated it was typical of the president himself to insert the lines about presidential responsibility in creating public awareness. Terry Edmonds, interview with the author, Washington, D.C., January 5, 2001.

18. Mike McCurry, interview with the author, Towson University course, "White House Communications Operations," Washington, D.C., March 1, 2004.

19. Mike McCurry, press briefing, Office of the Press Secretary, Dakar, Senegal, April 1, 1998.

20. For the development of the meetings, see Dick Morris, *Behind the Oval Office: Winning the Presidency in the Nineties* (New York: Random House, 1997), 26, 186–87.

21. Mike McCurry, interview with the author, Washington, D.C., April 7, 1999.

22. Rahm Emanuel, interview with the author, Chicago, Illinois, April 13, 2001. For a discussion of how President Clinton's national travels reflected his political priorities as well as his policy ones, see Charles O. Jones, "Campaigning to Governing: The Clinton Style," in *The Clinton Presidency: First Appraisals*, ed. Colin Campbell and Bert Rockman (Chatham, NJ: Chatham House, 1996), 30–36.

23. Mike McCurry, interview with the author, April 7, 1999, and Richard L. Berke, "After Hours at White House, Brain Trust Turns to Politics," Week in Review, *New York Times*, July 21, 1996.

24. Morris, *Behind the Oval Office*, 139–40.

25. Morris, *Behind the Oval Office*, 144.

26. Don Baer, interview with the author, Washington, D.C., August 14, 1996.

27. Ann Lewis, interview with the author, Washington, D.C., December 17, 1997.

28. Mike McCurry, interview with the author, Washington, D.C., April 7, 1999.

29. Joe Lockhart, interview with the author, Washington, D.C., June 29, 1998.

30. Rahm Emanuel, interview with the author, Chicago, Illinois, January 15, 1998.

31. For a discussion of the creation of the first Clinton State of the Union address, see Michael Waldman, *POTUS Speaks: Finding the Words that Defined the Clinton Presidency* (New York: Simon and Schuster, 2000), 92–114.

32. Ann Lewis, interview with the author, Washington, D.C., December 17, 1997.

33. Rahm Emanuel, interview with the author, Chicago, Illinois, January 15, 1998.

34. Ann Lewis, interview with the author, Washington, D.C., December 17, 1997.

35. For a discussion of the media environment during the Clinton impeachment case, see Jeffrey E. Cohen, "If the News Is So Bad, Why Are Presidential Polls So High? Presidents, the News Media, and the Mass Public in an Era of New Media," *Presidential Studies Quarterly* 34, no. 1 (March 2004): 493–515.

36. Gaggle by Press Secretary Mike McCurry, July 18, 1996, author's transcript.

37. Mike McCurry, interview with the author, "The President, the Press, and Democratic Society," University of California, Washington Center, March 1, 2004.

38. Harold Ickes, interview with the author, Washington, D.C., April 13, 2001.

39. Michael McCurry, interview with the author, Washington, D.C., February 10, 1998.

40. See "The 1992 Campaign: Clinton Denounces New Report of Affair," *New York Times*, January 24, 1992, and "The 1992 Campaign: Clintons to Rebut Rumors on '60 Minutes,'" *New York Times*, January 24, 1992.

41. Gwen Ifill, "The 1992 Campaign: Media; Clinton Defends His Privacy and Says the Press Intruded," *New York Times*, January 27, 1992.

42. Stephen Labaton, "Tape Links Clinton to Man Tied to Crime," *New York Times*, October 18, 1997. See also Susan Schmidt and Lena H. Sun, "On Tape, Clinton Links Lead in Polls, Issue Ads," *Washington Post*, October 16, 1997.

43. Labaton, "Tape Links Clinton."

44. Susan Schmidt and Amy Goldstein, "Enigma No More, Ex-Aide Emerges," *Washington Post*, March 17, 1998.

45. Lanny J. Davis, *Truth to Tell: Tell It Early, Tell It All, Tell It Yourself* (New York: Free Press, 1999), 60.

46. Davis, *Truth to Tell*, 61.

47. Davis, *Truth to Tell*, 62.

48. Jim Kennedy, interview with the author, Washington, D.C., August 10, 1998.

49. Mike McCurry, interview with the author, "The President, the Press, and Democratic Society," University of California, Washington Center, March 1, 2004.

50. Joe Lockhart, interview with the author, Washington, D.C., June 29, 1998.

51. Mike McCurry, interview with the author, "The President, the Press, and Democratic Society," University of California, Washington Center, March 1, 2004.

52. Michael McCurry, interview with the author, Washington, D.C., June 10, 1997. In the 1930s, the U.S. Public Health Service commenced the Tuskegee syphilis study, using as its subjects mostly poor African-American sharecroppers. In the study, there were two control groups, one of which did not receive medication. After penicillin was established as an antidote for the disease, the group that had not received medication was not informed of the solution to the problem—as ethics would obviously dictate. The study did not come to public light until the 1970s, when the question of compensating the victims of the study became an issue in the Congress and the courts. Clinton wanted to put a final stamp on the issue by publicly apologizing from the White House.

53. Mike McCurry, interview with the author, "The President, the Press, and Democratic Society," University of California, Washington Center, March 1, 2004.

54. Joe Lockhart, interview with the author, Washington, D.C., June 29, 1998.

55. David Gergen, interview with the author, Washington, D.C., September 27, 1995.

56. Ann Lewis, interview with the author, Washington, D.C., December 17, 1997.

57. Joseph Lockhart, interview with the author, Washington, D.C., February 10, 1999.

58. John Podesta, interview with the author, Washington, D.C., July 12, 2001.

59. Rahm Emanuel, interview with the author, Chicago, Illinois, January 15, 1998.

60. Bob Woodward, *The Agenda: Inside the Clinton White House* (New York: Simon and Schuster, 1994), 172.

61. John Podesta, interview with the author, Washington, D.C., July 7, 2001.

62. Mike McCurry, interview with the author, Washington, D.C., April 7, 1999.

63. Joe Lockhart, interview with the author, Washington, D.C., June 29, 1998.

64. John Podesta, interview with the author, Washington, D.C., December 10, 1997.

65. Michael McCurry, interview with the author, Washington, D.C., February 10, 1998.

66. John Podesta, interview with the author, Washington, D.C., December 10, 1997.

67. Jim Kennedy, interview with the author, Washington, D.C., August 10, 1998.

68. John Podesta, interview with the author, Washington, D.C., December 10, 1997.

69. Harold Ickes, interview with the author, Washington, D.C., April 13, 2001.

70. Joel Johnson, interview with the author, Washington, D.C., January 17, 2001.

Chapter 3. The Communications Operation of President George W. Bush

1. Karl Rove, interview with the author, Washington, D.C., February 5, 2007. For a discussion of their transition goals, see Clay Johnson, "The 2000–2001 Presidential Transition: Planning, Goals, and Reality," *PS: Political Science and Politics* 35, no. 1 (2002): 51–53 and Terry Sullivan, "Assessing Transition 2001," in *The Nerve Center, Lessons in Governing from the White House Chiefs of Staff*, ed. Terry Sullivan (College Station: Texas A&M University Press, 2004), 125–66.

2. Ken Herman, interview with the author, "The President, the Press, and Democratic Society," University of California, Washington Center, February 14, 2005.

3. Ken Herman, interviews with the author, Washington, D.C., October 5–6, 2005.

4. Ken Herman, "Bush Trip Steeped in History; Governor Asked to Clarify Remarks on," *Austin American-Statesman*, December 1, 1998. The article dealing with Bush's remarks portrayed him in the following way: "As he gazed out a hotel hallway at the Superdome and waited for an elevator, Bush—clearly going for a laugh at his own expense—said the first thing he was going to say to Israeli Jews was that they were all 'going to hell.' Bush, who has both a quick wit and generally good judgment on when to use it, made the comment to the same *Austin American-Statesman* reporter who had reported his 1993 comments about his religious beliefs."

5. Ken Herman, interviews with the author, Washington, D.C., October 5–6, 2005.

6. Mary Matalin, interview with the author, Washington, D.C., October 3, 2002.

7. Dan Bartlett, interview with the author, Washington, D.C., May 22, 2002.

8. "President's Remarks in Orlando, Florida," October 30, 2004. Available at www.whitehouse.gov/news/releases/2004/10/20041030-12.html.

9. CNN / USA Today / Gallup poll, October 22–24, 2004. Available at www .pollingreport.com.

10. Dan Bartlett, interview with the author, Washington, D.C., October 27, 2006.

11. Dan Bartlett, interview with the author, "The President, the Press, and Democratic Society," University of California, Washington Center, March 8, 2004.

12. Jason Piscia, "Pawnee 'Foster Grandparent' Earns Award for Her Efforts," [Springfield, Illinois] State Journal-Register, April 20, 2005.

13. Christie Bolsen, "She Cherishes Kiss from President Bush," South Bend [Indiana] Tribune, April 12, 2005.

14. Meg Jones, "Takes Five: Beverly Christy-Wright: Volunteer's Above-and-Beyond Service Recognized by Bush," Milwaukee Journal Sentinel, February 24, 2006.

15. Mike Barber, "Sacrifice in Iraq Leads to Visit with President; Servicemen's Families Will Greet Bush on Visit Here," Seattle Post-Intelligencer, June 16, 2006.

16. "Funeral Services for Founder of Challenger Boys and Girls Club," [Los Angeles] City News Service, July 14, 2006.

17. White House, USA Freedom Corps, "Presidential Greeters Program," November 17, 2006. Available at www.usafreedomcorps.gov/about_usafc/newsroom/local_vols.asp.

18. James Wilkerson, interview with the author, Washington, D.C., July 3, 2002.

19. Ari Fleischer, interview with the author, Washington, D.C., March 7, 2001.

20. Ari Fleischer, interview with the author, Washington, D.C., March 7, 2001.

21. Scott McClellan, interview with the author, "The President, the Press, and Democratic Society," University of California, Washington Center, May 6, 2004.

22. "The White House and the Press: Competitors in a Dependent Relationship," panel hosted by the American Political Science Association and the White House Historical Association, Washington, D.C., October 9, 2003.

23. President Bush, "Remarks at the Paul H. Nitze School of Advanced International Studies and a Question-and-Answer Session," April 10, 2006.

24. Scott Sforza, interview with the author, Washington, D.C., May 9, 2006.

25. For a discussion of President Bush's management principles and an earlier description of how the communications operation worked in the first term, see Martha Joynt Kumar, "Communications Operations in the White House of President George W. Bush: Making News on His Terms," Presidential Studies Quarterly 33, no. 2 (June 2003): 366–93.

26. Karl Rove, interview with the author, Washington, D.C, May 8, 2002.

27. Karen Hughes, interview with the author, Washington, D.C., June 13, 2002.

28. Mary Matalin, interview with the author, Washington, D.C., October 3, 2002.

29. Karl Rove, interview with the author, Washington, D.C, May 8, 2002.

30. Karl Rove, interview with the author, Washington, D.C., May 8, 2002.

31. Joshua Bolten, interview with the author, Washington, D.C., November 17, 2006.

32. Dan Bartlett, interview with the author, "The President, the Press, and Democratic Society," University of California, Washington Center, March 8, 2004.

33. Joshua Bolten, interview with the author, Washington, D.C., November 17, 2006.

34. Author's tabulation from Bureau of National Affairs, "Daily Report for Executives," White House Phone Book, no. 155, August 13, 2001, and no. 140, July 22, 2002.

35. Background interview, 2002.

36. Ari Fleischer, interview with the author, Washington, D.C., July 11, 2002.

37. Background interview, 2002.

38. Mary Matalin, interview with the author, Washington, D.C., October 3, 2002.

39. Karen Hughes, interview with the author, Washington, D.C., June 13, 2002.

40. Karl Rove, interview with the author, Washington, D.C., May 8, 2002.

41. Susan Neely, interview with the author, Washington, D.C., May 2, 2002.

42. Background interview, 2002.

43. Background interview, 2002.

44. Dana Perino, interview with the author, Washington, D.C., November 17, 2006.

45. "President Announces Tony Snow as Press Secretary," White House, April 26, 2006. Available at www.whitehouse.gov/news/releases/2006/04/20060426 .html.

46. Tony Snow, interview with the author, Washington, D.C., October 4, 2006.

47. Scott McClellan, interview with the author, "The President, the Press, and Democratic Society," University of California, Washington Center, May 6, 2004.

48. Dan Bartlett, interview with the author, "The President, the Press, and Democratic Society," University of California, Washington Center, March 8, 2004.

49. Dan Bartlett, "The White House and the Press" panel.

50. Ari Fleischer, interview with the author, Washington, D.C., July 11, 2002.

51. Nicolle Devenish, interview with the author, Washington, D.C., July, 2002.

52. Scott Sforza, interview with the author, Washington, D.C., May 9, 2006.

53. Dan Bartlett, interview with the author, "White House Communications Operations" course, Towson University, Towson, Maryland, March 8, 2004.

54. The two Radio Days were held October 30, 2002, and January 21, 2004. See Judy Keen, "Bush's 'Radio Day' Gets Static from Democrats," USA Today, October 30, 2002, and Bob Deans, "Low Frequency Radio, Usually Taciturn White House Figures Face Mikes," Atlanta Journal Constitution, January 22, 2004.

55. Karl Rove, interview with the author, Washington, D.C., May 8, 2002.

56. Scott Sforza, interview with the author, Washington, D.C., June 27, 2002.

57. Public Papers of the Presidents of the United States, William Jefferson Clinton (Washington, D.C.: Government Printing Office). The figures come from the "Document Category," "Addresses to the Nation," and counts of the individual items.

58. Figures come from counts of the following categories in issues of the Weekly Compilation of Presidential Documents from 2001 to January 2005: "Addresses to the Nation," "Addresses and Remarks," "Radio Addresses," "Bill Signings—Remarks," and "Meetings with Foreign and International Leaders."

59. Scott Sforza, interview with the author, Washington, D.C., June 27, 2002.

60. Scott Sforza, interview with the author, Washington, D.C., May 9, 2006.

61. David E. Sanger and Judith Miller, "Libya to Give Up Arms Programs, Bush Announces," New York Times, December 20, 2003. See also Robin Wright and Glenn Kessler, "Two Decades of Sanctions, Isolation Wore Down Gaddafi," Washington

Post, December 20, 2003. President Bush, "Remarks on the Decision by Colonel Muammar Abu Minyar al-Qadhafi of Libya to Disclose and Dismantle Weapons of Mass Destruction Programs," December 19, 2003, *Public Papers of the Presidents of the United States.* Available at www.presidency.ucsb.edu/ws.

62. Sanger and Miller, "Libya to Give Up Arms Programs."

63. Dana Milbank and Glenn Kessler, "Enron's Influence Reached Deep into Administration," *Washington Post,* January 18, 2002.

64. Jeanne Cummings, Jacob M. Schlesinger, and Michael Schroeder, "Bush Crackdown on Business Fraud Signals New Era," *Wall Street Journal,* July 10, 2002, and David E. Sanger, "How a Clear Strategy Got Muddy Results," *New York Times,* July 12, 2002.

65. "The White House and the Press" panel.

66. Dan Bartlett, interview with the author, Washington, D.C., October 27, 2006.

67. George W. Bush, "Address Before a Joint Session of the Congress on the State of the Union," January 28, 2003, *Public Papers of the Presidents of the United States.* Available at www.presidency.ucsb.edu/ws.

68. Walter Pincus and Dana Milbank, "Bush, Rice Blame CIA for Iraq Error; Tenet Accepts Responsibility for Clearing Statement on Nuclear Aims in Jan. Speech," *Washington Post,* July 12, 2003.

69. Dana Milbank, "Fleischer's Final Briefing Is Not Quite a Grand Slam," *Washington Post,* July 15, 2003.

70. Background briefing, July 18, 2003.

71. Dan Balz and Walter Pincus, "Why Commander in Chief Is Losing the War of the 16 Words," *Washington Post,* July 24, 2003.

72. Scott McClellan, press briefing, Office of the Press Secretary, White House, October 6, 2005.

73. Tucker Eskew, interview with the author, Washington, D.C., June 13, 2002.

74. White House Global Messenger, "Key Points," March 11, 2005.

75. Nicolle Devenish Wallace, interview with the author, "The President, the Press, and Democratic Society," University of California, Washington Center, May 9, 2005.

76. Secretary of State Condoleezza Rice, March 14, 2005, http://www.state.gov/secretary/rm200543385.htm.

77. Dan Bartlett, interview with the author, "The President, the Press, and Democratic Society," University of California, Washington Center, March 8, 2004.

78. Nicolle Devenish, interview with the author, "The President, the Press, and Democratic Society," University of California, Washington Center, May 9, 2005.

79. See www.shadowtv.com/PDF/ShadowTVmonitoring.pdf.

80. Scott Sforza, interview with the author, Washington, D.C., May 9, 2006.

81. Dan Bartlett, interview with the author, "The President, the Press, and Democratic Society," University of California, Washington Center, March 8, 2004.

82. Andrew Card, interview with the author, Washington, D.C., November 30, 2001.

83. Scott McClellan, interview with the author, "The President, the Press, and Democratic Society," University of California, Washington Center, May 6, 2004.

84. Mike Allen, "Management Style Shows Weaknesses: Delegation of Responsibility, Trust in Subordinates May Have Hurt Bush," *Washington Post*, June 2, 2004.

85. Thomas Griscom, interview with the author, Washington, D.C., May 3, 2006.

86. David S. Hilzenrath and Mike Allen, "Embattled Pitt Resigns as SEC Chief, Latest Controversy Cost Him White House Support," *Washington Post*, November 6, 2002.

87. Stephen Barr, "Bush Team Plays Down Recent Setbacks," *Washington Post*, September 14, 2003.

88. Andrew Card, interview with the author, Washington, D.C., November 30, 2001.

89. Tom Brune, "Cadre Grows to Rein in Message," *Newsday*, February 24, 2005.

90. Juliet Eilperin, "Climate Researchers Feeling Heat from White House," *Washington Post*, April 6, 2006.

91. Juliet Eilperin, "Debate on Climate Shifts to Issue of Irreparable Change; Some Experts on Global Warming Foresee 'Tipping Point' When It Is Too Late to Act," *Washington Post*, January 29, 2006.

92. "President Addresses American Society of Newspaper Editors Convention," White House, April 14, 2005. Available at www.whitehouse.gov/news/releases/2005/04/20050414-4.html.

93. Greg Toppo, "Education Department Paid Commentator to Promote Law," *USA Today*, January 7, 2005.

94. Jim Drinkard and Mark Memmott, "HHS Said It Paid Columnist for Help," *USA Today*, January 27, 2005.

95. Christopher Lee, "GAO Issues Mixed Ruling on Payments to Columnists," *Washington Post*, October 1, 2005.

96. Christopher Lee, "Prepackaged News Gets GAO Rebuke," *Washington Post*, February 21, 2005. Emphasis in GAO report.

97. James A. Baker III, interview with the author, Houston, Texas, May 14, 2001.

Chapter 4. White House Communications Advisers

1. An argument could be made that in the nineteenth century George Cortelyou, private secretary to Presidents McKinley and Roosevelt, and then William Loeb following him performed the functions of a modern-day press secretary and communications director. Both men briefed reporters and planned publicity events. For a discussion of William Loeb's work, see George Juergens, *News From the White House: The Presidential-Press Relationship in the Progressive Era* (Chicago: University of Chicago Press, 1981), 47–51. For a description of the work of George Cortelyou, see William Seale, *The President's House: The History of an American Idea* (Washington, D.C.: American Institute of Architects Press, 1992).

2. For a discussion of how James Hagerty fought off the efforts of others in the

White House to do publicity work with executive departments, see Karen Hult and Charles Walcott, *Governing the White House: From Hoover through LBJ* (Lawrence: University Press of Kansas, 1995), 57–58.

3. For an excellent examination of the development of the Office of Communications, see John Maltese, *Spin Control: The White House Office of Communications and the Management of Presidential News* (Chapel Hill: University of North Carolina Press, 1994), 28–74.

4. For organization charts of the office under various directors in particular years, see Maltese, *Spin Control*, 243–53.

5. Brit Hume, interview with the author, Washington, D.C., August 2, 1996.

6. David Hume Kennerly, interview with the author, Washington, D.C., June 6, 1996.

7. Terry Edmonds, interview with the author, Washington, D.C., January 5, 2001.

8. The Clinton figures do not cover all of the interviews the president had with reporters, as such figures are difficult to come by. I have Clinton White House lists for the president's radio and television interviews, but no list was maintained for his interviews with print reporters. By tradition, interviews that reporters conduct with presidents are regarded as the property of the news organization, not the White House. The decision to release the transcript is made by the news organizations, except in the case of interviews with foreign news organizations, where the White House releases the translated transcript.

9. See Martha Joynt Kumar and Terry Sullivan, "The White House Communications Director: Presidential Fire-Walker," paper presented to the Midwest Political Science Association, Chicago, Illinois, April 18–20, 1996.

10. George Stephanopoulos, interview with the author, Washington, D.C., September 9, 1995.

11. Don Baer, interview with the author, White House Interview Program, Washington, D.C., July 22, 1999.

12. Michael Deaver, interview with the author, White House Interview Program, Washington, D.C., September 9, 1999.

13. David Demarest, interview with the author, White House Interview Program, Washington, D.C., December 7, 1999.

14. Marlin Fitzwater, interview with the author, White House Interview Program, Deale, Maryland, October 21, 1999.

15. Tony Snow, interview with the author, Washington, D.C., January 11, 1993.

16. Terry Hunt, interview with the author, Washington, D.C., June 12, 1996.

17. Mari Maseng Will, interview with the author, Washington, D.C., May 18, 1993.

18. David Hume Kennerly, interview with the author, Washington, D.C., June 6, 1996.

19. John McConnell, interview with the author, Washington, D.C., December 4, 2006. The speech can be found at President George W. Bush, "Remarks on the Unveiling of the Official Portraits of President William J. Clinton and First Lady Hillary Clinton," June 14, 2004, *Public Papers of the Presidents of the United States.*

20. James A. Baker III, Interview no. 1, interview with the author and Terry Sullivan, White House Interview Program, Houston, Texas, July 7, 1999.

21. Michael Deaver, interview with the author, Washington, D.C., July 11, 1996.

22. James A. Baker III, Interview no. 1, July 7, 1999.

23. David Demarest, interview with the author, White House Interview Program, Washington, D.C., December 7, 1999.

24. Don Baer, interview with the author, White House Interview Program, Washington, D.C., July 22, 1999.

25. Samuel Kernell and Samuel Popkin, eds., *Chief of Staff: Twenty-Five Years of Managing the Presidency* (Berkeley: University of California Press, 1986), 27.

26. Nicolle Devenish Wallace, interview with the author, "White House Communications Operations" course, Towson University, Washington, D.C., May 9, 2005.

27. Kevin Sullivan, interview with the author, Washington, D.C., November 30, 2006.

28. Kevin Sullivan, interview with the author, Washington, D.C., November 30, 2006.

29. Joshua Bolten, interview with the author, Washington, D.C., November 17, 2006.

30. Background information from a White House source.

31. Robert Saliterman, interview with the author, Washington, D.C., December 11, 2006.

32. Kevin Sullivan, interview with the author, Washington, D.C., November 30, 2006.

33. The nine categories are "Morning Update," "In Case You Missed It," "Straight to the Point," "Fact Sheet," "What They're Saying," "The Briefing Breakdown," "By the Numbers," "Economy Watch," and "Medicare Check-Up."

34. Counts of various categories of e-mail message received by those on the press list. For the other positive message categories, in 2006 I received fewer than ten for "By the Numbers" and "What They're Saying" and around a dozen each for "Economy Watch" and "Medicare Check-Up."

35. December 6, 7, and 11, 2006.

36. December 5, 6, and 12, 2006.

37. Dana Perino, interview with the author, Washington, D.C., November 17, 2006.

38. September 8 and December 4, 2006.

39. David Wessel, "Once Unloved, Medicare's Prescription-Drug Program Defies Critics, but Issues Remain," *Wall Street Journal*, December 7, 2006.

40. "Setting the Record Straight," "The Rest of the Story," "Now and Then," "Myth/Fact," and "In Their Own Words." In 2006, the press list received fewer than ten each for all of the categories, except "Setting the Record Straight" (thirty). On the White House website, "The Rest of the Story" and "Myth/Fact" are included as part of its "Setting the Record Straight" category.

41. Howard Kurtz, "Tony Snow Knows How to Work More Than One Room; It's Gloves Off (and Pass the Hat) for Bush Spokesman," *Washington Post*, October 12, 2006.

42. May 8, 2006, Associated Press; May 9, *USA Today*; May 10, CBS News, *New York Times*; May 11, *Washington Post*, Associated Press. Available at www.whitehouse.gov/news/setting-record-straight/.

43. "Myth/Fact: Five Key Myths in Bob Woodward's Book," September 30, 2006. Available at www.whitehouse.gov/news/releases/2006/09/20060930-5.html.

44. Caren Bohan, "White House Lists Book's 'Five Key Myths,'" *Washington Post*, October 1, 2006.

45. Kevin Sullivan, interview with the author, Washington, D.C., November 30, 2006.

46. Kevin Sullivan, interview with the author, Washington, D.C., November 30, 2006.

47. Robert Saliterman, interview with the author, Washington, D.C., December 11, 2006.

48. John Maltese, *The White House Office of Communications and the Management of Presidential News* (Chapel Hill: University of North Carolina Press, 1994), 104–5.

49. Thomas Griscom, interview with the author, Washington, D.C., September 1995.

50. Michael Deaver, interview with the author, Washington, D.C., July 11, 1996.

51. "Buchanan's Greatest Hits," *Washington Post*, February 4, 1987; originally published March 5, 1986.

52. Lou Cannon, "White House Raises Stakes as Contra Vote Looms; Strategy Is to Place Onus on Democrats," *Washington Post*, March 9, 1986, p. A1.

53. Karl Rove, interview with the author, Washington, D.C., May 2002.

54. Karen Hughes, interview with the author, Washington, D.C., June 13, 2002.

55. Thomas Griscom, interview with the author, Washington, D.C., September 1995.

56. George Stephanopoulos, interview with the author, Washington, D.C., September 9, 1995.

57. Loretta Ucelli, interview with the author, Washington, D.C., January 2, 2001.

58. David Demarest, interview with the author, Washington, D.C., January 14, 1993.

59. Patrick Anderson, *The President's Men: White House Assistants of Franklin D. Roosevelt, Harry S Truman, Dwight D. Eisenhower, John F. Kennedy, and Lyndon B. Johnson* (Garden City, NY: Doubleday, 1968), 191.

60. Thomas Griscom, interview with the author, Washington, D.C., September, 1995.

61. Mari Maseng Will, interview with the author, May 18, 1993.

62. Background interview, 1989.

63. The legislation became law without President Reagan's signature in the fall of 1988. In May, he vetoed a similar provision that was included in the Omnibus Trade Bill. The discussion here refers to the May 1988 veto action.

64. Background interview, 1989.

65. Robert Beckel interview, Carter Presidency Project, White Burkett Miller Center of Public Affairs, University of Virginia, Charlottesville, Virginia, November 13, 1981.

66. Dan Bartlett, interview with the author, Washington, D.C., May 22, 2002.

67. Marion Blakey, director, Office of Public Affairs, interview with the author, Washington, D.C., January 17, 1989.

68. Background interview, 1989.

69. Don Baer, interview with the author, White House Interview Program, July 22, 1999.

70. Richard Moe, interview, Carter Presidency Project, White Burkett Miller Center of Public Affairs, University of Virginia, Charlottesville, Virginia, January 1982.

71. He did, however, give his radio address on a regular basis, and on four occasions he devoted it to Bork. Only one of those addresses, the July 4 one, addressed the Bork nomination prior to the beginning of the Senate confirmation hearings. From the viewpoint of the administration, the radio address was a good format for Reagan. "He can say whatever he wants," a staff member said. "And it makes the Saturday evening news and hits Sunday newspapers. It gives him a chance to control his message." The aide pointed out an additional advantage to the radio program: they turned it into a newspaper column sent to weekly newspapers. "It has proven to be a worthwhile effort," the person said. "One thousand one hundred are interested in using it out of the 1,300 sent the column." Elizabeth Board, interview with the author, Washington, D.C., January 12, 1989.

72. Memorandum for Senator Baker from John Tuck, "Summary of Senator Baker's Communications Activities and meetings on Behalf of Judge Bork," September 17, 1987, White House Central Files, Thomas C. Griscom Files, box 15149, Bork (3), Ronald Reagan Library.

73. Memorandum for Tom Griscom from Tom Gibson, "Advocacy Materials," July 22, 1987, White House Central Files, Thomas C. Griscom Files, box 15149, Bork (3), Ronald Reagan Library.

74. Memorandum for the Chief of Staff from Tom Gibson, "Office of Public Affairs Activities in Support of Judge Bork," October 15, 1987, White House Central Files, Thomas C. Griscom Files, box 15149, Bork (1), Ronald Reagan Library.

75. Memorandum for the Chief of Staff from Tom Gibson, "Office of Public Affairs Activities in Support of Judge Bork," October 15, 1987, White House Central Files, Thomas C. Griscom Files, box 15149, Bork (1), Ronald Reagan Library.

76. Memorandum for Leslye Arsht from Sue Richard and Elizabeth Board, "Media Plan for Support of Bork Nomination," July 23, 1987, White House Central Files, Thomas C. Griscom Files, box 15149, Bork (3), Ronald Reagan Library.

77. Memorandum for Howard H. Baker Jr., Kenneth M. Duberstein, William L. Ball III, Thomas C. Griscom from Arthur B. Culvahouse Jr., counsel to the president, "Bork Confirmation Status Report," September 8, 1987, White House Central Files, Thomas C. Griscom Files, box 15149, Bork (3), Ronald Reagan Library.

78. Elizabeth Board, interview with the author, Washington, D.C., January 12, 1989.

79. Memorandum for Tom Griscom from Elizabeth Board, "Media Activities #3," September 4, 1987, White House Central Files, Thomas C. Griscom Files, box 15149, Bork (3), Ronald Reagan Library.

80. Elizabeth Board, interview with the author, Washington, D.C., January 12, 1989.

81. Marion Blakey, interview with the author, Washington, D.C., January 17, 1989.

82. Stuart Taylor Jr., "Study Puts Bork to Right of Other Judges Named by Reagan," *New York Times,* July 28, 1987.

83. Stuart Taylor Jr., "Liberal Lawyers' Group Says Bork Favored Business in Court Rulings," *New York Times,* August 7, 1987.

84. Edward Walsh, "AFL-CIO Asks Senate to Disapprove Bork; Judge Tied to 'Agenda of the Right Wing,'" *Washington Post,* August 18, 1987.

85. "Bork's Nomination Opposed by the Women's Law Center," *New York Times,* August 19, 1987.

86. Mary Thornton, "Women's Law Group Urges Rejection of Bork," *Washington Post,* August 19, 1987.

87. Linda Greenhouse, "A.C.L.U., Reversing Policy, Joins the Opposition to Bork," *New York Times,* September 1, 1987.

88. Ruth Marcus, "White House Paper on Bork Inaccurate, Biden Aides Say," *Washington Post,* September 4, 1987.

89. Memorandum for Howard H. Baker Jr., Kenneth M. Duberstein, William L. Ball III, Thomas C. Griscom from Arthur B. Culvahouse Jr., counsel to the president, "Bork Confirmation Status Report," September 8, 1987, White House Central Files, Thomas C. Griscom Files, box 15149, Bork (3), Ronald Reagan Library.

90. Ruth Marcus, "Justice Dept. Hits Bork Critics," *Washington Post,* September 13, 1987.

91. Robin Toner, "Saying No to Bork, Southern Democrats Echo Black Voters," *New York Times,* October 8, 1987.

92. Stuart Taylor Jr., "Prepping the Nominee," *National Journal,* December 11, 2004.

Chapter 5. The Press Secretary to the President

1. For a history of press secretaries, see W. Dale Nelson, *Who Speaks for the President? The White House Press Secretary from Cleveland to Clinton* (Syracuse, NY: Syracuse University Press, 1998).

2. Ron Nessen, interview with the author, White House Interview Program, Washington, D.C., August 3, 1999.

3. Joseph C. Wilson, "What I Didn't Find in Africa," *New York Times,* July 6, 2003.

4. Robert Novak, "Mission to Niger," *Washington Post,* July 14, 2003.

5. "Press Briefing by Scott McClellan," White House, September 29, 2003. Available at www.whitehouse.gov/news/releases/2003/09/20030929-7.html.

6. Donnie Radcliffe, "The Last Word from Larry Speakes; The Spokesman Looks Back on Six Years at the Podium," *Washington Post,* January 30, 1987.

7. Established in 1865, the executive clerk's operation is the oldest office in the White House. See Bradley H. Patterson Jr., *The White House Staff: Inside the West Wing and Beyond* (Washington, D.C.: Brookings Institution Press, 2000), 359–62.

8. Roman Popadiuk, interview with the author, White House Interview Program, College Station, Texas, November 2, 1999.

9. Larry Speakes, interview with the author, White House Interview Program, Washington, D.C., June 26, 1999.

10. Larry Speakes, interview with the author, White House Interview Program, Washington, D.C., June 26, 1999..

11. Carol D. Leonnig and Jim VandeHei, "Testimony by Rove and Libby Examined; Leak Prosecutor Seeks Discrepancies," *Washington Post*, July 23, 2005.

12. Michael McCurry, interview with the author, White House Interview Program, Washington, D.C., March 27, 2000.

13. Jody Powell, interview with the author and Michael B. Grossman, Washington, D.C., May 21, 1981.

14. Background briefing, July 22, 1979.

15. Kenneth R. Bazinet, "Hil Worth 20M Outside the Senate," *New York Daily News*, March 12, 1999.

16. Howard Kurtz, "Reporter: Rove Told Him of Plame's CIA Tie," *Washington Post*, July 17, 2005.

17. Dan Bartlett, interview with the author, "The President, the Press, and Democratic Society," University of California, Washington Center, March 8, 2004.

18. Mike Allen, "In Private, Bush Sees Kerry as Formidable Foe; President Holds Unusual Meeting with Reporters as He Readies for Campaign," *Washington Post*, March 3, 2004.

19. Mike McCurry, interview with the author, Towson University course, "President, Press, and Democratic Society," Washington, D.C., March 8, 2004.

20. Cornwell, *Presidential Leadership of Public Opinion*, 100.

21. Dan Bartlett, interview with the author, Washington, D.C., October 27, 2006.

22. Tony Snow, interview with the author, Washington, D.C., October 4, 2006.

23. Mike McCurry, conversation with the author, Washington, D.C., October 25, 2006.

24. Dan Bartlett, interview with the author, Washington, D.C., October 27, 2006.

25. Tony Snow, "Doc Senator Misdiagnoses Embryonic Stem Cell Research," August 5, 2005.

26. "Press Briefing by Tony Snow," White House, July 21, 2006. www .whitehouse.gov/news/releases/2006/07/20060718.html.

27. "Meet the Press," NBC News Transcripts, July 23, 2006.

28. "Press Briefing by Tony Snow," White House, July 24, 2006. Available at www.whitehouse.gov/news/releases/2006/07/20060724-4.html.

29. Tony Snow, interview with the author, Washington, D.C., October 4, 2006.

30. Joshua Bolten, interview with the author, Washington, D.C., November 17, 2006.

31. Mike McCurry, interview with the author, Washington, D.C., June 10, 1997.

32. Marlin Fitzwater, interview with the author, Deale, Maryland, August 8, 1998.

33. Dawn Alexander, interview with the author, Washington, D.C., June 27, 1996.

34. Scott McClellan, interview with the author, Washington, D.C., March 12, 2001.

35. Mike McCurry, interview with the author, Washington, D.C., June 10, 1997.

36. Marlin Fitzwater, interview with the author, telephone, March 29, 1999.

37. Barry Toiv, interview with the author, Washington, D.C., March 27, 1998.

38. Michael McCurry, interview with the author, White House Interview Program, Washington, D.C., March 27, 2000.

39. Marlin Fitzwater, interview with the author, Deale, Maryland, August 8, 1998.

40. Bill Plante, interview with the author, Washington, D.C., December 8, 1995.

41. Terry Hunt, interview with the author, Washington, D.C., June 12, 1996.

42. Helen Thomas, interview with the author, Washington, D.C., January 4, 1985.

43. Terry Hunt, interview with the author, Washington, D.C., June 12, 1996.

44. Scott McClellan, interview with the author, Washington, D.C., June 4, 2003.

45. Joe Lockhart, interview with the author, Washington, D.C., August 25, 1997.

46. Marlin Fitzwater, interview with the author, White House Interview Program, Deale, Maryland, October 21, 1999.

47. Larry Speakes, interview with the author, White House Interview Program, Washington, D.C., June 26, 1999.

48. Marlin Fitzwater, interview with the author, Deale, Maryland, August 8, 1998.

49. Mike McCurry, interview with the author, Washington, D.C., February 10, 1998.

50. Gaggle notes, October 2, 2000.

51. Marlin Fitzwater, interview with the author, Deale, Maryland, August 8, 1998.

52. Ari Fleischer, interview with the author, Washington, D.C., March 7, 2001.

53. Scott McClellan, interview with the author, "The President, the Press, and Democratic Society," University of California, Washington Center, May 6, 2004.

54. Tony Snow, interview with the author, Washington, D.C., October 4, 2006.

55. Michael McCurry, interview with the author, White House Interview Program, Washington, D.C., March 27, 2000.

56. Mike McCurry, interview with the author, June 10, 1997.

57. Mike McCurry, interview with the author, November 3, 1997.

58. Marlin Fitzwater, interview with the author, telephone, October 31, 1997.

59. Roman Popadiuk, interview with the author, White House Interview Program, College Station, Texas, November 2, 1999.

60. Ann Devroy, interview with the author, August 16, 1995.

61. Mike Allen and Charles Lane, "Rice Helped Shape Bush Decision on Admissions," *Washington Post*, January 17, 2003.

62. Mike Allen, "Rice: Race Can Be Factor in College Admissions," *Washington Post*, January 18, 2003. Conversation with April Ryan, January 17, 2003.

63. Ron Fournier, "Rice Says Race Could Factor in Admissions," Associated Press, January 17, 2003.

64. Mike Getler, "Rice, Race, and Reporters," *Washington Post*, January 26, 2003.

65. J. Y. Smith, "Critic Paul Hume Dies; Drew Truman's Wrath," *Washington Post*, November 27, 2001.

66. Bernard Holland, "Paul Hume, 85, Washington Music Critic," *New York Times*, November 28, 2001.

67. Michael McCurry, interview with the author, White House Interview Program, Washington, D.C., March 27, 2000. Unless otherwise attributed, all quotations and information in this section come from McCurry.

68. Marlin Fitzwater, interview with the author, White House Interview Program, Deale, Maryland, October 21, 1999.

69. Joseph Lockhart, interview with the author, Washington, D.C., February 9, 1999.

70. Ari Fleischer, interview with the author, Washington, D.C., March 7, 2001.

71. Scott McClellan, interview with the author, Washington, D.C., June 4, 2003.

72. Marlin Fitzwater, interview with the author, White House Interview Program, Deale, Maryland, October 21, 1999.

73. Marlin Fitzwater, interview with the author, White House Interview Program, Deale, Maryland, October 21, 1999.

74. Marlin Fitzwater, interview with the author, White House Interview Program, Deale, Maryland, October 21, 1999.

75. At the death of her husband, Naomi Nover took over the news service portfolio of her husband, Bernard Nover. While she did no reporting, she continued to follow presidential events, including traveling with the press corps. A quirky individual, she was not always even-tempered. See Lloyd Grove, "Adding Punch to the Press Corps," *Washington Post*, April 27, 1995.

76. Marlin Fitzwater, interview with the author, White House Interview Program, Deale, Maryland, October 21, 1999.

Chapter 6. The Gaggle and the Daily Briefing

1. Terry Hunt, interview with the author, June 12, 1996.

2. Terry Hunt, interview with the author, August 17, 2006.

3. Joseph Lockhart, interview with the author, February 10, 1999.

4. Mark Knoller, interview with the author, June 6, 1996.

5. Marlin Fitzwater, interview with the author, telephone, March 29, 1999.

6. Marlin Fitzwater, interview with the author, telephone, March 29, 1999.

7. Joseph Lockhart, interview with the author, February 10, 1999.

8. Ari Fleischer, interview with the author, July 11, 2002.

9. Ari Fleischer, interview with the author, March 7, 2001.

10. Prior to the George W. Bush administration, the sessions did not have a transcript. In some cases I have created one on my own. The sessions I refer to here are ones from June 6, 18, and 19, 1996, and May 11, 1998.

11. Gaggle, June 20, 1996.

12. White House internal transcripts for July 11, 12, and 13, 2005. McClellan

answered 27, 18, and 23 questions and the sessions lasted 14, 14, and 12 minutes, respectively.

13. Mark Felsenthal, interview with the author, March 24, 1998.

14. Kenneth Bazinet, interview with the author, March 24, 1998.

15. Joseph Lockhart, interview with the author, February 10, 1999.

16. Background remarks, summer 1998.

17. Ari Fleischer, interview with the author, March 7, 2001.

18. Press Gaggle by Scott McClellan, internal transcript, Office of the Press Secretary, White House, September 28, 2005.

19. "Press Briefing by Scott McClellan," White House, September 28, 2005. Available at www.whitehouse.gov/news/releases/2005/09/20050928-2.html.

20. Joseph Lockhart, interview with the author, February 10, 1999.

21. Gaggle, June 18, 1996. Author's transcript.

22. Gaggle, February 7, 1998. From my own notes.

23. Author's recollection of the session.

24. Gaggle, February 4, 1998. Author's recollection of the session.

25. Gaggle, June 20, 1996. Author's transcription of the session.

26. Michael McCurry, interview with the author, White House Interview Program, Washington, D.C., March 27, 2000.

27. Joseph Lockhart, interview with the author, February 10, 1999.

28. Leo Rosten, *The Washington Correspondents* (New York: Harcourt, Brace, 1937), 65.

29. "Press Briefing by Scott McClellan," White House, September 16, 2003. Available at www.whitehouse.gov/news/releases/2003/09/20030910-5.html.

30. "Press Briefing by Scott McClellan," White House, October 10, 2003. Available at www.whitehouse.gov/news/releases/2003/10/20031010-6.html.

31. "Press Briefing by Scott McClellan," White House, July 11, 2005. Available at www.whitehouse.gov/news/releases/2005/07/20050711-3.html.

32. Ibid.

33. Terence Hunt, interview with the author, June 12, 1996.

34. Marlin Fitzwater, interview with the author, August 8, 1998.

35. James Fetig, interview with the author, White House Interview Program, Rockville, Maryland, February 2, 1999.

36. For photographs and a review of the history of the Press Room and the current Briefing Room, see the website of the White House Historical Association. Available at www.whitehousehistory.org/03/subs_press.

37. Tony Snow, interview with the author, Washington, D.C., October 4, 2006.

38. Background interview with a reporter who witnessed the exchange.

39. Background interview, 1998.

40. Background interview, 1999.

41. Laura Gibbons, ed., *News Media Yellow Book,* vol. 9, no. 3, Spring 1998, vii.

42. The Press Secretary's Briefing, January 21, 1998.

43. Mark Knoller, interview with the author, June 6, 1996.

44. Marlin Fitzwater, interview with the author, August 8, 1998.

45. Joseph Lockhart, interview with the author, February 10, 1999.

46. Brit Hume, interview with the author, August 2, 1996.

47. Michael McCurry, interview with the author, July 19, 1996.

48. Michael McCurry, interview with the author, February 10, 1998.

49. Joseph Lockhart, interview with the author, February 10, 1999.

50. Mary Ellen Glynn, interview with the author, May 23, 1999.

51. The White House, Office of the Press Secretary, Press Briefing by Secretary of State Madeline Albright, January 22, 1998.

52. The following were the organizations in the rotating pool. For newspapers: *Austin American Statesman, Baltimore Sun, Boston Globe, Chicago Tribune, Christian Science Monitor, Columbus Dispatch,* Copley News, Cox Newspapers, *Dallas Morning News, Denver Post, Financial Times,* Gannett News, Hearst Newspapers, *Houston Chronicle,* Knight Ridder, *Los Angeles Times,* McClatchy, Media News, *National Journal, Newsday, New York Daily News, New York Post, New York Times, Politico,* Scripps-Howard, United Press International, *USA Today, Wall Street Journal, Washington Examiner, Washington Post,* and *Washington Times.* For radio: ABC, American Urban Radio Networks, Associated Press, Bloomberg, CBS, NPR, Standard Radio News, Talk Radio, Voice of America. The five television networks were: ABC, CBS, CNN, Fox, and NBC. The magazine photographers in the rotation were from *Time* and *Newsweek.*

Chapter 7. Presidential Press Conferences

1. "National Thanksgiving Turkey Spared," White House, November 26, 2002. Available at www.whitehouse.gov/news/releases/2002/11/20021126-4.html.

2. December 2, 1953, Executive Office Building. *Public Papers of the Presidents of the United States, Dwight D. Eisenhower,* vol. I, 803.

3. James Russell Wiggins, "The Presidential Press Conference," *The Ellsworth American,* January 1, 1998, sect. II, 1.

4. "Remarks by President Bush and President Karzai of Afghanistan in a Press Availability," White House, June 15, 2004. Available at www.whitehouse.gov/news/releases/2004/06/20040615-4.html.

5. "President and Iraqi Interim President Al-Yawer Discuss Iraq Future," White House, December 6, 2004. Available at www.whitehouse.gov/news/releases/2004/12/20041206-2.html.

6. Dan Bartlett, interview with the author, Washington, D.C., June 12, 2003.

7. Helen Thomas, interview with the author, Washington, D.C., summer 1996.

8. Ken Auletta, "Fortress Bush," *New Yorker,* January 19, 2004, 53.

9. James A. Baker III, interview with the author, Houston, Texas, May 14, 2001.

10. Michael McCurry, interview with the author, Washington, D.C., February 10, 1998.

11. David Gergen, interview with the author, Washington, D.C., September 27, 1995.

12. Scott McClellan, interview with the author, Washington, D.C., June 4, 2003.

13. "The Press Secretary," written and produced by Theodore Bogosian for the Public Broadcasting Company, September 2001.

14. Michael McCurry, interview with the author, Washington, D.C., April 7, 1999.

15. Scott McClellan, interview with the author, Washington, D.C., June 4, 2003.

16. Mary Matalin, interview with the author, Washington, D.C., October 3, 2002.

17. President Theodore Roosevelt was the first president to meet regularly with reporters and explain his thinking and policies. His meetings with reporters were for those journalists he wanted in them. They were not open to all Washington reporters, nor were those of his successor, President William Howard Taft. What separated President Wilson's sessions from those of his two predecessors was the open access rule governing them, which allowed reporters from all news organizations to attend, rather than a select few, and the initial attempt to schedule them on a twice-weekly basis. This schedule was not maintained, but it was revived after President Harding came into office. See Cornwell, *Presidential Leadership of Public Opinion*, for his treatment of the development of presidential press conferences from Wilson through Lyndon Johnson.

18. See the fine article on the press conferences of President Coolidge, Elmer Cornwell, "Coolidge and Presidential Leadership," *Public Opinion Quarterly* 21, no. 2 (Summer 1957): 265–78.

19. Jonathan Daniels, ed., *Complete Presidential Press Conferences of Franklin Roosevelt* (New York: Da Capo Press, 1972), 263, January 4, 1936.

20. In assembling the information for this table, I have sought to make my counts consistent within each time period. In later periods, certain sessions might not be categorized as press conferences, but there is no reason to apply the rules of today retroactively in deciding which sessions should be counted. In tracking their development, the goal is to look at presidential press conferences as an evolving forum. The chart seeks to establish comparable criteria for what is counted as a press conference. It combines figures from publicly available transcripts with manuscript collections, such as the papers of Charles Swem at the Princeton University Library (Swem transcribed Woodrow Wilson's press conferences and speeches).

21. The dates are January 19, February 1, April 3, May 18, October 10, November 11, and December 31.

22. Examples of officials assisting on budget press conferences: December 6, 1965, December 2, 1966, and January 17, 1967. Secretary of Defense McNamara was in press conferences on November 5, 1966, December 6, 1966, and July 13, 1967.

23. Marlin Fitzwater, interview with the author, by telephone, November 22, 2002.

24. The White House, Office of the Press Secretary, Joint Press Conference by President Clinton and President Jerry Rawlings of Ghana, February 24, 1999. President William J. Clinton, "The President's News Conference with President Rawlings," February 24, 1999, *Public Papers of the Presidents of the United States*. Available at www.presidency.ucsb.edu/ws.

25. These numbers, based on internal counts kept by the Press Office staff, represent accurate numbers for television and radio interviews. The interviews with newspapers and magazines that are counted in this total, however, are ones for which the transcripts were publicly released. There were many print interviews where the transcripts were not released.

26. Michael McCurry, interview with the author, Washington, D.C., April 7, 1999.

27. Michael McCurry, interview with the author, Washington, D.C., April 7, 1999.

28. Background information from a reporter at the gaggle who lagged behind to see if someone took McCurry's bait and, if so, who did.

29. Michael McCurry, interview with the author, Washington, D.C., April 7, 1999.

30. See Michael Grossman and Martha Joynt Kumar, *Portraying the President*, 140–41.

31. "The Press Secretary," written and produced by Theodore Bogosian for the Public Broadcasting Company, September 2001.

32. Michael McCurry, interview with the author, Washington, D.C., April 7, 1999.

33. Harold Ickes, interview with the author, Washington, D.C., April 13, 2001.

34. "The Press Secretary," written and produced by Theodore Bogosian for the Public Broadcasting Company, September 2001.

35. Joseph Lockhart, interview with the author, Washington, D.C., June 29, 1998.

36. Michael McCurry, interview with the author, Washington, D.C., April 7, 1999.

37. President William J. Clinton, "The President's News Conference," April 30, 1998, *Public Papers of the Presidents of the United States, President Clinton*. Available at www.presidency.ucsb.edu/ws.

38. "The Press Secretary," written and produced by Theodore Bogosian for the Public Broadcasting Company, September 2001.

39. President William J. Clinton, "The President's News Conference," April 30, 1998, *Public Papers of the Presidents of the United States, President Clinton*. Available at www.presidency.ucsb.edu/ws. The transcript renders it as "independent council."

40. Susan Page, "A Duck by Any Other Name; New Words for No Comment," *USA Today*, May 1, 1998.

41. He was commenting on the press conference President Clinton held on March 19, 1999. Marlin Fitzwater, interview with the author, telephone, March 30, 1999.

Chapter 8. Managing the Message

1. Poll data available at pollingreport.com/social.htm.

2. James A. Baker III, interview with the author, Houston, Texas, May 14, 2001.

3. Marlin Fitzwater, interview with the author, Deale, Maryland, August 8, 1998.

4. Andrew Rosenthal, "President Announces Plan for More Latin Debt Relief," *New York Times*, June 27, 1990.

5. Martha Joynt Kumar and Terry Sullivan, eds., *White House World: Transitions, Organization, and Staff Operations* (College Station: Texas A&M University Press, 2003), 133.

6. Mike McCurry, interview with the author, "The President, the Press, and Democratic Society," University of California, Washington Center, April 19, 2006.

7. Karl Rove, interview with the author, May 2002.

8. President William J. Clinton, "The President's News Conference," January 29, 1993, *Public Papers of the Presidents of the United States*. Available at www.presidency.ucsb.edu/ws.

9. Mike McCurry, interview with the author, "The President, the Press, and Democratic Society," University of California, Washington Center, March 1, 2004.

10. Ann Devroy, interview with the author, August 1995.

11. Dan Bartlett, interview with the author, Washington, D.C., May 22, 2002.

12. White House internal transcript of session with reporters biking with him, August 13, 2005. Not a public document.

13. Evan Thomas et al., "How Bush Blew It," *Newsweek*, September 15, 2005, 26–40.

14. "Remarks on Departure for a Tour of Gulf Coast Areas Damaged by Hurricane Katrina," September 2, 2005, *Weekly Compilation of Presidential Documents*. Available at www.gpo.gov/nara/nara003.html.

15. "President Arrives in Alabama, Briefed on Hurricane Katrina," White House, September 2, 2005. Available at www.whitehouse.gov/news/releases/2005/09/20050902-2.html.

16. Andrew Rosenthal, "Bush Encounters the Supermarket, Amazed," *New York Times*, February 4, 1992.

17. Fitzwater, *Call the Briefing*, 328–32.

18. John E. Yang, "Bush Says Tax Plan Critics Are Divisive; President Goes to Grocers to Seek Support for Economic Incentives," *Washington Post*, February 4, 1992.

19. E-mail message from Marlin Fitzwater to Martha Kumar, October 27, 2005.

20. Jonathan Yardley, "President Bush, Checkout-Challenged," *Washington Post*, February 10, 1992, and Joel Achenbach, "Message for Rip Van Bush; A Primer on the Technology Thing," *Washington Post*, February 6, 1992.

21. Background interview.

22. Ron Nessen, interview with the author, White House Interview Program, Washington, D.C., August 3, 1999.

23. James A. Baker III, interview with the author, Houston, Texas, May 14, 2001.

24. Dan Bartlett, interview with the author, March 8, 2004. "The President, the Press, and Democratic Society," University of California, Washington Center.

25. Jonathan Weisman, "Bush, Adviser Assailed for Stance on 'Offshoring' Jobs," *Washington Post*, February 11, 2004.

26. Later in the month, Secretary of the Treasury John Snow refused to condemn the outsourcing of jobs: "I think American corporations need to do what they need to do to be competitive, and as they're competitive, it's good for their shareholders, it's good for their consumers and it's good for their employees, because enterprises—and I come out of the American business system. Enterprises that don't succeed don't create many jobs." Capital Report, CNBC News Transcripts, February 24, 2004.

Index